Jurisdictional Immunities of States and International Organizations

Jurisdictional Immunities of States and International Organizations

Edward Chukwuemeke Okeke

OXFORD
UNIVERSITY PRESS

OXFORD
UNIVERSITY PRESS

Oxford University Press is a department of the University of Oxford. It furthers the University's objective of excellence in research, scholarship, and education by publishing worldwide. Oxford is a registered trademark of Oxford University Press in the UK and certain other countries.

Published in the United States of America by Oxford University Press
198 Madison Avenue, New York, NY 10016, United States of America.

Library of Congress Cataloging-in-Publication Data

Names: Okeke, Edward Chukwuemeke, author.
Title: Jurisdictional immunities of states and international organizations / Edward Chukwuemeke Okeke.
Description: New York : Oxford University Press, 2018. | Includes bibliographical references and index.
Identifiers: LCCN 2017048644 | ISBN 9780190611231 ((hardback) : alk. paper)
Subjects: LCSH: Immunities of foreign states. | Jurisdiction (International law) |
International organizations.
Classification: LCC KZ4012 .O44 2018 | DDC 341.3/3—dc23
LC record available at https://lccn.loc.gov/2017048644

Note to Readers

This publication is designed to provide accurate and authoritative information in regard to the subject matter covered. It is based upon sources believed to be accurate and reliable and is intended to be current as of the time it was written. It is sold with the understanding that the publisher is not engaged in rendering legal, accounting, or other professional services. If legal advice or other expert assistance is required, the services of a competent professional person should be sought. Also, to confirm that the information has not been affected or changed by recent developments, traditional legal research techniques should be used, including checking primary sources where appropriate.

(Based on the Declaration of Principles jointly adopted by a Committee of the American Bar Association and a Committee of Publishers and Associations.)

Dedicated to my wife, Ijeoma, and my son, Nnamdi, without whom the book would have been finished much earlier but less up-to-date.

CONTENTS

FOREWORD

The law on jurisdictional immunities constitutes an important subfield of international law, safeguarding the sovereign equality of States and the effective functioning of international organizations alike. Jurisdictional questions involve evaluating the judicial authority of a State vis-à-vis other States and entities, including international organizations. State immunities, in this context, serve to delimit the scope of jurisdiction in line with the maxim of *par in parem non habet imperium*. Yet rules concerning jurisdictional immunities of States and international organizations do not exist in a vacuum. Immunities coexist with and sometimes conflict or compete with other norms of international law, which calls for the balancing of State sovereignty with those other norms. Jurisdictional immunities must be reconciled not only with a State's right to exercise its territorial jurisdiction over actors, organs, and property within its territory, but also, increasingly, with the growing body of human rights norms. Accordingly, immunities of States are far from absolute and, where applicable, their scope is not unlimited. The jurisdictional immunities of international organizations, despite sharing similarities with State immunities, are not analogous and rest rather on the functional necessity of certain immunities for international organizations to be able to operate independently despite being located within the territory of a sovereign State.

An important development over the past century that has affected jurisdictional immunities has been the evolution of international law away from its Westphalian origins in a purely State-centric system toward a system recognizing also individuals and peoples as legitimate subjects of international law. This development has been accompanied by the globalization of economic and financial transactions and the increasing emergence of intergovernmental organizations in many parts of the world. Moreover, the international community has developed an enhanced concern for human rights, for humanitarian law, and for violations of jus cogens norms. In this context, the aspiration to secure the rule of law on the international and extraterritorial scale has also grown in relevance.

However, access to justice, which is a vital prerequisite for the rule of law, depends largely on whether victims are able to establish jurisdiction vis-à-vis a feasible judicial forum. Immunities can act as a procedural bar to establishing such jurisdiction, even in cases where victims lack access to alternative venues. In the *Jurisdictional Immunities* case, the ICJ found no basis in State practice for the assertion "that international law makes the entitlement of a State to immunity dependent upon the existence of effective alternative means of securing redress."[1] The victims in that case were consequently left without access to a remedy, highlighting the continuing weight given to immunities by courts.

Immunity should not, however, be viewed as an immutable value in international law. While immunity has often been treated as a default rule, there is no reason it should always take precedence over equally important rules of international law. There might be a case for carving out a very limited exception to immunity in those circumstances where immunity may prevent the victims of war crimes, crimes against humanity, or fundamental human rights violations from otherwise obtaining an effective remedy or where no other means of redress is available. States and international organizations should not be able to hide behind a smokescreen of immunity in order to deny victims access to justice.

With regard to international organizations, a balance often needs to be struck between the interests of host States and the ability of international organizations to function effectively in the fulfillment of their aims. Sometimes, such interests involve legitimate concerns relating to issues of impunity, respect for human rights, and other important policies and norms. At the same time, the effective functioning of international organizations requires that host States can guarantee the general inviolability of an organization's property, staff, and representatives from the reach of the State's jurisdiction. The immunities of organizations, unlike those of States, are however constrained in scope by the treaties providing for those immunities as well as the aims of the organizations to function for the benefit of all their Member States, rather than in their own self-interest.

While much has been written regarding immunities of States and international organizations, respectively, there exist few comprehensive volumes on the topic. In light of the different conceptions concerning the scope and extent of immunities in State practice and international judicial organs, there is nonetheless room for further treatment and analysis of this topic. In this context, Mr. Okeke's book provides a notable contribution to the academic scholarship on immunities by reviewing a broad set of case law and literature relating to the immunities of

1. Jurisdictional Immunities of the State (*Germany v. Italy: Greece Intervening*), Judgment, 2012 I.C.J. Rep. 2012, para. 101.

States and international organizations alike, highlighting the differences between these two types of immunities, and tying the various approaches discussed together into a single volume. Mr. Okeke's long-standing experience working within international organizations on issues relating to jurisdictional immunities, including at UNESCO and the World Bank, makes him well positioned to write on this topic. His case-law based approach gives the work a very practical quality and contributes to its great value. Both scholars and practitioners working in the area of immunities will find this book to be a very useful resource.

Judge Abdulqawi Ahmed Yusuf
President, International Court of Justice

PREFACE AND ACKNOWLEDGMENTS

The idea of this book was conceived in March 2004 at the annual meeting of the Legal Advisers of the Specialized Agencies, Related and Other Organizations of the United Nations System, which was hosted by the then Legal Adviser of UNESCO in Paris, during a discussion on the practice of some national courts in applying the doctrine of restrictive State immunity, namely, the distinction between *acta jure imperii* and *acta jure gestionis* in their determination of the jurisdictional immunity of international organizations. It dawned on me that a major problem militating against the understanding of this arcane subject was the confusion of concepts between State immunity and the immunity of international organizations. Since the idea was conceived, I have devoted myself to researching the subject and discussing it with fellow scholars and practitioners alike, and ultimately distilling the idea into this book.

There exist very few, if any, original and unalloyed ideas in law. The nature of legal scholarship is such that one builds from the work of others. I am, therefore, indebted to all those whose scholarship I benefited from in the writing of the book. Equally, I am grateful to everyone who played a role in the conception, gestation, and publication of this book, especially the following: Abdulqawi Yusuf, Antigoni Axenidou, Gian Luca Burci, Olufemi Elias, Edward Kwakwa, Susan Karamanian, David Rivero, Don Wallace, Maurizio Ragazzi, Omri Sender, Neils Blokker, Mona Khalil, Ucheora Onwuamaegbu, Nora Muller, Duncan Kiara, Elsie Onubogu, Maria Dakolias, Kingsley Moghalu, Sidi Boubacar, Robert Williams, Nadine Chapman, Giuliana Dunham-Irving, Nneoma Nwogu, Victor Mosoti, Siobhán McInerney-Lankford, Vikram Raghavan, Frank Fariello, Kenneth Mwenda, Sean Murphy, Sandie Okoro, Charles Di Leva, Antonio Parra, Anna Chytla, Ijeoma Okeke, Nnamdi Okeke, Ilyasah Shabazz, Christian Tomas, Wendy Mills, Leonard Rosenbaum, and Monica Castro, as well as my editors at Oxford University Press, namely, Blake Ratcliff, Alden Domizio, Brooke Smith, David Lipp, and Bala Murugan.

I would like to acknowledge the unyielding support of my family, especially during the drawn-out period that I was consumed in the extracurricular writing of this book. I would be remiss if I did not particularly acknowledge my late father, Alfred Okeke, and my mother, Kate Obukwelu, who were my first teachers and editors.

Edward Chukwuemeke Okeke

Introduction

PURPOSE AND SCOPE OF THE BOOK

If you are expecting the hackneyed polemic about immunity and impunity, this is a different kind of book. Other books have assailed the doctrine of immunity, and have done it very well. Another such book does not add any value to that scholarship.

If you are expecting a doctrinal debate on jurisdictional immunity, the emphasis of this book is more on judicial dialogue by courts in their deciding cases than on doctrinal debates by scholars. Doctrines are prone to oversimplification. However, the book engages in doctrinal debates where it elucidates. Consequently, some theories about jurisdictional immunity are discussed, and discounted where warranted. Where they exist, the book examines the so-called majority and minority views for a better understanding of the salient principles at issue.

If you want a vade mecum on the law and practice of jurisdictional immunities of States and international organization, this is the book. Its purpose is to provide practitioners who are confronted with cases or controversies on jurisdictional immunity with a guide on both the state and the trend of the law. The choice of only jurisdictional immunities of States and international organizations as the subject of the book is purposeful, and is informed by the common thread that States and international organizations are the two recognized subjects of international law.

From the Peace of Westphalia in 1648[1] to the creation of the United Nations in 1945,[2] States were at the center of international law, as they were considered its sole subject in the sense that international law only applied to States. In its 1949 *Reparation for Injuries* advisory opinion, the International Court of Justice (ICJ) confirmed that international organizations are also subjects of international law even though they might not possess all the rights and responsibilities on the international plane as States.[3]

The book covers the relationship between the jurisdictional immunities of States and international organizations, addressing their similarities and dissimilarities. It is the author's belief that this is the best way to do justice to the subject, considering that the immunity of international organizations was historically conceived in terms of State immunity. The relationship of these immunities with diplomatic immunity is also examined.

The major aim of this book is to clarify the conceptual confusion that has often marred the understanding of the law of the (different but interrelated) jurisdictional immunities of both States and international organizations. The focus of the book is to holistically analyze and synthesize select and relevant opinions of international and national courts. To achieve this aim, the focus of the book is more to describe what the law is than to argue what the law should be. An understanding of the law is more useful to a practitioner than a criticism of it. This does not mean that there's not much to criticize about the state of the law, but it is more adroit, from a practitioner's perspective, to understand the law. A judge would give more credence to a counsel supporting his argument with case law than with commentary.

Jurisdictional immunities of States and international organizations are as controversial as they are confusing—a state of affairs that has been exacerbated by inconsistent and sometimes incomprehensible judicial decisions. To confound the confusion, what ought (*lex ferenda*) is often conflated with what is (*lex lata*),

1. The Peace of Westphalia were the treaties that ended the European Thirty Years' War (1618–1648) in the Holy Roman Empire, as well as the Eighty Years' War (1568–1648) between Spain and the Netherlands. It established the political order in Europe of coexisting sovereign States, which eventually became the basis of international law and world order.

2. The Charter of the United Nations was signed on June 26, 1945, in San Francisco, at the conclusion of the United Nations Conference on International Organization, and came into force on October 24, 1945. According to the Preamble of the Charter, the organization was established, among other purposes, to save succeeding generations from the scourge of war, and to establish conditions under which justice and respect for obligations arising from treaties and other sources of international law can be maintained. Article 2(1) of the Charter enshrines the "principle of the sovereign equality of all its Members."

3. *Reparation for Injuries Suffered in the Service of the United Nations*, Advisory Opinion, 1949 I.C.J. Rep. 174 (Reparation Case).

and vice versa. "In order to know what it is, we must know what it has been, and what it tends to become. . . . The history of what the law has been is necessary to the knowledge of what the law is."[4] Beyond the certainty of the existence of jurisdictional immunities, there is little clarity as to their nature and scope.

The book is not an exegesis on everything immunity. The jurisdictional immunities of heads of State and of diplomats are beyond the scope of this book, and are only tangentially examined. Also beyond its scope is the immunity from enforcement or execution[5] enjoyed by States and international organizations, which are distinct from but related to jurisdictional immunity. With respect to States, the ICJ

> observes that the immunity from enforcement enjoyed by States in regard to their property situated on foreign territory goes further than the jurisdictional immunity enjoyed by those same States before foreign courts. Even if a judgment has been lawfully rendered against a foreign State, in circumstances such that the latter could not claim immunity from jurisdiction, it does not follow *ipso facto* that the State against which judgment has been given can be the subject of measures of constraint on the territory of the forum State or on that of a third State, with a view to enforcing the judgment in question. Similarly, any waiver by a State of its jurisdictional immunity before a foreign court does not in itself mean that that State has waived its immunity from enforcement as regards property belonging to it situated in foreign territory. The rules of customary international law governing immunity from enforcement and those governing jurisdictional immunity (understood *stricto sensu* as the right of a State not to be the subject of judicial proceedings in the courts of another State) are distinct, and must be applied separately.[6]

Similarly, the law generally is that any waiver of jurisdictional immunity of international organizations shall not extend to any measure of execution.[7] The

4. Oliver Wendell Holmes, Jr., The Common Law 1 (1881).

5. There are three types of jurisdiction: (1) jurisdiction to prescribe is the authority of a State to make laws that are applicable within its jurisdiction, (2) jurisdiction to adjudicate is the authority of a State to subject persons and things to judicial process, and (3) jurisdiction to enforce is the authority of a State to compel compliance with its laws. Jurisdictional immunity extends to exemptions from the executive and administrative authorities of the forum State.

6. Jurisdictional Immunities of the State (*Germany v. Italy: Greece Intervening*), Judgment, 2012 I.C.J. Rep. 99, ¶ 113.

7. See, e.g., Article II, Section 2, of the Convention on the Privileges and Immunities of the United Nations, and Article III, Section 4, of the Convention on the Privileges and Immunities of the Specialized Agencies of the United Nations.

law in the case of some multilateral development banks, such as the World Bank, is somewhat different in that immunity from execution or enforcement operates only before the delivery of final judgment.[8] In other words, where there is no jurisdictional immunity and judgment is rendered against the Bank, there is no immunity from enforcement of that judgment.

NATURE OF JURISDICTIONAL IMMUNITY

Jurisdictional immunity, also known as immunity from legal or judicial process, bars a national court from subjecting certain legal persons to judicial process or adjudicating their legal relations. States claim jurisdiction over everyone and everything within their territories. The concept of jurisdiction covers the entire panoply of the judicial process, from the initiation of proceedings, trials, and orders such as interim measures, to judgments and execution of judgments. Jurisdiction includes:

> the power to administer justice [which] is indeed very comprehensive and wide-ranging. It is exercisable in some countries in the name of the king, in others on behalf of the people or of the State. The power is generally part of the functions entrusted to the judicial authorities, but in its actual administration several aspects are performed by other officers, such as the police, the administrative officer of a tribunal or a court or a local authority, or the department of public prosecution. Thus, the expression covers the issuance and service of summons or a warrant of arrest or search warrant and other types of writ to initiate proceedings, the arrest and detention of person, investigation and inquiry or inquest, the provision of security for costs, interim measures or injunction, attachment of property or freezing of assets, as well as other procedural steps before and during the hearing and trial by a court of law. It also includes the power of the judicial authority to pronounce judgment and to order measures to satisfy and execute the judgments rendered, as well as award of costs and charge of fees for the administration of justice. This should also cover all other administrative and executive powers . . . normally exercised by the judicial or administrative and police authorities of territorial State.[9]

8. Article VII, Section 3, of the Articles of Agreement of the International Bank for Reconstruction and Development provides pertinently: "The property and assets of the Bank shall, wheresoever located and by whomsoever held, be immune from all forms of seizure, attachment or execution before the delivery of final judgment against the Bank."

9. Sompong Sucharitkul, Second Report on Jurisdictional Immunities of States and Their Property, para. 45, p. 210, Document A/CN.4/331 and ADD.1 (11 April and 30 June 1981); [1980] 2(1) Y.B. Int'l Law Comm'n.

Immunity subsumes the existence of jurisdiction a priori. In other words, a court must have jurisdiction, ab initio, before it can examine the issue of immunity, which is a derogation from a national court's jurisdiction that renders domestic law unenforceable. As noted by the ICJ, "jurisdiction does not imply absence of immunity, while absence of immunity does not imply jurisdiction."[10] Immunity bars a court from hearing a case on its merits *in limine* but "an action against a State is not barred *in limine*: if the defendant State chooses to waive immunity, the action will proceed to a hearing and judgment. The grant of immunity is to be seen not as qualifying a substantive right but as a procedural bar on national courts' power to determine rights."[11] Where a party had argued that immunity should be denied because the "acts were contrary to international law, or to good faith, or were discriminatory, or penal," the court considered the argument invalid: "The whole purpose of the doctrine of state immunity is to prevent such issues being canvassed in the courts of one state as to the acts of another."[12]

Jurisdictional immunity is not applicable or available in proceedings before international tribunals or courts, as they are creatures of treaties or conventions, or the creation of international organizations, where submission to jurisdiction is subsumed.[13]

10. *Arrest Warrant* case, para. 59.

11. *McElhinney v. Ireland* [GC], no. 31253/96, ECHR 2001-XI, para. 25.

12. *I Congreso del Partido* [1981] 2 All ER 1064 at 1078, [1983] 1 AC 244 at 272 (Lord Wilberforce) cited in *Jones v. Saudi Arabia*, [2006] UKHL 26, [2007] 1 All ER 113, [2006] BHRC 621, para. 12.

13. See London Agreement for the International Military Tribunal at Nuremberg ("Nuremberg Tribunal"), Article 7, 82 UNTS 279 (1945) ("The official position of defendants, whether as Heads of State or responsible officials in Government Departments, shall not be considered as freeing them from responsibility or mitigating punishment."); Charter of the International Military Tribunal for the Far East ("Tokyo Tribunal"), Article 6, TIAS 1589 (1946) ("Neither the official position, at any time, of an accused, nor the fact that an accused acted pursuant to order of his government or of a superior shall, of itself, be sufficient to free such accused from responsibility for any crime with which he is charged, but such circumstances may be considered in mitigation of punishment if the Tribunal determines that justice so requires."); Statute of the International Criminal Tribunal for the Former Yugoslavia (ICTY), Article 7(2), UN SC Res 827 (1993) ("The official position of any accused person, whether as Head of State or Government or as a responsible Government official, shall not relieve such person of criminal responsibility nor mitigate punishment."); Statute of the International Criminal Tribunal for Rwanda (ICTR), Article 6(2), UN SC Res 995 (1994) (This provision is identical to the provision of the ICTY statute.); Rome Statute of the International Criminal Court (ICC), Article 27(1), 2187 UNTS 3 (1998) ("This statute shall apply equally to all persons without any distinction based on official capacity. In particular, official capacity as a Head of State or Government, a member of a Government or parliament, an elected representative or a government official shall in no case exempt a person from criminal responsibility under this Statute, nor shall it, in and of itself, constitute a ground for reduction of sentence.").

Jurisdictional immunity "is essentially procedural in nature"[14] and "is entirely distinct from the substantive law which determines whether that conduct is lawful or unlawful."[15] A national court must address immunity as a threshold matter before it can apply any other rule of law.[16] A court cannot determine liability without first establishing subject matter jurisdiction. A trial court's denial of a claim of immunity is an immediately appealable collateral order.[17] As immunity is a threshold issue that goes to a court's subject matter jurisdiction, the standard of review is de novo.[18] "The point of immunity is to protect a foreign state that is entitled to it from being subjected to the jurisdiction of courts in this country, protection which would be meaningless were the foreign state forced to wait until action is resolved on the merits to vindicate its rights not to be in court at all."[19] Similarly, questions regarding the jurisdictional immunity of international organizations should be decided at the outset as a threshold jurisdictional matter.[20]

Whenever the issue of immunity arises, a court must decide it as a preliminary matter by its procedure before the suit can proceed on the merits. "Where applicable, state immunity is an absolute preliminary bar, precluding any examination of the merits. A state is either immune from the jurisdiction of a foreign court or it is not. There is no half-way house and no scope for the exercise of discretion."[21] However, a defendant can waive jurisdictional immunity, which is distinct and separate from immunity from execution, and a waiver of immunity from jurisdiction does not mean a consent or submission to enforcement or execution of judgment. The defense of immunity can be raised by a defendant in a preliminary motion as a matter for summary judgment or at trial.[22] "Unlike a court faced with an allegation that a claim does not disclose a cause of action, a court faced with

14. Arrest Warrant (*Democratic Republic of Congo v. Belgium*), 2002 I.C.J. Rep. 25, ¶ 60.

15. Jurisdictional Immunities of the State (*Germany v. Italy: Greece Intervening*), Judgment, 2012 I.C.J. Rep. 99, ¶ 58.

16. See *NYSA-ILA Pension Trust Fund ex rel. Bowers v. Garuda Indonesia*, 7 F.3d 35, 39 (2d Cir. 1993).

17. See *Cohen v. Beneficial Indus. Loan Corp.*, 337 U.S. 541 (1949).

18. See *Cassirer v. Kingdom of Spain*, 616 F. 3d 1019 (2010).

19. *Id.* at 1025.

20. See *Tuck v. Pan Am. Health Org.*, 668 F. 2d 547, 549 (D.C. Cir. 1981) ("This shield would be lost if the merits of a complaint were fully tried before the immunity question was addressed."); *De Luca v. United Nations Org.*, 841 F. Supp. 531, 533 (S.D.N.Y. 1994) ("Properly invoked immunity shields a defendant not only from the consequences of litigation's results, but also from the burden of defending themselves.") (internal quotation marks and citation omitted).

21. *Jones v. Saudi Arabia*, para. 33 (Lord Bingham of Cornhill).

22. See *Schreiber v. Canada (Attorney General)*, 2002 SCC 62, para. 18.

an immunity claim cannot withhold its decision until the end of the trial. There can be no trial until the court decides whether the foreign state is subject to the court's jurisdiction."[23]

A defendant claiming sovereign immunity bears the burden of proof of establishing a prima facie case that it is an entity entitled to immunity. Then the burden of going forward shifts to the plaintiff to produce evidence that that entity is not entitled to immunity, but the ultimate burden of proving immunity rests with the entity claiming it.[24]

Jurisdictional immunity is a rule of international law that operates on the national plane. Put differently, it is the intersection of international law and national law in national legal systems. Although jurisdictional immunities are the subject of study in international law, it is debated whether it is imposed by international law or domestic law, as the law and practice of States differ in this regard. Lord Denning had wondered:

> I think that we should go back and look for the principles which lie behind the doctrine of sovereign immunity. Search as you will among the accepted sources of international law and you will search in vain for any set propositions. There is no agreed principle except this: that each state ought to have proper respect for the dignity and independence of other states. Beyond that principle there is no common ground. It is left to each state to apply the principle in its own way; and each has applied it differently. Some have adopted a rule of absolute immunity which, if carried to its logical extreme, is in danger of becoming an instrument of injustice. Others have adopted a rule of immunity for public acts but not for private acts which has turned out to be a most elusive test. All admit exceptions. There is no uniform practice. There is no uniform rule.[25]

Lord Hoffman, in *Jones v. Saudi Arabia,* took the view that State immunity is not "a matter of discretion, relax or abandon. It is imposed by international law without any discrimination between one state and another."[26] At any rate, "State

23. *FG Hemisphere Associates v. Democratic Republic of Congo,* [2010] 2 HKC 487 (Yeung JA, Court of Appeals), para. 241.

24. See *Keller v. Cent. Bank of Nigeria,* 277 F. 3d 811, 815 (6th Cir. 2002).

25. *Rahimtoola v. Nizam of Hyderabad* [1958] AC 379, [1957] 3 All ER 441 (Lord Denning).

26. *Jones v. Saudi Arabia,* [2006] UKHL 26, [2007] 1 All ER 113, [2006] BHRC 621, para. 101 (Lord Hoffmann), citing Lord Millett in *Holland v Lampen-Wolfe* [2000] 3 All ER 833 at 847–48, [2000] 1 WLR 1573 at 1588.

immunity is a complex doctrine that is shaped by constantly evolving international relations."[27]

Anglo-American legal opinion has long accepted that international law is incorporated into national law.[28] There exist the monist and dualist approaches to the incorporation of treaty law into national law. In the monist system, a treaty becomes part of the national law following ratification by the State, whereas in the dualist system, an enabling legislation is also required for the treaty to become part of the national law. For instance, the United Kingdom follows the dualist theory of treaty law and, as such, under the International Organisations Act 1968, an international organization can be declared by an Order in Council to have the legal capacity of a body corporate under English law. "Treaties, as it is sometimes expressed, are self-executing. Quite simply, a treaty is not part of English law unless and until it has been incorporated into the law by legislation. So far as individuals are concerned, it is *res inter alios acta* from which they cannot derive rights and by which they cannot be deprived of rights or subjected to obligations; and it is outside the purview of the court not only because it is made in the conduct of foreign relations, which are the prerogative of the Crown, but also because, as a source of rights and obligations, it is irrelevant."[29] Similarly, Canada follows the dualist approach: "This means that, unless a treaty provision expresses a rule of customary international law or a peremptory norm, that provision will only be binding in Canadian law if it is given effect through Canada's domestic law-making process."[30]

Except for the European Convention on State Immunity, there is no other treaty in force regarding State immunity.[31] The customary international law of State immunity is essentially developed by cases decided by national courts, as recognized by the ICJ in the *Jurisdictional Immunities of the State (Germany v. Italy: Greece Intervening)* case, where it extensively relied on national laws and court decisions as evidence of customary international law.[32] National legislation on State immunity are legally defensible as long as they do not violate rules of

27. *Kazemi Estate v. Islamic Republic of Iran*, [2014] S.C.J. No. 62, para. 169.

28. GERHARD VON GLAHN, LAW AMONG NATIONS 29 (4th ed. 1981).

29. *Rayner (J.H.) (Mincing Lane) Ltd. v. United Kingdom (Department of Trade and Industry)*, House of Lords, para. 57.

30. *Kazemi Estate*, para. 149.

31. United Nations Convention on Jurisdictional Immunities of States and Their Property is not yet in force.

32. See Jurisdictional Immunities of the State (*Germany v. Italy: Greece Intervening*), 2012 I.C.J. 143.

international law. Where there is no domestic legislation dealing with sovereign immunity, courts do have recourse to customary international law, and at issue usually is the content of the customary international law. In this regard, Lord Denning observed in 1977:

> Seeing that the rules of international law have changed—and do change—and that the courts have given effect to the changes without any Act of Parliament, it follows to my mind inexorably that the rules of international law, as existing from time to time, do form part of our English law. It follows, too, that a decision of this court, as to what was the ruling of international law 50 or 60 years ago, is not binding on this court today. International law knows no rule of *stare decisis*. If this court today is satisfied that the rule of international law on a subject has changed from what it was 50 or 60 years ago, it can give effect to that change, and apply the change in our English law, without waiting for the House of Lords to do it.[33]

The practice of most or the majority of States is that foreign States are generally immune from the jurisdiction of forum States, with some common exceptions, such as commercial activities, and a few controversial exceptions, such as terrorism. Sovereign immunity was originally concerned with a sovereign as a natural person and then developed to cover a foreign State as a legal person. Consequently, "sovereign immunity" and "State immunity" are used interchangeably. The concept has evolved from immunity *ratione personae* to immunity *ratione materiae,* which makes a distinction between acts *jure imperii* and acts *jure gestionis*. Originally, the classical or absolute doctrine of sovereign immunity was granted to or applied by all States, regardless of the nature of the act. Conversely, the contemporary concept of restrictive immunity makes a distinction between acts performed by a State in a sovereign or in a private capacity.

In some jurisdictions, the executive branch of government plays a role in the determination of State immunity. This was the case in the United States before the enactment of the Foreign Sovereign Immunities Act (FSIA),[34] when courts relied on the position of the State Department in determining whether to grant immunity. The proper role of the executive in the determination of sovereign immunity is with respect to the recognition of a sovereign for purposes

33. *Trendtex Trading Corporation, Ltd. v. Central Bank of Nigeria,* United Kingdom Court of Appeal, 13 January 1977, 1 ALL E.R. 881.

34. Foreign Sovereign Immunities Act (FSIA), enacted in 1976 and codified at Title 28, §§ 1330, 1332, 1391(f), 1441(d), and 1602–1611 of the United States Code.

of immunity.[35] In this regard, Lord Sumner stated in *Duff Development Co. Ltd v. Government of Kelantan*:

> It is the prerogative of the Crown to recognize or withhold recognition from States or chiefs of States, and to determine from time to time the status with which foreign powers are to be deemed to be invested. This being so, a foreign ruler, whom the Crown recognizes as a sovereign, is such a sovereign for the purposes of an English Court of law, and the best evidence of such recognition is the statement duly made with regard to it in His Majesty's name. Accordingly where such a statement is forthcoming no other evidence is admissible or needed. I think this is the real judicial explanation why it was held that the Sultan of Johore was a foreign sovereign. [Mighell v. Sultan of Johore [1894] 1 QBD 149.] In considering the answer given by the Secretary of State, it was not the business of the Court to inquire whether the Colonial Office rightly concluded that the Sultan was entitled to be recognized as a sovereign by international law. All it had to do was to examine the communication in order to see if the meaning of it really was that the Sultan had been and was recognized as a sovereign.[36]
>
> [D]ifferent states may, according to their own constitutional arrangements, allocate to different organs of government the responsibility for laying down the policy to be adopted on state immunity, including any exceptions to such immunity. An examination of the practice of the United Kingdom and the United States shows that such allocation of responsibility may change over time, such as by the legislature taking over responsibility from the executive (and, in the case of the United Kingdom, with the judiciary having assumed responsibility in the interim), especially where the pre-existing practice is thought to have given rise to inconsistencies.[37]

Although international organizations do not appear before national courts as much as States, the question of their jurisdictional immunity is by no means settled. The legal uncertainty about the jurisdictional immunity of international organizations derives mainly from the misunderstanding by some national courts of the conceptual underpinning of the immunity. The first sentence in *Atkinson v. Inter-American Development Bank* is very telling: "This case involves

35. See *Mighell v. Sultan of Johore*, [1894] 1 QB 149, where the question was whether the Sultan of Johore was an independent sovereign.

36. *Duff Development Co. Ltd v. Government of Kelantan* [1924] AC 797, 824.

37. *Democratic Republic of Congo v. FG Hemisphere Associates*, Court of Final Appeal, [2011] 4 HKC 151, para. 266.

a well-known method of enforcing a judgment and *a little-known immunity from judicial process*."[38] The arcana of the immunity of international organizations had also been underscored in a memorandum by the International Labour Organization:

> The nature and effect of these immunities are frequently misunderstood. The circumstances in which international immunity operates to except the person enjoying it from compliance with the law are altogether exceptional. Such immunity is not a franchise to break the law, but a guarantee of complete independence from interference by national authorities with the discharge of official international duties. In general such immunity confers only exemption from legal process and not exemption from the obligation to obey the law. . . ."[39]

The immunity of international organizations is founded on the principles that all member States are equal, and that the organizations and their officials shall be independent from the member States in the fulfillment of the functions for which the member States created the organizations. The jurisdictional immunity of international organizations protects them from the jurisdiction of national courts, and it is applicable in three major categories: (1) organizational immunity protects the organization qua organization from judicial or legal process, (2) official or staff immunity protects staff from judicial process for official acts, and (3) archival immunity protects the organization's documents from discovery, subpoena, or other involuntary disclosure. To subject international organizations and their officials to the jurisdiction of the courts of individual member States would infringe on the principles that underlie the immunity.

The immunity of officials of international organizations is *ratione materiae* (conduct-based), as opposed to the immunity of diplomats, which is *ratione personae* (status-based). Immunity *ratione materiae* attaches to conduct undertaken on behalf of an international organization. However, some legal instruments on privileges and immunities may additionally grant diplomatic immunities to some high-ranking and designated officials of international organizations, which also protect their private conduct. Most important, the immunity of officials

38. *Atkinson v. Inter-Am. Dev. Bank*, 156 F. 3d 1335 (D.C. Cir. 1998) (emphasis added). In this case, the United States Court of Appeals for the District of Columbia Circuit affirmed the decision of the District Court holding that the Inter-American Bank was entitled to immunity under the International Organizations Immunities Act in a garnishment action brought against the Bank by the former spouse of an employee of the Bank.

39. C. Wilfred Jenks, International Immunities 42 (1961).

derive from the immunity of the international organization and is imputed to the organization.

The major controversy about immunity is with access to courts and denial of justice. "Any time sovereign immunity is asserted, the inevitable result is that certain domestic parties will be left without legal recourse."[40] The same goes for the immunity of international organisations. As regrettable as this result might be, it is a policy choice that nations make in the interest of international comity and reciprocity.[41] "The principle of sovereign immunity is not founded on any technical rules of law; it is founded on broad considerations of public policy, international law and comity."[42] International organizations and their officials require autonomy and independence to function without undue interference by States. Immunity provides such autonomy and independence. Autonomy is not the opposite of accountability, as international organizations could still be held accountable for their conduct. Immunity is not a carte blanche or franchise for officials to be lawless.

Some have questioned whether immunities are a necessity or anachronism in the contemporary world. Even if one adopts a position that immunities are an anachronism, it subsumes that immunities were a necessity, although they may no longer be so. More important, the serious discourse on immunities has centered on whether immunities should be limited, not whether they should be eliminated. As a result, it is important to recognize why immunities are or were a necessity, ab initio, before addressing whether they are still a necessity. In any event, questioning the necessity of immunities is simply polemical and does not really help with understanding them. To understand immunities is to know their underpinning.

STRUCTURE OF THE BOOK

In addition to the Introduction and Conclusion, the book is divided into three parts. Part I is devoted to jurisdictional immunity of States and has four chapters. Chapter 1 examines the historical development of State immunity, including from the absolute to the restrictive doctrine that distinguishes between acts *jure imperii* and *jure gestionis*. The provenance of the law on the jurisdictional immunity of States is widely held to be the seminal case of *Schooner Exchange*.[43]

40. *Re Canada Labour Code* [1992] 2 S.C.R. 50.

41. *Id.*

42. *Rahimtoola v. Nizam of Hyderabad* [1958] AC 379, [1957] 3 All ER 441, Lord Reid judgment.

43. *The Schooner Exchange v. McFadden*, 11 U.S. 116 (1812).

Although *The Schooner Exchange* is, generally but not quite accurately, regarded as the authoritative anchor for the classical doctrine of absolute State immunity, Chief Justice John Marshall actually saw immunity as an exception to the absolute jurisdiction of a State within its own territory:

> The jurisdiction of the nation within its own jurisdiction is necessarily exclusive and absolute. It is susceptible of no limitation not imposed by itself. Any restriction upon it, deriving validity from an external source, would imply a diminution of its sovereignty to the same extent of restriction, and an investment of that sovereign to the same extent in that power which could impose such restriction. All exceptions, therefore, to the full and complete power of a nation within its own territories, must be traced to the consent of the nation itself.[44]

The extent of immunity that a foreign State is entitled to in a forum State does not depend on the extent of immunity available to the foreign State in its own courts. However, the extent of immunity that a forum State is entitled to in its own courts may have a bearing on the extent of immunity it may accord a foreign State. In fact, the limitation on foreign sovereign immunity emanated from the amenability of a (domestic) sovereign to suit in its own court for certain acts.

The chapter also examines the rationale of State immunity, which is anchored on the three major attributes of statehood: independence, equality, and dignity. The sovereignty of a State encompasses its jurisdiction over people and property within its territory. State immunity is a derogation of that jurisdiction. A major justification for State immunity is facilitation of international relations in conformity with international law.

Chapter 2 is an overview of the sources of the law of State immunity. It examines international law and some national legislation on State immunity. The section on international law, as a source of the law on State immunity, examines treaty law and customary international law. With respect to treaty law, it discusses the 2004 United Nations Convention of the Jurisdictional Immunity of States and Their Properties, and the 1972 European Convention on State Immunity. The 2004 United Nations Convention, which built on the experience of the 1972 European Convention, as well as the practice and legislation of various States, sought to provide a comprehensive approach to the complicated issue of State immunity and to codify the restrictive doctrine of State immunity. Although the 2004 United Nations Convention has not yet entered into force, some courts and commentators have referred to some of its provisions as evidence of existence of

44. *Id.* at 133.

customary international law on State immunity. As there is no treaty of universal participation, State immunity is effectively a principle of customary international law developed largely through judicial decisions of national courts. Considering that codification is a feature of the civil law tradition, it is ironic that the few countries that have enacted legislation on State immunity are mostly from the common law tradition.[45]

Chapter 3 deals with the scope of State immunity. It examines who and what benefits from the jurisdictional immunity of a State, and under what conditions or circumstances. State immunity belongs to the State itself; however, States as abstract entities can only act through agents or agencies. The chapter also examines the distinction between immunity *ratione personae* and immunity *ratione materiae,* between *acta jure imperii* and *acta jure gestionis* for purposes of the doctrine of restrictive State immunity. It analyzes the common exceptions to State immunity, as well as some controversial ones. The general rule is that a State is immune unless an exception applies. The commercial activity exception is the raison d'etre of the doctrine of restrictive State immunity. Although the concept of the exception is clear, its judicial determination is sometimes complicated. The chapter also examines what constitutes a waiver of State immunity. A waiver confers jurisdiction where there is no exception to immunity. However, some courts consider a waiver as an exception, which may be a vestige of the doctrine of absolute State immunity under which no suit could be brought against a State without its consent. In the end, exceptions and waivers have the same effect in the sense that immunity is denied the State.

Chapter 4 addresses competing or conflicting norms, as well as the related but different doctrine of Act of State. At issue is whether human rights and jus cogens norms trump the rule of State immunity.[46] It examines the various approaches courts employ in dealing with the issue. The chapter discusses the nature of the

45. The two major and dominant legal traditions in the world are the civil law and common law, which have also had the most influence on international law. The civil law tradition is older and more widespread than the common law tradition. The historical origin of the civil law tradition is Roman Law, with the Twelve Tables (Lex XII Tabularum) circa 450 B.C., and the Justinian Code (Corpus Juris Civiles) circa 534 A.D., which became the foundation of the (modern or Western) civil law tradition. The civil law tradition is in force in most of Europe, Latin America, and most parts of Africa and Asia. It is also in force in certain enclaves in the Americas: Louisiana, Puerto Rico, and Quebec. The origin of the common law tradition is traced to the Norman Conquest of England in 1066 A.D. The common law tradition is in force in Great Britain, Ireland, United States, Canada, Australia, and most of the nations in Asia and Africa that were colonialized by Great Britain.

46. The Judgment of the European Court of Human Rights in *Jones and Others v. United Kingdom* and that of the ICJ in *Jurisdictional Immunities of the State (Germany v. Italy: Greece Intervening)* are very illuminative.

Act of State doctrine and how it differs from State immunity. The Act of State doctrine, which is sometimes confused with State immunity, is a matter of justiciability, not jurisdiction.

Part II is dedicated to the jurisdictional immunity of international organizations, which are those organizations established by treaty or other legal instruments governed by international law and possessing their own legal personality. The importance of international organizations in international law and relations cannot be overemphasized:

> One of the most striking features of the development of international law during the twentieth century has been the growth of international organizations. Not only do they grow in number every year, but there is also an increasing tendency to define their competence in ever wider terms, and to give them more far-reaching powers of independent action and decision. In every sphere of international relations, from the regulation of commodity prices to the protection of human rights, from technical assistance to the preservation of international peace, international organizations have a part to play which is constantly becoming more and more important.[47]

The relevance of international organizations is even more apparent and pronounced in the twenty-first century.

Chapter 5 addresses the nature of international organizations and the purpose of their immunity. International organizations are created by their constituent member States to discharge vital functions and responsibilities on their behalf, and in some cases on behalf of the world community as a whole. They are established to offer cooperative and concerted approaches to common challenges and myriad problems that have the best chance of being solved through multilateral actions. Although States remain the primary actors in international relations, international organizations have joined them as they provide the platform that enables different States to work together. International cooperation by States is indispensable in the contemporary world, which is the impetus for the creation of the United Nations and many other international organizations.

To achieve their objectives, international organizations are granted certain privileges and immunities by their member States; in particular, jurisdictional immunity, which protects them from legal process. The justification for the immunities of international organizations is primarily functional necessity. It is well-settled, under international law, that international organizations require

47. M.B. Akehurst, The Law Governing Employment in International Organizations 3 (1967).

those immunities that are necessary for them to fulfill their functions. This concept of functional necessity is to be found, for instance, in Article 105 of the United Nations Charter, and in Article VII, Section 1, of the Articles of Agreement of the International Bank for Reconstruction and Development.

Chapter 6 addresses the legal status of international organizations in both international and domestic spheres, examining their international and legal personalities that enable them to participate in international and national life. To carry out their functions, international organizations must have the requisite legal status, which also has a bearing on their jurisdictional immunity.

Chapter 7 examines the sources of the immunity of international organizations, which is mainly treaty law. The basic text or constituent instrument by which member States establish international organizations usually provides for the organizations' privileges and immunities. Provisions on privileges and immunities are also found in national legislation, and bilateral agreements, such as headquarters agreements or establishment agreements. The chapter also examines whether the immunity of international organizations is governed by customary international law, as well as the interrelationship between treaty and customary international law, and the relationship between international law and national law.

Chapter 8 deals with the most contentious aspects of the immunity of international organizations: its determination and scope.[48] The actual scope of the jurisdictional immunity of an international organization depends upon the interpretation of the applicable legal instrument. The chapter deals with the beneficiaries of the immunity of international organizations, the functions of international organizations, and official activities or acts. It also examines what may constitute waiver of or exception to immunity, and distinguishes them. International organizations are normally immune from legal process unless the organization expressly waives the immunity.[49] "In the context of sovereign, diplomatic and other immunity, a crucial distinction is made between adjudicative and enforcement jurisdictions. Waiver of immunity from one does not waive immunity from the other, even in respect of the same claim."[50] The Articles of Agreement of some multilateral development banks, such as the World Bank, provide for an exception to their jurisdictional immunity.[51] This exception to immunity has been inaccurately characterized as a

48. See, e.g., Difference Relating to Immunity from Legal Process of a Special Rapporteur of the Commission on Human Rights, [Cumaraswamy Case] Advisory Opinion, 1999 I.C.J. Rep. 62.

49. See Article II, Section 2, of the Convention on the Privileges and Immunities of the United Nations ("General Convention") Article III, Section 4, Convention on the Privileges and Immunities of the Specialized Agencies of the United Nations ("Specialized Agencies Convention").

50. *Re International Tin Council*, 1 All ER 890, [1987], 2 WLR 1229, [1987].

51. Article VII, Section 3, Articles of Agreement, The World Bank.

"charter-based waiver" by some courts.[52] The chapter further examines whether human rights concepts of access to court and denial of justice place any limitation on the jurisdictional immunity of international organizations. A denial of justice is inherent in a grant of immunity.[53] In that regard, the European Court of Human Rights landmark *Waite and Kennedy*[54] and *Beer and Regan* cases,[55] and the *Stitching Mothers of Srebrenica* case[56] are discussed.

Part III is devoted to cross-cutting and confused concepts. Chapter 9 examines the similarities and differences between the immunities of States and international organizations, as well as their interrelationship with diplomatic immunities. It also points out the pitfalls of analogies between the various immunities. The analogy between the immunities of States and international organizations might have proved promising when international organizations came into existence in the twentieth century, but it is now fraught with pitfalls. In an attempt to restrict the jurisdictional immunity of international organizations, it has been analogized to State immunity, but such an analogy is inapt even though the immunity of international organizations had roots in diplomatic and State immunities. Although the immunity of international organizations originated as "a general principle resting on the questionable analogy of diplomatic immunities[,] it has become a complex body of rules set forth in detail in conventions, agreements, statutes and regulations."[57]

The book concludes by making the case that the jurisdictional immunities of States and international organizations are not only sustainable but also necessary for international relations and cooperation. Contrary to the polemic that immunity breeds impunity, jurisdictional immunities promote respect for international law rather than undermine it. Even where a State or an international organization is immune, it may still be responsible for a wrongful act. To be sure, immunities can be abused. However, abuse of immunity is a different question from the necessity of immunity. The proverbial baby should not be thrown away with the dirty bath water.

52. See *Mendaro v. World Bank*, 717 F. 2d 610 (D.C. Cir. 1983).

53. *FG Hemisphere Associates LLC v. Democratic Republic of Congo*, [2010] 2 HKC 487, para. 165 ("The fact that the justice of a case might be defeated by claims to State immunity is nothing new.")

54. *Waite and Kennedy*, Application No. 26083/94, European Court of Human Rights, 18 February 1999.

55. *Beer and Regan*, Application No. 28934/95, European Court of Human Rights, 18 February 1999.

56. *Stitching Mothers of Srebrenica and Others v. the Netherlands*, (dec.), no. 65542/12, § 139 (e), 11 June 2013.

57. C. Wilfred Jenks, International Immunities xxxv (1961).

PART ONE

State Immunity

1

Historical Development and Rationale

DEFINITION OF STATE

A State is a polity with (1) international personality, (2) legal personality, (3) permanent population, (4) defined territory, and (5) its own government.[1] Vatican City, established by the 1929 Lateran treaty between Italy and the Holy See, is the smallest State in the world by both area and population, consisting of about 110 acres and fewer than 1,000 citizens. There are two theories on Statehood in international law. Under the declaratory theory, the existence of a State is a matter of fact in that an entity becomes a State upon the satisfaction of the criteria of Statehood. Under the constitutive theory, the existence of a State is a matter of law that requires recognition by other States.[2] Normally, satisfaction of the requirements of Statehood is manifest in admission of membership in an international organization, such as the United Nations, whose membership is open only to

1. See Article 1, Montevideo Convention on the Rights and Duties of States, 1933, 165 L.N.T.S. 19; § 201, RESTATEMENT (THIRD) OF THE FOREIGN RELATIONS LAW OF THE UNITED STATES (AM. LAW. INST. 1985) ("RESTATEMENT (THIRD)").

2. See generally JAMES R. CRAWFORD, THE CREATION OF STATES IN INTERNATIONAL LAW, published to Oxford Scholarship Online in February 2010.

Jurisdictional Immunities of States and International Organizations. Edward Chukwuemeke Okeke.

States.[3] However, in the case of Palestine, its claim to sovereign immunity was denied by a U.S. court in *Ungar v. Palestinian Liberation Organization (PLO)*, where the court noted that "neither political recognition of the PLO nor United Nations support for self-governance is sufficient to signify that the Restatement's conditions for statehood have been met."[4] The court noted: "We recognize the status of the Palestinian territories is in many ways sui generis."[5] State immunity does not revolve on the recognition of a foreign State by a forum State, but the recognition of a government may play a role in the determination of a beneficiary of State immunity. The recognition of a State, which is the formal affirmation by a State of another entity's Statehood, is different from the recognition of a government, which is the "formal acknowledgment that a particular regime is the effective government of a state."[6] Although there are different and competing approaches to recognition of government, the Estrada Doctrine is the only one that makes sense in the context of State immunity. The doctrine, which was first articulated by the Mexican Foreign Minister Don Genaro Estrada in 1930, espouses the recognition of only States, and not governments, so as to avoid the interference with the internal affairs of one State by another through the granting or withholding of recognition of the government. Thus, the Estrada Doctrine accords with the basis of Statehood, namely, independence, sovereign equality and dignity of States.

DEVELOPMENT FROM ABSOLUTE TO RESTRICTIVE STATE IMMUNITY

State immunity, also known as foreign sovereign immunity,[7] prevents the courts of a forum State from adjudicating or enforcing claims against a foreign State. The law of State immunity started to take root in the nineteenth century in Europe and the United States, when the nations of Africa, Asia, and Latin America had other concerns:

> Countries belonging to the developing continents such as Africa, Asia and Latin America were preoccupied with other problems. Africa was not

3. See Comment h, § 201, Restatement (Third).

4. 402 F. 3d 274, 291 (1st Cir. 2005).

5. *Id.* at 292.

6. See Comment a, § 203, Restatement (Third).

7. State immunity, sovereign immunity, and foreign sovereign immunity would be used interchangeably, without any change in meaning of the terms intended.

> composed of many independent sovereign States; people were struggling to assert their self-determination and to regain complete political independence.... Asia was also partially colonized. The Asian countries that maintained their sovereign independence throughout the nineteenth century and all through their national history did not escape subjection to a so-called "capitulation regime", whereby some measures of extraterritorial rights and power were recognized in favor of foreign States and their subjects. The question of State immunity was relatively insignificant, since even foreigners were outside the competence of the territorial authorities, administrative and judicial.... The Latin American continent was comparatively more recent in its emergence as a new continent of thriving independent sovereign independent sovereign nations.[8]

State immunity "derives from the principle of sovereign equality of States, which, as Article 2, paragraph 1, of the Charter of the United Nations makes clear, is one of the fundamental principles of the international legal order. This principle has to be viewed together with the principle that each State possesses sovereignty over its own territory and that there flows from that sovereignty the jurisdiction of the State over events and persons within that territory."[9]

Common Law Tradition

The Napoleonic Wars gave rise to *The Schooner Exchange v. McFaddon* case, which is heralded as the provenance of classical doctrine of absolute State immunity.[10] The *Schooner Exchange*, a merchant vessel owned by two Americans, was sailing from the United States to Spain when it was captured and condemned as a prize of war.[11] The vessel was turned into a Napoleonic man-of-war and renamed the *Balaou*. The American libellants brought an *in rem* action to repossess the French warship that had been located at a U.S. port where it had docked under the stress of bad weather. The seminal opinion of Chief Justice John Marshall of the United States Supreme Court was *ex nihilio*, as the issue presented by the case was uncharted waters: "In exploring an unbeaten path, with few, if any, aids from precedents or written law, the court has found it necessary to rely much on general

8. Second Report on Jurisdictional Immunities of States and Their Property, U.N. Document A/CN.4/331 and Add.1, pp. 219, 220, para. 83 (11 April and 30 June 1981).

9. Jurisdictional Immunities of the State (*Germany v. Italy: Greece Intervening*), Judgment, 2012 I.C.J. Rep. 99, ¶ 57.

10. *The Schooner Exchange v. McFaddon*, 11 U.S. 116, 7 Cranch 116 (1812).

11. The United States was neutral in the war at sea between Britain and France.

principles, and on a train of reasoning, founded on cases in some degrees analogous to this."[12] Chief Justice Marshall analogized to what is now characterized as diplomatic and head-of-State immunities, considering that the sovereign was then the personification of the State. He emphasized that the absolute jurisdiction of a sovereign within its own territory "is susceptible of no limitation not imposed by itself," but, as a matter of comity, "all sovereigns have consented to a relaxation in practice, in cases under certain peculiar circumstances, of that absolute and complete jurisdiction within their respective territories which sovereignty confers."[13] The decision noted that jurisdictional immunity is based on the "perfect equality and absolute independence of sovereigns."[14] It held:

> [T]he *Exchange*, being a public armed ship, in the service of a foreign sovereign, with whom the government of the United States is at peace, and having entered an American port open for her reception, on the terms on which ships of war are generally permitted to enter the ports of a friendly power, must be considered as having come into the American territory, under an implied promise, that while necessarily within it, and demeaning herself in a friendly manner, she should be exempt from the jurisdiction of the country.[15]

Until the mid-twentieth century, the doctrine of absolute State immunity was the order of the day and found expression in the decisions of other national courts. In England, the doctrine was applied in *The Parlement Belge*, which was an in rem action against the eponymous vessel owned by the king of Belgium that was used to carry mails, as well as passengers and merchandise.[16] After canvassing a host of cases, including *The Schooner Exchange*, the Court of Appeal stated:

> The principle to be deduced from all these cases is that, as a consequence of the absolute independence of every sovereign authority and of the international comity which induces every sovereign state to respect the independence and dignity of every other sovereign state, each and every one declines to exercise by means of its courts any of its territorial jurisdiction over the person of any sovereign or ambassador of any other state,

12. *Schooner Exchange*, 11 U.S. at 136.

13. *Id.*

14. *Id.* at 137.

15. *Id.* at 147.

16. *The Parlement Belge*, [1874–1880] All ER Rep 104.

> or over the public property of any state which is destined to public use, or over the property of any ambassador, though such sovereign, ambassador, or property be within its territory, and therefore, but for the common agreement, subject to its jurisdiction.[17]

In holding that the Admiralty Court had no jurisdiction over the *Parlement Belge*, the Court of Appeal noted that an independent sovereign is immune even if it "has carried on a private trading adventure and [i]f the remedy sought by an action *in rem* against public property is, as we think it is, an indirect mode of exercising authority of the court against the owner of the property, then the attempt to exercise such an authority is an attempt inconsistent with the independence and equality of the state which is represented by such owner."[18]

In *Mighell v. Sultan of Johore*, a breach of marriage promise action against a sovereign prince, the Court of Appeal stated that *The Parlement Belge* was binding on it even though it did not altogether agree with that judgment. It construed *The Parlement Belge* to have "laid down an absolute rule, without any exception or qualification whatever. No mention was made there of the case of a sovereign voluntarily submitting himself to the authority of a foreign court."[19] The Court of Appeal dismissed the appeal because the defendant has not submitted to the jurisdiction of the English courts despite the argument that the Sultan of Johore had lived and acted in England as a private individual under an assumed name.[20]

Another celebrated English case espousing the doctrine of absolute immunity was *The Porto Alexandre*,[21] where the Portuguese government had claimed and was granted immunity in an in rem action for salvage charges for a vessel owned by it and solely used for the carriage of freight. The Court of Appeal considered itself bound by *The Parlement Belge*, which it (mis)construed to mean that any ship owned or possessed by a sovereign was entitled to immunity regardless of the type of activity in which it was engaged. To that effect, it had cited the following passage in *The Parlement Belge*:

> [T]he public property of a government in use for public purposes is beyond the jurisdiction of the courts of either its own or any other State, and that the ships of war are beyond such jurisdiction, not because they are ships of

17. *Id.*

18. *Id.*

19. *Mighell v. Sultan of Johore*, [1893] All ER Rep 1019.

20. *Id.*

21. *The Porto Alexandre*, [1919] All ER Rep 615.

> war, but because they are public property. It puts all the public movable property of a State which is in its possession for public purposes, in the same category of immunity from jurisdiction as the person of the sovereign, or of an ambassador, or of ships of war, and exempts it from the jurisdiction of all courts for the same reason—viz, that the exercise of such jurisdiction is inconsistent with the independence of the sovereign authority of the State.[22]

The Court of Appeal concluded that the immunity of a sovereign and its property know no limitation. However, it noted the problems posed by State immunity in circumstances of burgeoning commercial trading by national ships, but was of the opinion that the remedies do not lie with the courts:

> If ships of the State find themselves left on the mud because no one will salve them when the State refuses any legal remedy for salvage, their owners will be apt to change their views. If the owners of cargoes on national ships find that the ship runs away and leaves them to bear all the expenses of salvage, there may be found a difficulty in finding cargoes for national ships. These are matters to be dealt with by negotiations between governments, and not by governments exercising their power to interfere with the property of other States, contrary to the principles of international courtesy which govern relations between independent and sovereign States.[23]

At the heels of the *Porto Alexandre* decision came *The Tervate*, where the Court of Appeal determined that *The Parlement Belge* compelled the decision that a maritime lien against a public vessel of the State of Belgium cannot exist at all as it would be inconsistent "with the rule of immunity laid down by the law of nations."[24] It noted that "it is now established that procedure *in rem* is not based upon wrongdoing of the ship personified as an offender, but is the means of bringing the owner of the ship to meet his personal liability by seizing his property."[25] Consequently, the Court of Appeal concluded that as the Belgian government could not have been sued in personam, its ship could not be arrested in rem because "by the comity of nations no process can be brought in the courts against the person or the property of a foreign sovereign."[26]

22. *Id.*

23. *Id.*

24. *The Tervate*, [1922] All ER Rep 387.

25. *Id.*

26. *Id.*

Under the then prevalent doctrine of absolute State immunity in England, a sovereign is not subject to jurisdiction for engaging in private trading business, and an agreement to arbitrate a contractual dispute does not waive the immunity.[27] The doctrine of absolute immunity also held sway in an action in rem addressed to "the steamship Jupiter and all persons claiming any right or interest in the said steamship," where the court decided "that this process by the very nature of it is an attempt to implead the Russian Soviet government" and that the English courts cannot exercise such jurisdiction over a sovereign independent State.[28]

Back in the United States, the doctrine of absolute State immunity reached its zenith in *Pesaro*, a libel in rem against the steamship *Pesaro* for breach of contract to ship certain artificial silk from Italy to New York.[29] At issue was whether a ship owned and possessed by a foreign State, and operated by it for commercial purposes, was immune.[30] The U.S. Supreme Court noted that although *The Schooner Exchange* did not refer to merchant ships owned and operated by governments, "the principles are applicable alike to all ships held and used by a government for a public purpose, and that when, for the purpose of advancing the trade of its people or providing revenue for its treasury, a government acquires, mans and operates ships in the carrying trade, they are public ships in the same sense that war ships are."[31] The Court also found support in *The Parlement Belge*, which had reviewed *The Schooner Exchange* and many other cases bearing on the question, and had been consistently followed in England.[32] The Court decided that the public ship of a friendly foreign government is immune from a libel in rem. It extended absolute immunity to "all ships held and used by a government . . . for the purpose of advancing the trade of its people or providing revenue for its treasury [which] are public ships in the same sense that warships are."[33] The Court decided the case without the benefit of a suggestion of immunity by the State Department.

27. See *Compania Mercantil Argentina v. United States Shipping Board*, [1924] All ER Rep 186, where the Court of Appeal held that a foreign sovereign does not lose its immunity in an action arising out of a trading contract or from an agreement to arbitrate.

28. *The Jupiter*, [1924] All ER Rep 405.

29. *Berizzi Brothers Co. v. Steamship Pesaro*, 271 U.S. 562 (1926) ("Pesaro").

30. *Id.* at 570.

31. *Id.* at 574.

32. *Id.* at 575, 576.

33. *Id.* at 574.

The doctrine of absolute State immunity in England reached its apogee in *The Cristina*.[34] The *Cristina* was a vessel owned by a Spanish shipping company, Compania Naviera Vascongada, which had been requisitioned for public use by the recognized government of Spain during the Spanish Civil War, after it left Spain but before it entered into a British port. The prerequisition owners of the vessel took out a writ in rem against the vessel and all persons claiming an interest in it, and asked to have possession of the vessel adjudged to them. The Spanish government filed a motion to set aside the writ, the arrest, and all subsequent proceedings on the grounds that the vessel was its property and in its possession, and that the action impleaded it.[35] The House of Lords unanimously held that the writ should be set aside. It also determined that the rule of absolute immunity is not limited to ownership and that the requisitioning of the *Cristina* by the Spanish government gave it a right or interest in the *Cristina* that was immune from interference from the courts of England.

Both Lords Atkin and Wright in their judgments stated that as a rule of customary international law, which rule was part of English common law, property owned and controlled by a foreign sovereign cannot be seized or detained by legal process. In the context of the vessel having been requisitioned for public use, the speeches of Lords Atkin and Wright received the concurrence of Lords Thankerton, Macmillan, and Maugham who reserved judgment on whether immunity extended to the property of a foreign sovereign that was not destined for public use but was instead in commercial use.

Lords Macmillan and Maugham both recognized the emergence of the doctrine of restrictive immunity. Lords Thankerton, Macmillan, and Maugham all expressed their reservation about the rule of absolute immunity as rendered by the Court of Appeal in *The Porto Alexandre*.

Lord Atkin delivered the leading judgment and stated:

> The foundation for the application to set aside the writ and arrest the ship is to be found in two propositions of international law engrafted on our domestic law which seem to me to be well-established and to be beyond dispute. The first is that the courts of a country will not implead a foreign sovereign. That is, they will not by their process make him against his will a party to legal proceedings, whether the proceedings involve process against his person or seek to recover from him specific property or damages. The second is that they will not by their process, whether the sovereign is a party

34. *Compania Naviera Vascongado v. Steamship "Cristina" and Persons Claiming an Interest therein ("The Cristina")*, [1938] A.C. 485.

35. See *id.* at 486.

> to the proceedings or not, seize or detain property which is his, or of which he is in possession or control. There has been some difference in the practice of nations as to possible limitations of this second principle, as to whether it extends to property used only for the commercial purposes of the sovereign or to personal private property. In this country, it is my opinion, well-settled that it applies to both.
>
> I draw attention to the fact that there are two distinct immunities appertaining to foreign sovereigns: for at times they tend to become confused: and it is not always clear from the decisions whether the judges are dealing with one or the other or both. It seems to me clear that, in a simple case of a writ *in rem* issued by our admiralty court in a claim for collision damage against the owners of a public ship of a sovereign state in which the ship is arrested, both principles are broken. The sovereign is impleaded and his property is seized.[36]

Lord Thankerton doubted the absoluteness of the proposition that a foreign sovereign cannot be impleaded. He argued "that an action *in rem* against property of the sovereign which is engaged in private trading, and which is not dedicated to public uses, is not to be regarded as inconsistent with the independence and equality of the state represented by such owners, and that any other view would lead to absolute exemption of all property owned by the sovereign, and not the exemption of some property only."[37]

Lord Macmillan shared his reservation:

> I confess that I should hesitate to lay down that it is part of the law of England that an ordinary foreign trading vessel is immune from civil process within this realm by reason merely of the fact that it is owned by a foreign State, for such principle must be an importation from international law and there is no proved consensus of international opinion or practice to this effect. On the contrary, the subject is one on which divergent views exist and have been expressed among the nations. When the doctrine of the immunity of the person and property of foreign sovereigns from the jurisdiction of the Courts of this country was first formulated and accepted, it was a concession to the dignity, equality and independence of foreign sovereigns which the comity of nations enjoined. It is only in modern times that sovereign States have so far condescended to lay aside their dignity as to enter competitive

36. *Id.* at 490–91.

37. *Id.* at 495–96.

> markets of commerce, and it is easy to see that different views may be taken as to whether an immunity conceded in one set of circumstances should to the same extent be enjoyed in totally different circumstances.[38]

Lord Wright noted that even though the immunity of ships was first recognized in *The Schooner Exchange* with respect to a warship in that particular case, the immunity appertained to the sovereign and was not dependent on the peculiar nature or the particular use of the ship. According to him, this principle was developed during the First World War and "was most uncompromisingly expressed in a judgment of the Supreme Court of the United States in *Berizzi Brothers Co. v. S.S. Pesaro*."[39] He, however, noted:

> This modern development of the immunity of public ships has not escaped severe, and, in my opinion, justifiable criticism on practical grounds of policy, at least as applied in times of peace. The result that follows is that Governments may use vessels for trading purposes, in competition with private ship-owners, and escape liability for damage, and salvage claims. Various international conventions have discussed this problem, which culminated in the International Convention for the Unification of Certain Rules concerning the Immunity of State-owned Ships, of 10 April 1926. The general purpose of the Convention was to provide that ships owned or operated by States were to be subject to the same rules of liability as privately-owned vessels, ships of war, State-owned yachts, and various other vessels owned or operated by a State on Government and non-commercial service were excepted.[40]

Lord Maugham had issues with "the recent current of authority in our Courts as regards State-owned trading ships [and felt] that it is high time steps were taken to put an end to a state of things which, in addition to being anomalous, is most unjust to our own nationals."[41] He continued:

> Half a century ago foreign Governments were seldom embarked in trade with ordinary ships, though they not infrequently owned vessels destined for public uses, and, in particular, hospital vessels, supply-ships, and

38. *Id.* at 498.

39. *Id.* at 511 [citation omitted].

40. *Id.* at 512.

41. *Id.* at 521.

> surveying or exploring vessels. There were doubtless very strong reasons for extending the privileges long possessed by ships of war to public ships of the nature mentioned, but there has been a very large development of state-owned commercial ships since the Great War, and the question whether the immunity should continue to be given to ordinary trading ships has become acute.
>
> I am far from relying merely on my own opinion as to the absurdity of the position which our courts are in if they must continue to disclaim jurisdiction in relation to commercial ships owned by foreign Governments. The matter has been considered over and over again of late years by foreign jurists, by English lawyers, and by business men, and with practical unanimity they are of the opinion that, if Governments or corporations formed by them choose to navigate and trade as ship-owners, they ought to submit to the same legal remedies and actions as any other shipowner.
>
> There is no doubt that the practice as to the immunity of state-owned merchant ships has been, and still is, far from uniform. France and Belgium, for example, grant only a limited immunity, and Italy grants no immunity at all.[42]

Across the Atlantic, the U.S. courts were also still wrestling with the issue of vessels of foreign States. Warships have always been accorded immunity, but the change in politico-economic circumstances of the nineteenth century when States started operating trading vessels brought controversy to the doctrine of absolute immunity.

Ex Parte Republic of Peru was an in rem action in admiralty against Peru for breach of a charter party to carry a cargo of sugar from Peru to the United States.[43] Peru moved for the release of its steamship, *Ucayali*, on the grounds of sovereign immunity. The U.S. Supreme Court noted:

> The case involves the dignity and rights of a friendly sovereign state, claims against which are normally presented and settled in the course of the conduct of foreign affairs by the President and by the Department of State. When the Secretary elects, as he may and as he appears to have done in this case, to settle claims against the vessel by diplomatic negotiations between the two countries rather than by continued litigation in the courts, it is of public importance that the action of the political arm of the Government

42. *Id.* at 521–23 [Citations omitted].

43. *Ex Parte Republic of Peru*, 318 U.S. 578 (1943).

> taken within its appropriate sphere be promptly recognized, and that the delay and inconvenience of a prolonged litigation be avoided by prompt termination of the proceedings in the district court.[44]

The Court considered the suggestion of immunity by the State Department as dispositive in the case: "The certification and the request that the vessel be declared immune must be accepted by the courts as a conclusive determination by the political arm of the Government that the continued retention of the vessel interferes with the proper conduct of our foreign relations."[45]

Two years after *Ex Parte Peru*, the Supreme Court, in *Mexico v. Hoffmann*, an in rem action by the owners of an American fishing vessel, *Lottie Carson*, denied immunity to a merchant ship, *Baja California*, owned but not possessed by the Mexican government, for allegedly colliding and damaging the *Lottie Carson* in Mexican waters. In an opinion by Chief Justice Stone, the Supreme Court held:

> It is . . . not for the courts to deny an immunity which our government has seen fit to allow, or to allow an immunity on new grounds which the government has not seen fit to recognize. The judicial seizure of property of a friendly state may be regarded as such affront to its dignity and so may affect our relations with it, that it is an accepted rule of substantive law governing the exercise of the jurisdiction of the courts that they accept and follow the executive determination that the vessel shall be treated as immune. But recognition by the courts of an immunity upon principles which the political department of government has not sanctioned may be equally embarrassing to it in securing the protection of our international interests and for recognition by other nations.[46]

The State Department declined to express its opinion on the claim of immunity through the usual suggestion of immunity: "The State Department has certified that it recognizes such ownership, but it has refrained from certifying that it allows the immunity or recognizes ownership of the vessel without possession by the Mexican government as a ground for immunity."[47] The Supreme Court ruled that "[i]n the absence of the recognition of the claimed immunity by the political

44. *Id.* at 586–87.

45. *Id.* at 589.

46. *Republic of Mexico v. Hoffman*, 324 U.S. 30, 35–36 (1945).

47. *Id.* at 36.

branch of the government, the courts may decide for themselves whether all the requisites of immunity exist."[48]

Ex Parte Peru and *Mexico v. Hoffman* provided the impetus for the so-called Tate Letter, by which the Acting Legal Adviser to the United States Department of State on May 19, 1952, conveyed the Department's new policy of restrictive immunity to the Acting Attorney General Philip B. Perlman.[49] The letter stated:

> [T]he granting of sovereign immunity to foreign governments in the courts of the United States is most inconsistent with the action of the Government of the United States in subjecting itself to suit in these same courts in both contract and tort and with its long established policy of not claiming immunity in foreign jurisdictions for its merchant vessels. Finally, the Department feels that the widespread and increasing practice on the part of governments of engaging in commercial activities makes necessary a practice which will enable persons doing business with them to have their rights determined in the courts. For these reasons it will hereafter be the Department's policy to follow the restrictive theory of sovereign immunity in the consideration of requests of foreign governments for a grant of sovereign immunity.[50]

Thus, the U.S. Department of State adopted the doctrine of restrictive State immunity, which the Supreme Court recognized in *Alfred Dunhill of London v. Republic of Cuba,* where a plurality declared that the commercial transactions of a foreign State would no longer benefit from State immunity

Back in England, now the bastion of absolute State immunity, Lord Denning adumbrated the doctrine of restrictive State immunity in *Rahimtoola v. The Nizam of Hyderabad,*[51] *Thai-Europe Tapioca Service Ltd. v. Government of*

48. *Id.* at 34–35.

49. Letter from Jack B. Tate, Acting Legal Adviser, Department of State, to Philip B. Perlman, Acting Attorney General, Department of Justice (May 19, 1952) ["Tate Letter"], reprinted in 26 Dep't St. Bull. 984-85 (1952) and *Alfred Dunhill v. Republic of Cuba*, 425 U.S. 682, 711–15 (1976). Before the codification of FSIA by the legislative branch of the U.S. government, determinations of the immunity of States were made by the executive branch through the Department of State to the judiciary branch in the form of a "suggestion of immunity," which is a formal communication to the court of its decision to recognize a defendant's immunity. The suggestions of immunity were sometimes informed by expediency, not principle. Thus, the FSIA removed the decision-making on State immunity from the Department of State to the courts.

50. Tate Letter, "Changed Policy Concerning the Granting of Sovereign Immunity to Foreign Governments," 26 Department of State Bulletin (1952), p. 985.

51. *Rahimtoola v. The Nizam of Hyderabad*, AC 379 (1958); 24 ILR 175.

Pakistan,[52] and *Trendtex Trading Corporation v. Central Bank of Nigeria*.[53] In his dissenting opinion in *Rahimtoola v. Nizam of Hyderabad*, he called for the reconsideration of State immunity for commercial activities: "[If] the dispute concerns, for instance, the commercial transactions of a foreign government (whether carried on by its own departments or agencies or by setting up separate legal entities), and it arises properly within the territorial jurisdiction of our courts, there is no ground for granting immunity."[54]

In *Trendtex*, the Central Bank of Nigeria had invoked State immunity when it was sued in respect of a letter of credit that it had issued. Lord Denning reiterated the views that he had restated in *Thai-Europe Tapioca*:

> [A] foreign sovereign has no immunity when it enters into a commercial transaction with a trader here and a dispute arises which is properly within the territorial jurisdiction of our courts. If a foreign government incorporates a legal entity which buys commodities on the London market; or if it has a state department which charters ships on the Baltic Exchange: it thereby enters into the market places of the world: the international comity requires that it should abide by the rule of the market.[55]

Lord Denning noted that the United States and some European countries have abandoned the doctrine of absolute immunity and embraced restrictive immunity:

> In the last 50 years there has been a complete transformation in the functions of a sovereign state. Nearly every country now engages in commercial activities. It has its department of state—or creates its own legal entities—which go into the market places of the world. They charter ships. They buy commodities. They issue letters of credit. This transformation has changed the rules of international law relating to sovereign immunity. Many countries have now departed from the rule of absolute immunity. So many have departed from it that it can no longer be considered a rule of international law. It has been replaced by the doctrine of restrictive immunity. This doctrine gives immunity to acts of a governmental nature, described

52. *Thai-Europe Tapioca Service Ltd. v. Government of Pakistan*, 1 LR 1 (UK, CA, 1975), [1975], 1 WLR 1485.

53. *Trendtex Trading Corporation v. Central Bank of Nigeria*, QB 529 (K, CA, 1976).

54. [1958] A. C. 379.

55. *Trendtex Trading Corporation v. Central Bank of Nigeria* [1977] 1 QB 529, [1976] 3 All ER 437, [1977] 2 W.L.R. 356, 368.

in Latin as *jure imperii*, but no immunity to acts of a commercial nature, *jure gestionis*.[56]

The Phillipine Admiral decision by the Privy Council was the first attempt under the English common law to move from absolute to restrictive State immunity. It was an in rem action, on appeal from the Supreme Court of Hong Kong, which was then Hong Kong's court of last resort. The Privy Council held that although the courts have held that absolute immunity applies to in personam actions on commercial activities, it does not apply to in rem actions:

> The rule that no action *in personam* can be brought against a foreign sovereign State on a commercial contract has been regularly accepted by the Court of Appeal in England and was assumed to be the law even by Lord Maugham in the *The Cristina*. It is no doubt open to the House of Lords to decide otherwise but it may fairly be said to be at the least unlikely that it would do so.

The Privy Council declined to follow *The Porto Alexander* and held that restrictive State immunity was more consonant with justice, and that as a trading vessel, *The Phillipine Admiral*, was not immune even though she was government-owned.

In 1976, the United States codified the doctrine of restrictive State immunity in the Foreign Sovereign Immunities Act (FSIA). Following the lead of the United States, the United Kingdom in 1978 codified the doctrine in the State Immunity Act (SIA).

In *I Congreso del Partido*, the House of Lords confirmed the doctrine of restrictive immunity and stated it is "clear that international law, in a general way, in 1978, gave support to a 'restrictive' theory of state immunity. We do not need the statute to make this good."[57] The House of Lords took judicial notice of judicial decisions and academic commentaries across the world to conclude that a customary international law of restrictive State immunity has developed and that the common law has incorporated it. The Court also stated:

> The relevant exception, or limitation, which has been engrafted upon the principle of immunity of states, under the so-called "restrictive theory," arises from the willingness of states to enter into commercial, or other private law, transactions with individuals. It appears to have two main

56. *Id.* at 366.

57. *Playa Larga v. I Congreso del Partido ("I Congresso")*, [1983] 1 A.C. 244, 260. The dispute had arisen before but was decided after the enactment of the SIA based on the common law.

> foundations: (a) It is necessary in the interest of justice to individuals having such transactions with states to allow them to bring such transactions before the courts. (b) To require a state to answer a claim based upon such transactions does not involve a challenge to or inquiry into any act of sovereignty or governmental act of that state. It is, in accepted phrases, neither a threat to the dignity of that state, nor any interference with its sovereign functions.[58]

Lord Wilberforce stated: "I would unhesitatingly affirm as part of English law the advance made by *The Philippine Admiral* [1977] AC 373 with the reservation that the decision was perhaps unnecessarily restrictive in, apparently, confining the departure made to actions *in rem*."[59]

Civil Law Tradition

Because State immunity was primarily a question of competence in civil law countries, the development of the principle there took a different route from that followed by common law jurisdictions.[60] The doctrine of restrictive State immunity accorded better with the civil law jurisdictions, where different types of courts adjudicated different types of disputes. The courts of Belgium, France and Italy, as well as the Mixed Courts of Egypt,[61] were in the vanguard of the development of the doctrine of restrictive State immunity.[62]

58. *I Congreso del Partido*, [1983] 1 A.C. 244, 262 (Lord Wilberforce).

59. *Id.*

60. See Second Report on the Jurisdictional Immunities of States and Their Property, U.N. Document A/CN.4/331 and Add.1, p. 218, para. 77 (11 April and 30 June 1981).

61. The Mixed Courts of Egypt arose out of the capitulatory system that placed foreigners in an "extraterritorial" position in Egypt, and the bench was recruited from the nationals of the capitulary powers, namely, Austria-Hungary, Belgium, England, Denmark, France, Germany, Holland, Italy, Portugal, Russia, Sweden, and the United States, including Egypt as the capitulary State. The court had territorial jurisdiction over Egypt, and jurisdiction in civil and commercial cases that involved a foreigner. It was organized on the basis of French law, but followed the jurisprudence of Belgium and Italian courts. It operated from 1876 until 1949.

62. See Sompong Sucharitkul, *Immunities of Foreign States Before National Authorities*, 149 Recueil des 87 (1976), pp. 126–46; Draft Articles on Jurisdictional Immunities of States and Their Property, with commentaries (1991), Commentary on Article 10(3)(b), para. (16); Hersch Lauterpacht, *The Problem of Jurisdictional Immunities of Foreign States*, 28 BRIT. Y.B. INT'L L. 220 (1951), pp. 227–28, 251–56.

The Italian courts were among the first to apply the doctrine.[63] The French Court of Cassation applied the doctrine in *Spanish Government v. Lambege et Pujol* in an action brought by a Frenchman for the attachment of debt and held:

> The reciprocal independence of states is one of the most universally respected principles of international law, and it follows as a result therefrom that a government cannot be subjected to the jurisdiction of another against its will, and that the right of jurisdiction of one government over litigation arising from its own acts is a right inherent to its sovereignty that another government cannot seize without impairing their mutual relations.[64]

Similarly, in *Societe Anonyme des Chemins de Fer Liegeois Luxembourgeois v. the Netherlands,* the Belgian Court of Cassation held that a foreign State is immune when it is acting in a sovereign role, but is amenable to the jurisdiction of Belgium just like any private person when the dispute concerns the commercial activities of that State.[65]

RATIONALE AND STATE OF THE LAW

At its origin, State immunity was founded on the sovereignty principles of independence, equality, and dignity of States, which are the basis of the maxim *par in parem non habet imperium.*

> The basis of immunity has been the sovereignty of the foreign sovereign in a way analogous to or comparable with that of the local sovereign. In the "*Prins Frederich*" case (1820), the first English case that contained a pronouncement on the principle of international law relating to jurisdictional immunities of foreign States and their property, as well as in the subsequent cases in which jurisdictional immunity was accorded to foreign States,

63. See *Dralle v. Republic of Czechoslovakia,* Supreme Court of Austria, May 10, 1950, 1950 International Law Report 155, 158 ("The first court to enunciate the principle that in matters belonging to the realm of private law foreign States cannot claim immunity was the Court of Cassation of Naples in a judgment of March 27, 1886. . . . A few months later the Court of Cassation of Florence . . . followed this decision. The Court of Cassation of Rome did likewise on July 1 and October 12, 1893.")

64. *Spanish Gov't v. Lambège et Pujol,* Court of Cassation (France), D. 1849 1, 5, 9 (translated and excerpted in Barry E. Carter & Phillip R. Trimble, International Law 588 (2d ed. 1995)). See also N.C.H. Dunbar, 132 Recueil Des Cours, Collected Course, 1971, at 206–09 (Martinus Nijhoff 1972).

65. See *Société anonyme des chems de fer liégeois-luxembourgeois c. Etat néerlandais (Ministère du Waterstaat),* Pasicrisie 1903, I, 294–303, Base de données de CAHDI "Les Immunités des État et des organistions international"—contribution de Belgique—Jurisprudence du 11/06/1903.

the court declined jurisdiction on the grounds that the foreign State as personified by the foreign sovereign was equally sovereign and independent and that to implead him would insult his "regal dignity."[66]

In *The Cristina*, Lord Wright stated:

> [State immunity] is sometimes said to flow from international comity or courtesy, but may now more properly be regarded as a rule of international law, accepted among the community of nations. It is binding on municipal Courts of this country in the sense and to the extent that it has been received and enforced by these Courts. It is true that it involves a subtraction from the sovereignty of the State, which renounces *pro tanto* the competence of its Courts to exercise their jurisdiction even over matters occurring within its territorial limits, though to do so is prima facie an integral part of sovereignty. The rule may be said to be based on the principle "*par in parem non habet imperium*", no State can claim jurisdiction over another sovereign State. Or it may be rested on the circumstance that in general the judgment of a municipal Court could not be enforced against a foreign sovereign State, or that the attempt to enforce might be regarded as an unfriendly act. Or it may be taken to flow from reciprocity, each sovereign State within the community of nations accepting some subtraction from its full sovereignty in return for similar concessions on the side of the others. I need not discuss other possible explanations. The rule is naturally subject to waiver by the consent of the sovereign, who may desire a legal adjudication as to his rights.[67]

The European Court of Human Rights has also held that "sovereign immunity is a concept of international law, developed out of the principle *par in parem non habet imperium*, by virtue of which one State shall not be subject to the jurisdiction of another State. The grant of sovereign immunity to a State in civil proceedings pursues the legitimate aim of complying with international law to promote comity and good relations between States through the respect of another State's sovereignty [citations omitted]."[68] "Whatever the legal foundation of the doctrine of State immunity, whether historically it is based on the analogy with the immunity of the local sovereign, or is merely an inevitable extension of

66. Sompong Sucharitkul, Second Report on Jurisdictional Immunities of States and Their Property, para. 68, p. 216, A/CN.4/331 and ADD.1 (11 April and 30 June 1981).

67. *Compania Naviera Vascongado v. Steamship "Cristina" and Persons Claiming an Interest therein ("The Cristina")*, [1938] A.C. 485, 502.

68. *Jones v. United Kingdom*, (Applications nos. 34356/06 and 40528/06), ECtHR Judgment, para. 188.

diplomatic immunities, or whether analytically it is founded on the principles of sovereignty, independence, equality and dignity of States, or additionally on reciprocity, comity of nations and avoidance of political embarrassment in international relations, the principle of State immunity should be taken as a point of departure in any logical treatment of the topic. State immunity [is] the general rule."[69]

The "principle of State immunity which was formulated in the early nineteenth century and was widely accepted in common law countries as well as in large number of civil law countries in Europe in that century, has later been adopted as a principle of customary international law on a solid and uncontested basis in the general practice of States."[70] The law of State immunity is that under the doctrine of absolute immunity, a State could not, without its consent, be made a defendant in a foreign court, notwithstanding the type or nature of the legal relationship or proceedings. Under the doctrine of restrictive immunity, a State is immune only in suits involving what is considered sovereign or public acts but not in cases arising out of the State's commercial activities. Although there is no treaty of universal application, considering that the United Nations Convention on the Jurisdictional Immunities of States and Their Property is not yet in force, the restrictive immunity codified in the Convention is construed by some courts as declaratory of customary international law.

In sum, State immunity is a rule of international law that has developed from the decisions of national and international courts, based variously on rationales of sovereignty, independence, equality, dignity, comity, and *par in parem non habet imperium*. The current state of the law of State immunity is that despite the prevalence of the doctrine of restrictive immunity, there is still residual absolute immunity even though it has fallen into disrepute.[71] The United States was first to enact national legislation to codify the doctrine of restrictive State immunity in the FSIA in 1976. The United Kingdom was next with SIA in 1978. Next were Australia and other Commonwealth countries: Singapore in 1979, Pakistan in 1981, South Africa in 1981, Canada in 1982, Australia in 1985, and Argentina in 1995.

69. Preliminary Report on the Topic of Jurisdictional Immunities of States and Their Property, U.N. Document A/CN.4/323, p. 240, para. 59 (18 June 1979).

70. Second Report on Jurisdictional Immunities of States and Their Property, U.N. Document A/CN.4/331 and Add.1, p. 220, para. 84 (11 April and 30 June 1981).

71. See *Democratic Republic of Congo v. FG Hemisphere Associates*, [2011] 4 HKC 151 (Court of Final Appeal).

2

Overview of Sources of Law of State Immunity

INTERNATIONAL LAW

State immunity is a rule of international law that renders a foreign State immune from the jurisdiction of a forum State. The international law of State immunity is made up of customary international law and treaty law.[1]

Customary International Law

The English position on the source of the law on State immunity is that it "is a creature of customary international law and derives from the equality of sovereign states. It is not a self imposed restriction on the jurisdiction of its courts which the United Kingdom has chosen to adopt. It is a limitation imposed from without upon the sovereignty of the United Kingdom itself."[2] In the same vein, the preamble of the 2004 United Nations Convention on the Jurisdictional Immunities of States and Their Property states that "the jurisdictional immunities of States

1. See Article 38 of the Statute of the International Court of Justice on the sources of international law.

2. *Holland v. Lampen-Wolfe*, per Lord Millett, [2000] 1 WLR 1573, 1588; [2002] 3 All ER 833; [2002] UKHL 40; 119 ILR 367.

and their property are generally accepted as a principle of customary international law." State immunity is, therefore, "a general rule of customary international law solidly rooted in the current practice of States."[3]

There are two components of customary international law: settled State practice and *opinio juris*.[4] The International Court of Justice (ICJ) has ruled:

> State practice of particular significance is to be found in the judgment of national courts faced with the question whether a foreign State is immune, the legislation of those States which have enacted statutes dealing with immunity, the claims to immunity advanced by States before foreign courts and the statements made by States, first in the course of the extensive study by the International Law Commission and then in the context of the adoption of the United Nations Convention. *Opinio juris* in this context is reflected in particular in the assertion by States claiming immunity that international law accords them a right to such immunity from the jurisdiction of other States; in the acknowledgment by States granting immunity, that international law imposes upon them an obligation to do so; and, conversely, in the assertion by States in other cases of a right to exercise jurisdiction over foreign States.[5]

State practice, in the opinion of the ICJ, evinces "that there is a right to immunity under international law, together with a corresponding obligation on the part of other States to respect and give effect to that immunity."[6] The ICJ also opines that the State practice "is confirmed by the record of national legislation, judicial decisions, assertions of a right to immunity and the comments of States to what became the United Nations Convention."[7]

In sum, customary international law does not require unanimous practice and acceptance by States, but a settled and generally accepted practice and a belief by States that the practice is obligatory as a matter of law. "[C]ustomary international law is, by its very nature, unequivocal. It is not binding law if it is equivocal. In the absence of consistent state practice one way or another, and of *opinio juris*

3. [1980] 2(2) Y.B. INT'L LAW COMM'N 147, ¶ 26; Jurisdictional Immunities of the State (*Germany v. Italy: Greece Intervening*), Judgment, 2012 I.C.J. Rep. 99, ¶ 56.

4. See *North Sea Continental Shelf (Federal Republic of Germany/Denmark; Federal Republic of Germany/Netherlands)*, Judgment, 1959 I.C.J. Rep. ¶ 77.

5. Jurisdictional Immunities of the State, ¶ 55.

6. Jurisdictional Immunities of the State, ¶ 56.

7. *Id.*

as to the binding effect of a state practice, no rule of customary international law is established."[8]

Treaty Law

A treaty creates international legal obligations between the parties. "A treaty is a contract between the governments of two or more sovereign states."[9] In terms of functions, a treaty may be contractual, dispositive, constitutive, or lawmaking.[10] A lawmaking treaty "is an instrument through which a substantial number of states declare their understanding of what a particular rule of law is; by which new general rules for the future conduct of the ratifying or adhering states are laid down; by which some existing customary or convention rule of law is abolished, modified, or codified; or by which some new international agency is created."[11] Thus, lawmaking treaties are those that declare, codify, or establish rules of law. Sometimes, for its proper execution, observance and implementation, a treaty may call for change in the domestic law of countries. A country is required to bring its domestic law in conformity with a treaty that it has accepted.

European Convention on State Immunity

The European Convention on State Immunity of 1972 ("European Convention" or "Basle Convention")[12] is the first multilateral treaty on State Immunity in effect even though it applies obviously only among the European Contracting States.[13] The Preamble of the Basle Convention points out its purpose and affirms the doctrine of restrictive immunity: "Taking into account the fact that

8. Kazemi Estate v. Islamic Republic of Iran, 2014 SCC 62 ¶ 102, [2014] 3 S.C.R. 176 (Can.).

9. *Rayner (J.H.) (Mincing Lane) Ltd. v. United Kingdom (Department of Trade and Industry)*, House of Lords, para. 4.

10. Constitutive treaties are those that establish international organizations.

11. Gerhard von Glahn, Law Among Nations 17 (4th ed. 1981).

12. European Convention on State Immunity (opened for signature on May 16, 1972, entered into force on June 11, 1976), ETS No. 74. As of 2016, only eight members of the Council of Europe have ratified or acceded to the Convention. The Explanatory Report on the European Convention on State Immunity and the Additional Protocol (1972) does not constitute authoritative interpretative instruments of the Convention even though it may facilitate the application of the Convention's provisions.

13. The International Convention for the Unification of Certain Rules Concerning the Immunity of State-Owned Ships signed in Brussels on April 10, 1926 ("Brussels Convention") dealt only with the immunity of State-owned vessels.

there is in international law a tendency to restrict cases in which a State may claim immunity before foreign courts."[14] The Basle Convention explicitly adopts the distinction between *acta jure imperii* and *acta jure gestionis* that is the raison d'être of the doctrine of restrictive State immunity.[15] Its general rule is that a Contracting State is immune from the jurisdiction of another Contracting State. "A Contracting State shall be entitled to immunity from the jurisdiction of the courts of another Contracting State if the proceedings do not fall within Article 1 to 14; the court shall decline to entertain such proceedings even if the State does not appear."[16] It starts by listing situations where a State should not have immunity. The actual substantive exceptions are contained in Articles 1 to 12, with clarifications in Articles 13 and 14. In any situation not within the listed exceptions, the Contracting State is immune, even for *acta jure gestionis*.[17] The Basle Convention requires each Contracting State to give effect to judgments against it by courts of another Contracting State. Even though entities established by Contracting States do not enjoy immunity under the Convention, the courts of a Contracting State may still not entertain certain proceedings brought against such entities.

A Contracting State that institutes or intervenes in proceedings before the court of another Contracting State assents to the jurisdiction of that State for purposes of those proceedings.[18] However, where a Contracting State would ordinarily have been entitled to immunity as a defendant, it does not assent to the jurisdiction of another Contracting State by merely intervening in a proceeding in which it is not a party to claim a right or interest in property that is the subject matter.[19] A Contracting State may submit expressly to the jurisdiction of the courts of another Contracting State by international agreement, written contract, or consent after a dispute between the parties has arisen.[20] However, a choice-of-law clause in a contract is not to be construed as submission to jurisdiction.[21]

14. Preamble, Basle Convention.

15. See Articles 24(1), 27(2).

16. Article 15.

17. Explanatory Report, paras. 56 and 96.

18. Article 1(1).

19. Article 13. The exception under this Article excludes cases where the contract is between States, or the parties to the contract have agreed otherwise in writing, or the contract is concluded in the foreign State and the obligation is governed by that State's administrative law.

20. Article 2.

21. See Explanatory Report, para. 24.

Where a Contracting State has participated in a proceeding regarding the merits, it is deemed as having forfeited its immunity unless it is not aware of the essential facts to its claim of immunity and provided it claims immunity promptly.[22] But a Contracting State is not deemed to have waived its immunity if its appearance before a court is for assertion of immunity.[23]

A Contracting State is not immune from the jurisdiction of the courts of another Contracting State in proceedings about its contractual obligations in another Contracting State.[24] Similarly, a Contracting State is not immune in proceedings about a contract of employment between that State and an individual regarding work to be performed in the forum State.[25] This exception excludes cases where the employee is a national of the foreign State or a foreigner that has been locally recruited.

Where a Contracting State participates with a private person in a company, association, other person, or entity with its seat, office, or principal place of business in the forum State, it is not immune in proceedings regarding that business relationship, unless it is otherwise agreed in writing.[26] In the same vein, unless otherwise agreed in writing by the parties, a Contracting State is not immune in proceedings relating to activities in connection with its office, agency, or other establishment in the forum State through which it engages in an industrial, commercial, or financial activity just like a private person.[27]

The immunity of a Contracting State is also abrogated in proceedings involving the following situations: intellectual property;[28] immovable property;[29] and movable or immovable property arising by way of succession, gift, or *bona vacantia*.[30] The exceptions to immunity with respect to intellectual property and immovable property require a nexus between the property right and the forum State.

A Contracting State is not entitled to immunity in proceedings for compensation for tort in a forum State, if the tortfeasor was present in the territory of the forum State when the events causing the personal injury or property damage

22. Article 3(1).

23. Article 3(2).

24. Article 4.

25. Article 5(1).

26. Article 6.

27. Article 7(1).

28. Article 8.

29. Article 9. See Explanatory Report, para. 44; Article 32.

30. Article 10. See Explanatory Report paras. 47–49.

occurred.[31] Although the territorial tort exception applies to *acta jure imperii*, it has an exclusion for military forces abroad.[32]

A Contracting State is precluded from claiming immunity in proceedings relating to an arbitration agreement or award in the courts of another Contracting State in whose territory or under whose law an arbitration has taken place or will take place, unless the arbitration agreement provides otherwise.[33]

Thus, Articles 1 to 3 deal with waiver of immunity, whereas Articles 4 to 12 deal with exceptions to immunity. As Articles 1 to 14 concern only civil matters, it can be concluded that States enjoy complete immunity with regard to criminal proceedings under that Convention. A Contracting State is entitled to jurisdictional immunity from another Contracting State even if that foreign State does not appear, unless the proceedings fall within Articles 1 to 14 of the Basle Convention.[34]

The Convention provides for procedural rules for the service of process and the time limits for entering an appearance or appealing against a judgment.[35] It also has general provisions.[36] A "Contracting State" does not include any legal entity that is distinct and capable of suing or being sued even if entrusted with public functions.[37] Political subdivisions or State agencies, such as central banks or railway administrations, are examples of such entities.[38] Under Article 27(2), proceedings may be instituted against an Article 27(1) entity in the same manner as against a private person, except in respect of acts performed in the exercise of sovereign authority (*acta jure imperii*).

Political subdivisions or constituent States of Federation do not enjoy immunity unless the Contracting States make a declaration that the Convention will apply to its constituent States.[39] To that effect, on ratification, Austria, Belgium, and Germany respectively made the necessary declaration that their constituent States were to have the same rights and obligations as those Contracting States themselves.[40] "The effect of the declaration is that the provisions of the

31. Article 11.

32. Article 31.

33. Article 12(1).

34. See Article 15.

35. Articles 16 to 19.

36. See Chapter V of the Convention.

37. See Article 27(1).

38. See Explanatory Report, para. 109.

39. Article 28.

40. See Chart of signatures and ratifications of Treaty 074, European Convention on State Immunity, ETS No. 074.

Convention on immunity and non-immunity from jurisdiction, on immunity from execution and on the effects of judgments given against a State, become applicable in proceedings instituted against a constituent State of the federation before the courts of a foreign State."[41]

The Basle Convention excludes from its application proceedings concerning social security; damage or injury in nuclear matters; and custom duties, taxes or penalties.[42] These specific exclusions do not preclude the application of other rules independent of the Basle Convention.[43] Other exclusions concern proceedings in respect of claims relating to the operation of seagoing vessels owned or operated by a Contracting State or to the carriage of cargoes and passengers by such vessels, or to the carriage of cargoes owned by a Contracting State and carried on board merchant vessels.[44] Also excluded are the privileges and immunities of the armed forces of a Contracting State when in the territory of another Contracting State.[45] Diplomatic and consular privileges and immunities are also excluded under Article 32.[46] Article 33 excludes existing or future international agreements in special fields that relate to matters dealt with in the Basle Convention, and is also intended to prevail over treaties dealing with enforcement of judgments.[47] The Basle Convention excludes proceedings introduced before its entry into force or proceedings arising out of, or judgments based on, omissions or facts prior to the date on which the Basle Convention is opened for signature.[48]

In the event of a dispute between Contracting States regarding the interpretation or application of the Basle Convention, the parties shall refer it to the ICJ if they cannot agree on a different mode of dispute settlement.[49]

41. Article 28, Explanatory Report, para. 110.

42. See Article 29; Explanatory Report, paras. 113 and 114.

43. See Explanatory Report, para. 114.

44. Article 30. It excluded matters that are already governed by the International Convention for the Unification of Certain Rules relating to the Immunity of State-Owned Vessels (signed on April 10, 1926) and Additional Protocol (signed on May 24, 1934), ("Brussels Convention") 176 LNTS 199.

45. Article 31. The Status of Forces Agreement (SoFA) of the North Atlantic Treaty Organization (NATO) contains such privileges and immunities.

46. Explanatory Report, para. 117, declares that the provisions of the Convention will prevail in the event of any conflict with other international agreements governing diplomatic or consular privileges and immunities.

47. Explanatory Report, para. 118.

48. Article 35.

49. Article 34.

The Basle Convention provides for an Optional Regime to which Contracting States may subscribe additionally. Under this regime, a Contracting State may declare that, in cases falling within Articles 1 to 13, its courts shall be entitled to entertain proceedings against another Contracting State to the extent that its courts are entitled to entertain proceedings against States not party to the Basle Convention, except for *acta jure imperii*.[50]

United Nations Convention on Jurisdictional Immunities of States and Their Properties

The United Nations Convention on Jurisdictional Immunities of State and Their Property ("United Nations Convention"),[51] which was adopted by General Assembly Resolution 59/38 of 2 December 2004, was the culmination of the work of the International Law Commission, the open-ended Working Group of the Sixth Committee, and the Ad Hoc Committee on the Jurisdictional Immunities of States and Their Property, pursuant to various General Assembly resolutions.[52] The United Nations Convention, which built on the experience of the Basle Convention, as well as the practice and legislation of various States, seeks to provide a comprehensive approach to the complicated issue of State immunity. It is a compromise convention that sought to codify the doctrine of restrictive State immunity. Its Preamble recites "that the jurisdictional immunities of States and their property are generally accepted as a principle of customary international law." It also recites "that an international convention on the jurisdictional immunities of States and their property would enhance the rule of law and legal certainty, particularly in dealings of States with natural or juridical persons, and would contribute to the codification and development of international law and the harmonization of practice in this area." Although it has not yet entered into force, some national and international courts have construed some of the provisions of the United Nations Convention as codification of customary international law on State immunity. In sum, the Convention is in some aspects declaratory of customary international law and in other aspects legislative where

50. Article 24(1). Declarations under Article 24(1) may be rescinded in accordance with Article 24(4).

51. United Nations Convention on Jurisdiction Immunities of States and Their Property, G.A. Res. 59/38, U.N. Doc. A/Res/59/38 (Dec. 2, 2004) In accordance with its Article 30, the United Nations Convention "shall enter into force on the thirtieth day following the date of deposit of the thirtieth instrument of ratification, acceptance, approval or accession with the Secretary-General of the United Nations." So far, it is not yet in force, as it has only 28 signatories and 21 parties.

52. See Resolutions 32/151 of 19 December 1977, 46/55 of 9 December 1991, 49/61 of 9 December 1994, 52/151 of 15 December 1997, 54/101 of 9 December 1999, 55/150 of 12 December 2000, 56/78 of 12 December 2011, 57/16 of 19 November 2002, and 58/74 of 9 December 2003.

its provisions "sought to resolve differences rather than to recognise existing consensus."[53]

In the typical fashion of most national legislation on State immunity, the United Nations Convention provides for a general rule of State immunity subject to enumerated exceptions. It is divided into six Parts (Introduction, General Principles, Proceedings in which State immunity cannot be invoked, State immunity from measures of constraint in connection with proceedings before a court, Miscellaneous provisions, and Final clauses) and consists of a Preamble, 33 Articles, and an Annex.

Applicability and Scope

The United Nations Convention applies to the immunity of a State and its property from the jurisdiction of the courts of another State.[54] The immunity from jurisdiction extends to all adjudicative, administrative, and executive authority exercised in a proceeding. It covers the entire judicial process, from the institution of proceedings through the disposition of the suit. It does not apply to criminal proceedings.[55] As a general principle, Article 5 provides that a State enjoys immunity from the jurisdiction of the courts of another State, whereas Article 6 provides the modalities for giving effect to State immunity. Accordingly, the courts of a forum State shall refrain from exercising jurisdiction over a foreign State and shall determine on their own initiative whether the foreign State enjoys immunity. The obligation of the court includes a determination of whether the proceedings are against the foreign State. A proceeding is against a foreign State if the State is a named party, or if it affects the property, rights, or activities of that State. Of course, the issue of "immunity arises only when the defendant State is unwilling or does not consent to be proceeded against. It does not arise if the State agrees to become a party to the proceeding."[56]

Article 2 defines "State" to include the State itself and its various organs of government. A State also includes constituent units of a federal State or political subdivisions of the State, which are entitled to perform acts in the exercise of sovereign authority, and are acting in that capacity; agencies and instrumentalities of the State or other entities to the extent that they are entitled to perform and

53. *Benkharbouche (Respondent) v Secretary of State for Foreign and Commonwealth Affairs (Appellant) and Secretary of State for Foreign and Commonwealth Affairs and Libya (Appellants) v Janah (Respondent)* [2017] UKSC 62, para. 32.

54. United Nation Convention, Article 1.

55. See General Assembly Resolution 59/38 of 2 December 2004.

56. Draft articles on Jurisdictional Immunities of States and Their Property, with commentaries (1991) ("Draft Articles and Commentaries"), Article 6(2)(a), Commentary (8).

are actually performing acts in the exercise of sovereign authority of the State; and representatives of States acting in that capacity. The following entities and individuals benefit from the immunity of the State: sovereign or head of State, the head of government, the central government, various ministries and departments of government, and branches of government. A foreign State may take the form of a kingdom, empire, republic, federation, or confederation.[57] The constituent units of a federal State or political subdivisions of the State enjoy immunity only when they "are entitled to perform acts in the exercise of sovereign authority, and are acting in that capacity," whereas the counterpart agencies and instrumentalities of the State or other entities benefit from immunity only when "they are entitled to perform and are actually performing acts in the exercise of sovereign authority of the State."[58] The distinction is intended to accord the constituent units of federal States that are regarded as States, which may be distinguishable from agencies and instrumentalities, the same immunities as those of the State, without the additional requirement that they perform acts in the exercise of the sovereign authority of the State.[59]

Submission to Jurisdiction

A foreign State is not immune where it has expressly consented to the jurisdiction of a forum State.[60] Such consent can be by an international agreement, a written contract, a declaration before the court, or a written communication in a specific proceeding. However, an agreement by a foreign State for the application of the law of another State does not constitute a consent to the exercise of jurisdiction by that other State.[61] Submission to jurisdiction by way of consent extends to all proceedings in all instances of the courts, but not to enforcement or execution of any judgment.[62] Also, this consent shall not imply consent to the application of measures of constraint.[63]

A foreign State cannot invoke its immunity if it participates in a proceeding before a court of a forum State by instituting the proceeding, or intervening in the

57. See Draft Articles and Commentaries, Article 2, Commentary.

58. Draft Articles and Commentaries, Article 2(1)(b)(iv), Commentary (14).

59. See Draft Articles and Commentaries, Article 2(1)(b)(ii), Commentary (11).

60. See United Nations Convention, Article 7.

61. See United Nations Convention, Article 7(2); Draft Articles and Commentaries, Article 7, Commentary (13) ("Questions of consent to the exercise of jurisdiction and applicable law to the case must be treated separately.").

62. See Draft Articles and Commentaries, Article 7(1), Commentary (12).

63. See United Nations Convention, Article 20.

proceeding, or taking any other steps relating to the merits in the proceedings.[64] Consent is evinced through participation in the proceedings.[65] Such participation is considered an implicit waiver of immunity. However, a participation in a proceeding is not a consent "if the State satisfies the court that it could not have acquired knowledge of facts on which a claim to immunity can be based until after it took such a step . . . provided it does so at the earliest possible moment."[66] A participation in a proceeding simply to invoke immunity, or to assert a right or interest at issue in that proceeding is not considered a consent to the exercise of jurisdiction.[67] Similarly, the appearance of a representative of a foreign State as a witness shall not be interpreted as consent. It is the right of a foreign State not to submit to the jurisdiction of a court entertaining a proceeding and, as such, failure to enter an appearance in a proceeding shall not be interpreted as consent.[68]

A foreign State forfeits its immunity in any counterclaim arising out of the same legal relationship or facts as the principal claim in the proceedings initiated by it.[69] Also, a foreign State cannot invoke immunity in a counterclaim arising out of the same legal relationship or facts as the claim presented by the foreign State in its intervention to present that claim in a proceeding.[70] Furthermore, a foreign State forfeits its immunity in the principal claim in a proceeding instituted against it if it makes a counterclaim.[71] As an implicit waiver of immunity, counterclaims against the foreign State require the nexus of the same factual or legal relationship with the principal claim, but counterclaims by the foreign State do not require the same factual or legal connection with the principal claim. This means that the foreign State remains immune against independent counterclaims, unless they fall within the exceptions enumerated under Part III of the Convention.

In sum, Articles 7, 8, and 9 together address how a foreign State submits to jurisdiction through express or implied consent. They have the same result of denying a foreign State the immunity to which it would have been entitled under Article 5.[72]

64. See United Nations Convention, Article 8.

65. See Draft Articles and Commentaries, Article 8, Commentary (1).

66. United Nations Convention, Article 8(1)(b).

67. United Nations Convention, Article 8(2).

68. United Nations Convention, Article 8(3).

69. United Nations Convention, Article 9(1).

70. United Nations Convention, Article 9(2).

71. United Nations Convention, Article 9(3).

72. See Draft Articles and Commentaries, Article 9, Commentary (1).

Exceptions to and Limitation on Immunity

The Convention enumerates the kind of proceedings in which State immunity cannot be invoked.[73] It distinguishes between acts or activities where State immunity is applicable or absent. "In the attempt to specify areas of activity to which State immunity does not apply, several distinctions have been made between acts or activities to which State immunity is applicable and those not covered by State immunity."[74] The distinction considered the dual capacity and personality of the State, and the differentiation between *acta jure imperii* and *acta jure gestionis*, as well as the situations involved and the practice of States.[75]

A State does not enjoy immunity for "commercial transactions," which are transactions for the sale of goods or supply of services; immunity for a loan or other transactions of a financial nature; or immunity of a commercial, industrial, trading, or professional nature, but not including employment contracts.[76] In the determination of what is a commercial transaction, the nature of the contract or transaction is examined first, but the purpose should also be considered if the parties to the contract or transaction so agreed or if it is the practice in the forum State for such determination.[77] Article 10 does not apply in commercial transactions between States, or if the parties to the commercial transaction have expressly agreed otherwise.[78] The Article leaves intact the immunity of a foreign State in a proceeding regarding a commercial transaction by a State enterprise with its own independent legal personality.[79] The immunity of the State itself is not affected in a legal dispute arising out of the commercial transactions of a State entity with an independent legal personality as the State is not a party to the transaction.[80]

73. See Draft Articles and Commentaries, Part III, Commentary (1). Part III of the Convention is captioned "Proceedings in which State Immunity cannot be invoked" to reconcile the position of some States who favored the term "limitation" as consistent with the notion that contemporary international law did not recognize the jurisdictional immunity of States in the areas covered under Part III, with the position of those other States who favored the term "exception" under the notion that it accurately depicts that jurisdictional immunity was the rule of international law and subject only to the exceptions expressed in Part III.

74. Draft Articles and Commentaries, Part III, Commentary (3).

75. *Id.*

76. See United Nations Convention, Articles 10 and 2(1)(c).

77. See United Nations Convention, Article 2(2).

78. See United Nations Convention, Article 10(2).

79. See United Nations Convention, Article 10(3).

80. See Draft Articles and Commentaries, Article 10(3), Commentary (9).

Article 11 provides that a foreign State cannot invoke immunity in a forum State in a proceeding about a contract of employment between the foreign State and an individual for work performed or to be performed in the territory of the forum State, unless otherwise agreed between the States. The exception to immunity applies to disputes about the terms and conditions in the contract of employment. The exception does not apply if the employee is engaged to perform particular functions in the exercise of governmental authority, such as those entrusted with State security functions.[81] The exception also does not apply if the employee is a diplomatic agent or consular officer, or covered by a different international immunity regime.[82] The foreign State also retains its immunity in proceedings about the recruitment, renewal of employment, or reinstatement of an employee.[83] Furthermore, the exception does not apply where the subject-matter of the proceeding is dismissal or termination and the foreign State determines that the proceeding will interfere with its security interests.[84] The foreign State is immune if the employee is its national, unless the employee is also a permanent resident of the forum State.[85] Finally, the foreign State is immune if it has so agreed in writing with the employee, subject to public policy considerations conferring exclusive jurisdiction on the forum State because of the subject-matter of the proceedings.[86]

Under Article 12, a foreign State is not immune in proceedings for pecuniary compensation for personal injuries and damage to property, where it would have been liable under the *lex loci delicti commissi*.[87] This exception does not revolve around the distinction between *acta jure imperii* and *acta jure gestionis*. It is intended to provide relief for individuals who suffer personal injury, death, or physical damage to or loss of personal property caused by a foreign State intentionally, accidentally, or negligently on the territory of the forum State.[88] It requires a territorial connection between the forum State and the tortfeasor, that is, the cause of action must relate to physical damage occurring in the forum State, with

81. See United Nations Convention, Article 11(2)(a); Draft Articles and Commentaries, Article 11, Commentary (9).

82. See United Nations Convention, Article 11(2)(b).

83. United Nations Convention, Article 11(2)(c).

84. United Nations Convention, Article 11(2)(d).

85. United Nations Convention, Article 11(2)(e).

86. United Nations Convention, Article 11(2)(f).

87. See Draft Article and Commentaries, Article 12, Commentary (2) and (3).

88. *Id.*

the perpetrator of the damaging act or omission physically present during the occurrence.[89]

Other exceptions apply with respect to ownership, possession, and use of property;[90] intellectual and industrial property;[91] participation in companies or other collective bodies;[92] ships owned or operated by a State;[93] and arbitration agreements.[94] An arbitration agreement regarding a "commercial arbitration" has the effect of denying a foreign State immunity "relating to the supervisory jurisdiction of a court of another State which is otherwise competent to determine questions connected with the arbitration agreement, such as the validity of the obligation to arbitrate or go to arbitration or to compel the settlement of a difference by arbitration, the interpretation and validity of the arbitration clause or agreement, the arbitration procedure and the setting aside of arbitral awards."[95]

Immunity from Measures of Constraint

Under the Convention, a foreign State is immune from both prejudgment and post-judgment measures of constraint in connection with proceedings before a forum court. Part IV deals with measures of constraint, such as attachment, and arrest and execution, upon the use of property. Article 20 makes clear that submission to jurisdiction under Article 7 shall not imply consent to the taking of measures of constraint where consent to such measures is required under Articles 18 and 19. Article 21 provides protection for specific categories of property, which shall not be considered as specifically in use or intended for use by

89. See Draft Article and Commentaries, Article 12, Commentary (9).

90. See United Nations Convention, Article 13, which is an important exception to State immunity and distinct from the immunity in respect to attachment of or execution on property. This exception is, however, without prejudice to the privileges and immunities enjoyed under international law as recognized under Article 3 of the Convention.

91. See United Nations Convention, Article 14.

92. See United Nations Convention, Article 15.

93. See United Nations Convention, Article 16.

94. See United Nations Convention, Article 17. An arbitration agreement regarding a "commercial arbitration" has the effect of denying a foreign State immunity "relating to the supervisory jurisdiction of a court of another State which is otherwise competent to determine questions connected with the arbitration agreement, such as the validity of the obligation to arbitrate or go to arbitration or to compel the settlement of a difference by arbitration, the interpretation and validity of the arbitration clause or agreement, the arbitration procedure and the setting aside of arbitral awards." Draft Articles and Commentaries, Article 17, Commentary (1).

95. Draft Articles and Commentaries, Article 17, Commentary (1).

the foreign State for other than government noncommercial purposes under Article 19(c).

Part V of the Convention contains miscellaneous provisions for the service of process,[96] default judgment,[97] and privileges and immunities during court proceedings.[98] Part VI, final clauses, provides that the Annex to the Convention is an integral part of it. Article 26 deals with the relationship between the Convention and other already existing international agreements on State immunity between the same parties. Article 27 provides for the dispute settlement mechanism for the interpretation or application of the Convention.

EXAMPLES OF NATIONAL LEGISLATION

Although State immunity is a rule of international law, there exist national legislation on State immunity that are virtually from the common law tradition. In civil law jurisdictions, "the principle of State immunity has been established in several countries as a result of judicial interpretation or application of legal provisions, such as the restrictive application of article 14 of the French Civil Code or articles 52 and 54 of the Belgian Civil Code, resulting in non-exercise of territorial jurisdiction."[99] The United States and the United Kingdom were the first two countries to enact national legislation on State immunity. Both enactments capture the diversity and paradigm of the law on restrictive State immunity.[100] Other nations have enacted legislation: 1979 Singapore State Immunity Act, 1981 South Africa Foreign Sovereign Immunity Act, 1981 Pakistan State Immunity Ordinance, 1985 Australia Foreign States Immunities Act, 1985 Canada State Immunity Act, 1995 Argentina Immunidad Jurisdiccional de los Estados Extranjeros ante los Tribunales Argentinos, 2008 Israel Foreign States Immunity Law, and 2009 Japan Act on Civil Jurisdiction over Foreign States.

The U.S. and the UK laws provide respectively that they are the only basis for adjudicating State immunity claims. They both codify the doctrine of restrictive immunity by providing for the general rule that States are immune except where enumerated exceptions apply. The UK legislation enumerates more exceptions

96. See United Nations Convention, Article 22.

97. See United Nations Convention, Article 23.

98. United Nations Convention, Article 24.

99. Second Report on the Jurisdictional Immunities of States and Their Property, U.N. Document A/CN.4/331 and Add.1, p. 225, para. 106 [citations omitted] (11 April and 30 June 1981).

100. It is beyond the scope of this book to review legislation other than those of the United States and the United Kingdom. Both legislations have similarities and dissimilarities, and all the other legislations are variations of them.

and provides more comprehensive definitions of them than its U.S. counterpart. The UK statute has these additional exceptions: contracts of employment between the foreign State and an individual where the contract was made or performed in the United Kingdom,[101] intellectual property,[102] foreign State's membership in a body corporate,[103] submission of dispute to arbitration,[104] and taxation and duties.[105] Another difference between the two legislations is with respect to the procedure for service of process on foreign States. The U.S. statute provides for four specific means,[106] whereas the UK enactment provides only for service through diplomatic channels.[107] Both statutes take different approaches toward default judgment. Under the U.S. statute, a default judgment will not be entered against a foreign State "unless the claimant established his claim or right to relief by evidence satisfactory to the court."[108] The UK legislation, on the other hand, does not require a decision on the merits but a court can enter a default judgment against a foreign State if it is satisfied that service was proper and the time for appearance has expired.[109]

United States Foreign Sovereign Immunities Act

Applicability and Scope

The United States enacted the Foreign Sovereign Immunities Act (FSIA)[110] in 1976, which has been amended several times ever since. The FSIA was the outcome of a consensus bill in Congress with various stakeholders in the U.S. government, and 10 years of work over three administrations. It has been subjected to significant judicial interpretation, which has helped resolve most of the ambiguity or confusion with some of the statutory language and complex structure.

101. See State Immunity Act (SIA), Section 4.

102. See SIA, Section 7.

103. See SIA, Section 8.

104. See SIA, Section 9.

105. See SIA, Section 11.

106. See Foreign Sovereign Immunities Act, 28 U.S.C. §§ 1330, 1608 (2016) ["FSIA"].

107. SIA, Section 12(1).

108. FSIA, 28 U.S.C. § 1608(e) (2016).

109. SIA, Section 12(4).

110. FSIA 28 U.S.C. 1602–1611 (2016); H.R. Rep. No. 1487, 94th Cong., 2d Sess. 7-8 (1976) ("H.R. Report"). The House Report is the operative legislative history as the House bill was passed in lieu of the Senate bill.

The Act has benefitted from extensive commentary over the years.[111] Although the FSIA was enacted in 1976, and became effective on January 19, 1977, the U.S. Supreme Court has held that the Act applies retroactively.[112] The Supreme Court considered the preamble of the FSIA as an expression of "Congress' understanding that the Act would apply to all post-enactment claims of sovereign immunity."[113] In other words, the statute applies to acts that took place before its enactment.[114]

The declared purpose of the FSIA was to depoliticize foreign sovereign immunity decisions and provide a clear statutory basis for the adjudication of State immunity claims:

> The Congress finds that the determination by United States courts of the claims of foreign states to immunity from the jurisdiction of such courts would serve the interests of justice and would protect the rights of both foreign states and litigants in United States courts. Under international law, states are not immune from the jurisdiction of foreign courts insofar as their commercial activities are concerned, and their commercial property may be levied upon for the satisfaction of judgments rendered against them in connection with their commercial activities. Claims of foreign states to immunity should henceforth be decided by courts of the United States and of the States in conformity with the principles set forth in this chapter.[115]

111. See, e.g., DAVID P. STEWART, THE FOREIGN SOVEREIGN IMMUNITIES ACT: A GUIDE TO JUDGES (2013); JOSEPH W. DELLAPENNA, SUING FOREIGN GOVERNMENTS AND THEIR CORPORATIONS (2d ed. 2003); *Report of the ABA Working Group, Reforming the Foreign Sovereign Immunities Act*, 40 COLUM. J. TRANSNAT'L L. 489 (2002) RESTATEMENT (THIRD) OF THE FOREIGN RELATIONS LAW OF THE UNITED STATES §§ 451–460 (AM. LAW INST. 1987); DAVID EPSTEIN & JEFFREY L. SNYDER, INTERNATIONAL LITIGATION: A GUIDE TO JURISDICTION, PRACTICE AND STRATEGY ch. 7 (2d ed. 1996); BARRY E. CARTER & PHILLIP R. TRIMBLE, INTERNATIONAL LAW ch. 6 (2d ed. 1995); LOUIS HENKIN, RICHARD PUGH, OSCAR SCHACHTER & HANS SMIT, INTERNATIONAL LAW 1126–87 (3d ed. 1993); Ernesto J. Sanchez, Foreign Sovereign Immunites Act Deskbook (American Bar Association 2014).

112. *Republic of Austria v. Altman*, 541 U.S. 677, 697 (2004) ("we find clear evidence that Congress intended the Act to apply to preenactment conduct.").

113. *Id.* "Claims of foreign states to immunity should henceforth be decided by courts of the United States and of the States in conformity with the principles set forth in this chapter." 28 U.S.C. § 1602 (2016).

114. See *id.* at 699 ("Congress' purposes in enacting such a comprehensive jurisdictional scheme would be frustrated if, in post-enactment cases concerning pre-enactment conduct, courts were to continue to follow the same ambiguous and politically charged 'standards' that the FSIA replaced.")

115. 28 U.S.C. § 1602 (2016).

The Act is basically a jurisdictional statute in that where a foreign State does not enjoy immunity federal courts have both personal and subject matter jurisdictions over claims against that State.[116] "[J]urisdictional statutes speak to the power of the court rather than to the rights or obligations of the parties."[117] The structure of the FSIA is such that jurisdictional immunity, personal jurisdiction, and subject matter jurisdiction are intertwined. As a result, if a foreign State is properly served in accordance with 28 U.S.C. § 1608, then statutory personal jurisdiction exists for claims where there is subject matter jurisdiction. Conversely, where one of the enumerated exceptions to immunity does not apply, the court lacks both subject matter and personal jurisdiction over the foreign State. Territoriality is key in the statutory scheme as it is not the intent of the Act to turn U.S. courts into international claims courts.[118]

Under the FSIA, federal courts have jurisdiction over suits against foreign States even in the absence of diversity and federal question.[119] The FSIA governs all suits in both state and federal courts against foreign States, including their "agencies and instrumentalities." The Act contains a "comprehensive set of legal standards governing claims of immunity in every civil action against a foreign state or its political subdivisions, agencies or instrumentalities"[120] and "provides the sole basis for obtaining jurisdiction over a foreign state in the courts of this country."[121]

There is a statutory presumption of immunity, and the specific exceptions to the jurisdictional immunity of a foreign state are enumerated in Sections 1605–1607. The exceptions include waiver;[122] commercial activities occurring in the United States or causing a direct effect in the United States;[123] property expropriated in

116. 28 U.S.C. § 1330(a) (2016) provides; "The district courts shall have original jurisdiction without regard to amount in controversy of any nonjury civil action against a foreign state as defined in section 1603(a) of this title as to any claim for relief *in personam* with respect to which the foreign state is not entitled to immunity under sections 1605–1607 of this title or under any applicable international agreement." 28 U.S.C. § 1330(b) (2016) provides: "Personal jurisdiction over a foreign state shall exist as to every claim for relief over which the district courts have [subject-matter] jurisdiction under subsection (a) where service has been made under [28 U.S.C. § 1608]."

117. *Landgraf v. USI Film Prods.*, 511 U.S. 244, 274 (1994).

118. See *Argentina Republic v. Amerada Hess Shipping Corp.*, 488 U.S. 428 (1989).

119. See *Verlinden B.V. v. Central Bank of Nigeria*, 461 U.S. 480, 489–94, 103 S. Ct. 1962 (1983); 28 U.S.C. § 1330(a) (2016).

120. *Verlinden*, 461 U.S. at 488.

121. *Samantar v. Yousuf*, 560 U.S. 305, 314 (2010) citing Amerada Hess.

122. See 28 U.S.C. § 1605(a)(1) (2016).

123. See 28 U.S.C. § 1605(a)(2) (2016).

violation of international law;[124] inherited, gift, or immovable property located in the United States;[125] noncommercial torts or personal injury occurring in the United States;[126] maritime liens;[127] arbitration;[128] counterclaims;[129] and terrorism.[130] If the defendant qualifies as a foreign State and no exception applies, the defendant is immune, and the court is ousted of any personal or subject-matter jurisdiction that the court may have had. Conversely, if the defendant qualifies as a foreign State but the claim falls within an exception under the statute, and if service of process has been made as provided by the statute, then the court has and can exercise personal and subject-matter jurisdiction over the defendant.

Consequently, a State is immune from the jurisdiction of U.S. courts, unless the suit falls within the exceptions set forth in the statute.[131] The FSIA not only provides foreign States with immunity from jurisdiction but also immunity from execution of judgments and attachments. Consequently, even when a foreign State is determined to be not immune from jurisdiction, the separate immunity from enforcement may still insulate the State from execution of a resulting judgment. FSIA has also a so-called preexisting treaty exception as its grant of sovereign immunity is "[s]ubject to existing international agreements to which the United States [was] a party at the time of enactment of th[e] Act."[132] Examples of such international agreements are the North Atlantic Treaty Organization (NATO) Status of Force Agreement, commercial contracts or agreements to which the United States is party and that calls for nonjudicial remedies through arbitration or other dispute resolution mechanism.[133] In other words, where there is conflict between that treaty and the FSIA, the provisions of that treaty would trump the FSIA.[134]

124. See 28 U.S.C. § 1605(a)(3) (2016).

125. See 28 U.S.C. § 1605(a)(4) (2016).

126. See 28 U.S.C. § 1605(a)(5) (2016).

127. See 28 U.S.C. § 1605(b) (2016).

128. See 28 U.S.C. § 1605(a)(6) (2016).

129. See 28 U.S.C. § 1607 (2016).

130. See 28 U.S.C. § 1605A (2016).

131. See 28 U.S.C. § 1604 (2016).

132. See 28 U.S.C. § 1604 (2016).

133. See H.R. Report p. 17.

134. See *de Csepel v. Republic of Hungary*, 714 F.3d 591, 601 (D.C. Cir. 2013); *Abelesz v. Magyar Nemzeti Bank*, 692 F.3d 661, 669 (7th Cir. 2012); *Moore v. United Kingdom*, 384 F.3d 1079, 1085 (9th Cir. 2004).

In sum, the FSIA addresses subject-matter and personal jurisdiction,[135] venue and removal to federal court,[136] procedural issues,[137] general principle of immunity of foreign States,[138] exceptions to immunity,[139] extent of liability,[140] and execution upon property of foreign States.[141] Section 1330(a) of FSIA specifically states that the Act does not apply to criminal proceedings.

PROCEDURES

The architecture of the FSIA is atypical: a court must determine whether a foreign State is immune before it determines whether it has personal and subject-matter jurisdiction. Ordinarily, immunity subsumes the existence of jurisdiction a priori. However, the formulation of 28 U.S.C. § 1330(a)[142] conditions subject-matter jurisdiction on the absence of immunity. Consequently, before a court must decide whether it has subject-matter jurisdiction, it must first determine whether the defendant is a "foreign state" as defined in Section 1603(a) and then whether any of the exceptions to immunity under Section 1605(a) or Section 1605A is applicable. "[E]ven if the foreign state does not enter an appearance to assert an immunity defense, a District Court still must determine that immunity is unavailable under this Act."[143]

Thus, a court lacks both personal and subject-matter jurisdiction if it determines first that the foreign State is immune. On the other hand, if the foreign State is not immune because an exception to immunity under the FSIA is applicable, and if proper service has been made, then the court automatically has personal and subject-matter jurisdiction.

135. See 28 U.S.C. §§ 1330(a) and 1332(a)(4) (2015).

136. See 28 U.S.C. §§ 1391(f) and 1441(d) (2011).

137. See 28 U.S.C. §§ 1330(a) and 1608 (2015).

138. See 28 U.S.C. § 1604 (2016).

139. See 28 U.S.C. §§ 1605 and 1607 (2016).

140. See 28 U.S.C. § 1606 (2016).

141. 28 U.S.C. §§ 1609–1611 (2016).

142. Under 28 U.S.C. § 1330(a), federal courts have "original jurisdiction without regard to amount in controversy of any nonjury civil action against a foreign state as defined in section 1603(a) of this title as to any claim for relief *in personam* with respect to which the foreign state is not entitled to immunity either under sections 1605–1607 of this title or under any applicable international agreement. 28 U.S.C. § 1330(a) (2010).

143. *Verlinden B.V. v. Central Bank of Nigeria*, 461 U.S. 480, 495 n.20 (1983).

Sovereign immunity is an affirmative defense, where the defendant must make a prima facie showing that it is a foreign sovereign or its subdivision, agency, or instrumentality, and then the burden shifts to the plaintiff to present evidence showing that an exception to the FSIA applies. Thus, the defendant retains the ultimate burden of persuasion on proving that it is immune.[144] FSIA limits the jurisdiction of American courts to hear claims against foreign States but it does not create any cause of action. "The language and history of the FSIA clearly establish that the Act was not intended to affect the substantive law determining liability of a foreign state or instrumentality."[145]

In *Saudi Arabia v. Nelson*, the presumption of immunity under the FSIA received the imprimatur of the Supreme Court: "Under the [FSIA], a foreign state is presumptively immune from jurisdiction of United States courts; unless a specified exception applies, a federal court lacks subject matter jurisdiction over a claim against a foreign state."[146]

The foreign State bears the burden to produce prima facie evidence that it is the defendant and that the plaintiff's claim relates to the public act of the foreign State. The burden then shifts to the plaintiff to produce evidence establishing that the foreign State is not entitled to immunity, but the ultimate burden of proving immunity rests with the foreign State.[147]

Beyond the issue of jurisdictional immunity, the FSIA grants foreign States certain protections such as a separate and formalized scheme for serving process on the foreign State proper or its agency or instrumentality; additional time to respond to actions; venue and the right of removal to federal court; right of bench, instead of jury, trial; and certain rights with respect to attachment and execution on the property of the foreign State. These other jurisdictional, procedural, and evidentiary issues, raised by suits under FSIA, are beyond the scope of this book.[148]

144. See H.R. Rep. No. 1487, 94th Cong., 2d sess., reprinted in 1976 U.S. Code Cong. & Admin. News 6604, 6616; *Matar v. Dichter*, 563 F.3d 9, 12 (2d Cir. 2009), also stating that the Court of Appeals' standard of review of the district court's decision regarding subject matter jurisdiction is for clear error as to factual findings, and de novo as to legal conclusions [Citations omitted].

145. *First Nat'l City Bank v. Banco Parra El Comercio*, 462 U.S. 611, 620 (1983); H.R. Rep. No. 94-1487, at 12 (1976), *as reprinted* in 1976 U.S.C.C.A.N. 6604, 6610.

146. *Saudi Arabia v. Nelson*, 507 U.S. 349 (1993).

147. See H.R. Report, p. 17.

148. A very useful discussion of these issues is found in David P. Stewart, The Foreign Sovereign Immunities Act: A Guide for Judges, published by the Federal Judicial Center (2013).

United Kingdom State Immunity Act

Applicability and Scope

The United Kingdom enacted the State Immunity Act 1978 (SIA)[149] and then ratified the European Convention on State Immunity ("Basle Convention") of 1972, which it had earlier signed.[150] Although the SIA was designed to implement the Basle Convention, which has been in force since 1976, it is broader in scope than the Basle Convention. The SIA, for the most part, treats all States alike but reserves more favorable treatment for the Contracting States of the Basle Convention in such areas as "procedural privileges and immunities, recognition of judgments and security for costs."[151]

The SIA, which adopts the doctrine of restrictive State immunity,[152] starts with the general rule that a State, including its head of State, government, and governmental departments, is immune from suit in the courts of the United Kingdom.[153] The SIA confers privileges and immunities to foreign and commonwealth States that are recognized by the United Kingdom. The SIA extends immunity to "separate entities," that is, bodies distinct from the executive organs of the central government of the foreign State and that have legal capacity, *if and only if* the proceedings against the entity relate to its exercise of sovereign authority, and the circumstances are such that the State itself would have been immune.[154] Constituent territories of a federal State are treated like separate entities unless they are invested with immunity like a State by an Order in Council.[155] Under the general rubric of Exceptions from Immunity, the SIA

149. The SIA is variously similar to the FSIA in some respects and to the Basle Convention in other respects.

150. Section 23(3) provides that the SIA does not have retroactive effect in that it does not apply to proceedings in respect of matters that occurred before it entered into force. In those instances, the common law would apply as was the case in *I Congreso del Partido* [1981] 3 WLR 328 (House of Lords).

151. See Andrew Dickinson, Rae Lindsay & James P. Loonam, State Immunity: Selected Materials and Commentary (2004).

152. Before the enactment of the SIA, the Court of Appeal of England and Wales had rejected the doctrine of absolute immunity in favor of restrictive immunity, notably in *The Philippine Admiral*, *Trendtex* and *I Congreso del Partido*, but these decisions were not binding outside England in the rest of the United Kingdom, namely Scotland, Wales, and Northern Ireland.

153. See SIA, Section 14(1).

154. See SIA, Section 14(2).

155. See SIA, Section 14(5).

recognizes several exceptions to immunity, including waiver and arbitration.[156] The SIA applies to immunity from jurisdiction and immunity from execution.

Part I of the SIA has 17 sections and is concerned with proceedings in the United Kingdom by or against foreign States. Section 1 provides for a rule of general immunity of States from jurisdiction, and Sections 2 to 11 provide for specific exceptions to that immunity. To satisfy the exercise of jurisdiction by States under customary international law, most of these exceptions require a nexus between the claim and the United Kingdom. Section 3(1)(a), however, does require a link between the case and the United Kingdom. The Act also applies to the immunity of heads of State.[157]

Section 23(3) provides that the provisions of Parts I and II of the SIA do not operate retrospectively, but makes no mention of Part III.

Section 2 deals with situations where a State is not immune because it is deemed to have submitted to the jurisdiction of the courts of the United Kingdom.[158] This waiver of immunity is based on the conduct of the State.[159] Such conduct may be an appearance of a foreign State as a plaintiff or a defendant on the merits;[160] however, a foreign State does not waive its immunity if it intervenes merely to assert its immunity or an interest in property.[161] A foreign State does not waive its immunity if its conduct is "in ignorance of facts entitling it to immunity if those facts could not reasonably have been ascertained and immunity is claimed as soon as reasonably practicable."[162] In addition to conduct that may be construed as an implied waiver, a foreign State may waive expressly its immunity by prior written agreement but a provision in any agreement that it will be governed by the law of the United Kingdom is not to be regarded as a waiver of immunity.[163] If a waiver of immunity derives from contract, then "any person who has entered

156. See SIA, Sections 2 to 12. These sections are similar to Articles 1 to 14 of the Basle Convention.

157. See long title of Act and Section 20.

158. SIA, Section 2 is comparable to Section 1605 of FSIA, which also provides for explicit or implicit waiver of immunity by a foreign State.

159. Although "submission to jurisdiction" is classified under "exceptions from immunity," it is really a waiver, which is different from an exception. Also, waiver focuses on the conduct of the State as opposed to exception, which focuses on the nature of the act.

160. See SIA, Section 2(3).

161. See SIA, Section 2(4).

162. SIA, Section 2(5).

163. See SIA, Section 2(2). This provision reverses the common law rule of *Kahan v. Pakistan Federation* [1951] 2 K.B. 1003 (C.A.) that submission to jurisdiction could be made only in the face of the court and not by prior written agreement.

into a contract on behalf of and with the authority of a State shall be deemed to have authority to submit on its behalf in respect of proceedings arising out of the contract."[164] A submission to jurisdiction "in respect of any proceedings extends to any appeal but not to any counter-claim unless it arises out of the same legal relationship or facts as the claim."[165]

Section 3 provides for exception from immunity for "commercial transactions and contracts" in the United Kingdom. This exception, in contrast to the corresponding exception in FSIA,[166] does not require that the commercial transaction have any nexus with the United Kingdom other than that which is necessary to establish the jurisdiction of the court in the first place.[167] Also, the commercial transaction exception may be excluded by the parties to the dispute in a written agreement.[168] This provision defines "commercial transaction" as:

> (a) Any contract for the supply of goods or services;
> (b) Any loan or other transaction for the provision of finance and any guarantee or indemnity in respect of any such transaction or any other financial obligation; and
> (c) Any other transaction or activity (whether of a commercial, industrial, financial, professional or other similar character) into which a State enters or in which it engages otherwise than in the exercise of sovereign authority.[169]

Under Section 4, a foreign State is not immune with respect to contracts of employment made in the United Kingdom or to be performed wholly or partly

164. See SIA, Section 2(7), which also provides that the "head of State's diplomatic mission in the United Kingdom . . . shall be deemed to have authority to submit on behalf of the State in respect of any proceedings."

165. SIA, Section 2(6). This provision is in contrast with Section 1607 of FSIA, under which the amount of relief sought cannot exceed the amount sought by the foreign State if the counterclaim does not arise from the same transaction in dispute.

166. See FSIA, 18 U.S.C. § § 1603(e), 1605(a) (2) (2016).

167. See SIA, Section 3(1).

168. See SIA, Section 3(2).

169. SIA, Section 3(3). This definition of "commercial transaction" is more specific than the so-called definition of "commercial activity" found in Section 1603(d) of FSIA. Also, the Section does not have the limitation of Sections 1603(e) and 1605 of FSIA in that the exception may apply to commercial transactions of the foreign State carried out in the United Kingdom.

in the United Kingdom, unless the employee is not a resident or national of the United Kingdom, or the parties have otherwise agreed in writing. Foreign States are not immune in proceedings in respect of personal injuries and damage to property, pursuant to Section 5 of the Act. Similarly, foreign States are generally not immune in proceedings relating to ownership, possession, and use of property;[170] intellectual property;[171] membership in bodies corporate, incorporated bodies, or partnerships;[172] or submissions to arbitration in the United Kingdom, unless otherwise excluded in the arbitration agreement.[173] Other exceptions from immunity under the Act deal with ships used for commercial purposes;[174] and certain taxes, duties, levies and rates.[175] Section 16(4) of SIA specifically states that the Act does not apply to criminal proceedings.

Procedures

On questions of what or who is a State for purposes of State immunity, a certificate by or on behalf of the UK secretary of state shall be conclusive evidence.[176] Procedure for service of process and judgments in default of appearance is found in Section 12 of SIA, which provides that any necessary documents required to institute proceedings against a foreign State shall be served by transmission to the foreign ministry of the State through the Foreign and Commonwealth Office.[177] Service shall be deemed to have been effected upon receipt at the ministry, and any time for entering appearance shall begin to run two months after the date of receipt.[178] No judgment in default against a State shall be entered except upon proof of service of process through diplomatic channels in

170. See SIA, Section 6.

171. See SIA, Section 7.

172. See SIA, Section 8.

173. See SIA, Section 9.

174. See SIA, Section 10, which relates to admiralty proceedings, and provides that a foreign State is not immune with respect to suits in rem and in personam concerning ships belonging to it if the vessel was in use or intended for use by it when the cause of action arose.

175. See SIA, Section 11.

176. See SIA, Section 21.

177. See SIA, Section 12(1).

178. See SIA, Section 12(2).

accordance with this Section.[179] However, service of a writ or other document in any manner to which the State has agreed is permissible.[180] In addition, the procedure for service of process under the SIA "shall not be construed as affecting any rules of court whereby leave is required for the service of process outside the jurisdiction."[181]

179. See SIA, Section 12(4).

180. See SIA, Section 12(6).

181. SIA, Section 12(7).

3

Scope of State Immunity

WHO AND WHAT ARE COVERED BY STATE IMMUNITY

Who and what are covered by State immunity are questions about the scope of the immunity. State immunity protects a foreign State qua State, as a sovereign and international person, from the jurisdiction of a forum State.[1] The government of a State is a beneficiary of State immunity, and a suit against a foreign government is an action against the foreign State itself, as the government acts on behalf of the State. The government is usually composed of subsidiary organs and departments that act on behalf of the government. "In the actual operation of the doctrine of State immunity, many categories of persons, institutions, agencies, instrumentalities, and properties have enjoyed the benefit of immunities in the name or on behalf of the State."[2] The "reality is that governmental decisions are carried out by a state's servants and agents. States are abstract entities that can only act through individuals."[3]

1. State immunity does not only foreclose proceedings or judgment on the merits but also protects the property of the State against any measures, such as seizure or attachment, in connection with the proceedings.

2. Sompong Sucharitkul, *Immunities of Foreign States Before National Authorities*, 149 Recueil des cours 87, 96 (1976).

3. Kazemi Estate v. Islamic Republic of Iran, 2014 SCC 62 ¶ 85, [2014] 3 S.C.R. 176 (Can.).

Jurisdictional Immunities of States and International Organizations. Edward Chukwuemeke Okeke.

Distinction between Immunities *Ratione Personae* and *Ratione Materiae*

Issues of immunity normally revolve around the status or conduct of the person or entity, which has a bearing on the availability or scope of immunity if accorded. It must be recalled that State immunity historically originated from the immunity of the sovereign, who was the personification of the State. Diplomatic immunity also had its historical origin in the immunity of the sovereign, as the diplomat was the representative of the sovereign and was afforded the same immunity as the sovereign. The primary rationale for the immunity of the sovereign and his diplomatic representative was that it would be an affront on the dignity of the sovereign for jurisdiction to be exercised over them. Over time the immunity was bifurcated into two separate immunities.

International law recognizes two different types of immunities, which also have different rationales, namely immunity *ratione personae* and immunity *ratione materiae*.[4] Immunity *ratione personae*, that is, immunity by reason of the person, is a status-based immunity that protects the individual from suit while still in office. It attaches to the position or office of the person but not to the conduct of the person. Heads of State, heads of government, and ministers of foreign affairs are deemed to represent their States, and by virtue of their high-ranking positions enjoy immunity *ratione personae*.[5] If the *Arrest Warrant* judgment is any guide, then immunity *ratione personae* may apply to other high-ranking State officials other than the troika of head of State, head of government, and minister of foreign affairs.

Immunity *ratione materiae*, that is, immunity by reason of the matter, is functional or official immunity. As States act through officials, functional immunity operates to protect States from being sued for acts performed by their officials on behalf of the States. Immunity *ratione materiae* is a conduct-based immunity that protects the official from suit based on the type of act performed, and it continues to cover the official after leaving office. The immunity belongs not to the official or individual but to the State, and may be waived by the State itself.

At issue usually is what constitutes an official act so as to benefit from sovereign immunity. A rationale for immunity *ratione materiae* is sovereign equality of States because to sue an individual regarding the conduct of the State's affairs or activities is tantamount to indirectly suing the State itself. Immunity *ratione*

4. See *R v. Bow Street Metropolitan Stipendiary Magistrate and others, ex parte Pinochet Ugarte (Amnesty International and others intervening) (No 3)*, ("*Ex Parte Pinochet 3*"), [2000] 1 AC 147, [1999] 2 ALL ER 97, [1999] 2 WLR 827 (Lord Millett).

5. See Arrest Warrant of 11 April 2000 (Democratic Republic of the Congo v. Belgium), Judgment, I.C.J. Rep. 2002, p. 3 ("*Arrest Warrant*"), para. 51.

materiae is a subject matter immunity that covers official conduct or a governmental act, and is the same no matter the rank of the official.[6]

The scope of immunity *ratione materiae* of a former head of State was the subject of the *Pinochet* case, where the question before the House of Lords was whether the former head of State of Chile was entitled to immunity *ratione materiae* for alleged acts of torture committed by him as head of State.[7] In his judgment, Lord Browne-Wilkinson noted: "Immunity *ratione materiae* applies not only to ex-heads of state and ex-ambassadors but to all state officials who have been involved in carrying out the functions of the state. Such immunity is necessary in order to prevent state immunity being circumvented by prosecuting or suing the official."[8]

Immunity *ratione materiae* is paradoxically both broader and narrower than immunity *ratione personae*. It is broader in the sense that it covers all official acts and lasts beyond the tenure in office, and narrower because it applies only to official acts and not to personal acts. Immunity *ratione personae*, on the other hand, covers acts performed before the person took office and personal acts performed while in office, but it is *ratione temporis* as the immunity terminates with the office. Immunity *ratione personae* and immunity *ratione materiae* are not mutually exclusive, as a person can have both (e.g., diplomatic agents).

Heads of State

Heads of State bear diverse titles, which have no bearing on their entitlement to immunity. They may perform either ceremonial or executive functions, or both. A head of State may not necessarily be the head of government of a State. For instance, in the United States, the president is both the head of State and the head of government, but in the United Kingdom, the monarch (queen or king) is the head of State and the prime minister is the head of the government.

The origin of head of State immunity dates to when the sovereign was both the embodiment and personification of the State, as immortalized by the statement of King Louis XIV of France: "*L'etat, c'est moi.*" In the United Kingdom, the immunity of foreign sovereigns originated from the practice that the domestic sovereign cannot be sued in his courts.[9] Heads of State, as sovereigns, have been identified

6. See *Ex Parte Pinochet (3)* (Lord Millett).

7. See *Ex Parte Pinochet (3)*.

8. *Id.*

9. See *De Haber v. Queen of Portugal*, (1851–1852) 17 QB 196, 117 E.R. 1255.

with the States that they head, and are usually included in the definition of State so much that "sovereign immunity" and "State immunity" are used interchangeably.[10] "[T]he older law not only treated Heads of States as entitled to very special legal considerations, but also frequently made no clear distinction between the Head of State on the one hand, and the State itself on the other hand. With international relations having that more personal quality than is usual today, issues of sovereign immunity were mainly concerned with protecting the position of the Head of State."[11] The immunity is based on customary international law: "Under traditional customary law the Head of State was seen as personifying the sovereign State. The immunity to which he was entitled was therefore predicated on status, just like the State he or she symbolized."[12] Thus, head of State immunity is an autonomous and distinct rule of customary international law, even though it is subsumed in State immunity under some national legislation.[13]

> It is well established that, put broadly, a Head of State enjoys a wide immunity from the criminal, civil and administrative jurisdiction of other States. This immunity—to the extent that it exists—becomes effective upon his assumption of office, even in respect of events occurring earlier."[14]
>
> "A Head of State's immunity is enjoyed in recognition of his very special status as a holder of his State's highest office."[15]
>
> "A former Head of State is entitled under international law to none of the facilities, immunities and privileges which international law accords to heads of States in office."[16]
>
> "After his loss of office he may be sued in relation to his private activities, both those taking place while he was still Head of State, as well as those

10. See Sompong Sucharitkul, *Immunities of Foreign States Before National Authorities*, 149 Recueil des cours 87, 97 (1976).

11. Arthur Watts, *Legal Position in International Law of Heads of States, Heads of Governments and Foreign Ministers* (1994) 247 Recueil des Cours at p. 35 ("Watts, 247 RDC").

12. See Arrest Warrant of 11 April 2000 (Democratic Republic of the Congo v. Belgium), Judgment, I.C.J. Rep. 2002, p.b3, Joint Separate Opinion of Judges Higgins, Kooijmans, and Buergenthal, para. 80.

13. See Section 36 of Australian Foreign Sovereign Immunity Act; Section 2(a) of Canadian State Immunity Act; Section 15(1)(a) of Pakistani State Immunity Ordinance No. VI of 1981; Section 16(1) of Singaporean State Immunity Act; Section 2(a) of South African Foreign Sovereign Immunity Act No. 87 of 1981.

14. Watts, 247 RDC at 53 [citations omitted].

15. *Id.*

16. *Id.* at 88.

> occurring before becoming Head of State or since ceasing to be Head of State."[17]
>
> "A Head of State's official acts, performed in his public capacity as Head of State, are however subject to different considerations. Such acts are acts of the State rather than the Head of State's personal acts, and he cannot be sued for them even after he has ceased to be Head of State. The position is similar to that of acts performed by an ambassador in the exercise of his functions, for which immunity continues to subsist even after the ambassador's appointment has come to an end.[18]

The immunity of a head of State results from his or her superior status in the apparatus of the State:

> The immunity of a serving head of state is enjoyed by reason of his special status as the holder of his state's highest office. He is regarded as the personal embodiment of the state itself. It would be an affront to the dignity and sovereignty of the state which he personifies and a denial of the equality of sovereign states to subject him to the jurisdiction of the municipal courts of another state, whether in respect of his public acts or private affairs. His person is inviolable; he is not to be arrested or detained on any ground whatever.[19]

A head of State enjoys immunity from all forms of judicial process, which includes both civil and criminal proceedings.[20] The immunity is both *ratione personae* and *ratione materiae*. Heads of State enjoy immunity *ratione personae* for as long as they remain in office. The person of a foreign Head of State is inviolable, as he cannot be arrested or detained or be subjected to judicial process in a forum State while he is in office. However, once heads of State leave office they may be sued for personal acts they performed while in office because those acts are not covered by immunities *ratione materiae*. Thus, the status of heads of State guarantees their immunity while in office but any residual immunity they may have while out of office would depend on the nature of the conduct, that is, whether the act was in a public or private capacity. The immunity of a head of State for nonofficial acts is *ratione temporis* in the sense that there is a temporal limitation to it. The

17. *Id.* [citations omitted].

18. *Id.* at 89 [citations omitted].

19. *Ex Parte Pinochet* (3), (Dissent of Lord Millett).

20. See *Arrest Warrant Case*, para. 51.

immunity for such acts is no longer available once the status as head of State is no more.[21]

The issue is usually whether the person claiming immunity as head of State is actually recognized as such by the forum State. This is one of the questions addressed in a suit for damages against a vessel belonging to the Khedive of Egypt: "Is the international status of the Khedive that of a sovereign prince of Egypt?"[22] After a historical inquiry about the status of his Highness the Khedive, the court concluded that Egypt was then considered as one of the provinces of the then Ottoman Empire and lacked conditions of sovereignty such as *jus legationis*.[23] The court also considered the opinion of the British Foreign Office that "the Khedive has not been and is not now recognised by Her Majesty as reigning sovereign of the state of Egypt."[24] The court held "that his highness the Khedive, however exalted his position and distinguished his rank, has failed to establish that he is entitled to the privileges of a sovereign prince, according to the criteria of sovereignty required by the reason of the thing, and by the usage and practice of nations as expounded by accredited writers upon international jurisprudence."[25]

When Panamanian strongman Manuel Antonio Noriega fell out of favor with the U.S. government, Panama was invaded by the United States and he was captured and brought to the United States for trial on drug-related charges. Noriega's claim of head of State immunity was denied by the U.S. courts because the U.S. government never recognized him "as Panama's legitimate, constitutional ruler."[26] In other words, the United States did not recognize Noriega as the de jure head of State of Panama even though he was the de facto head of State and served as the commander of the Panamanian Defense Forces. The position of the executive branch of the U.S. government on the head of State immunity was vital, as the Foreign Sovereign Immunity Act (FSIA) addresses neither head of State immunity nor foreign official immunity in the criminal context. "Generally, the Executive Branch's position on head-of-state immunity falls into one of three

21. See *Ex-King Farouk of Egypt v. Christian Dior*, 24 ILR 228-9 (1957). The Court of Appeals of Paris, France, held that King Farouk of Egypt, following his abdication, was no longer entitled to head of State immunity from the jurisdiction of the French courts.

22. *The Charkieh (6200)* [1873] L.R. 4 A. & E.59 at p.75 (Sir Robert Phillimore).

23. *Id.* at. 84.

24. *Id.* at 86.

25. *Id.* at 100.

26. See *United States of America v. Manuel Antonio Noriega*, 117 F. 3d 1206, 1211 (11th Cir. 1997).

categories: the Executive Branch (1) explicitly suggests immunity; (2) expressly declines to suggest immunity; or (3) offers no guidance."[27]

In support of its determination that Noriega was not entitled to immunity, the Court reasoned that the U.S. government's capture and prosecution of Noriega manifested its clear position that Noriega should be denied immunity:

> Moreover, given that the record indicates that Noriega never served as the constitutional leader of Panama, that Panama has not sought immunity for Noriega and that the charged acts relate to Noriega's private pursuit of personal enrichment, Noriega likely would not prevail even if this court had to make an independent determination regarding the propriety of immunity in this case.[28]

In the United States, "[t]he obligation of the Judicial Branch is clear—a determination by the Executive Branch that a foreign head of state is immune from suit is conclusive and a court must accept such a determination without reference to the underlying claim of the plaintiff."[29]

The United Kingdom State Immunity Act (SIA) includes head of State in its definition of foreign State."[30] Section 20(1) provides pertinently: "Subject to the provisions of this section and to any necessary modifications, the Diplomatic Privileges Act 1964 shall apply to . . . a sovereign or head of State . . . as it applies to the head of a diplomatic mission."[31] The House of Lords addressed the immunity of a head of State in the *Pinochet* case.

The *Pinochet* case arose out of the arrest by English authorities of the former president of Chile in 1998 during a private visit to the United Kingdom for medical treatment, pursuant to an international warrant issued by a Spanish judge for extradition to Spain to answer charges for alleged crimes committed. Pinochet applied to quash the arrest warrant on the grounds that he enjoyed immunity from criminal proceedings as a former head of State. The House of Lords (Lords Browne-Wilkinson, Hope of Craighead, Hutton, Saville of Newdigate, Millett, Phillips of Worth Matravers, with Goff of Chieveley dissenting) held by a majority of six to one that Pinochet did not enjoy immunity for the alleged crime.

27. *Id.* at 1212.

28. *Id.*

29. *Ye v. Zemin*, 383 F.3d 620, 626 (7th Cir. 2004) [citation omitted].

30. United Kingdom SIA, Sections 14(1)(a), and 20(1).

31. Diplomatic Privileges Act 1964 ("Diplomatic Act") gave effect to the Vienna Convention on Diplomatic Relations 1961 ("Vienna Convention").

In arriving at their judgments, the Law Lords examined the scope of immunity of heads of State under SIA.

As recognized by Lord Goff, the "problem is, of course, how to identify the 'necessary modifications' when applying the Vienna Convention to heads of State." The problem was with scope of immunity of Pinochet as a former head of State, as the scope of immunity of a serving head of State was not in dispute. He held that Pinochet benefitted from immunity *ratione materiae* as a former head of State.

Lord Hope believed SIA restricts the immunity of a head of State in civil proceedings as it does for diplomats but does not do the same for criminal proceedings, and that the Act codified the customary international law of immunity of both serving and former heads of State. Regarding the question of the "necessary modification" to be made to Article 39(2) of the Vienna Convention[32] in its application to a former head of State, he concluded that the residual immunity *ratione materia* should cover all acts that the person has performed in the exercise of governmental functions and protects those acts from further analysis. He, however, believes that the immunity is subject to two exceptions: criminal acts by the head of State for his own pleasure or benefit, and crimes with the status of jus cogens.

Lord Hutton considered "Section 20 . . . a difficult section to construe" but that it "did not change the law in relation to the immunity from criminal jurisdiction to which a former head of state was entitled in the United Kingdom." Lord Phillips did not think that Section 20 of the SIA applies to the conduct of a head of State outside the United Kingdom, and that immunity *ratione materiae* extends to "actions that are prohibited as criminal under international law."

Lord Saville noted that a former head of State has immunity *ratione materiae,* which belongs to the State, and that Section 20 of SIA gave statutory force to the customary international law principle. Lord Millett agreed that the "immunity which is in question in the present case, therefore, belongs to the Republic of Chile, not to Senator Pinochet."

The House of Lords unanimously held that a serving head of State enjoyed absolute immunity from criminal proceedings even for alleged international crime, but disagreed as to the scope of residual immunity *rationae materiae* of a former head of State.

32. Article 39(2) of the Vienna Convention provides:

> When the functions of a person enjoying privileges and immunities have come to an end, such privileges and immunities shall normally cease at the moment when he leaves the country, or on expiry of a reasonable period in which to do so, but shall subsist until that time, even in case of armed conflict. However, with respect to acts performed by such a person in the exercise of his functions as a member of the mission, immunity shall continue to subsist.

The state of the law is that an incumbent head of State has both immunity *ratione personae* and immunity *ratione materiae*, but a former head of State is left with only immunity *ratione materiae*.

Foreign Officials

The immunity of officials of foreign States derives from the immunity of the States, as the acts that are the subject of the immunity are imputable to the States. Consequently, only the foreign State can assert or waive the immunity of a foreign official. "[A]s a matter of international law, the same immunity against suit in a foreign domestic court which protects the state itself also protects the individuals for whom the state is responsible. . . . The traditional way of expressing this principle in international law is to say that the acts of state officials acting in that capacity are not attributable to them personally but only to the state."[33] The imputation of acts of foreign officials as acts of the foreign State for purposes of State immunity has a corollary in the international law of State responsibility. International law is concerned more with the conduct of States and less with the conduct of individuals. Under international law, individuals are not responsible for wrongs committed by the State even though the individual may have committed the wrongful act at the behest of the State or under color of law. The limited international norms on individual responsibility are the province of international criminal law,[34] international humanitarian law, and international human rights law, whose very purpose is to hold individuals, including officials, responsible for their acts even when acting for the State. The principle of individual responsibility for international crimes was pioneered by the Nuremberg Tribunal:

> The principle of international law which, under certain circumstances, protects the representatives of a state, cannot be applied to acts which are condemned as criminal by international law. The authors of these acts cannot shelter themselves behind their official position in order to be freed from punishment in appropriate proceedings.[35]

The immunity of foreign officials was at issue in *Jones v. Saudi Arabia*, where the claimant had sued the Kingdom of Saudi Arabia and its officials for aggravated

33. *Jones v. Saudi Arabia*, [2006] UKHL 26, [2007] 1 All ER 113, [2006] BHRC 621, para. 66.

34. See International Military Tribunal at Nuremberg, Judgments and Sentences, October 1, 1946, reproduced in 41 American Journal of International Law 172, 221 (1947) ("Crimes against international law are committed by men, not abstract entities, and only by punishing individuals who commit such crimes can the provisions of international law be enforced.")

35. *In re Goering*, 13 ILR 203, 221 (1946) [citation omitted].

and exemplary damages for assault and battery, trespass to the person, false imprisonment, and torture in the Kingdom.[36] The House of Lord noted that the applicable law is the SIA, which provides that a State is immune from the jurisdiction of the courts of the United Kingdom except in the specific proceedings under Sections 2–11 of Part 1 of the Act. Section 14(1) defines a State to include (1) the sovereign or other head of that State in his public capacity, (2) the government of that State, and (3) any department of that government. Section 16(4) provides that Part 1 of the Act does not apply to criminal proceedings. The SIA does not use the term "official."

The House of Lords observed:

> While the 1978 Act explains what is comprised within the expression "State", and both it and the [Basle] Convention govern the immunity of separate entities exercising sovereign powers, neither expressly provides for the case where suit is brought against the servants or agents, officials or functionaries of a foreign state (servants or agents) in respect of acts done by them as such in the foreign state. There is, however, a wealth of authority to show that in such case the foreign state is entitled to claim immunity for its servants as it could if sued itself. The foreign state's right to immunity cannot be circumvented by suing its servants or agents.[37]

It concluded:

> (1) that all the individual defendants were at the material times acting or purporting to act as servants or agents of the Kingdom; (2) that their acts were accordingly attributable to the Kingdom; (3) that no distinction is to be made between the claim against the Kingdom and the claim against the personal defendants; and (4) that none of these claims falls within any of the exceptions specified in the 1978 Act. . . . On a straightforward application of the 1978 Act, it would follow that the Kingdom's claim to immunity for itself and its servants or agents should succeed, since this is not one of those exceptional cases, specified in Pt 1 of the 1978 Act, in which a state is not immune, and therefore the general rule of immunity prevails.[38]

36. *Jones v. Saudi Arabia*, [2006] UKHL 26, [2007] 1 All ER 113, [2006] BHRC 621. Judgment of Lord Bingham of Cornhill, with which Lord Hoffman, Lord Rodger of Earlsferry, Lord Walker of Gestingthorpe, and Lord Carswell agree.

37. *Jones v. Saudi Arabia*, [2006] UKHL 26, [2007] 1 All ER 113, [2006] BHRC 621, para. 10.

38. *Id.*, para. 13.

To the claimants' argument that the Kingdom of Saudi Arabia's claim to immunity for itself and the individual defendants would be incompatible with their right of access to a court under Article 6 of the European Convention on Human Rights (ECHR), the House of Lord held that "Pt 1 of the 1978 Act is not shown to be disproportionate as inconsistent with a peremptory norm of international law, and its application does not infringe the claimants' convention right under art 6 of the European Convention (assuming it to apply)."[39] It, therefore, dismissed the claims on grounds of State immunity.

The *Jones* case made it to the European Court of Human Rights (ECtHR), where applicants alleged that the grant of immunity in civil proceedings to the Kingdom of Saudi Arabia amounted to a disproportionate interference with their right of access to court under Article 6 of the ECHR.[40] The ECtHR stated:

> The first question is whether the grant of immunity *ratione materiae* to State officials reflects generally recognised rules of public international law. The Court has previously accepted that the grant of immunity to the State reflects such rules. Since an act cannot be carried out by a State itself but only by individuals acting on the State's behalf, where immunity can be invoked by the State then the starting point must be that immunity *ratione materiae* applies to the acts of State officials. If it were otherwise, State immunity could always be circumvented by suing named officials. This pragmatic understanding is reflected by the definition of 'State' in the 2004 UN Convention . . . which provides that the terms includes representatives of the State acting in that capacity.[41]

The ECtHR noted:

> There is also extensive case-law at national and international level which concludes that acts performed by State officials in the course of their service are to be attributed, for the purposes of State immunity, to the State on whose behalf they act. Thus in *Propend*, the English Court of Appeal held that immunities conferred on the State pursuant to the 1978 Act must be read as affording to individual State officials "protection under the same cloak as protects the State itself". . . . In Canada, the Court of Appeal in *Jaffe* concluded that the notion of "State"' in the SIA covered employees of the State acting in the course of their duties. . . . In *Fang*, the High Court

39. *Id.*, para. 28.

40. *Jones v. United Kingdom*, [2014] ECtHR, *Applications nos. 34356/06 and 40528/06.*

41. *Id.*, para. 202.

in New Zealand held that State immunity incidentally conferred immunity *ratione materiae* in claims against individuals whose conduct in the exercise of the authority of the State was called into question. . . . In *Zhang*, an Australian Court of Appeal held that individual officers were covered by the Immunities Act since they were entitled to immunity at common law and this had not been changed by the Act. . . . Although the United States Supreme Court in *Samantar* held that officials did not fall under the notion of "State" within the meaning of the FSIA, it clarified that their immunities were governed by common law, as the statute was deemed to be only a partial codification of immunity rules in the United States. . . . The Court of Appeal (Fourth Circuit) subsequently accepted that, in principle, State officials could enjoy immunity for acts performed in the course of their employment by the State

In *Blaškić*, the ICTY described State officials acting in their official capacity as "mere instruments of a State" and explained that they enjoyed "functional immunity". . . . In *Djibouti v. France*, the ICJ referred to the possibility open to the Djibouti government to claim that the acts of two State officials were its own acts, and that the officials were its organs, agencies or instrumentalities in carrying them out.

The weight of authority at international and national level therefore appears to support the proposition that State immunity in principle offers individual employees or officers of a foreign State protection in respect of acts undertaken on behalf of the State under the same cloak as protects the State itself."[42]

The United States Foreign Sovereign Immunity Act (FSIA) provides that "a foreign state shall be immune from the jurisdiction" of U.S. courts, unless a specified exception in the statute applies.[43] The statute defines a "foreign state" to include "a political subdivision of a foreign state or an agency or instrumentality of foreign state" as also defined in the statute.

"An 'agency or instrumentality of a foreign state' means any entity—(1) which is a separate legal person, corporate or otherwise, and (2) which is an organ of a foreign state or political subdivision thereof, or a majority of whose shares or other ownership interest is owned by a foreign state or political subdivision thereof, and (3) which is neither a citizen of a State of the

42. *Id.*, para. 203-4.

43. Foreign Sovereign Immunity Act (FSIA), 28 U.S.C. §§ 1330, 1604, 1605–1607 (2008); *Saudi Arabia v. Nelson*, 507 U.S. 349, 355 (1993).

> United States as defined in section 1332 (c) and (e) of this title, nor created under the laws of any third country."[44]

In *Samantar v. Yousuf*,[45] the United States Supreme Court decided the narrow question of whether the FSIA provides a foreign official with immunity from suit based on actions taken in his official capacity, and unanimously held that the FSIA did not govern the determination of the petitioner's immunity from suit. The petitioner had served as first vice president and minister of defense of Somalia, and from 1987 to 1990 he served as its prime minister. The respondents are natives of Somalia who alleged that they, or members of their families, were the victims of torture and extrajudicial killings during those years. They sought damages from the petitioner based on his alleged authorization of those acts.

The Supreme Court considered the argument that either "foreign state" or "agency or instrumentality" under § 1603 of the FSIA could be read to include a foreign official, but stated that its review of the text, purpose, and history of the FSIA led the Court to the conclusion that the FSIA did not govern the petitioner's claim of immunity.[46] It stated that the FSIA did not deprive the District Court of subject-matter jurisdiction in the case, but emphasized the narrowness of its holding.[47] It also stated: "Whether petitioner may be entitled to immunity under the common law, and whether he may have other valid defenses to the grave charges against him, are matters to be addressed in the first instance by the District Court on remand."[48]

The Supreme Court further stated:

> And we think this case, in which respondents have sued petitioner in his personal capacity and seek damages from his own pockets, is properly governed by the common law because it is not a claim against a foreign state as the Act defines that term. Although Congress clearly intended to supersede the common-law regime for claims against foreign states, we find nothing in the statute's origin or aims to indicate that Congress similarly wanted to codify the law of foreign official immunity.[49]

44. 28 U.S.C. § 1603 (2008). (Definitions).

45. *Samantar v. Yousuf*, 560 U.S. 305, 130 S. Ct. 2278; 176 L. Ed. 2d 1047 (2010).

46. See *id.*, 560 U.S. at 325.

47. *Id.*

48. *Id.*, 560 U.S. at 325–26.

49. *Id.*, 560 U.S. at 325.

Furthermore, the Court pointed out: "Because we are not deciding that the FSIA bars petitioner's immunity but rather that the Act does not address the question, we need not determine whether declining to afford immunity to petitioner would be consistent with international law."[50]

Thus, the holding in *Samantar* revolved on the specific language of § 1603 of FSIA. The Supreme Court reasoned that although an individual official could be an agency or instrumentality in the sense of someone or something through which action is accomplished, Congress's specific definition of "agency or instrumentality" did not countenance such a broad definition. According to the Court, an "agency or instrumentality" means an "entity" that meets three specified characteristics under the FSIA, which would exclude individual officials.[51] The Court also examined other provisions of the Act and concluded:

> Reading the FSIA as a whole, there is nothing to suggest we should read "foreign state" in § 1603 (a) to include an official acting on behalf of the foreign state, and much to indicate that this meaning was not what Congress enacted. The text does not expressly foreclose petitioner's reading, but it supports the view of respondents and the United States that the Act does not address an official's claim to immunity.[52]

Thus, an individual sued for conduct undertaken in an official capacity is not a "foreign state" within the meaning of the FSIA.

Following the enactment of the FSIA, the courts had been split on whether the immunity of foreign officials comes under the purview of the Act, whose main purpose was to codify the customary international law rules governing the immunity of foreign states. The majority view among the circuits was that the FSIA applied to claims against the individual government officials for actions taken in an official capacity.[53] The Supreme Court resolved the issue in favor of the minority view, and held that the FSIA does not govern whether an individual foreign official enjoys immunity from civil suit.[54] The Court however noted that "even if a suit is not governed by the Act, it may still be barred by foreign sovereign immunity under the common law,"[55] and that "it may be the case that some actions

50. *Id.*, 560 U.S. at 320, n.14.

51. See *id.*, 560 U.S. at 315.

52. *Id.*, 560 U.S. at 319 [citation omitted].

53. See *Chuidian v. Philippine National Bank*, 912 F.2d 1095 (9th Cir. 1990) and its progeny.

54. See *Samantar*, 560 U.S. 305.

55. *Id.*, 560 U.S. at 324.

against an official in his official capacity should be treated as actions against the foreign state itself, as the state is the real party in interest."[56]

Following the Supreme Court's decision and on remand to the District Court, Samantar sought dismissal of the claims against him on the grounds that under common law heads of State and foreign officials are immune for acts performed in their official capacity. The District Court rejected the common law immunity claim and denied the motion to dismiss, and the Court of Appeals affirmed the decision. In the proceedings, the State Department provided a Statement of Interest (SOI) opposing immunity for Samantar. According to the SOI, as the immunity that benefits foreign officials for their official acts belongs to the State, Samantar's claim for immunity is undermined by the nonexistence of a recognized government in Somalia to assert or waive his immunity, or to take a position as to whether the acts were taken in an official capacity. Samantar's permanent resident status in the United States militated against his claim of immunity as United States "residents like Samantar who enjoy the protections of U.S. law ordinarily should be subject to the jurisdiction of our courts, particularly when sued by U.S. residents."[57] Because the State Department has not officially recognized a Somali government, the court did not face the usual risk of offending a foreign State by exercising jurisdiction over the plaintiff's claims. Likewise, as a permanent legal resident, Samantar has a binding tie to the United States and its court system.

The Court of Appeals held "that Samantar is not entitled to conduct-based official immunity under the common law, which in this area incorporates international law."[58] The Court of Appeals admitted that the SOI provided additional reason for its holding. The Court's reliance on the SOI begs the question whether its conclusion would have been different if Somalia was not a failed State and had a recognized and functioning government to assert immunity on behalf of Samantar. If the conclusion is precisely that foreign officials are not immune for acts of torture and extrajudicial killings as claimed in the *Samantar* case, then the SOI regarding the political instability or failed Statehood of Somalia is nugatory. Thus, the reasoning of the Court, as provided in the SOI, presents the decision with an inherent inconsistency. The Supreme Court denied certiorari, ending an attempt by the former prime minister of Somalia to claim that the torture and extrajudicial killing for which he had admitted responsibility in court were official acts entitled to immunity.

56. *Id.*, 560 U.S. at 325.

57. *Yousuf v. Samantar*, 699 F. 3d 763, 767 (4th Cir. 2012).

58. *Id.* at 778.

Before the enactment of the FSIA, courts deferred to the State Department's suggestion of immunity concerning both foreign States and foreign officials. Now, since the Supreme Court has ruled that the FSIA does not apply to foreign officials, their immunity requires the courts to follow the determination of the executive branch. The determination involves a two-step procedure: a foreign State requests a suggestion of immunity for itself, or its official, from the State Department, and if the State Department accepted its request and filed a suggestion of immunity, then the court will relinquish its jurisdiction, but if the State Department denies the request or takes no position, then the court can decide for itself whether immunity existed.[59]

What the FSIA and the Supreme Court interpretation of the statute in *Samantar* did is decide that the immunity of foreign States and that of foreign officials have different sources of law in the United States. The *Samantar* decision has, therefore, narrowed the definition of a foreign State in a very important aspect that is at variance with most other national legislation on State immunity. A critique of the decision is that it will have the effect of reintroducing political considerations in the determination of the immunity, which Congress had sought to address by enacting the FSIA and reposing such determination in the hands of the courts. In fairness to the Supreme Court, it was merely interpreting a statute, and if Congress sees a continuing problem with the executive branch's role in the determination of immunity of foreign officials, it can always legislate to address the problem.

In *Kazemi Estate*,[60] the Canadian Supreme Court examined whether foreign officials (acting in their official capacity) are included in the term "government" as used in Section 3(1) of the State Immunity Act.[61] The Court noted:

> On the plain wording of the Act, it is unclear which actors Parliament intended to capture when it included the term "government" in the definition of "foreign state." The term "government" is capable of referring to many different entities and individuals, including but not limited to: legislatures, the executive, entities receiving government funding and which are subject to government control, and public officials. The absence of an explicit reference to "public officials" in the Act requires that the term "government" be interpreted in context, and . . . against the backdrop of international law.[62]

59. See *Samantar*, 560 U.S. at 312. ("Although cases involving individual foreign officials as defendants were rare, the same two step procedure was typically followed when a foreign official asserted immunity.")

60. Kazemi Estate v. Islamic Republic of Iran, 2014 SCC 62, [2014] 3 S.C.R. 176 (Can.).

61. State Immunity Act, RSC 1985, c S-18.

62. *Kazemi Estate*, para. 84.

The Canadian Supreme Court also noted:

> [T]the definition of the term "foreign state" at s. 2 of the *SIA* is open-ended, as indicated by the use of the word "includes". When this statutory language is placed in context, in conjunction with the purpose of the Act, it becomes clear that public officials must be included in the meaning of "government" in s. 2 of the *SIA*. The reality is that governmental decisions are carried out by a state's servants and agents. States are abstract entities that can only act through individuals. Significantly, s. 14(1)(c) of the Act provides that a certificate issued by the Minister of Foreign Affairs as to whether a person or persons are to be regarded as the head or government of a foreign state is conclusive evidence of any matter that is stated in it. It is difficult to conceive a reason for which "persons" might be regarded as "government" under the Act if not to be provided immunity pursuant to s. 3(1).[63]

The Canadian Supreme Court further noted:

> In practice, suing a government official in his or her personal capacity for acts done while in government has many of the same effects as suing the state, effects that the *SIA* seeks to avoid. Allowing civil claims against individual public officials would in effect require our courts to scrutinize other states' decision making as carried out by their public officials.[64]

The Canadian Supreme Court distinguished the *Kazemi Estate* case from *Samantar* where the United States Supreme Court interpreted the FSIA as not including within the definition of "foreign state" an official acting on behalf of the foreign state:

> The decision in *Samantar* hinged on the specific language found at s. 1603 of the *FSIA*. A number of differences between Canadian and U.S. legislation render *Samantar* inapplicable to the case at hand. First . . . the *FSIA* does not contain a definition of "foreign state" which includes "government", the precise word our Court is tasked with interpreting in the instant case. Second, in the *FSIA*, when Congress intended to refer to officials, it did so expressly. The express mention of officials in some parts of the *FSIA* but not in the definition of "foreign state" indicates that Congress did not intend to

63. *Id.*, para. 85.

64. *Id.*, para. 90.

> include officials in the broader definition of "foreign state" under s. 1603. Unlike the *FSIA*, express reference to officials can be found nowhere in the *SIA*. Therefore, the statutory interpretation argument of "implied exclusion", which was helpful to the U.S. Supreme Court in *Samantar*, cannot be made in our case.[65]

The Canadian Supreme Court concluded that "public officials, being necessary instruments of the state, are included in the term 'government' as used in SIA. That being said, public officials will only benefit from state immunity when acting in their official capacity."[66]

Thus, even in a proceeding against a foreign official, the foreign State is the proper defendant. Considering that States act through their officials, State immunity would be illusory if it does not extend to and cover also the official acts of foreign officials. It is widely accepted that foreign officials are immune for their official acts, but it remains controversial what acts are official as to be covered by State immunity.

Ministers of foreign affairs are a special category of foreign officials. "In customary international law, the immunities accorded to Ministers for Foreign Affairs are not granted for their personal benefits, but to ensure the effective performance of their functions on behalf of their respective States."[67] The International Court of Justice (ICJ) has observed "that a Minister for Foreign Affairs, responsible for the conduct of his or her State's relations with all other States, occupies a position such that, like the Head of State or the Head of Government, he or she is recognized under international law as representative of the State solely by virtue of his or her office."[68] In light of the nature of the functions exercised by a minister for foreign affairs, the ICJ concluded that the official enjoys immunity throughout the duration of his or her office for acts performed in both official and private capacities, as well as those performed before assumption of office or while in office.[69]

65. *Id.*, para. 92.

66. *Id.*, para. 93.

67. Arrest Warrant of 11 April 2000 (Democratic Republic of the Congo v. Belgium), Judgment, I.C.J. Rep. 2002, p. 3, para. 53.

68. *Id.*

69. See *id.*, paras. 53 and 54.

Entities or Organs of a Foreign State

Political Subdivisions of a Foreign State

A State may have a federal, confederate, or unitary political structure or system, which reflects how political authority is distributed among different parts and levels of the State. Certain political subdivisions of a foreign State benefit from State immunity. Article 2(1)(b)(ii) of the United Nations Convention provides for the constituent units of a federal system to be regarded as a State for purposes of State immunity, and distinguished them from the political subdivisions referred to in Article 2(b)(iii), namely, agencies and instrumentalities of the State.[70]

Section 1603(a) of FSIA defines "foreign state" broadly and extends State immunity to political subdivisions: "A 'foreign state,' except as used in section 1608 of this title, includes a political subdivision of a foreign state or an agency or instrumentality of a foreign state."[71] Thus, ministries of national governments are considered as a "foreign state," for purposes of State immunity. In the same vein, political subdivisions, such as states, provinces, prefectures, cantons, counties, etc., under the respective systems of government of the foreign State, would come under the definition of foreign state even though the FSIA does not define political subdivisions. According to the legislative history, political subdivisions include "all governmental units beneath the central government, including local governments."[72] Political subdivisions must have a separate legal personality, as well as the capacity to engage in commercial transaction, and must function as part of the government structure of the foreign State.

Agencies and Instrumentalities of a Foreign State

Article 2(1)(b)(iii) of the United Nations Convention includes in the term of State "agencies or instrumentalities of the State or other entities, to the extent that they are entitled to perform and are actually performing acts in the exercise of sovereign authority of the State."[73] A foreign State encompasses those entities that are "entitled to perform acts in the exercise of sovereign authority as well as acts of a private nature" but they may invoke immunity only in respect of the

70. See Draft Articles and Commentaries, Article 2(1)(b)(ii), Commentary (11).

71. The FSIA's definition of a foreign State is circular, but any State as recognized under international law would fit this definition. Moreover, there is no statutory requirement of diplomatic or political recognition by the U.S. government.

72. H.R. Rep. No. 1487, 94th Cong., 2d Sess. 12, at 15–16 (1976), as reprinted in 1976 U.S.C.C.A.N. 6604, 6613.

73. *Id.*

acts performed in the exercise of sovereign authority.[74] The reference to "other entities" covers nongovernmental entities that in exceptional cases are entrusted with authority to perform certain governmental functions, such as the practice of some governments entrusting commercial banks to deal with import and export licensing.[75] Thus, where an entity is entitled to perform acts in the exercise of sovereign authority as well as acts of a private nature, immunity may be invoked only in respect of the acts performed in the exercise of sovereign authority. However, entities, such as State enterprises, established to perform commercial transactions, as a rule, are not entitled to invoke State immunity under Article 10(10)(3) of the Convention.[76] "Agencies" or "instrumentalities" are used interchangeably under the Convention, with no particular difference in meaning intended.[77] "Proceedings against an entity of a foreign State, whether or not incorporated as a separate entity, could be considered to be a proceeding against the foreign State, particularly when the cause of action relates to the activities conducted by the agency or instrumentality of a foreign State in the exercise of sovereign authority of that State."[78]

State Entities with Separate Legal Personality

Departments of a foreign State benefit from the immunity of that State. However, it has been contested whether the immunity applied where that entity has a separate legal existence. In a suit for damages for an alleged libel against the Soviet news agency, Tass, the English court determined that the "sole question is whether a body called the Tass Agency of Moscow has established that it is part and parcel of a sovereign independent State. . . . It is common ground that the onus of establishing that lies on them. Furthermore, it is common ground that the certificate of their ambassador in this country is not conclusive of the matter, though, no doubt, it is evidence of very high evidential value."[79] The court continued:

> I should desire to reserve for future consideration the question whether or not the mere fact of a separate legal existence is necessarily inconsistent with the entity being part and parcel of a sovereign independent state. There

74. See Draft Articles and Commentaries, Article 2(1)(b)(iv), Commentary (14).

75. *Id.* Commentary (15).

76. *Id.*

77. *Id.* Commentary (16).

78. *Id.*

79. *Krajina v. Tass Agency* [1949] 2 All ER 274 (Tucker LJ).

> again, it must depend on the foreign law. It may be that under some foreign systems of law such a separate existence might be considered inconsistent, but it is clear from our Acts of Parliament that we do not consider the fact that a government department may have a separate legal juristic existence as necessarily incompatible with it being a department of State for which immunity can be claimed.[80]

Article 27 of the Basle Convention excludes from the expression "Contracting State" "any legal entity of a Contracting State which is distinct therefrom and is capable of suing or being sued, even if that entity has been entrusted with public function." It treats that entity as a private person but "the courts may not entertain proceedings in respect of acts performed by the entity in the exercise of sovereign authority (*acta jure imperii*)." Also, the entity does not have immunity if a Contracting State would not have immunity in corresponding circumstances.[81] The intent is to treat this legal entity as a private person when it is not exercising public functions.[82]

In *Trendtex Trading Corp. v. Central Bank of Nigeria*,[83] the English Court of Appeal considered whether the Central Bank of Nigeria is a department of the Federal Republic of Nigeria. Trendtex Trading Corporation had sued Central Bank of Nigeria for damages on a letter of credit concerning an order for cement for the construction of army barracks in Nigeria, and the Bank had claimed sovereign immunity. The Court of Appeal considered the Nigeria Statute of 1958 under which the Central Bank of Nigeria was established, and of the amendments to it by later decrees. It concluded: "(i) The Central Bank of Nigeria is a central bank modelled on the Bank of England. (ii) It has governmental functions in that it issues legal tender; it safeguards the international value of the currency; and it acts as banker and financial adviser to the government. (iii) Its affairs are under a great deal of government control in that the Federal Executive Council may overrule the board on monetary and banking policy and on internal administrative policy. (iv) It acts as banker for other banks in Nigeria and abroad, and maintains accounts with other banks. It acts as banker for the states within the federation: but has few, if any, private customers."[84]

80. *Id.*

81. See Article 27 of Basle Convention.

82. See Explanatory Report on Article 27. These entities may include national bank or railway administrations.

83. [1977] 1 QB 529; [1977] 2 W.L.R. 356.

84. *Id.* at 371.

Lord Denning MR then stated: "In these circumstances I have found it difficult to decide whether or not the Central Bank of Nigeria should be considered in international law a department of the Federation of Nigeria, even though it is a separate legal entity. But, on the whole, I do not think it should be."[85] He, nevertheless, ruled that the suit related to a commercial transaction and that there was no immunity for commercial transactions even for a government department.

According to Lord Shaw:

> The cardinal question is whether the Central Bank is properly to be regarded as a department of the Government of Nigeria in the guise of a bank, or whether it is in truth a bank to which the execution of specific aspects of government control of finance has been delegated. In the first case the Central Bank may be entitled to immunity from suit in the courts of this country; in the second case it can claim no such immunity. There can be no intermediate hybrid status occupied by the bank wherein it is to be regarded as a government department for certain purposes and as an ordinary commercial or financial institution for different purposes. It must be one or the other.[86]

Lord Shaw then ruled:

> Whether a particular organisation is to be accorded the status of a department of government or not must depend on its constitution, its powers and duties and its activities. These are the basic factors to be considered. The view of the government concerned must be taken into account but is not of itself decisive (*Krajina v. Tass Agency* [1949] 2 All E.R. 274); it does not relieve a court before which the issue of sovereign immunity arises of the responsibility of examining all the relevant circumstances.[87]

Under Section 14(1) of the SIA, a department of government is entitled to immunity for its own acts even though it has a separate legal personality under the law of the foreign State. However, an entity that is separate and distinct from the executive organs of the government of the foreign State and is capable of suing and being sued is not considered as a State entitled to immunities under Section 14 of SIA.

Under Section 14(2) of the SIA, a separate entity is immune "if, and only if (a) the proceedings relate to anything done by it in the exercise of sovereign

85. *Id.*

86. *Id.* at 382.

87. *Id.* at 383.

authority; and (b) the circumstances are such that a State . . . would have been so immune."[88] In *Kuwait Airways Corp. v. Iraqi Airways Co.*, the issue was whether Iraqi Airways Company (IAC) was entitled immunity under Section 14(2) of the Act as a separate entity from the government of Iraq that was capable of suing and being sued. The case arose out of the 1990 Iraqi invasion and occupation of Kuwait. The proceedings concerned a fleet of 10 civil aircraft belonging to Kuwait Airways Corporation (KAC) that Iraq seized and incorporated into the fleet of IAC. KAC brought an action in England to claim delivery of the aircraft together with consequential damages or compensatory damages for the value of the aircraft. The trial judge decided that IAC was not entitled to immunity, but the Court of Appeal decided that IAC was entitled to immunity under Section 14(2) of the SIA. KAC appealed to the House of Lord,[89] which allowed the appeal by KAC so that proceedings against IAC should go on. Lord Mustill and Lord Slynn dissented, in part, and stated that they would have upheld IAC's claim to immunity in relation to the whole claim.

IAC had challenged the jurisdiction of the English courts on the grounds that, as a separate entity, it was entitled to immunity under Section 14(2) of the Act because the proceedings related to things done by it in the exercise of sovereign authority.

Before the House Lords, Lord Goff, in his judgment, stated that for IAC to be immune, it must satisfy both conditions of Section 14(2), that is, the proceedings must relate to acts performed by the separate entity in the exercise of sovereign authority, and that the circumstances must be such that a State itself would have been immune.[90] He noted that the Section derived from Article 27 of the Basle Convention and, as such, the phrase "in the exercise of sovereign authority" must be construed in accordance with the accepted meaning of "*acta jure imperii*" in the Convention.[91] Regarding the act done by IAC to which the proceedings relate, he stated: "The essential things done which constitute the gravamen of the proceedings against IAC are (1) the removal of the aircraft from Kuwait Airport to Iraq, and (2) the treatment of the aircraft by IAC as part of its fleet after [Iraqi Revolutionary Command Council] RCC) Resolution 369," which purportedly dissolved KAC and transferred its assets to IAC.[92] With this categorization of the

88. Section 14 of SIA.

89. The appeal was heard before Lord Goff of Chieveley, Lord Jauncey of Tullichettle, Lord Mustill, Lord Slynn of Hadley, and Lord Nicholls of Birkenhead.

90. *Kuwait Airways Corp. v. Iraqi Airways Co.*, [1995] 3 All E.R. 694, para. 27.

91. *Id.* para 28.

92. *Id.* para. 34.

acts of IAC, Lord Goff ruled that IAC was acting in the exercise of sovereign authority in its involvement with the State of Iraq in the seizure of the aircraft and their removal to Iraq to be used as directed by the government of Iraq.[93] However, he ruled that the situation changed after RCC Resolution 369 came into effect, and that IAC's retention and use of the aircraft as its own were not acts done in the exercise of sovereign authority.[94] He "cannot see that the characterization as an act '*jure imperii*' of the earlier involvement by an entity in the act of seizure can, on the facts of the present case, be determinative of the characterization of the subsequent retention and use of the property by the state entity following the vesting of the property by a legislative act of the state."[95]

Lord Mustill disagreed with Lord Goff's characterization of the successive events because he believed "IAC was not acting autonomously, but in harness with the Republic of Iraq, and under the shadow of the sovereign authority by which the latter itself was acting, so that its acts were a manifestation of that authority."[96] Lord Slynn also disagreed with the change in the characterisation of the acts, and believed that the nature of IAC's acts, that is, the seizure, removal, and use of the aircraft, remained the same throughout and were done in the exercise of sovereign authority.[97] The disagreements, which revolve around the characterization of the acts, highlight the difference in the immunity determination of a separate entity vis-à-vis the State:

> [Section] 14 as a whole assumes that the state may be immune in circumstances where an entity is not. The immunities of the sovereign and of the entity are of an entirely different character. The former is a matter of status, inherent in the nature of the person or body claiming it, and all-embracing except where specifically excluded by the Act. By contrast the separate entity has no status entitling it to a general immunity, and is endowed by s. 14 only with a case-by-case immunity in the situations where described. Moreover, the immunities differ in extent as well as kind, for there must be many activities of separate entities which could not on any view be described as done under sovereign authority for the purposes of s. 14(2)(a), but which if done by the sovereign would be outside the

93. *Id.* para. 38.

94. *Id.* para. 39.

95. *Id.*

96. *Id.* para. 63.

97. *Id.* Paras. 78 and 79.

"commercial transaction" exception and all the other exceptions in Part I of the Act, and hence would attract the general immunity under s.1.[98]

A determination of whether an act was done "in the exercise of sovereign authority" calls for a distinction between *acta jure imperii* and *acta jure gestionis* because the second prong of Section 14(2) revolves on whether "the circumstances are such that a State would have been immune.[99] Thus, if the circumstances are such that it falls under the commercial exception, for example, the entity would not be immune.

The FSIA extends immunity to an "agency or instrumentality" of a foreign State, which is defined as any separate legal person that is either an organ of a foreign State or political subdivisions, or majority-owned by the foreign State or its political subdivisions, or is neither a citizen of the United States nor created under the laws of any third country.[100] A separate legal person is, therefore, an entity created under the law of the foreign State with the legal capacity to sue or be sued, contract, and acquire property, in its own name.[101] An agency or instrumentality of a foreign state "could assume a variety of forms, including a state trading corporation, a mining enterprise, a transport organization such as a shipping line or airline, a steel company, a central bank, an export association, a governmental procurement agency or a department or ministry which acts and is suable in its own name."[102]

Whether an entity is an "agency or instrumentality" of a foreign State matters because the FSIA treats it differently from the State itself. The FSIA applies less protective rules and standards to agencies and instrumentalities than it does for the State itself. The differences in treatment are with respect to service of process, venue, punitive damages, and attachment of assets.[103]

98. *Id.* para. 62.

99. See Section 14(2)(b) of SIA.

100. See 28 U.S.C. § 1603(b) (2005).

101. See H.R. Rep. No. 1487, 94th Cong., 2d Sess. 12, at 15–16 (1976), as reprinted in 1976 U.S.C.C.A.N. 6604, 6614.

102. *Id.*

103. See 28 U.S.C. §§ 1608, 1391, 1610 (2008). For example, Section 1608 has different requirements for service of process between political subdivisions and agency or instrumentality. Under subsection (a), for a political subdivisions, absent a special agreement, service is proper only if made according to an applicable international convention or if process is sent by mail, return receipt requested, by the clerk of the court to the head of the Ministry of Foreign Affairs of the foreign State. Also, service by the clerk of the court must include a translation of each document into the official language of the foreign State. Subsection (b), on the hand, provides that for an agency or instrumentality, service is proper if made according to a special arrangement between the parties,

In *Bancec*,[104] the question before the Supreme Court was whether Citibank may obtain a setoff in its counterclaim against Bancec, which was established by the Cuban government as a separate juridical entity. Bancec had sued to collect on a letter of credit issued in its favor by First National City Bank ("Citibank"), which counterclaimed and asserted a right to set off its nationalized Cuban assets. Bancec contended that its separate juridical status shielded it from liability for the acts of the Cuban government. The District Court disagreed and concluded that Bancec is an alter ego of the Cuban government, and granted judgment in favor of Citibank. The Court of Appeals for the Second Circuit reversed but was in turn reversed by the Supreme Court.

The Supreme Court concluded that the FSIA was not intended to affect the substantive law about the liability of a foreign State or instrumentality and, as such, does not control whether Citibank may set off the value of its seized Cuban assets against Bancec's claim. Regarding Bancec's separate juridical status, it decided that this is generally determined by the law of the state of incorporation, but that law should not always be given a conclusive effect.[105] It described the characteristics that should be considered in the determination of whether an entity is an instrumentality of a foreign State:

> The instrumentality is typically established as a separate juridical entity, with the powers to hold and sell property and to sue and be sued. Except for appropriations to provide capital or to cover losses, the instrumentality is primarily responsible for its own finances. The instrumentality is run as a distinct economic enterprise; often it is not subject to the same budgetary and personnel requirements with which government agencies must comply.[106]

The Supreme Court noted that separate legal personality is regarded as an almost indispensable aspect of an instrumentality, which has been construed to waive its

or the applicable international convention, or by delivery of a copy of the summons and complaint to an officer of the agency, or a managing agent or general agent, or to any other agent authorized by appointment or by law to receive service of process in the United States. Service of process on a political subdivisions is more demanding. With respect to venue, Section 1391(f) makes the federal district court for the District of Columbia the proper venue for suits against a foreign State and its subdivisions, but the venue for an agency or instrumentality of a foreign State can be "any judicial district in which the agency or instrumentality is licensed to do business or is doing business."

104. *First National City Bank v. Banco Para El Commercio Exterior De Cuba (Bancec)*, 462 U.S. 611 (1983).

105. *Id.* at 621–22.

106. *Id.* at 624 [citation omitted].

sovereign immunity.[107] Thus, instrumentalities of foreign States "established as juridical entities and independent from their sovereign should normally be treated as such."[108] It found support in the legislative history of the FSIA for the presumption of separateness of instrumentalities of foreign States,[109] but held that the presumption may be overcome in certain circumstances such as when the entity is so controlled by its owner that an agency/principal relation is created. It can also be overcome by equitable principles such as when recognition would work fraud or injustice, or defeat legislative or public policy.[110] The Supreme Court, therefore, held that Citibank may set off the value of its assets seized by the Cuban government against the amount sought by Bancec because to give to Bancec separate juridical status would absolve the Cuban government of liability when it is the real beneficiary of Bancec's action.[111]

Most circuit courts apply the "core function" test in their determination of whether an entity is an agency or instrumentality of a foreign State. In *Transaero, Inc. v. La Fuerza Aerea Boliviana*, which is regarded as the leading case applying the core function test, the Bolivian Air Force argued that it had not been properly served process as a political subdivisions of a foreign State.[112] To decide whether the Bolivian Air Force counts as a political subdivisions or an agency or instrumentality, the District of Columbia (D.C.) Circuit Court of Appeals adopted a categorical approach of whether the core functions of the foreign entity are predominantly governmental or commercial, an approach that was also urged by the United States as amicus curiae.[113] Thus, if the core function is commercial, then the entity should be an instrumentality.[114] The D.C. Circuit Court of Appeals held that the core functions of the armed forces of a foreign State are governmental, and "that armed forces are as a rule so closely bound up with the structure of the state that they must in all cases be considered as the 'foreign state' itself, rather than a separate 'agency or instrumentality' of the state."[115]

107. *Id.* at 625.

108. *Id.* at 627.

109. *Id.* at 628; citing H.R. Rep. No. 94-1487, pp. 29–30 (1976).

110. *Id.* at 629–30.

111. *Id.* at 633.

112. *Transaero, Inc. v. La Fuerza Aerea Boliviana*, 30 F.3d 148 (D.C. Cir. 1994).

113. *Id.* at 151.

114. *Id.* at 151–52.

115. *Id.* at 153.

In *MOD v. Cubic*,[116] the Ninth Circuit Court of Appeals adopted the core function test, joining the D.C. Circuit,[117] the Second Circuit,[118] and the Fifth Circuit.[119] The case arose out of a wrongful death default judgment against Iran and the attempt to attach the judgment of an American defense contractor, Cubic Defense Systems ("Cubic"), who had contracted with the Ministry of Defense and Support of the Armed Forces of the Islamic Republic of Iran ("MOD"). The issue was whether MOD constituted a foreign State or an agency or instrumentality, that is, whether MOD "is inherently a part of the political state or a commercial actor."[120] The Court adopted the reasoning of the D.C. Circuit in *Transaero* that the armed forces are so intimately connected to a State's sovereignty but declined to follow its categorical rule that the armed forces will always be part of the foreign State itself. The Court imagined a situation where a foreign State could outsource "its defense to paramilitary groups or mercenary forces that would not properly count as part of the state but rather as 'separate legal person[s].' "[121] It held that there is a strong presumption that the armed forces constitute a part of the foreign State itself and that the presumption has not been rebutted because no evidence was presented that MOD is a "separately constituted legal entity" distinct from the State of Iran.[122] It stated that there was no evidence that "MOD is 'primarily responsible for its own finances,' that it is run as a 'distinct economic enterprise,' that it operates with 'independence from close political control,' or that it exhibits any of the traits—other than the capacity to sue and be sued—that the Court has identified as characteristic of a 'separately constituted legal entity.' "[123]

In contrast to the core-function test, other courts have adopted the "legal characteristic" test, and *Hyatt Corp. v. Stanton*[124] is considered the leading case applying that test. Hyatt Corporation, incorporated in Delaware, United States, had sued Stanton, the senior vice president of Skopbank, a Finnish bank owned

116. *Ministry of Def. & Support for the Armed Forces of the Islamic Republic of Iran v. Cubic Def. Sys. (MOD v. Cubic)*, 495 F.3d 1024 (9th Cir. 2007).

117. See *Transaero*, 30 F.3d 148, 151; *Roeder v. Iran*, 333 F.3d 228, 234 (D.C. Cir. 2003).

118. See *Garb v. Poland*, 440 F.3d 579, 594 (2d. Cir. 2006).

119. *Magness v. Russia*, 247 F.3d 609, 613 n.7 (5th Cir. 2001).

120. *MOD v. Cubic*, 495 F.3d at 1035.

121. *Id.*, 495 F.3d 1024.

122. *Id.*

123. *Id.* citing *First Nat'l City Bank v. Banco Para El Comercio Exterior De Cuba (Bancec)*, 462 U.S. 611, 624 (1983).

124. *Hyatt Corp. v. Stanton*, 945 F. Supp. 675 (S.D.N.Y. 1996), Judge Michael Mukasey.

by the Finnish Government Guarantee Fund (GGF) in New York state court for various torts. Stanton moved for removal from state court to federal court.[125] In opposition, Hyatt argued that Skopbank is owned by GGF, which is an "agency or instrumentality of a foreign state" and cannot itself be an agency or instrumentality as to qualify as a foreign States under the FSIA, and as no foreign State is involved, the case must be remanded to State court.

According to the court, to determine whether Skopbank is an agency or instrumentality, it had to first determine whether GGF is a political subdivisions, or an agency or instrumentality of the Finnish government. It noted that some courts distinguished a political subdivisions from an agency or instrumentality based on the "legal characteristics" test, that is, an entity is an agency or instrumentality if, under the law of the foreign State where it was created, the entity has the capacity to sue and be sued in its own name, contract in its own name, or hold property in its own name.[126] The court decided that the proper test is the "legal characteristics" one because it "most closely approximates Congress's intent, as indicated by both the text and the legislative history of the statute."[127] It declined to follow the "core function" test believing that it departed from the text of FSIA by its distinction between commercial and governmental entities in the definition of agency or instrumentality, as well as the legislative history, which gave examples of both commercial and noncommercial entities in describing these entities.[128] It, therefore, held[129] that based on the legal characteristics test GGF is an agency or instrumentality of Finland, and that Skopbank, a majority of whose shares are owned by GGF, is not a foreign State under the FSIA.

The Ninth Circuit Court of Appeals has criticized the legal characteristics test as illogical because the FSIA presupposes that a foreign State is capable of suing and being sued, and the provision would be superfluous if it is "the touchstone of an 'agency or instrumentality.'"[130]

125. See 28 U.S.C. § 1441(d) (2005) provides: "Any civil action brought in a State court against a foreign state as defined in section 1603(a) of this title may be removed by the foreign state to the district court of the United States for the district and division embracing the place where such action is pending. Upon removal the action shall be tried by the court without jury."

126. *Hyatt*, 945 F. Supp. at 681, *citing Bowers v. Transportes Navieros Ecuadorianos (Transnave)*, 719 F. Supp. 166, 170 (S.D.N.Y. 1989); *Unidyne Corp. v. Aerolineas Argentinas*, 590 F. Supp. 398, 400 (E.D. Va. 1984).

127. *Hyatt*, 945 F. Supp. at 683–84.

128. *Id.*

129. *Id.* at 690.

130. *Ministry of Def. & Support for the Armed Forces of the Islamic Republic of Iran v. Cubic Def. Sys. (MOD v. Cubic)*, 495 F.3d 1024, 1035 (9th Cir. 2007).

No matter the test for the determination of agency or instrumentality status of an entity, there is no gainsaying that many agencies and instrumentalities are commercial enterprises.[131]

Organ of a Foreign State

In addition to having a separate legal personality, an agency or instrumentality of a foreign State under the FSIA must be "an organ of a foreign state or political subdivision thereof, or a majority of whose shares or other ownership interest is owned by a foreign state or political subdivision thereof."[132] The term "organ" is not defined in the FSIA, but courts have devised tests to determine whether an entity is an organ. "Although there is no specific test for 'organ' status under the FSIA, various factors are relevant: (1) whether the foreign State created the entity for a national purpose; (2) whether the foreign state actively supervises the entity; (3) whether the foreign state requires the hiring of public employees and pays their salaries; (4) whether the entity holds exclusive rights to some right in the [foreign] country; and (5) how the entity is treated under foreign state law."[133] Courts also examine the circumstances surrounding the entity's creation, its organizational structure, the purpose of its activities, and the level of governmental supervision and financial support, as well as whether the foreign State requires the hiring of public employees and pays their salaries, and the entity's status, obligations, and privileges under the foreign State's law.[134] Under these tests, no single factor is determinative or dispositive, and all factors need not be present for the determination that an entity is an organ under FSIA.

Whether an entity, with a separate legal personality, is "an organ of a foreign state or political subdivision thereof, or a majority of whose shares or other ownership interest is owned by a foreign state or political subdivision thereof" may raise the so-called "tiering"[135] and "pooling"[136] issues. Courts have struggled with determining whether entities indirectly owned by a foreign State or owned by

131. See *Transaero, Inc. v. La Fuerza Aerea Boliviana*, 30 F.3d 148, 155 (D.C. Cir. 1994). (dissent of Mikva J).

132. 28 U.S.C. § 1603(b)(2) (2005).

133. *Filler v. Hanvit Bank*, 378 F.3d 213, 217 (2d Cir. 2004) [citations omitted].

134. See, e.g., *Alperin v. Vatican Bank*, 360 F. App'x 847, 849 (9th Cir. 2009) (Vatican Bank qualifies as an "organ" and therefore "agency or instrumentality").

135. "Tiering" is when an entity is majority owned by another entity that is in turn majority owned by a foreign State.

136. "Pooling" is when an entity is directly majority owned by two or more foreign States, that is, two or more foreign States have pooled majority ownership of the entity.

two or more foreign States qualify as an "organ" of a foreign State under FSIA. Agencies and instrumentalities, as well as political subdivisions, are subsumed within the definition of a foreign State under the FSIA, but these entities do not equate with the foreign State "and, therefore, cannot confer agency or instrumentality status on corporate entities further down the chain of ownership."[137] With respect to pooling, a court has ruled, through a purposive interpretation of the FSIA, that a separate entity that is majority owned by more than one foreign State meets the definition of "agency or instrumentality" even though Section 1603(b)(2) does not explicitly so provide.[138] In this regard, the Supreme Court has held that an entity is an "agency or instrumentality of a foreign state" only if the State (or its political subdivisions) directly owns a majority of the entity's shares.[139] It ruled that "[m]ajority ownership by a foreign state, not control, is the benchmark of instrumentality status."[140] Thus, under *Dole* a tiered subsidiary—an entity wholly owned by a corporate parent that is in turn wholly owned by a foreign State—does not qualify as an "agency or instrumentality of a foreign state." Determining when a defendant qualifies as a foreign State or its agency or instrumentality is important in cases where the status of the defendant has changed between when the act giving rise to the claim occurred and when the claim is filed. The Supreme Court has also held that the status of the entity must be determined as of the time that the suit is filed, not when the underlying cause of action occurred: "We think the plain text of [28 U.S.C. § 1603(b)(2)], because it is expressed in the present tense, requires that instrumentality status be determined at the time suit is filed."[141]

DISTINCTION BETWEEN ABSOLUTE IMMUNITY AND RESTRICTIVE IMMUNITY

The classical doctrine of absolute sovereign immunity was based on the principle of *par in parem non habet imperium* (equals do not have authority over one another).[142] Under this principle, "the courts of a country will not implead a foreign

137. *Filler v. Hanvit Bank*, 378 F.3d 213, 219 (2d Cir. 2004).

138. See *LeDonne v. Gulf Air, Inc.*, 700 F. Supp. 1400 (E.D. Va. 1988).

139. *Dole Food Co. v. Patrickson*, 538 U.S. 468, 477, 123 S. Ct. 1655, 1663 (2003) ("A corporation is an instrumentality of a foreign state under the FSIA only if the foreign state itself owns a majority of the corporation's shares.").

140. *Id.* at 477.

141. *Id.* at 478.

142. See *The Schooner Exchange v McFadden*, 11 U.S. 116 (1812).

sovereign, that is, they will not by their process make him against his will a party to legal proceedings whether the proceedings involve process against his person or seek to recover from him specific property or damages."[143] The transition from the doctrine of absolute to the restrictive State immunity reflects the economic and political realities of increased commercial activities by States. The increased participation of States in international trade and commerce was the impetus for the adoption of the doctrine of restrictive State immunity. Under the doctrine of restrictive immunity, "the trading or commercial activities of states are not protected."[144]

> The rationale of the common law doctrine of restrictive immunity . . . is that where the sovereign chooses to doff his robes and descend into the market-place he must take the rough with the smooth and having condescended to engage in mundane commercial activities he must also condescend to submit himself to an adjudication in a foreign court on whether he has in the course of those activities undertaken obligations he has failed to fulfil.[145]

Belgium and Italy were at the vanguard of the doctrine of restrictive sovereign immunity when they started denying immunity in cases stemming from commercial activities. With the issuance of the so-called Tate Letter in 1952 by the State Department, the United States declared its policy of restrictive State immunity and distinguished it from absolute State immunity:

> A study of the law of sovereign immunity reveals the existence of two conflicting concepts of sovereign immunity, each widely held and firmly established. According to the classical or absolute theory of sovereign immunity, a sovereign cannot, without his consent, be made a respondent in the courts of another sovereign. According to the newer or restrictive theory of sovereign immunity, the immunity of a sovereign is recognized with regard to sovereign or public acts (*jure imperii*) of a state, but not with respect to private acts (*jure gestionis*). . . . [I]t will hereafter be the [State] Department's policy to follow the restrictive theory. . . . "[146]

143. *Compania Naviera Vascongado v. The Cristina*, [1938] AC 485, 490 (Lord Atkin).

144. See *Holland v. Lampen-Wolfe*, [2000], 1 WLR 1573, 1578 (Lord Cooke).

145. *Kuwait Airways Corp v Iraqi Airways Co and others*, [1995] 3 All ER 694, 718, [1995] 1 WLR 1147, [1995] 2 Lloyd's Rep 317 (Lord Mustill).

146. Letter of Jack B. Tate, Acting Legal Adviser of the Department of State, to Acting Attorney General (May, 19, 1952) ("Tate Letter"), reprinted in 26 Department of State Bulletin, 984–85 (1952), and in *Alfred Dunhill of London v. Republic of Cuba*, 425 U.S. 682, 711 (1976).

In sum, "the doctrine of restrictive immunity, which is not the antithesis of absolute immunity—for absolute immunity remains the starting point—but a qualification to the rule."[147]

Distinction between *Acta Jure Imperii* and *Acta Jure Gestionis*

The distinction between *acta jure imperii* and *acta jure gestionis* is the raison d'etre of the doctrine of restrictive State immunity. *Acta jure gestionis* are private, commercial, or non-sovereign acts, whereas *acta jure imperii* are public, governmental, or sovereign acts. "It is certainly difficult to draw the line between sovereign acts and the private law activities of States. Difficulties of this kind are often met in international law, however; they cannot lead to the abandonment of the distinction."[148] In *Holland v. Lampen-Wolfe*, Lord Clyde stated: "Difficult as the distinction may be at common law, we have to do the best we can to apply it."[149] He continued:

> The solution in any particular case where the question of state immunity arises at common law has to be one of the analysis of the particular facts against the whole context in which they have occurred. There is little if anything to be gained by trying to fit the case into a particular precedent or to devise categories of situations which may or may not fall on the side of the line or the other. It is the nature and character of the activity on which the claim is based which has to be studied, rather than the motive or purpose of it. The solution will turn upon an assessment of the particular facts. The line between sovereign and non-sovereign state activities may sometimes be clear, but in other cases may well be difficult to draw. In some cases . . . even when the relevant activity has been identified it may have a double aspect, being at once sovereign and commercial, so that it may then have to be determined precisely to which aspect the proceedings in question relate.[150]

In *Holland v. Lampen-Wolfe*, Holland, a citizen of the United States, sued Lampen-Wolfe, a fellow citizen of the United States, for defamation in relation to education service at a U.S. military base in the United Kingdom. Lampen-Wolfe

147. *FG Hemisphere Associates LLC v. Democratic Republic of Congo & ORS*, [2010] 2 HKC 487 (Court of Appeal), para. 65.

148. *Claim Against the Empire of Iran Case*, Federal Constitutional Court, Federal Republic of Germany (30 April 1963), p. 76, 45 ILR 57 (1963).

149. *Holland v. Lampen-Wolfe*, para. 16.

150. *Id.*, para. 17.

applied to set the writ aside for impleading a foreign State and asserted that the proceedings were covered by immunity under both the common law and the UK State Immunity Act. The United States invoked immunity in behalf of Lampen-Wolfe, who is an official of its Department of Defense. Lord Millett seized the occasion to expound on the doctrine of State immunity:

> It is an established rule of customary international law that one state cannot be sued in the courts of another for acts performed "*iure imperii*". The immunity does not derive from the authority or dignity of sovereign states or the need to protect the integrity of their governmental functions. It derives from the sovereign nature of the exercise of the state's adjudicative powers and the basic principle of international law that all states are equal. The rule is "*par in parem non habet imperium*" . . . it is a subject matter immunity. It operates to prevent the official and governmental acts of one state from being called into question in proceedings before the courts of another. The exercise of the doctrine is confirmed by the European Convention on State Immunity 1972, the relevant provisions of which are generally regarded as reflecting customary international law. In according immunity from suit before the English courts to foreign states the State Immunity Act 1978 and the common law give effect to the international obligations of the United Kingdom.
>
> Where the immunity applies, it covers an official of the state in respect of acts performed by him in an official capacity.[151]

The Court noted that Lampen-Wolfe had acted in his capacity as an official of the United States Department of Defense and that the United States has asserted immunity in his behalf. Thus, if the United States is entitled to the claimed immunity, then the proceedings are barred.[152] It also noted that the SIA has no exception in respect for actions for defamation, and that the "exceptions relied upon in the present case are contained in s. 3, which is concerned with commercial transactions and contracts to be performed in the United Kingdom."[153] It then held that this exception does not apply as the proceedings did not relate to any such contract.[154]

151. *Id.*, paras. 31–32.

152. *Id.*, para. 32.

153. *Id.*, para. 34.

154. *Id.*, para. 46.

As sound as the theory behind the distinction may be, as a practical matter, it is difficult to categorize some activities as quintessentially sovereign or otherwise.[155] Even though the distinction between *acta jure imperii* and *acta jure gestionis* may be difficult, some acts are much more discernible as public than as private. Although States can engage in all sorts of private acts, there are some acts that are still the exclusive preserve of States. A typical sovereign act is expropriation. The distinction between *acta jure imperii* and *acta jure gestionis* is not only difficult but also dynamic: "The meaning of these two notions is not carved in stone, however; it is subject to a continuously changing interpretation which varies with time reflecting the changing priorities of society."[156]

According to the ICJ, an illegal or unlawful act can be *acta jure imperii* at the same time.

> [T]he terms "*jure imperii*" and "*jure gestionis*" do not imply that the acts in question are lawful but refer to whether the acts in question fall to be assessed by reference to the law governing the exercise of sovereign power (*jus imperii*) or the law concerning non-sovereign activities of a State, especially private and commercial activities (*jus gestionis*). To the extent that this distinction is significant for determining whether or not a State is entitled to immunity from the jurisdiction of another State's court in respect of a particular act, it has to be applied before that jurisdiction can be exercised, whereas the legality or illegality of the act is something which can be determined only in the exercise of that jurisdiction.[157]

"The fact that conduct was unlawful or objectionable was not, of itself, a ground for refusing immunity."[158]

155. See Jean-Flavien Lalive, L'Immunité de juridiction des états et des organisations internationales, (1953) Recueil des Cours de l'Académie de Droit International, 205, 282-83 (« *Les distinction entre les actes de l'Etat sont empiriques et souvent arbitraires. Tout d'abord ceux qui parlent d'une double personnalité de l'Etat,—comme si celui-ci était un Janus, dont une face serait tournée vers les fonctions dites "publiques" et l'autre face orientée vers les activités privées—font de la poésie et non du droit.* »); Kuljit Ahluwalia, The Legal Status, Privileges and Immunities of the Specialized Agencies of the United Nations and Certain Other International Organizations (The Hague: Martinus Nijhoff Year), p. 22 (As has been universally voiced, it is difficult to draw a clear line of demarcation between the two sets of activities and to place that distinction on a sound and logical footing.).

156. *Arrest Warrant Case*, Separate Opinion of Judges Higgins, Kooijmans, and Buergenthal, p. 3, para. 72.

157. Jurisdictional Immunities of the State (*Germany v. Italy: Greece Intervening*), Judgment, I.C.J. Reports 2012, p. 99, para. 60.

158. *Jones and Others v. United Kingdom*, European Court of Human Rights, 2014 Judgment, para. 26.

Purpose, Nature or Context Test

In distinguishing between acta jure imperii and acta jure gestionis under the doctrine of restrictive State immunity, courts apply the purpose, nature or context test. For instance, the Federal Constitutional Court of (then) Federal Republic of Germany stated:

> The distinction between sovereign and non-sovereign State activities cannot be drawn according to the purpose of the State transaction and whether it stands in a recognizable relation to the sovereign duties of the State. For, ultimately, activities of State, if not wholly then to the widest degree, serve sovereign purposes and duties, and stand in a still recognizable relationship to them. Neither should the distinction depend on whether the State has acted commercially. Commercial activities of States are not different in their nature from other non-sovereign State activities.
>
> As a means for determining the distinction between acts *jure imperii* and *jure gestionis* one should rather refer to the nature of the state transaction or the resulting legal relationships, and not to the motive or purpose of the State activity. It thus depends on whether the foreign State has acted in exercise of its sovereign authority, that is in public law, or like a private person, that is in private law.[159]

Characterization of a claim is very critical in the distinction between *acta jure imperii* and *acta jure gestionis*. To this effect, Lord Wilberforce provided the following guidance in *I Congreso*:

> The conclusion which emerges is that in considering, under the "restrictive" theory whether state immunity should be granted or not, the court must consider the whole context in which the claim against the state is made, with a view to deciding whether the relevant act(s) upon which the claim is based, should, in that context, be considered as fairly within an area of activity, trading or commercial, or otherwise of a private law character, in which the state has chosen to engage, or whether the relevant act(s) should be considered as having been done outside that area, and within the sphere of governmental or sovereign activity.[160]

159. *Claim Against the Empire of Iran* Case, 45 ILR 57, 79–80 (Federal Constitutional Court of the Federal Republic of Germany, 1963).

160. *I Congreso*, [1983] 1 A.C. 244, 267.

He went on to approve the reasoning of *Claim against the Empire of Iran Case,*[161] but noted: "I agree that the purpose is not decisive but it may throw some light upon the nature of what was done."[162]

Where a plaintiff had argued that there is no immunity in personal injury claims because it is presumed that such tort is an act *jure gestionis* in the sense that anyone can do it, the court ruled that it "has to look at all the circumstances in relation to the nature of the activity and its context and decide whether those factors together (no one factor being in itself determinative) characterise the activity as sovereign or non-sovereign."[163] The court considered that the activity in the case was the medical treatment of a member of the U.S. armed forces by the U.S. government in its military base hospital in the United Kingdom, and concluded it was an act *jure imperii* based on the nature of the treatment, the parties, and the place of occurrence:

> The context in which the act took place was the maintenance by the United States of a unit of the US Strategic Air Force in the United Kingdom. This looks about as imperial an activity as could be imagined. But it would be facile to regard this context as determinative of the question. Acts done within the context could range from arrangements concerning the flight of the bombers (plainly *jure imperii*) to ordering milk for the base from a local diary or careless driving by off-duty airmen on the roads of Suffolk. Both of the latter would seem to me to be jure gestionis, fairly within an area of private law activity. I do not think that there is a single test or "bright line" by which cases on either side can be distinguished. Rather, there are a number of factors which may characterise the act as nearer to or further from the central military activity.
>
> Some acts are wholly military in character, some almost entirely private or commercial and some in between.[164]

In *Weltover,* the United States Supreme Court had stated:

> we conclude that when a foreign government acts, not as regulator of a market, but in the manner of a private player within it, the foreign sovereign's actions are "commercial" within the meaning of the FSIA. Moreover,

161. *Id.* at 263.

162. *Id.,* 1 AC 244, 272; 64 ILR 307, 323.

163. *Littrell v. United States of America (No 2)* [1994] 4 All ER 203, [1995] 1 WLR 82 (Rose LJ).

164. *Id.* (Hoffmann LJ).

> because the Act provides that the commercial character of an act is to be determined by reference to its "nature" rather than its "purpose," *28 U. S. C. § 1603(d)*, the question is not whether the foreign government is acting with a profit motive or instead with the aim of fulfilling uniquely sovereign objectives. Rather, the issue is whether the particular actions that the foreign state performs (whatever the motive behind them) are the *type* of actions by which a private party engages in "trade and traffic or commerce".[165]

In *Kuwait Airways Corp.*, the Canadian Supreme noted:

> [I]n both U.S. and English law, the characterization of acts for purposes of the application of state immunity is based on an analysis that focusses on their nature. It is therefore not sufficient to ask whether the act in question was the result of a state decision and whether it was performed to protect a state interest or attain a public policy objective. If that were the case, all acts of a state or even of a state-controlled organization would be considered sovereign acts. This would be inconsistent with the restrictive theory of state immunity in contemporary public international law and would have the effect of eviscerating the exceptions applicable to acts of private management, such as the commercial activity exception.[166]

The Canadian Supreme Court also noted:

> [The] Canadian commercial activity exception requires a court to consider the entire context, which includes not only the nature of the act, but also its purpose: "It seems to me that a contextual approach is the only reasonable basis of applying the doctrine of restrictive immunity. The alternative is to attempt the impossible—an antiseptic distillation of a "once-and-for-all" characterization of the activity in question, entirely divorced from its purpose. It is true that purpose should not predominate, as this approach would convert virtually every act by commercial agents of the state into an act *jure imperii*. However, the converse is also true. Rigid adherence to the "nature" of an act to the exclusion of purpose would render innumerable government activities *jure gestionis*."[167]

165. *Argentina v. Weltover*, 504 U.S. 607, 614 (1992) [citations omitted].

166. Kuwait Airways Corp. v. Iraq, 2010 SCC 40, [2010] 2 S.C.R. 571 (Can.), para. 30.

167. *Id.*, para. 31 [citation omitted].

Judge Vincent in *Reid* articulated the context test as follows:

> In some situations, for example, the divorcement of act, motive, or purpose may not be possible. In other words, the motive or purpose underlying particular conduct may constitute part of the definition of the act itself, while in others the nature or quality of the act performed may not be ascertainable without reference to the context within which it is carried out. Further, even if the "relevant act" can be isolated, a plethora of possible relationships to the exercise of sovereign power can exist, the character and proximity of which would be dependent upon the perception held or policy adopted within the jurisdiction in which the matter arises as to attributes of sovereign itself.[168]

The French position is articulated as follows: "Foreign State and organs which constitute an emanation of these States enjoy jurisdictional immunity in so far as the act giving rise to the dispute between the parties, by its *nature or purpose*, is an exercise of the sovereign of such States and is therefore not a normal act of administrative management."[169] In Italy, the nature of the activities of a foreign State may be determined by examining its purpose: "Thus it is essential, in deciding the question of immunity, to determine the nature of the activities of the foreign State, that is whether these were intended to achieve public, institutional ends."[170] In a suit by two Italian firms seeking return of their property that had been confiscated by Libya, the Italian Court of Cassation held that Libya enjoyed sovereign immunity because under "international customary rule . . . foreign States are not subject to Italian jurisdiction only in cases of acts performed (even on Italian soil) in the exercise of functional activities within the foreign country's sphere of public law and intended to achieve public ends. Foreign States do not enjoy State immunity in cases of acts of a merely private nature, which are not intended to achieve public ends."[171]

In sum, in the distinction between *acta jure imperii* and *acta jure gestionis*, most courts give regard solely to the nature of the act. A few may apply the purpose test alone. A good many others consider the context of the act, which looks at both

168. *Reid v. Nauru*, Australia, 1992 [1993] 1 VR 251, 253; 104 ILR 193, 195–96.

169. *X v. Saudi School in Paris and Kingdom of Saudi Arabia*, Court of Cassation (Mixed Chamber), France, 20 June 2003 [emphasis added], 127 I.L.R. 163, 166.

170. *Libya v. Imprese Marittime Frassinetti*, [Italy, Court of Cassation] 78 I.L.R. 90, 92 (1979).

171. *Id.*

the purpose and the nature. The United Nations Convention favors the context approach:

> In determining whether a contract or transaction is a "commercial transaction" [under the Convention], reference should be made primarily to the nature of the contract or transaction, but its purpose should be taken into account if, in the practice of the State which is party to it, that purpose is relevant to determining the non-commercial character of the contract or transaction.[172]

COMMON EXCEPTIONS

> The principle of State immunity has long ceased to be a blanket rule exempting States from the jurisdiction of courts of law. . . . [I]t may be said that the edifice of absolute immunity of jurisdiction (and even of execution) began to crumble, in the first quarter of the twentieth century, with the advent of State trading: why should States, when engaging in commercial activities like individuals, be treated more favourably than the latter and, thus, enjoy a competitive advantage? By the same token, why should a foreign country locally hiring employees who will engage directly in diplomatic or consular activities on behalf of that country be exempted from the operation of local law? And why should a State be so exempted when appearing, like a private person, in the guise of an heir or legatee, or as the owner of industrial or intellectual property? Why, finally . . . should a State not be accountable, before the courts of another State, for injury and damage inflicted by its agents on individuals or their property on the territory of that other State, just as it would be if the tort had been caused, not by an agent of that other State, but by an individual?

172. Article 2 of the United Nations Convention. Article 2, Commentary (26), Draft Articles and Commentaries states: "This two-pronged approach, which provides for the consideration not only of the nature, but in some instances also of the purpose of the contract or transaction, is designed to provide an adequate safeguard and protection for developing countries, especially in their endeavours to promote national economic development. Defendant States should be given an opportunity to prove that, in their practice, a given contract or transaction should be treated as non-commercial because its purpose is clearly public and supported by *raison d'Etat*, such as the procurement of food supplies to feed a population, relieve a famine situation or revitalize a vulnerable area, or supply medicaments to combat a spreading epidemic, provided that is the practice of that State to conclude such contracts or transactions for such public ends. It should be noted, however, that it is the competent court, and not the defendant State, which determines in each case the commercial or non-commercial character of a contract or transaction taking into account the practice of the defendant State."

> The above exceptions to absolute immunity have gradually come to be recognised by national legislators and courts, initially in continental western Europe and, much later, in common-law countries. For obvious reasons, they have been slower to emerge in the former socialist bloc, long dominated by State trading and the absence of competition.
>
> The exceptions . . . have also found their way into the international law on State immunity.[173]

The doctrine of restrictive State immunity starts with the premise that States are generally immune with few exceptions, which revolve on the subject matter of the suit.[174] Treaties and national legislation on State immunity have in common the following exceptions: commercial activity,[175] immovable property,[176] territorial tort,[177] and employment contract.[178]

Commercial Activity or Transaction

The burgeoning engagement of States in commercial activities in the twentieth century was the catalyst for the development of the doctrine of restrictive State immunity. Although the doctrine is well-settled as customary international law, the commercial activity or transaction is the most litigated. This is so because there is no satisfactory definition of commercial activity. Most legal instruments do not define it, and the few that do, do so in a circular way, thereby, presenting problems of interpretation and application for the courts and litigants alike. Descriptions of commercial activities often masquerade as definition.

173. *McElhinney v. Ireland* [GC], no. 31253, ECHR 2001-XI (Joint Dissenting Opinion of Judges Caflisch, Cabral Barreto, and Vajic).

174. See, e.g., United Nations Convention, Art. 5; Basle Convention, Art. 15; SIA, Sec. 1; and FSIA, Sec. 1602.

175. United Nations Convention, Article 10; Basle Convention, Articles 4 and 7; FSIA, Section 1605(a)(2); SIA, Section 3; Canada SIA, Section 5; Singapore SIA, Section 5; Australia FSIA, Section 11.

176. United Nations Convention, Article 13; Basle Convention, Article 9; FSIA, Section 1605(a)(4); SIA, Section 6; Canada SIA, Section 8; Singapore SIA, Section 8; and Australia FSIA, Section 14.

177. United Nations Convention, Article 12; Basle Convention, Article 11; FSIA, Section 1605(a)(5); SIA, Section 5; Singapore SIA, Section 7; Canada SIA, Section 6; and Australia FSIA, Section 13.

178. United Nations Convention, Article 11; Basle Convention, Article 5; SIA, Section 4; Australia FSIA, Section 12; Singapore SIA, Section 6; and FSIA, Section 1605(a)(2) (commercial activity subsumes employment contract under the Act).

Treaty Provisions

According to Article 2(1) of the United Nations Convention, a "commercial transaction" is:

(i) any commercial contract or transaction for the sale of goods or supply of service;
(ii) any contract for a loan or other transaction of a financial nature, including any obligation of guarantee or of indemnity in respect of any such loan or transaction;
(iii) any other contract or transaction of a commercial, industrial, trading or professional nature, but not including a contract of employment of persons.

Article 10 of the United Nations Convention provides that a foreign State cannot invoke immunity in a proceeding in a forum State regarding its commercial transaction, except if the parties to the transaction have agreed otherwise. The exception, of course, does not apply to commercial transactions between States, and presupposes a preexisting jurisdiction of the forum State under its internal law.[179]

Article 2(2) of the United Nations Convention provides:

> In determining whether a contract or transaction is a "commercial transaction" . . . reference should be made primarily to the nature of the contract or transaction, but its purpose should also be taken into account if the parties to the contract or transaction have so agreed, or if, in the practice of the State, that purpose is relevant to determining the non-commercial character of the contract or transaction.

Article 4 of the Basle Convention denies immunity to a Contracting State "if the proceedings relate to an obligation of the State, which, by virtue of a contract, falls to be discharged in the territory of the State of the forum." However, "the State may invoke its immunity if two conditions are fulfilled, that is to say, if the contract has been concluded on its territory and if the obligation of the State is governed by the administrative law of that State." The exception also does not apply where the parties have a written agreement to the contrary, for example, if they agree that courts other than in the place of performance should have jurisdiction, or to submission to arbitration. Article 7 of the Basle Convention provides: "A Contracting State cannot claim immunity from the jurisdiction of a court of another Contracting State if it has on the territory of the State of the

179. Article 10, Commentary (3), Draft Articles and Commentaries.

forum an office, agency or other establishment through which it engages, in the same manner as a private person, in an industrial, commercial or financial activity, and the proceedings relate to that activity of the office, agency or establishment." The narrow scope of Article 7, which covers the *acta jure gestionis* of a State, and broad scope of Article 4 balance out to create the traditional commercial activity exception. The activities covered by Article 7 must have a territorial connection with the forum State.[180]

Territoriality

Although much more evident in tort cases, the territoriality principle could be a factor in commercial cases. In *Borga*, the Italian Court of Cassation ruled that "when a foreign state carries out, in the territory of another state, an economic activity which could be performed by a private person, it thereby divests itself of its public law personality and it cannot claim immunity from the jurisdiction of that other State."[181] Similarly, Swiss courts require a connection between a commercial activity and the territory of Switzerland in their determination on sovereign immunity. For example, in *UAR v. Mrs. X*, the Swiss Court ruled: "A distinction must be made according to whether the foreign State acts in the exercise of its sovereign (*iure imperii*) or in a private law capacity (*iure gestionis*) . . . In the latter case . . . a foreign State may be sued before the Swiss courts and may be subjected in Switzerland to enforcement measures, on condition that the legal relationship to which it is a party is connected with Swiss territory [*rattache au territoire de ce pays*]. This condition requires that the relationship has its origin in Switzerland, fails to be performed there, or at least that the debtor has taken certain steps capable of making Switzerland a place of performance."[182]

United States

FSIA defines "commercial activity" tautologically as "either a regular course of commercial conduct or a particular commercial transaction or act. The commercial character of an activity shall be determined by reference to the nature of the course of conduct or particular transaction or act, rather than by reference to its purpose."[183] The exception is the "most significant of the FSIA's exceptions."[184]

180. See Explanatory Report on Articles 4 and 7 ("most industrial, commercial or financial activities carried on by a State on the territory of another State where it has no office, agency or establishment would probably give rise to contractual obligation which are dealt with by Article 4.")

181. *Borga v. Russia*, 22 ILR 235, 238 (1953).

182. *UAR v. Mrs. X*, Switzerland, 65 ILR 385, 389 (1960).

183. 28 U.S.C. § 1603(d) (1976).

184. See *Argentina v. Weltover*, 504 U.S. 607, 611; 112 S. Ct. 2160, 2164 (1992).

The U.S. Supreme Court has elaborated on the criterion for determining commercial activity as follows:

> [W]hen a foreign government acts not as regulator of a market, but in the manner of a private player within it, the foreign sovereign's actions are "commercial" within the meaning of the FSIA. Moreover, because the Act provides that the commercial character of an act is to be determined by reference to its "nature" rather than its "purpose"... the question is not whether the foreign government is acting with profit motive or instead with the aim of fulfilling uniquely sovereign objectives. Rather, the issue is whether the particular actions that the sovereign state performs (whatever the motive behind them) are the *type* of actions by which a private party engages in "trade and traffic or commerce." Thus, a foreign government's issuance of regulations limiting foreign currency exchange is a sovereign activity, because such authoritative control of commerce cannot be exercised by a private party; whereas a contract to buy army boots or even bullets is a "commercial" activity, because private companies can similarly use sales contracts to acquire goods.[185]

Examples of commercial activity include the "production, sale or purchase of goods; hiring or leasing of property; borrowing or lending of money; performance of or contracting for the performance of services; and similar activities carried on by natural or juridical persons."[186]

The commercial activity exception under FSIA, which has three clauses or prongs that require varying degrees of nexus with the United States, provides:

> A foreign state shall not be immune from the jurisdiction of the courts of the United States... in any case in which the action is based [1] upon a commercial activity carried on in the United States by the foreign state; or [2] upon an act performed in the United States in connection with a commercial activity of the foreign state elsewhere; or [3] upon an act outside of the territory of the United States in connection with a commercial activity of the foreign state elsewhere and that act causes a direct effect in the United States.[187]

185. *Id.* at 614–15 (Citations omitted].

186. RESTATEMENT THIRD OF FOREIGN RELATIONS § 453, Comment b. (AM. LAW. INST. 1987).

187. 28 U.S.C. § 1605(a)(2) (2012).

First Clause

The first clause deals with action *based upon a commercial activity carried on in the United States*. Although the FSIA does not define the phrase "based upon," the U.S. Supreme Court has interpreted the exception to mean that the commercial activity must have "substantial contact" with the United States.[188] According to the legislative history, this clause applies to "cases based on commercial transactions performed in whole or in part in the United States, import-export transactions involving sales to, or purchases from, concerns in the United States . . . financing from a private or public lending institution located in the United States."[189] A claim is based upon the commercial activity exception under the FSIA if it establishes an element of the claim that, if proven, would entitle the plaintiff to relief.[190] Thus, the first clause requires that the plaintiff's claim be based upon a commercial activity that has substantial contact with the United States.

In *OBB v. Sachs*,[191] the plaintiff had purchased a Eurail pass in the United States for rail travel in Europe and had suffered injuries when boarding a train in Austria. Plaintiff sued the railway, which is State-owned by Austria, in the United States courts. She argued that her suit was not barred by State immunity and that the commercial activity exception under the FSIA was applicable because the suit is "based upon" the railway's sale of the pass in the United States.

The Supreme Court used the opportunity to elaborate on the first clause of the commercial activity exception and upon the guidance provided by its decision in *Saudi Arabia v. Nelson*. It stated that the inquiry on "based upon" requires a court to identify the particular conduct on which the plaintiff's suit is based by looking at those elements of a claim that if proven would entitle the plaintiff to relief.[192] It discounted, as an over-reading of *Saudi Arabia v. Nelson*, the one-element test by which a court identifies all the elements of each claim in a complaint before the court may dismiss those claims as not falling under the commercial activity exception.[193] It stated that *Saudi Arabia v. Nelson* "teaches that an action is 'based upon' the 'particular conduct' that constitutes the 'gravamen' of the suit."[194]

188. *Saudi Arabia v. Nelson*, 507 U.S. 349, 356 (1993).

189. H.R. Rep. No. 1487, 94th Cong., 2d Sess. 12, reprinted in 1976 U.S. Code Cong. & Admin. News at 6615–16 ("1976 U.S.C.C.A.N.").

190. See *Saudi Arabia v. Nelson*, 507 U.S. 349, 357 (1993).

191. *OBB Personenverkehr v. Carol Sachs*, 136 S. Ct. 390 (2015) ("OBB").

192. *Id.* at 395 [citation and quotation marks omitted].

193. *Id.* at 396.

194. *Id.*

The Supreme Court construed *Saudi Arabia v. Nelson* and concluded that this plaintiff's claims were not "based upon" the sale of rail tickets in the United States but that "the conduct constituting the gravamen of Sach's suit plainly occurred abroad. All of her claims turn on the same tragic episode in Austria, allegedly caused by wrongful conduct and dangerous conditions in Austria, which led to injuries suffered in Austria."[195] The Supreme Court reiterated its caution in *Saudi Arabia v. Nelson* that "[d]omestic conduct with respect to different types of commercial activity may play a more significant role in other suits under the first clause of § 1605(a)(c). In addition, we consider here only a case in which the gravamen of claim is found in the same place."[196]

Second Clause

The second clause concerns action *based upon an act performed in the United States in connection with a commercial activity of the foreign state elsewhere.*[197] The requirement would be satisfied when an act occurs in the United States and has a nexus with a commercial activity outside of the United States. Moreover, when the act that is performed in the United States is significant enough on its own, it might qualify as commercial activity in the United States and satisfy the first clause. Thus, the first and second clauses may overlap. The legislative history of FSIA gives the following examples of acts or conduct in the United States in connection with commercial activity outside the United States that satisfy the requirement of the second clause: a representation in the United States leading to a claim for unjust enrichment, an act in the United States that violates the federal securities laws, or the wrongful discharge in the United States of an employee working on commercial activity carried on in a third country.[198] The act of the foreign State in the United States does not necessarily have to be commercial in nature, but in addition to the act in the United States by the foreign State being in

195. *Id.*

196. *Id.* at 397, n.2. Before the Supreme Court, the plaintiff raised a new argument "that OBB's entire railway enterprise constitutes the 'commercial activity' that has the requisite 'substantial contact with the United States,' because OBB reaches out to American customers by marketing and selling Eurail passes in the United States." The argument that jurisdiction was justified under the second clause of the commercial activity exception was forfeited because it was never raised before the District Court or Court of Appeals, and the Supreme Court did not find unusual circumstances to warrant entertaining the argument that was not presented to any lower court. *Id.* at 397–98.

197. See 1976 U.S.C.C.A.N. at 6618.

198. 1976 U.S.C.C.A.N. at 6617–18.

connection with the commercial activity of the foreign State, it must be sufficient to form the basis of the claim.[199]

Third Clause

The third clause is about actions *based upon an act outside of the territory of the United States in connection with a commercial activity of the foreign state elsewhere and that act causes a direct effect in the United States.* With respect to the degree of connection to the United States, this clause is the most attenuated and, as such, has engendered the most judicial analysis and commentary. According to the legislative history, this clause "would embrace commercial conduct abroad having direct effects within the United States which would subject such conduct to the exercise of jurisdiction by the United States consistent with principles set forth in section 18, Restatement of the Law, Second, Foreign Relations Law of the United States 1965)."[200]

In *Argentina v. Weltover*, the U.S. Supreme Court provided guidance on the type of conduct that satisfies the "direct effect" requirement.[201] The case was about a breach-of-contract claim against Argentina for her unilateral decision to reschedule payment on government bonds ("Bonods") in United States dollars through transfer on the London, Frankfurt, Zurich, or New York markets, at election of the creditors. The plaintiffs, two Panamanian corporations and a Swiss bank, who held the Bonods refused to accept the rescheduling and insisted on full payment in New York. In considering whether Argentina's unilateral

199. *Id.* at 6618. ("Although some or all of these acts might also be considered to be a 'commercial activity carried on in the United States,' as broadly defined in section 1603(e), it has seemed advisable to provide expressly for the case where a claim arises out of a specific act in the United States which is commercial or private in nature and which relates to a commercial activity abroad. It should be noted that the acts (or omissions) encompassed in this category are limited to those which in and of themselves are sufficient to form the basis of a cause of action.")

200. 1976 U.S.C.C.A.N. at 6618 Section 18 of the Restatement provides: "A state has jurisdiction to prescribe a rule of law attaching legal consequences to conduct that occurs outside its territory and causes an effect within its territory, if either (a) the conduct and its effect are generally recognized as constituent elements of a crime or tort under the law of states that have reasonably developed legal systems, or (b) (i) the conduct and its effect are constituent elements of activitity to which the rule applies; (ii) the effect within the territory is substantial; (iii) it occurs as a direct and foreseeable result of the conduct outside the territory; and (iv) the rule is not inconsistent with principles of justice generally recognized by states that have reasonably developed legal systems."; See *Argentina v. Weltover*, 504. U.S. 607 (1992) ("Section 18 states that American laws are not given extraterritorial application except with respect to conduct that has, as a 'direct and foreseeable result,' a 'substantial' effect within the United States. Since this obviously deals with jurisdiction to *legislate* rather than jurisdiction to *adjudicate*, this passage of the House Report has been charitably described as 'a bit of a *non sequitur*.'") [citations omitted; emphasis in original.]

201. *Argentina v. Weltover*, 504. U.S. 607 (1992).

rescheduling of the Bonods had a "direct effect" in the United States, the Supreme Court ruled that "an effect is 'direct' if it follows 'as an immediate consequence of the defendant's . . . activity."[202] According to the Supreme Court, a direct effect need not be substantial or foreseeable.[203] An effect is direct if it is the immediate consequence of a defendant's activity.[204] The Court concluded that Argentina's act had a "direct effect" in the United States because the plaintiffs "had designated their account in New York as the place of payment, and Argentina made some interest payments into those accounts before announcing that it was rescheduling the payment."[205] The Court also rejected the notion that the "direct effect" requirement cannot be met where the plaintiff is a foreign corporation, reiterating "that the FSIA permits 'a foreign plaintiff to sue a foreign sovereign in the courts of the United States, provided the substantive requirements of the Act are satisfied.' "[206]

Based upon Requirement

The commercial exception requires that the claim must be *based upon* a relevant commercial activity in the United States or elsewhere with a nexus to the United States.

In *Odhiambo*,[207] the plaintiff, a Kenyan citizen, was a whistleblower under a rewards program developed by the Kenyan Revenue Authority to get information about tax evasion by offering whistleblowers a share of the proceeds. The District of Columbia Court of Appeals held that Odhiambo's breach-of-contract claim is not "*based upon*" the alleged instances of commercial activity by Kenya that had substantial contact with the United States, including the meetings that Kenyan officials held with him in the United States to discuss the disputed rewards. The Court discounted any contention that Odhiambo's meetings with Kenyan officials in the United States established any fact without which his breach-of-contract claim will fail. Consequently, the plaintiff could not proceed under clause one of the commercial exception. The Court noted that under its case law mere business meetings in the United States do not suffice to create substantial contact with the United States, and "that clause one requires a plaintiff's

202. *Id.* at 616 [citation omitted].

203. See *Id.* at 618.

204. *Id.*

205. *Id.* at 619.

206. *Id.*

207. *Odhiambo v. Kenya*, 764 F.3d 31 (D.C. Cir. 2014).

claim to be 'based upon' *the aspect of the foreign state's commercial activity that establishes substantial contact with the United States.*"[208]

Regarding clause two of the commercial activity exception, the Court stated that the plaintiff's "clause two argument falters on the same grounds as his clause one argument: His breach-of-contract claim is not *based upon* any alleged 'act performed in the United States in connection with' Kenya's commercial activity." It ruled that "based upon" means the same thing in both clauses. It, therefore, held that none of the acts alleged by Odhiambo satisfied the test of clause two: it applies only if the act performed in the United States in connection with a commercial activity of the foreign State elsewhere establishes a fact without which the plaintiff will lose.[209]

With respect to clause three, the Court agreed with the plaintiff that "his claim is based upon the 'act' of Kenya's alleged breach of contract, which happened outside the United States in connection with the rewards offer—a presumptively commercial activity of the Kenyan government."[210] Notwithstanding, the Court still had to determine whether the alleged breach of contract caused a "direct effect in the United States" given that Odhiambo now resides in the United States. The Court construed *Republic of Argentina v. Weltover, Inc.*, 504 U.S. 607 (1992), the leading Supreme Court case on the meaning of "direct effect," as well as its own direct effect cases involving alleged breaches of contract, which have turned on whether the contract established the United States as a place of performance. It reasoned that the text and purpose of the FSIA support the position that 'breaching a contract that establishes the United States as a place of performance will have a *direct* effect here, whereas breaching a contract that establishes a different or unspecified place of performance can affect the United States only *indirectly*, as the result of some intervening event such as the plaintiff's move to this country."[211] The Court restated the clear distinction that its case law draws:

> For purposes of clause three of the FSIA commercial activity exception, breaching a contract that establishes or necessarily contemplates the United States as a place of performance causes a direct effect in the United States, while breaching a contract that does not establish or necessarily contemplate the United States as a place of performance does not cause a direct effect in the United States.[212]

208. *Id.* at 36–37 (emphasis in original).

209. *Id.* at 38.

210. *Id.*

211. *Id.* at 40.

212. *Id.*

The Court pointed out that a plaintiff's presence in or citizenship of the United States alone does not suffice to create a direct effect in the United States.[213] It noted that Kenya did not promise to perform any specific obligations in the United States, as nothing in the rewards offer suggested that the United States might be the place of performance. It held that Kenya's alleged breach of its obligations therefore did not create a *direct* effect in the United States, and that any effect in the United States arose only after a variety of intervening events that occurred in Kenya before Odhiambo took refuge in the United States.[214]

Canada

The Canada State Immunity Act provides: "A foreign state is not immune from the jurisdiction of a court in any proceedings that relate to any commercial activity of the foreign state."[215] It defines commercial activity as "any particular transaction, act or conduct or any regular course of conduct that by reason of its nature is of a commercial character."[216] The Act favors the generalized definition of commercial activity in FSIA over the comprehensive but possibly limiting definition in the United Kingdom State Immunity Act (SIA).[217] Unlike the FSIA, the SIA does not bar explicitly consideration of the purpose of an activity.

In *Re Canada Labour Code*,[218] the Canadian Supreme Court decided that labor relations at a foreign military base does not constitute "commercial activity" under Section 5 of the Canada State Immunity Act[219] so as to constitute an exception to sovereign immunity. The Court examined whether employment at the U.S. naval base in Argentia, Newfoundland, Canada, constituted commercial activity, and whether a union certification proceeding in respect of Canadian civilian employees before the Canada Labour Relations Board related to that activity. It determined that there are aspects of the employment that are commercial, whereas others are

213. *Id.*

214. *Id.* at 41.

215. 1980-81-82-83, c. 95, s. 5.

216. *Id.* s. 2.

217. See generally *The Canadian State Immunity Act*, 14 Law & Pol'y Int'l Bus. 1197 (1982–1983); *Re Canada Labour Code*, [1992] 2 S.C.R. 50 ("Parliament chose to follow the American model for the codification of the rules regarding the restrictive theory of sovereign immunity, in that both Canada and the United States define 'commercial activity' in a general fashion, leaving it to the courts to develop a workable definition. This model can be contrasted with the English State Immunity Act . . . which carves out a specific exception for contracts of employment.")

218. *Re Canada Labour Code* [1992] 2 S.C.R 50.

219. Section 5 provides: "A foreign state is not immune from the jurisdiction of a court in any proceedings that relate to any commercial activity of the foreign state."

sovereign and, as such, "the certification proceeding affects both the commercial and sovereign aspects of employment at the base."[220]

The Canadian Supreme Court concluded that the commercial aspect of the employment was "merely incidental" and not sufficiently strong to trigger the commercial activity exception under Section 5 of the Canadian SIA. It noted:

> I find it difficult if not impossible to distinguish in a principled manner between the nature and purpose of employment relationships, and I would thus decline to follow this approach. Nature and purpose are interrelated, and it is impossible to determine the former without considering the later. I do not accept that the definition of "commercial activity" in the Act precludes consideration of its purpose. That definition, in circuitous fashion, defines "commercial activity" as conduct that "by reason of its nature is of a commercial character". In many cases, it may be unnecessary to delve into metaphysical distinctions between the ontology and teleology of the activity in question. However, if consideration of purpose is helpful in determining the nature of an activity, then such considerations should be and are allowed under the Act. Further, when an activity is multifaceted in nature (as in the instant case) consideration of its purpose will assist in determining which facets are truly "related" to the proceedings in issue.[221]

The Canadian Supreme Court reasoned that "employment at a military base is a multi-faceted relationship"[222] and gave the example that "the right to be paid is for the most part a commercial aspect of the employment relationship"[223] but "the right to dismiss an employee without notice for security reasons is a sovereign attribute of the relationship."[224] It concluded: "I cannot think of no activity of a foreign state that is more inherently sovereign than the operation of such a base. As such, the United States government must be granted unfettered authority to manage and control employment activity at the base."[225]

The Supreme Court pointed out that a mere employment contract for services at the base is intrinsically a commercial activity but that the management and operation of a military base is patently a sovereign activity. With respect to whether

220. *Re Canada Labour Code* [1992] 2 S.C.R 50, 69.

221. *Re Canada Labour Code* [1992] 2 S.C.R 50, p. 70.

222. *Id.* at 76.

223. *Id.* at 77.

224. *Id.*

225. *Id.* at 78.

the certification proceedings "relate" to the commercial aspect of the employment so as to fall under the commercial activity exception, the Court ruled that "it is not enough that the proceedings merely 'touch on' or 'incidentally affect' affect the hiring of civilian labour at the base."[226] It reasoned "that there is too tenuous a connection between the U.S. Navy's base entering the local labour market for the purpose of hiring individual employees and non-consensual labour management relations imposed under the Canada Labour Code to create the requisite nexus for commercial activity to be brought into play in this case."[227] It held: "The union certification procedure relates most obviously and directly to the sovereign attributes of a foreign state, which must remain immune from such proceedings."[228]

The Supreme Court canvassed the case law in other jurisdictions that have recognized immunity from national labor relations tribunals. It distinguished the present case from the U.S. case of *Goethe House New York, German Cultural Center v. NLRB*, where the Second Circuit Court of Appeals of the United States overturned the decision of the District Court that granted the West German government petition for a preliminary injunction, enjoining the National Labor Relations Board from processing a representation application for non-German employees at the Goethe House, a nonprofit cultural center sponsored by Germany.[229] "The factual distinction between a cultural centre and a military base must be . . . emphasized."[230]

United Kingdom

Section 3 of the UK SIA provides: "A State is not immune as respects proceedings relating to (a) a commercial transaction entered into by the State; or (b) an obligation of the State which by virtue of a contract (whether a commercial transaction or not) falls to be performed wholly or partly in the United Kingdom." It defines "commercial transaction" as:

> (a) any contract for the supply of goods or services; (b) any loan or other transaction for the provision of finance and any guarantee or indemnity in respect of any such transaction or of any other financial obligation; and (c) any other transaction or activity (whether of a commercial, industrial,

226. *Id.* at 80.

227. *Id.* at 81.

228. *Id.* at 89.

229. See *Goethe House New York, German Cultural Center v. NLRB*, 869 F.2d 75 (2d Cir. 1988).

230. *Re Canada Labour Code* [1992] 2 S.C.R 50, p. 87.

> financial, professional or other similar character) into which a State enters or in which it engages otherwise than in the exercise of sovereign authority; but [excludes] a contract of employment between a State and an individual.

In *NML Capital v. Republic of Argentina*,[231] NML had obtained a summary judgment in a New York court in relation to bonds issued by Argentina. It sought to enforce and recognize the judgment in the English Commercial Court, and it prevailed, but the judgment was reversed by the Court of Appeal on the ground that Argentina was protected by State immunity. One of the issues considered by the Supreme Court of the United Kingdom was whether the proceedings for the recognition and enforcement of the New York court's judgment were proceedings "relating to a commercial transaction" within the meaning of Section 3 of SIA. All five justices agreed that the expression 'relating to' is capable of bearing a broader or narrower meaning, but by a majority of three (Lords Mance, Collins, and Walker) to two (Lords Phillips and Clark), the Supreme Court held that Section 3 of SIA does not extend to enforcement of foreign judgments. However, they all agreed that there was no need for a link between a commercial transaction and the United Kingdom.

Lord Mance did not think that the drafters of the SIA or Parliament contemplated that Section 3(1)(a) should apply to a foreign judgment against a foreign State.[232] He distinguished between the pursuit of a cause of action without the benefit of a foreign judgment and a suit based on a foreign judgment given in respect of a cause of action.[233] According to him, "it stretches language beyond the admissible to read 'proceedings relating to . . . a commercial transaction' as covering proceedings relating to a judgment which itself relates to a commercial transaction."[234]

Lord Collins (with whom Lord Walker agreed) thought that the expression should be given a narrower meaning because the "proceedings in England relate to the New York judgment and not the debt obligations on which the New York proceedings were based."[235] He noted that a "wider meaning would give effect to the practical reality that the proceedings relate to liability under the bonds, the issue of which was plainly a commercial transaction for the purposes of section 3."[236]

231. *NML Capital Limited v. Republic of Argentina* [2011] UKSC 31.

232. *Id.*, para. 84.

233. *Id.*, para. 85.

234. *Id.*, para. 86.

235. *Id.*, para. 116

236. *Id.*, para. 111.

Lord Phillips thought that the expression "relating to" should be given a wider meaning, which requires an examination of the underlying transaction that led to the New York judgment.[237]

Lord Clarke observed that "it is common ground that the New York proceedings in which NML obtained the judgment against Argentina were . . . proceedings [relating to a commercial transaction within the meaning of Section 3 of SIA]."[238] He agreed with NML's argument that "if the New York proceedings related to a commercial transaction, it is but a short step to hold that these proceedings, which were brought in order to enforce a judgment in respect of a liability under the bonds, are also proceedings 'relating to a commercial transaction.'"[239] He thought so because both proceedings "have the same purpose, namely to enforce Argentina's liabilities under commercial bonds."[240] He opined that it is in accord with the statutory purpose of the SIA to give it an updated meaning and consider the context of the proceedings, that is, enforcement of Argentina's liabilities under the commercial bonds. He framed the issue in the proceedings as simply whether Argentina enjoys State immunity, and that the answer to the question depends on whether its liability arises out of *acta jure imperii* or *acta jure gestionis*.[241]

Notwithstanding their disagreement about whether a claim falls within the scope of Section 3 of SIA, the Supreme Court nevertheless unanimously held that Argentina is not immune because of Section 31 of the Civil Jurisdiction and Judgments Act 1982, and its submission and waiver of immunity in the bonds.

Immovable Property

The immovable property exception existed even under the doctrine of absolute sovereign immunity.[242] Immovable property has always been regarded to be part of the territory of a forum State under the legal doctrine of *lex rei sitae*: rights in real property depend on and are determined according to the law of the situs of

237. *Id.*, para. 29.

238. See *id.*, para. 139.

239. *Id.*

240. *Id.*

241. See *id.*, para. 148.

242. See *Schooner Exchange v. McFaddon*, 11 U.S. 116, 7 Cranch 116, 144–45 (1812) ("A prince, by acquiring private property in a foreign country, may possibly be considered as subjecting that property to the territorial jurisdiction; he may be considered as so far laying down the prince, and assuming the character of a private individual.")

the property[243] Jurisdiction in relation to immovable property, such as land, is local and not transitory. Article 13(a) of the United Nations Convention provides that a foreign State cannot invoke immunity in a forum State in a proceeding that relates to the determination of "any right or interest of the State in, or its possession or use of, or any obligation of the State arising out of its interest in, or its possession or use of, immovable property situated in the State of the forum." "[T]he expression 'right or interest' . . . gives rise to some semantic difficulties. The law of property, especially real property, contains many peculiarities. What constitutes a right in property in one system may be regarded as an interest in another system. Thus, the combination of 'right or interest' is used as a term to indicate the totality of whatever right or interest may have under any legal system."[244]

This exception has no bearing on a foreign State's immunity in respect of its property from attachment and execution, and is without prejudice to the privileges and immunities enjoyed by the State under international law with respect to property of diplomatic missions and other representative offices of a government of the State.[245] The exception "is not intended to confer jurisdiction on any court where none exists."[246]

Article 9 of the Basle Convention provides that a Contracting State cannot claim immunity in a proceeding in a forum State relating to "its rights or interest in, or its use or possession of, immovable property; or its obligations arising out of its rights or interests in, or use or possession of, immovable property" where the property is situated in the forum State. Article 9 must be read in conjunction with Article 32, which provides: "Nothing in the present Convention shall affect privileges and immunities relating to the exercise of the functions of diplomatic missions and consular posts and of persons connected with them."[247] The immovable property exception covers inter alia:

> 1. proceedings against States concerning their rights in immovable property in the State of the forum; 2. proceedings relating to mortgages whether the foreign State is mortgagor or mortgagee; 3. proceedings relating to nuisance; 4. proceedings arising from the unauthorised (permanent or temporary)

243. See Draft Articles and Commentaries, Article 13, Commentary (4).

244. *Id.*

245. See Draft Articles and Commentaries, Article 13, Commentary (1).

246. *Id.*

247. Explanatory Report on Article 32 makes clear that in the event of a conflict between the Basle Convention and the Vienna Conventions on diplomatic and on consular immunities and privileges, the provisions of those conventions shall prevail.

> use of immovable property including actions in trespass, whether an injunction is claimed or damages or both; 5. proceedings concerning rights to the use of immovable property in the State of the forum, for example, actions to establish the existence or non-existence of a lease or tenancy agreement, or for possession or eviction; 6. proceedings relating to payments due from a State for the use of immovable property, or of a part thereof, in the State of the forum, with the exception of dues or taxes . . . ; 7. proceedings relating to the liabilities of a State as the owner or occupier of immovable property in the State of the forum (for example accidents caused by the dilapidated state of the building, *actio de eiectis vel effusis*).[248]

The FSIA provides that a foreign State shall not be immune in any case where "rights in immovable property situated in the United States are in issue."[249] Rights in immovable property within the contemplation of the FSIA include property interest in real estate, such as leasehold, easement, or servitude; possessory rights; or compensation rights secured by property interest.[250] The District of Columbia Circuit Court of Appeals has ruled that the "exception was not intended broadly to abrogate immunity for any action touching upon real estate."[251] In an action by a citizens' association to collect damages from Peru for conversion of a property to a chancery, which the association alleged violated local zoning laws, the court held that the claim makes no claim to any interest in the property. If anything, the "complaint sounds not in the law of real property at all, but the law of nuisance."[252]

It applies only to rights in property, which may be read broadly as was done by the U.S. Supreme Court in *Permanent Mission of India to the United Nations v. City of New York*,[253] where the Court held that the FSIA does not provide immunity to a foreign State from a lawsuit to declare the validity of a tax lien on its immovable property.[254] New York law exempts real property held by a foreign State from taxation when used by its diplomats. In this case, part of the property was used to house non-diplomatic staff and their families, and New York City levied property

248. Explanatory Report on Article 9.

249. 28 U.S.C. § 1605(a)(4) (2012).

250. See *Asociacion de Reclamantes v. Mexico*, 735 F.2d 1517 (D.C. Cir. 1984).

251. *MacArthur Area Citizens Ass'n v. Peru*, 809 F.2d 918, 921 (D.C. Cir. 1987).

252. *Id.*

253. *Permanent Mission of India to the United Nations v. City of New York*, 551 U.S. 193 (2007).

254. *Id.* at 195.

tax on that portion. The diplomatic mission refused to pay the taxes, and the unpaid taxes were converted into tax liens held by the City against the property by operation of New York state law. The Supreme Court ruled that the FSIA's immovable property exception focuses more broadly on "rights in" property and was not limited to cases concerning rights to title, ownership, or possession. It also ruled that the exception does not exclude cases in which the validity of a lien is disputed. Based on its ruling, it had to determine whether a suit seeking a declaration of the validity of a tax lien implicates rights in immovable property and concluded that it establishes an interest in such property.[255] The Supreme Court noted: "As a threshold matter, property ownership is not an inherently sovereign function. . . . In addition, the FSIA was also meant "to codify . . . the pre-existing real property exception to sovereign immunity recognized by international practice."[256]

Territorial Tort

Territorial tort exception to State immunity allows a forum State to exercise jurisdiction over a foreign State for torts allegedly committed within the territory of the forum State, without allowing it to exercise extraterritorial jurisdiction. This exception relates generally to acts or omissions by a foreign State in the territory of a forum State that cause death or personal injury, or damage or loss of tangible property. Territoriality is the key to the tort exception, which does not distinguish between *acta jure imperii* and *acta jure gestionis*.[257]

Article 12 of the United Nations Convention provides:

> Unless otherwise agreed between the States concerned, a State cannot invoke immunity from jurisdiction before a court of another State which is otherwise competent in a proceeding which relates to pecuniary compensation for death or injury of the person, or damage to or loss of tangible property, caused by an act or omission which is alleged to be attributable to the State, if the act or omission occurred in whole or in part in the territory of that other State and if the author of the act or omission was present in that territory at the time of the act or omission.

255. The dissent was of the opinion that the "case is not about the validity of . . . title to immovable property, or even the validity of its automatic prejudgment lien. Rather, it is a dispute over a foreign sovereign's tax liability." *Id.* at 204.

256. *Id.* at 199–200 [citations omitted].

257. See *Littrel v. United States of America (No 2)* [1994] 4 All ER 203, [1995] 1 WLR 82.

The exception applies to provide relief to individuals who suffer personal injury, death, or physical damage to or loss of property caused by an act or omission in the forum State, which might be intentional, accidental, or caused by negligence attributable to a foreign State, and which is actionable under the *lex loci delicti commissi*.[258] The exception is geared toward principally insurable risks, but it also covers intentional physical harm such as assault and battery, arson, or homicide.[259]

The FSIA tort exception provides that a foreign State shall not be immune from jurisdiction for acts "in which money damages are sought against a foreign state for personal injury or death, or damage to or loss of property, occurring in the United States and caused by the tortious act or omission of that foreign state or of any official or employee of that foreign State while acting within the scope of his office or employment."[260] The United States Supreme Court has ruled that the territorial tort exception of FSIA applies only to noncommercial torts, that is, tort actions not encompassed within the commercial activity exception: "Congress' primary purpose in enacting § 1603(a)(5) was to eliminate a foreign state's immunity for traffic accidents and other torts committed in the United States, for which liability is imposed under domestic tort law."[261] According to the legislative history of the FSIA, the noncommercial tort exception "is directed primarily at the problem of traffic accidents but is cast in general terms as applying to all tort actions for money damages, not otherwise encompassed by [the commercial activity exception]."[262] This does not mean "that the exception applies only to traffic accidents; rather, the point is that the legislative history counsels that the exception should be narrowly construed so as to not encompass the farthest reaches of common law."[263] The legislative history also states that the "tortious act or omission" under this exception "is meant to include causes of action which are based on strict liability as well as on negligence."[264]

The territorial scope of the tort exception may be "susceptible to the interpretation that only the effect of the tortious action need occur here, where Congress

258. See Draft Articles and Commentaries, Article 12, Commentary (1), (2), (3) and (4).

259. *Id.*

260. 28 U.S.C. § 1605 (a)(5) (2012).

261. *Amerada Hess*, 488 U.S. at 439–40.

262. 1976 U.S.C.C.A.N. at 6619.

263. *MacArthur Area Citizens Ass'n v. Peru*, 809 F.2d 918, 921 (D.C. Cir. 1987) [citations omitted].

264. 1976 U.S.C.C.A.N. at 6620; See *O'Bryan v. Holy See*, 556 F.3d 361 (6th Cir. 2009).

intended such a result in the FSIA it said so more explicitly."[265] Even though the text of the FSIA states that the injury or damage must occur within the United States, there is no express requirement that the tortious act or omission must also occur within the United States. Notwithstanding, some courts have adopted the "entire tort" interpretation of the tort exception and held that both the tortious act or omission and the injury or damage must occur in the United States.[266] Dicta by the Supreme Court seems to support the view that injury must also occur within the United States: "Because respondent's injury unquestionably occurred well outside the 3-mile limit then in effect for the territorial waters of the United States, the exception for noncommercial torts cannot apply."[267] For instance, where plaintiffs had sued instrumentalities of a foreign State for damages and losses resulting from the September 11, 2001, terrorist attacks, which they claim resulted from the instrumentalities allegedly contributing financial and other resources to the terrorists, but did not claim the actions by the instrumentalities occurred in the United States, the Court held that the exception did not apply because the alleged tort by the instrumentalities occurred outside the United States.[268]

The territorial tort exception has two exclusions: it does not apply where the claim is (1) based on the performance or failure to perform a discretionary function, or (2) arises out of malicious prosecution, abuse of process, libel, slander, misrepresentation, deceit, or interference with contract rights.[269] For the exception to apply, the tort must involve a non-discretionary act. Although discretionary function is excluded from the tort exception, the scope of that limitation is not very certain. The discretionary function exclusion is modeled on a similar provision in the Federal Tort Claims Act ("FTCA"),[270] which governs suits against the U.S. federal government. According to the FTCA, discretionary functions leave "room for policy judgment and decision"[271] and are designed to

265. *Asociacion de Reclamantes v. Mexico*, 735 F.2d 1517, 1524 (D.C. Cir. 1984), citing 28 U.S.C. § 1605(a)(2) (2012) [commercial activity exception].

266. See, e.g., *Frolova v. Union of Soviet Socialist Republics*, 761 F.2d 370, 379–80 (7th Cir. 1985); *MacArthur Area Citizens Ass'n v. Peru*, 809 F.2d 918, 921 (D.C. Cir. 1987). Cf. Article 12 of the United Nations Convention, which provides an exception to immunity if the act or omission occurred "in whole or in part" in the territory of the forum State.

267. See *Argentine Republic v. Amerada Hess Shipping Corp.*, 488 U.S. 428, 441 (1989).

268. *O'Neill v. Saudi Joint Relief Comm. (In re Terrorist Attacks on September 11, 2001 (Saudi Joint Relief Comm.))*, 714 F3d 109 (2d Cir. 2013).

269. 28 U.S.C. § 1605(a)(5)(A) and (B) (2012).

270. See 28 U.S.C § 2680(a) and (h) (2006); see also 1976 U.S.C.C.A.N. at 6620.

271. *Dalehite v. United States*, 346 U.S. 15, 35–36 (1953).

"prevent judicial 'second-guessing' of legislative and administrative decisions grounded in social, economic, and political policy through the medium in an action in tort."[272] A function is not discretionary "when a federal statute, regulation, or policy specifically prescribes a course of action for an employee to follow [because] the employee has no rightful option but to adhere to the directive."[273] It is "the nature of the conduct, rather than the status of the actor, that governs whether the discretionary function applies in a given case."[274]

Article 11 of the Basle Convention provides:

> A Contracting State cannot claim immunity from the jurisdiction of a court of another Contracting State in proceedings which relate to redress for injury to the person or damage to tangible property, if the facts which occasioned the injury or damage occurred in the territory of the State of the forum, or if the author of the injury or damage was present in the territory at the time when those facts occurred.

The exception does not apply "[w]here there has been no physical injury and no damage to tangible property."[275] The exception requires that the author of the damage or tortfeasor must have been in the forum State when the damage was caused, but this requirement does not apply to the person whose liability is at issue.[276]

Although the territorial tort exception to State immunity does not distinguish between *acta jure imperii* and *acta jure gestionis*, it does not apply in certain circumstances when such act or omission is committed *jure imperii,* as was decided in *McElhinney v. Ireland.* In that case, the applicant, an Irish citizen, alleged that sovereign immunity did not apply to claims against two defendants, namely, a British soldier and the British secretary of state for Northern Ireland, for damages for personal injury caused by torts that took place within the territory of the forum State. His claim was dismissed by the Irish Supreme Court because "the facts alleged did not relate to any commercial activity, and it was not established that, as a principle of public international law, immunity no longer applied

272. *United States v. Varig Airlines*, 467 U.S. 797, 814 (1984).

273. *Berkovitz v. United States*, 486 U.S. 531, 536 (1988).

274. *Varig Airlines*, 467 U.S. at 813.

275. Explanatory Report, para. 48.

276. See Explanatory Report, para 49 ("For example, when a vehicle belonging to a State is involved in a traffic accident, then, provided the driver of the vehicle was present, the State as owner or possessor of the vehicle may be sued, even though the plaintiff does not seek to establish the personal liability of the driver.")

in respect of personal injuries caused by the tortious act of a foreign State's servant or agent acting within the sphere of sovereign activity (*de jure imperii*)."[277] The court took note of Article 11 of the Basle Convention,[278] but also noted that an exclusion of the exception is provided in Article 31 of the same Convention:

> Nothing in [the] Convention shall affect any immunities or privileges enjoyed by a Contracting State in respect of anything done or omitted to be done by, or in relation to, its armed forces, when on the territory of another Contracting State.[279]

The ECtHR agreed with the Supreme Court and stated: "Certainly, it cannot be said that Ireland is alone in holding that immunity attaches to suits in respect of such torts committed by *acta jure imperii* or that, in affording this immunity, Ireland falls outside any currently accepted international standards."[280]

In the *Jurisdictional Immunities of the State* case between Italy and Germany, the ICJ examined also whether State immunity "is applicable to acts committed by the armed forces of a State . . . in the course of conducting an armed conflict" where both parties agree that *acta jure imperii* are generally entitled to State immunity.[281] The Court of Cassation (Italy), in *Ferrini v. German*, held that Italian courts have jurisdiction over compensation claims for forced labor in Germany during World War II. Germany challenged the ruling of the Court of Cassation before the ICJ, requesting the Court to find that Italy has violated its obligation under international law to respect Germany's jurisdictional immunity. Germany's argument before the ICJ was that "there is no relevant limitation on the immunity to which a State is entitled in respect to *acta jure imperii*."[282] Italy counterargued:

> Germany is not entitled to immunity in respect of the cases before the Italian courts for two reasons: first, that immunity as *to acta jure imperii* does not extend to torts, or delicts occasioning death, personal injury or damage to property committed on the territory of the forum State, and, secondly, that irrespective of where the relevant acts took place, Germany

277. *McElhinney v. Ireland* [GC] no. 31253/96, ECHR 2001-XI, para. 15.

278. *Id.*, para. 15.

279. *Id.*

280. *Id.*, para. 38.

281. Jurisdictional Immunities of the State (*Germany v. Italy: Greek Intervening*), Judgment, I.C.J. Rep. 2012, p. 99, ¶ 60.

282. *Id.*

> was not entitled to immunity because those acts involved the most serious violations of rules of international law of a peremptory character for which no alternative means of redress was available.[283]

The ICJ considered whether customary international law has developed to the point where there is a territorial tort exception to State immunity applicable to *acta jure imperii,* and noted that the national legislation that provide for such an exception do not expressly distinguish between *acta jure imperii* and *acta jure gestionis.*[284] After a comprehensive examination and analysis of the Basle Convention and the United Nations Convention,[285] national legislation on State immunity,[286] and judgments of national courts, the ICJ opined:

> State practice in the form of judicial decisions supports the proposition that State immunity for *acta jure imperii* continues to extend to civil proceedings for acts occasioning death, personal injury or damage to property committed by the armed forces and other organs of a State in the conduct of armed conflict, even if the relevant acts take place on the territory of the forum State. That practice is accompanied by *opinio juris,* as demonstrated by the positions taken by States and the jurisprudence of a number of national courts which have made clear that they considered that customary international law required immunity. The almost complete absence of contrary jurisprudence is also significant, as is the absence of any statements by States in connection with the work of the International Law Commission regarding State immunity and the adoption of the United

283. *Id.*, para. 61.

284. *Id.* at paras. 64 and 65.

285. The Court noted that the Conventions is not in effect between the parties, and that its relevance is limited to whether "their provisions and the process of their adoption and implementation shed light on the content of customary international law." *Id.*, para. 66.

286. *Id.*, para. 70. ("Turning to State practice in the form of national legislation, the Court notes that nine of the ten States referred to by the Parties which have legislated specifically for the subject of State immunity have adopted provisions to the effect that a State is not entitled to immunity in respect of torts occasioning death, personal injury or damage to property occurring on the territory of the forum State (United States of America Foreign Sovereign Immunities Act 1976, 28 *USC*, Sect. 1605 (*a*) (5); United Kingdom State Immunity Act 1978, Sect. 5; South Africa Foreign States Immunities Act 1981, Sect. 6; Canada State Immunity Act 1985, Sect. 6; Australia Foreign States Immunities Act 1985, Sect. 13; Singapore State Immunity Act 1985, Sect. 7; Argentina Law No. 24.488 (Statute on the Immunity of Foreign States before Argentine Tribunals) 1995, Art. 2 (*e*); Israel Foreign State Immunity Law 2008, Sect. 5; and Japan, Act on the Civil Jurisdiction of Japan with respect to a Foreign State, 2009, Art. 10). Only Pakistan's State Immunity Ordinance 1981 contains no comparable provision."

> Nations Convention or, so far as the Court has been able to discover, in any other context asserting that customary international law does not require immunity in such cases.[287]

The ICJ, therefore, ruled that "customary international law continues to require that a State be accorded immunity in proceedings for torts allegedly committed on the territory of another State by its armed forces and other organs of State in the course of conducting an armed conflict. That conclusion is confirmed by the judgments of the European Court of Human Rights to which the Court has referred."[288] It then concluded "that, contrary to what had been argued by Italy in the present proceedings, the decision of the Italian courts to deny immunity to Germany cannot be justified on the basis of the territorial tort principle."[289]

In *Schreiber v. Canada (Attorney General)*,[290] the Supreme Court of Canada determined whether a claim of mental distress, denial of liberty, and damage to reputation suffered due to wrongful arrest and imprisonment was "personal injury" under the tort exception in Section 6(a) of the State Immunity Act of Canada, which provides: "A foreign state is not immune from the jurisdiction of a court in any proceedings that relate to any death or personal injury, or any damage to or loss of property that occurs in Canada." The appellant had sued Germany for damages for personal injury suffered as a result of his arrest and detention in Canada, pursuant to an arrest warrant by a German court for his extradition for tax evasion and other offenses. The Court determined:

> [A] legislative intent to create an exception to state immunity which would be restricted to a class of claims arising out of a physical breach of personal integrity [which] could conceivably cover an overlapping area between physical harm and metal injury, such as nervous stress; however, the mere deprivation of freedom and the normal consequences of lawful imprisonment, as framed by the claim, do allow the appellant to claim an exception to the *State Immunity Act*.[291]

The Court consequently dismissed the claim, holding that Section 6(a) of the Act did not deprive Germany of the immunity to which it is entitled under

287. *Id.*, para. 77.

288. *Id.*, para. 78.

289. *Id.*, para. 79.

290. *Schreiber v. Canada* (Attorney General), 2002 SCC 62, [2002] 3 S.C.R. 269 (Can).

291. *Id.*, para. 80.

Section 3(1) of the Act. The Canadian Supreme Court again addressed the tort exception in *Kazemi Estate*,[292] where the plaintiff had instituted civil proceedings against Iran and its officials, seeking damages for himself and the estate of his mother who was detained and tortured in Iran. He sought damages on behalf of his mother's estate for her physical, psychological, and emotional pain and suffering as well as damages for the psychological and emotional prejudice that he sustained as the result of the loss of his mother. The Iranian defendants moved to dismiss the action on the basis of State immunity. In response, plaintiff and her mother's estate raised certain exceptions provided in the Canada State Immunity Act. The case was appealed to the Canadian Supreme Court, which noted that the wordings of Section 6(a) could be interpreted to mean "either (1) that the injury manifest itself in Canada, even where the acts causing the death or the injury occurred outside Canada, or (2) that the acts causing the injury or death occur in Canada."[293] But it found the second interpretation more tenable when the words of Section 6(a) are examined in conjunction with the purpose of the Act, which is to ensure that the principle of sovereign equality that underpins of State immunity is upheld in Canada.[294] It also noted that interpreting Section 6(a) to require only that the death or injury occur in Canada would yield absurd results.[295] "It accords with the theory of sovereign equality to allow foreign states to be sued in Canada for torts allegedly committed by them within Canadian boundaries."[296] The Court, therefore, held that with regard to Section 6(a) of SIA, the territorial tort exception "does not apply where the impugned event, or the tort causing the personal injury or death, did not take place in Canada."[297]

Employment Contracts

Most national legislations on State immunity have an exception for contracts of employment.[298] Sometimes, this exception is subsumed in the commercial

292. Kazemi Estate v. Islamic Republic of Iran, 2014 SCC 62 ¶ 102, [2014] 3 S.C.R. 176 (Can.).

293. *Id.*, para. 69.

294. *Id.*, para. 70.

295. *Id.*, para. 71.

296. *Id.*, para. 72.

297. *Id.*, para. 73.

298. See *Cudak v. Lithuania*, Application 15869/02 [2010] ECHR 370, para. 63. National legislation on immunity: Section 4(2)(b) of SIA; Section 4(a)(3) of Israeli Foreign States Immunity Law 5769-2008; Section 6(2)(b) of Pakistani State Immunity Ordinance of 1981; Article 6(2)(b)

activity exception.[299] Courts determine whether a foreign State enjoys immunity in employment disputes based on any or a combination of these criteria: (1) the nature of the workplace, (2) the status of the employee, (3) the connection between the forum State and the employee or the employment, and (4) the nature of the claim.[300] The claims usually concern breaches of an employment contract or violations of labor and employment law, and deal with employment at diplomatic or consular missions, or military bases, or other foreign State-owned entities. The exception sometimes incorporates elements of diplomatic or consular immunities. The difficulty of drawing the distinction between *acta jure imperii* and *acta jure gestionis* is more apparent in employment disputes involving diplomatic missions where the approaches of various national courts are diverse and varied.

Article 5 of the Basle Convention provides:

> 1. A Contracting State cannot claim immunity from the jurisdiction of a Court of another Contracting State if the proceedings relate to a contract of employment between the State and an individual where the work has to be performed in the territory of the State of the forum.
> 2. Paragraph 1 shall not apply where: the individual is a national of the employing State at the time when the proceedings were brought; at the time when the contract was entered into the individual was neither a national of the State of the forum nor habitually a resident in that State; or the parties to the contract have otherwise agreed in writing, unless, in accordance with the law of the State of the forum, the courts of that State have exclusive jurisdiction by reason of the subject-matter.
> 3. Where the work is done for an office, agency or other establishment referred to in Article 7, paragraphs 2 (a) and (b) of the present Article apply only if, at the time the contract was entered into, the individual had his habitual residence in the Contracting State which employs him.

The exception is circumscribed by the consideration that it is justifiable in certain circumstances for the foreign State to retain immunity when the employee

of Singaporean State Immunity Act; and Section 5(1)(b) of the South African Foreign States Immunities Act 87 of 1981.

299. The U.S. FSIA does not have a specific provision for exception to immunity regarding contracts of employment, but they are covered by the exception for "commercial activity carried on in the United States by a foreign State." Section 1605(a)(2).

300. See *Cudak v. Lithuania*, Application 15869/02 [2010] ECHR 370, para. 18.

is a national of the foreign (defendant) State when the suit is brought, or was neither a national nor a habitual resident of the forum State when the contract was executed, that is, where the employee is a foreign worker who has not been locally recruited. The justification is that the nexus between the employee and the foreign State is usually closer than that between the employee and the forum State.[301]

The exception under Article 5 has an exclusion in Article 32, which provides: "Nothing in the present Convention shall affect privileges and immunities relating to the exercise of the functions of diplomatic missions and consular posts and of persons connected with them."[302]

Section 4(1) of the State Immunity Act (SIA) provides: "A State is not immune as respects proceedings relating to a contract of employment between the State and an individual where the contract was made in the United Kingdom or the work is to be wholly or partly performed there." However, where the employee was not habitually resident in the United Kingdom when the contract of employment was entered, Section 4(2) excludes the case from the application of the exception to immunity established by Section 4(1). The exception also has an exclusion under Section 16(1)(a), which provides:

> This Part of this Act does not affect any immunity or privilege conferred by the Diplomatic Privileges Act 1964 or the Consular Relations Act 1968; and (a) Section 4 above does not apply to proceedings concerning the employment of the member of a mission within the meaning of the Convention scheduled to the said Act of 1964 or of the member of a consular post within the meaning of the Convention scheduled to said Act of 1968.

Article 1 of the Vienna Convention on Diplomatic Relations (VCDR) provides pertinently: "(b) the 'members of the mission' are the head of the mission and the members of the staff of the mission; (c) the 'members of staff of the mission' are the members of the diplomatic staff or the administrative and technical staff, and of the service staff of the mission."

In *Fogarty v. United Kingdom,*[303] the applicant, an Irish national, was employed as an administrative assistant at the U.S. embassy in London. When her employment was terminated, she brought proceedings against the U.S. government

301. See Explanatory Report, para. 30.

302. *Id.*, para 30: "As regards contracts of employment with diplomatic missions or consular posts, Article 32 shall be taken into account."

303. *Fogarty v. United Kingdom* [GC], no. 37112/97, ECHR 2001-XI.

before the North London Industrial Tribunal, claiming sex discrimination. Her claim was upheld by the Tribunal. Subsequently, the applicant applied unsuccessfully for other posts at the embassy. She brought further proceedings at the Tribunal, claiming that she has been victimized and discriminated in violation of the U.K. Sex Discrimination Act. The U.S. government invoked immunity pursuant to Sections 1 and 16(1)(a) of the SIA, and averred that the posts for which the applicant had applied were part of the administrative and technical service of the embassy and, as such, came under the purview of Section 16(1)(a).

For foreign State employers at diplomatic and consular missions, Section 16 provides a saving clause. It excludes certain matters from the scope of Part 1 of the Act, with the effect that the exception created under Section 4 does not apply to such matters and the foreign State consequently retains immunity under Section 1(1). The ECtHR "recall[ed] that in *Pellegrin v. France* ([GC], no. 28541/95, ECHR 1999-VIII) it adopted a functional test for the purposes of determining the applicability of Article 6 § 1 [of the European Convention on Human Rights] to employment disputes involving public servants, based on the nature of the employee's duties and responsibilities. An employment dispute is excluded from the scope of Article 6 § 1 if it concerns a public servant whose duties typify the specific activities of the public service in so far as he or she acts as the depository of public authority responsible for protecting the general interests of the State."[304]

The ECtHR observed:

> [O]n the material before it (see paragraphs 16–20, 29 and 31 above), there appears to be a trend in international and comparative law towards limiting State immunity in respect of employment-related disputes. However, where the proceedings relate to employment in a foreign mission or embassy, international practice is divided on the question whether State immunity continues to apply and, if it does so apply, whether it covers disputes relating to the contracts of all staff or only more senior members of the mission. Certainly, it cannot be said that the United Kingdom is alone in holding that immunity attaches to suits by employees at diplomatic missions or that, in affording such immunity, the United Kingdom falls outside any currently accepted international standards.[305]
>
> [T]he proceedings which the applicant wished to bring did not concern the contractual rights of a current embassy employee, but instead related to alleged discrimination in the recruitment process. Questions relating to the recruitment of staff to missions and embassies may by their very nature

304. *Id.*, para. 28.

305. *Id.*, para. 37.

> involve sensitive and confidential issues, related, *inter alia*, to the diplomatic and organisational policy of a foreign State. The Court is not aware of any trend in international law towards a relaxation of the rule of State immunity as regards issues of recruitment to foreign missions.[306]

The ECtHR ruled that under the circumstances of the case, the conferral of immunity on the United States did not violate Article 6 of ECHR and was based on Sections 1 and 16(1)(a) of the SIA "which confer an immunity in respect of proceedings concerning employment within the staff, including the administrative and technical staff, of an embassy. This immunity applies in relation to all such employment-related disputes, irrespective of their subject matter and of the sex, nationality, place of residence or other attributes of the complainant."[307]

Article 11 (Contracts of Employment) of the United Nations Convention provides:

> 1. Unless otherwise agreed between the States concerned, a State cannot invoke immunity from jurisdiction before a court of another State which is otherwise competent in a proceeding which relates to a contract of employment between the State and an individual for work performed or to be performed, in whole or in part, in the territory of that other State.
> 2. Paragraph 1 does not apply if: (a) the employee has been recruited to perform particular functions in the exercise of governmental authority; (b) the employee is:
>   (i) a diplomatic agent, as defined in the Vienna Convention on Diplomatic Relations of 1961; (ii) a consular officer, as defined in the Vienna Convention on Consular Relations of 1963; (iii) a member of the diplomatic staff of a permanent mission to an international organization or of a special mission, or is recruited to a State at an international conference; or (iv) any other person enjoying diplomatic immunity; the subject-matter of the proceeding is the recruitment, renewal of employment or reinstatement of an individual; the subject-matter of the proceeding is the dismissal or termination of employment of an individual and, as determined by the head of State, the head of Government or the Minister of Foreign Affairs of the employer State, such a proceeding would

306. *Id.*, para. 38.

307. *Id.*, paras. 40 and 42.

> interfere with the security interest of that State; the employee is a national of the employer State at the time when the proceeding is instituted, unless this person has the permanent residence in the State of the forum; or the employer State and the employee have otherwise agreed in writing, subject to any considerations of public policy conferring on the courts of the State of the forum exclusive jurisdiction by reason of the subject-matter of the proceedings.

The United Nations Convention, therefore, provides an exception to immunity where the contract is to be performed in the forum State, but the exception is excluded where the employee is neither a national nor a resident of the forum State when the contract was entered. It is also excluded where the employee was a national of the foreign State at the time of the court proceedings. Immunity is, however, retained where "the employee has been recruited to perform functions closely related to the exercise of governmental authority."

Most courts take the position that the United Nations Convention on Jurisdictional Immunities of States and Their Property ("United Nations Convention") is a codification of customary international law on State immunity, even though it has not come into effect. Consequently, the provisions of the United Nations Convention and the customary international law it codifies are binding, even on States that have not ratified the Convention.[308] In this regard, Article 11 reflects the trend in the legislative and treaty practice of States in that endeavor.[309]

Under the United Nations Convention, the exception to immunity in employment contracts with staff of diplomatic and consular missions is subject to exclusions in the following cases: recruitment, renewal of employment, or reinstatement of an employee; dismissal or termination of an employee where the employer State determines that the proceedings will interfere with its security interest; where the employee was a national of the employer State; or where the employer State and employee had otherwise agreed in writing.[310]

308. See *Cudak v. Lithuania*, Application No. 15869/02, European Court of Human Rights (2010).

309. See Draft Articles and Commentaries, Article 11, Commentary (14).

310. *Id.*, Article 11(2)(b), Commentary (10) ("[Article 11(2)(c), (d), (e) and (f)] is designed to confirm the existing practice of States in support of the rule of immunity in the exercise of the discretionary power of appointment or non-appointment by the State of an individual to any official post or employment. This includes actual appointment which under the law of the employer State is considered to be the unilateral act of governmental authority. So also are the acts of 'dismissal' or 'removal' of a government employee by the State, which normally take place after the conclusion of an inquiry or investigation as part of the supervisory or disciplinary jurisdiction exercised by the employer State. This subparagraph also covers cases where the employee seeks renewal of his employment or reinstatement after untimely termination of his engagement. The rule of immunity

In *Cudak v. Lithuania*,[311] the applicant, who was born and lived in Vilnius, Lithuania, was recruited by the Polish embassy in Vilnius as a secretary and switchboard operator. When she was dismissed, she brought a claim for unlawful dismissal before the Vilnius Regional Court. Poland claimed immunity and the court proceedings were discontinued. The Court of Appeal upheld the decision, which was appealed to the Lithuanian Supreme Court, which considered it appropriate to decide according to "general principles of international law, in particular the 1972 European Convention on State Immunity."[312] The Lithuanian Supreme Court had held:

> [I]n the Supreme Court's view, it is possible to apply the principle of restrictive immunity to the Republic of Poland. Having regard to the fact that Lithuania recognises that foreign nationals may bring actions in respect of private-law disputes, it must be accepted that, in order to defend their rights, individuals or entities from the Republic of Lithuania are entitled to take proceedings against foreign States.
>
> It is thus necessary to establish in the present case whether the relationship between the claimant and the Republic of Poland was one of a public-law nature (*acta jure imperii*) or a private-law nature (*acta jure gestionis*). Besides that, other criteria are applicable and should allow [the court] to determine whether the State concerned enjoys immunity . . . in employment disputes. These criteria include, in particular, the nature of the workplace, the status of the employee, the territorial connection between the country of employment and the country of the court, and the nature of the claim.
>
> Regard being had to the plea of immunity by the Ministry of Foreign Affairs of the Republic of Poland . . . it is possible to conclude that there was a public-service relationship governed by public law (*acta jure imperii*) between the claimant and the embassy of the Republic of Poland, and that the Republic of Poland may lay claim to immunity from the jurisdiction of foreign courts. This conclusion is supported by other criteria. With regard to the nature of the workplace, it should be noted that the main function of the embassy . . . is directly related to the exercise of sovereignty of the Republic of Poland. With respect to the status of [the] employee . . . while the parties

applies to proceedings for recruitment, renewal or employment and reinstatement of an individual only. It is without prejudice to the possible recourse which may still be available in the State of the forum for compensation or damages for 'wrongful dismissal' or for breaches of obligation to recruit or to renew employment.")

311. *Cudak v. Lithuania* [2010] ECHR 370, Application No. 15869/02.

312. *Id.*, para. 17.

had entered into a contract of employment, the very fact that the employee was a switchboard operator implies that the parties developed a relationship akin to that which characterises a public-service function. . . . The court was unable to obtain any information allowing it to establish the scope of the claimant's actual duties. Thus, merely from the title of her position, it can be concluded that the duties entrusted to her facilitated, to a certain degree, the exercise by the Republic of Poland of its sovereign functions. . . . It must also be established whether the country of employment is the country of the court, since a court in the country of employment is best placed to resolve a dispute that has arisen in that country. In this respect, it is to be recognised that the exercise of the sovereign powers of the forum State is severely restricted with regard to an embassy, even though it is not a foreign territory as such (section 11(2) of the Status of Diplomatic Missions of Foreign States Act). As to the nature of the claim . . . it should be noted that a claim for recognition of unlawful dismissal and for compensation cannot be regarded as violating the sovereignty of [another] State, since such a claim pertains solely to the economic aspect of the impugned legal relationship[;] there is no claim for reinstatement. . . . However, by reason of this criterion alone, it cannot be unconditionally asserted that the Republic of Poland cannot invoke State immunity in this case. . . . [The claimant] has submitted no [other] evidence to confirm the inability for the Republic of Poland to enjoy State immunity (Article 58 of the Code of Civil Procedure).

Against the background of the above criteria, [in view of] the aspiration of Lithuania and Poland to maintain good bilateral relations . . . and respect the principle of sovereign equality between States . . . , the chamber concludes that the courts [below] properly decided that they had no jurisdiction to entertain this case.

The Supreme Court notes that both the Regional Court of Vilnius and the Court of Appeal based the decision to apply jurisdictional immunity to the Republic of Poland merely on the fact that the latter had refused to appear in the proceedings. Those courts did not examine the question of the application of restrictive jurisdictional immunity in the light of the criteria developed by the Supreme Court. However, this breach of procedural rules does not constitute, in the Supreme Court's view, a ground for quashing the decisions of the courts below. . . .

The application of jurisdictional immunity by the courts of the Republic of Lithuania does not prevent the claimant from taking proceedings before the Polish courts.[313]

313. *Id.*, para. 18 (Excerpt of the Judgment of the Lithuanian Supreme Court).

The ECtHR noted that in a subsequent case similar to that of the applicant's, the Supreme Court of Lithuania noted that the United Nations Convention could be taken into account as it reflects a trend in the international law of State immunity.[314] It observed that there was no legally binding international rule that staff of a diplomatic mission who participated in the exercise of sovereign authority could be distinguished from other members of staff.[315]

The ECtHR noted that Lithuania and Poland are not parties to the Basle Convention. The Court distinguished the case of Cudak "from that of Fogarty in that it does not concern recruitment but rather the dismissal of a member of the local staff of an embassy."[316] It recalled that in *Fogarty* it found "that there was a trend in international and comparative law towards limiting State immunity in respect of employment-related disputes, with the exception, however, of those concerning the recruitment of staff in embassies."[317] It noted:

> The 1991 Draft Articles, on which the 2004 United Nations Convention (and Article 11 in particular) was based, created a significant exception in matters of State immunity by, in principle, removing from the application of the immunity rule a State's employment contracts with the staff of its diplomatic missions abroad. However, that exception was itself subject to exceptions whereby, in substance, immunity still applied to diplomatic and consular staff in cases where: the subject of the dispute was the recruitment, renewal of employment or reinstatement of an individual; the employee was a national of the employer State; or, lastly, the employer State and the employee had otherwise agreed in writing.[318]

The ECtHR considered that Article 11 of the United Nations Convention could apply to Lithuania under customary international law.[319] It then noted that the applicant was not covered by any of the exceptions under Article 11, as "she did not perform any particular functions closely related to the exercise of governmental authority. In addition, she was not a diplomatic agent or consular officer, nor was she a national of the employer State. Lastly, the subject

314. *Id.*, para. 23.

315. *Id.*, para. 24.

316. *Id.*, para. 62.

317. *Id.*, para. 63.

318. *Id.*, para. 65.

319. *Id.*, para. 67.

matter of the dispute was linked to the applicant's dismissal."[320] The ECtHR particularly noted:

> [T]he applicant was a switchboard operator at the Polish embassy whose main duties were: recording international telephone conversations, typing, sending and receiving faxes, photocopying documents, providing information and assisting with the organisation of certain events. Neither the Lithuanian Supreme Court nor the respondent Government have shown how these duties could objectively have been related to the sovereign interests of the Polish government. While the schedule to the employment contract stated that the applicant could have been called upon to do other work at the request of the head of mission, it does not appear from the case file—nor have the Government provided any details in this connection—that she actually performed any functions related to the exercise of sovereignty by the Polish State.[321]

The ECtHR concluded that there has not been a showing that the applicant's duties were of importance to Poland's security interests as enshrined in Article 11(2)(d) of the United Nations Convention, noting that the proceedings arose from acts of sexual harassment and the subsequent dismissal of applicant.[322] The Court then held that the Lithuanian courts by declining jurisdiction based on State immunity to hear applicant's claim had violated Article 6 of ECHR.[323]

The ECtHR applied also the United Nations Convention in *Sabeh El Leil v. France*, where the employee who was employed as an accountant in the Kuwaiti Embassy in Paris was terminated on economic grounds.[324] The Court determined that the dispute did not fall within the exhaustively enumerated exceptions in Article 11 of the Convention as the applicant was not a diplomat, a consular agent, or a national of Kuwait.[325] It noted that the applicant was not employed to perform functions in the exercise of governmental authority, and that there was no establishment of any risk of interference with the security interest of the State of Kuwait.

320. *Id.*, para. 69.

321. *Id.*, para. 70.

322. *Id.*, para. 72.

323. *Id.*, paras. 74–75.

324. *Sabeh El Leil v. France*, Application No. 34869/05 [2011] ECHR 1055.

325. See *id.*, para 60.

In *Benkharbouche & Anor v. Embassy of the Republic of Sudan*, the question was whether a member of the service staff of a diplomatic mission to the United Kingdom is barred by State immunity from bringing an action against the employer foreign State to assert employment rights.[326] Benkharbouche, a Moroccan national, was dismissed as a cook at the Sudanese embassy in London, and she sued the embassy for unfair dismissal and violation of English labor laws. The embassy pled immunity under Section 1 of the SIA, which was upheld by the employment judge who dismissed the claim. The other plaintiff, Janah, also a Moroccan national, who had lived in the United Kingdom since 2005 and was employed as a domestic staff at the Libyan embassy in London brought claims against Libya for unfair dismissal, arrears of pay, racial discrimination, and harassment, as well as breach of English labor laws. Libya pled immunity, which was upheld by the Employment Judge. Because it was conceded that Janah was not habitually resident in the United Kingdom, Section 4(2) of the SIA dis-applied the exception under Section 4(1).

The employment dispute was appealed to the Employment Appeal Tribunal and then to the England and Wales Court of Appeal. The Court of Appeal noted that Section 16(1) of SIA had the effect of excluding proceedings concerning employment of members of a diplomatic or consular mission from the application of the exception to immunity under Section 4 and of restoring the immunity under Section 1 of the Act. It ruled that the plaintiffs were, therefore, barred by the provisions of the SIA from pursuing their claims against their former employers in the jurisdiction of the United Kingdom.[327] It then considered whether the applicable provisions of the SIA are compatible with Article 6 of ECHR and Article 47 of the European Union (EU) Charter. After a comprehensive review of the national and international laws, as well as decisions of national and international courts, it concluded that Section 16(1)(1) of the SIA, in its application to the claims brought by the plaintiffs, infringed on Article 6 of ECHR, and that also Section 4(2)(b) of the SIA in its application to the claims brought by plaintiffs infringed on Article 6 and 14 of ECHR. The decision of the Court of Appeal was appealed to the Supreme Court, where the issue was whether granting immunity from suit under the State Immunity Act 1978 engages, and breaches, the Respondents' rights under the ECHR and EU Charter.

The United Kingdom Supreme Court "conclude[d] that unless international law requires the United Kingdom to treat Libya and Sudan as immune as regards the claims of Janah and Benkharbouche, the denial to them of access to

326. *Benkharbouche & Anor v. Embassy of the Republic of Sudan* (Rev 1) [2016] 1 All ER 816, [2015] 3 WLR 301.

327. *Id.*, para. 9.

the courts to adjudicate on their claim violates article 6 of the Human Rights Convention."[328] According to the Supreme Court, despite the drafting technique employed in the SIA, as well as other legal instruments on State immunity, the starting point or default position is that a foreign State is entitled to immunity under customary international law only for *acta jure imperii*.[329] "As a matter of customary international law, if an employment claim arises out of an inherently sovereign or governmental act of the foreign state, the latter is immune."[330] Such a claim will depend on the employment relationship and on the functions of the employee.[331] However, the Court cautioned that the character of the employment is not "always and necessarily decisive" and gave two examples.[332] A State may be immune where its sovereign interest is engaged even though the employment contract was not in the exercise of sovereign authority.[333] In the same vein, territorial nexus between the claimant and the forum or foreign State may be relevant in the determination of immunity even though it has nothing to do with the distinction between *acta jure imperii* and *acta jure gestionis*.[334] The Supreme Court construed the SIA "as giving effect to customary international law only so far as it distinguishes between exercises of sovereign authority and acts of a private law character, and requires immunity to be conferred on the former but not the latter. There is no basis in customary international law for the application of state immunity in an employment context to acts of a private law character."[335]

The Supreme Court stated that Section 4(2)(b) of the SIA, which extends immunity to claims brought by national or habitual residents of third countries, is not required under customary international law.[336] It also stated: "Since section 16(1)(a) extends state immunity to the claims of any employee of a diplomatic mission, irrespective of the sovereign character of the employment or the acts of the state complained of, it is plain that it cannot be justified by reference to

328. *Benkharbouche (Respondent) v Secretary of State for Foreign and Commonwealth Affairs (Appellant) and Secretary of State for Foreign and Commonwealth Affairs and Libya (Appellants) v Janah (Respondent)* [2017] UKSC 62, para. 34 (Judgment of Lord Sumption with which Lord Neuberger, Lady Hale, Lord Clarke and Lord Wilson agree.)

329. See *Id.* at paras. 37 and 38.

330. *Id.* at para. 53.

331. See *Id.* at para. 54.

332. *Id.* at para. 57.

333. *Id.* at para. 58.

334. *Id.* at para. 59.

335. *Id.* at para. 63.

336. See *Id.* at para. 67.

any general principle of immunity based on the restrictive doctrine."[337] It ruled that the employment of the claimants "were clearly not exercises of sovereign authority, and nothing about their alleged treatment engaged the sovereign interests of their employers. Nor are they seeking reinstatement in a way that would restrict the right of their employers to decide who is to be employed in their diplomatic missions."[338] It, therefore, held that as a matter of customary international law, neither Libya nor Sudan is entitled to immunity in the employment claims, and that Sections 4(2)(b) and 16(1)(a) of the SIA are incompatible with Article 6 of ECHR.[339]

The FSIA does not have an expressly enumerated exception for contracts of employment.

The House Report states: "Also public or governmental and not commercial in nature, would be the employment of diplomatic, civil service, or military personnel, but not the employment of American citizens or third country nationals by the foreign state in the United States."[340] It also states that the "employment or engagement of laborers, clerical staff or public relations or marketing agents" would come within the definition of commercial activity.[341] The legislation, therefore, treats some employment contracts as coming within the ambit of the express exception for commercial activities or transactions. However, a Court of Appeals has held "that a *per se* rule of non-immunity for a foreign state's employment of third country nationals is inconsistent with Congress' intent to immunize foreign governmental activity from suit in American courts."[342] In *El-Hadad v. UAE*, an Egyptian citizen and former employee of the embassy of the United Arab Emirates (UAE) in the United States had sued both the embassy and UAE, after his employment was terminated, for breach of contract and defamation. UAE contended that El-Hadad was a civil servant and that his termination was therefore noncommercial and immune from suit in the United States. The District Court had discounted UAE's contention and held that the employment of El-Hadad was commercial because he was not a national of UAE. The Court of Appeals construed the legislative history of the FSIA but concluded that "the language that must control our decision is that of the statute rather than of the somewhat muddy legislative history. Under the FSIA, the immunity

337. *Id.* at para. 69.

338. *Id.* at para. 76.

339. *Id.*

340. House Report No. 94-1487, p. 16 (1976).

341. *Id.* at 16.

342. *El-Hadad v. United Arab Emirates* (UAE), 216 F. 3d 29, 33 (D.C. Cir. 2000).

exception depends solely on whether the action is based upon a 'commercial activity,' without any mention of the nationality of the participants. *See* 28 U.S.C. § 1605(a)(2)."[343] It held that the employment of civil servants is noncommercial for purposes of the FSIA, and suggested a multifactor inquiry for the determination of whether an employee is a civil servant.[344]

In sum, under the doctrine of restrictive State immunity, employment is generally treated as *acta jure gestionis*. In employment, there is no gainsaying that a forum State has an interest in enforcing its labor laws and protecting its nationals or residents in its territory. At the same time, this interest must be balanced with respect of the sovereignty of the foreign State. The balance accounts for the respect of the immunity of a foreign State if the employment is of a sovereign character or in a sovereign context. Consequently, the immunity of the foreign State is usually recognized with respect to employment in military establishments, and diplomatic and consular missions where the denial of immunity might intrude on the sovereignty of the foreign State. Factors that inform the determination of the employment contract exception to State immunity have been categorized, while recognizing that the factors are not mutually exclusive.[345] Whatever the category, it involves a balancing test of the territorial jurisdiction of the forum State and the sovereignty of the foreign State. For example, immunity is granted for employment at military bases on the grounds that adjudication of such disputes would infringe or intrude on the sovereignty of the foreign State. The status of the employee may also be determinative on the question of immunity, if the employment dispute involves a senior employee, in which case the foreign State will be immune. The nature of the claim may also have a bearing on the determination of immunity. For instance, the foreign State would be immune if the employment dispute implicates a matter of State security into which the forum court would be loath to inquire.

CONTROVERSIAL (OR UNCOMMON) EXCEPTIONS

Terrorism

The terrorism exception to State immunity is peculiar to North America: only the United States and Canada have such an exception under their respective

343. *Id.*

344. *Id.* at 34.

345. See Richard Garnett, *State Immunity in Employment Matters*, 46 INT'L & COMPARATIVE L.Q. 81–124 (1997); Philippa Webb, *The Immunity of States, Diplomats and International Organizations in Employment Disputes: The New Human Rights Dilemma?*, 27(3) EJIL 745–67 (2016).

national legislation. It is purely a foreign policy tool targeting certain designated States for specific acts of terrorism, often resulting in a clash between the executive and legislative branches of the U.S. government.[346] A criticism is that some countries that are considered hotbeds of terrorism are not designated as state-sponsors of terrorism. Some States that are the targets of the U.S. legislation, or fear that they may be swept in by the reach of the legislation, have threatened their own reciprocal or retaliatory law, which may lead to a "beggar-thy-neighbor" politicization of the (international) law of State immunity, which could weaken the international legal order of State sovereignty and immunity. Even when plaintiffs prevail in their suit against the States under the terrorism exception to immunity and obtain judgments, usually by default,[347] they "have often faced practical and legal difficulties" enforcing their judgment because the FSIA also "shields foreign State property from execution."[348] The difficulty in enforcement or execution of these judgments has led to the criticism that the legislation offers only pious hope to plaintiffs and has not had any deterrence on State-sponsored terrorism.

In 1996, the United States Congress amended the FSIA and enacted the Anti-Terrorism and Effective Death Penalty Act (AEDPA), which created the terrorism exception to allow American victims of terrorism to sue foreign States that the U.S. government has designated as State sponsors of terrorism.[349] The AEDPA

346. Legislation relating to the terrorism exception to FSIA has been enacted against opposition from the executive branch. For example, President Obama vetoed the Justice Against Sponsors of Terrorism Act (JASTA) because it "would upset longstanding international principles regarding sovereign immunity, putting in place rules that, if applied globally, could have serious implications for U.S. national interests," but Congress overrode the veto. The European Union has also criticized JASTA because "it would be in conflict with fundamental principles of international law and in particular the principle of State sovereign immunity." See http://www.europarl.europa.eu/RegData/etudes/BRIE/2016/593499/EPRS_BRI(2016)593,99_EN.pdf.

347. Although the foreign States have frequently declined to appear in court to defend the lawsuit, under 28 U.S.C. § 1608(e), plaintiffs can establish their claims by evidence satisfactory to the court.

348. 28 U.S.C. § 1609 (1976); *Bank Markazi v. Peterson*, 578 U.S. __ (2016). To address the issue of availability of certain assets of foreign States for satisfaction of judgments rendered under the terrorism exception, Congress enacted the Iran Threat Reduction and Syria Human Rights Act of 2012, 22 U.S.C. § 8772. The United States Supreme Court considered it "an unusual statute: It designates a particular set of assets and renders them available to satisfy the liability and damages judgments underlying a consolidated enforcement proceeding that the statute identifies by the District Court's docket number." At issue was whether the statute violated the separation of powers by purporting to change the law for, and directing a particular result in, a single pending case, and the Court held that it transgresses the constraints placed by the United States Constitution on Congress and the president. *Id.*

349. Public Law No. 104-132, Title II, § 221 (April 24, 1996); 110 Stat. 1241; 28 U.S.C. § 1605(a)(7) (1996).

provides that a foreign State is not immune in cases where "money damages are sought against a foreign state for personal injury or death that was caused by an act of torture, extrajudicial killing, aircraft sabotage, hostage taking, or the provision of material support or resources . . . for such an act or provision of material support is engaged in by an official, employee, or agent of such foreign state while acting within the scope of his or her office, employment or agency. . . ."[350] Jurisdiction under AEDPA required two conditions: (1) the State must have been designated a State sponsor of terrorism at the time that the act occurred or subsequently because of the act, and (2) the claimant must have a been a national of the United States when the act upon which the claim is based occurred.[351]

After a federal court ruled that the AEDPA did not create a federal cause of action, Congress passed the "Flatow Amendment" so as to create such a cause of action for conduct described in § 1605(a)(7).[352] The Flatow Amendment, as part of the 1996 Omnibus Consolidated Appropriation Act, was construed as establishing a federal cause of action.[353] However, the District of Columbia Circuit Court of Appeals limited the reach of the Flatow Amendment to only individuals when it ruled that there is no private federal right of action against the foreign State itself.[354] The terrorism exception was expanded in 2008 as the National Defense Authorization Act and codified at 28 U.S.C. § 1605A,[355] which created a cause of action against foreign States as well as their agents, officials, and employees. The 2008 version of the exception is significant in that it clearly provides for a private right of action under federal law for money damages against the designated foreign States, and specifies the damages that may be claimed. It also provides that the foreign State can be held vicariously liable for the actions of its agents, employees, or officials. Furthermore, it extended jurisdiction beyond cases involving U.S. citizens as victim or claimant, and expressly includes U.S. nationals as defined by the Immigration and

350. *Id.*

351. See *Jerez v. Cuba*, 775 F.3d 419, 421–22 (D.C. Cir. 2014).

352. See Civil Liability for Acts of State Sponsored Terrorism, Public Law No. 102-208, § 589, 110 Stat. 3009-172 (1996). The Flatow Amendment was named after Alisa Flatow, who died in a terrorist bombing in Gaza. See *Flatow v. Iran*, 999 F. Supp. 1 (D.D.C. 1998).

353. See Omnibus Consolidated Appropriation Act of 1996, Pub. L. 104-208, Section 589, 110 (1996), 110 Stat. 3009-1, 3009-172 (codified at 28 U.S.C. Section 1605).

354. See *Cicippio-Puleo v. Iran*, 353 F.3d 1024, 1029 (D.C. Cir. 2004).

355. National Defense Authorization Act for Fiscal Year 2008, Public Law No. 110-181, § 1083 (NDAA). The jurisdictional provision of Section 1605A is identical to that of the repealed 1605(a)(7).

Naturalization Act,[356] members of the United States Armed Forces, and government employees and contractors acting within the scope of their employment when the act upon which the claim is based occurred.[357] Section 1605A has retroactive application and is construed in *pari materia* with the repealed Section 1605(a)(7). To that effect, actions under Section 1605(a)(7) could be converted into Section 1605A under certain conditions.[358]

In sum, the terrorism exception, under the NDAA, applies only in money damages and only if (1) the foreign State had been formally designated as a state sponsor of terrorism at the time of the terrorist act or as a result of the act;[359] (2) the claimant or victim was a national of the United States, a member of the armed forces, or an employee or contractor of the U.S. government acting within the scope of employment;[360] and (3) for acts occurring in the foreign State concerned, the State had a "reasonable opportunity to arbitrate the claim in accordance with the accepted international rules of arbitration."[361] A foreign State is a designated state-sponsor of terrorism when the secretary of state so determines pursuant to Section 6(j) of the Export Administration Act of 1979, Section 620A of the Foreign Assistance Act of 1961, Section 40 of the Arms Export Control Act, or any other relevant provision of law.

In 2016, Congress further amended the FSIA by enacting the Justice Against Sponsors of Terrorism Act (JASTA), which is not limited to designated State sponsors of terrorism.[362] JASTA provides:

> A foreign state shall not be immune from the jurisdiction of the courts of the United States in any case in which money damages are sought against a

356. See 8 U.S.C.A. §§ 1101 et seq. (2012).

357. See 28 U.S.C. § 1605A(c)(3) (2008).

358. See *Van Beneden v. Al-Sanusi*, 709 F.3d 1165, 1166 (D.C. Cir. 2013).

359. See 28 U.S.C. § 1605A(a) (2008).

360. See 28 U.S.C. § 1605A(c) (2008). See Leibovitch v. Iran, 697 F.3d 561 (7th Cir. 2012) (foreign national family members of U.S. citizens do not have a private right of action under the terrorism exception.)

361. 28 U.S.C. § 1605A(a)(2)(iii) (2008).

362. See 28 U.S.C. §1605B (2016) ("Responsibility of foreign states for international terrorism against the United States"). The impetus for JASTA was the allegation linking Saudi Arabia (or some of its officials or instrumentalities) to 9/11 terrorist attacks on the United States and the pressure from victims of the attack in their bid to be able to haul Saudi Arabia into court to answer for its purported complicity in the attack. But JASTA, unlike other legislation on the terrorism exception, does not target Saudi Arabia specifically. It instead creates a broad exception that is potentially applicable to any foreign State—hence, adding to the controversy of the terrorism exception.

foreign state for physical injury to person or property or death occurring in the United States and caused by (1) an act of international terrorism in the United States; and (2) a tortious act or acts of the foreign state, or of any official, employee, or agent of that foreign state while acting within the scope of his or her office, employment, or agency, regardless where the tortious act or acts of the foreign state occurred.[363]

JASTA expanded the scope of the terrorism exception by creating a cause of action that a national of the United States may bring a claim against a foreign State in accordance with 18 U.S.C § 2333,[364] notwithstanding 18 U.S.C. 2337(2).[365] JASTA contains a stay-of-actions clause that authorizes the court to grant a renewable 180-day stay upon a showing by the executive branch that the U.S. government is engaged in good faith discussions with the foreign State or any parties as to the resolution of the claims.[366] JASTA has retroactive effect and will apply to any civil action pending on or commenced on or after its date of enactment, as well as to any civil action "arising out of an injury to a person, property, or business, on or after September 11, 2001."[367]

Although JASTA is under the rubric of the terrorism exception of FSIA, it broadens the territorial tort exception to sovereign immunity in that it permits suit for monetary damages based on "an act of terrorism in the United States" and injury or death "occurring in the United States." It abrogates the "entire tort"

363. 28 U.S.C. § 1605B(b) (2016). 18 U.S.C. § 2331 defines "international terrorism" as activities that—"(A) involve violent acts or acts dangerous to human life that are a violation of the criminal laws of the United States or of any State, or that would be a criminal violation if committed within the jurisdiction of the United States or of any State; (B) appear to be intended—(i) to intimidate or coerce a civilian population; (ii) to influence the policy of a government by intimidation or coercion; or (iii) to affect the conduct of a government by mass destruction, assassination, or kidnapping; and (C) occur primarily outside the territorial jurisdiction of the United States, or transcend national boundaries in terms of the means by which they are accomplished, the persons they appear intended to intimidate or coerce, or the locale in which their perpetrators operate or seek asylum."

364. 18 U.S.C § 2333 provides: "(a) ACTION AND JURISDICTION.—Any national of the United States injured in his or her person, property, or business by reason of an act of international terrorism, or his or her estate, survivors, or heirs, may sue therefor in any appropriate district court of the United States and shall recover threefold the damages he or she sustains and the cost of the suit, including attorney's fees."

365. 18 U.S.C § 2337(2) provides: "No action shall be maintained under section 2333 of this title against . . . a foreign state, an agency of a foreign state, or an officer or employee of a foreign state or an agency thereof acting within his or her official capacity or under color of legal authority."

366. See Sections 5(b) and 5(c), of JASTA.

367. See Section 7 of JASTA.

rule with respect to cases involving international terrorism, thereby subjecting foreign States to jurisdiction regardless of where the tortious act or acts of the foreign State occurred. Thus, unlike in *Argentina v. Amerada Hess Shipping Corp.*,[368] where the Supreme Court interpreted the tort exception of the FSIA as applying only where both the tortious act and the injury occur in the United States, JASTA allows suit for an alleged tort committed anywhere in the world provided there is a connection to a terrorist act in the United States. However, it excludes from the exception an omission or "mere negligence" by the foreign State.

JASTA also amends the federal criminal code to permit civil claims against foreign States or officials for injuries, death, or damages from an act of international terrorism, unless the foreign State is immune under FSIA, as amended by JASTA. Furthermore, it expands the liability of foreign officials in civil actions for terrorist acts by imposing liability on a person who commits, or aids, abets, or conspires to commit, an act of international terrorism against a national of the United States.

The terrorism exception has the distinction, unlike the other exceptions in the FSIA, of applying to foreign officials.[369] It is not mutually exclusive with the noncommercial tort exception, but provides an additional basis for jurisdiction.[370]

After abortive attempts at legislation by its parliament since 2005, Canada finally joined what has been termed an "American Anomaly" when it enacted the Justice for Victims of Terrorism Act (JVTA) on March 13, 2012, which amended the State Immunity Act and created a new Section 6.1 that provides: "A foreign state that is set out on the list referred to in subsection (2) is not immune from the jurisdiction of a court in proceedings against it for the support of terrorism on or after January 1, 1985."[371] The stated primary purposes of JVTA for allowing plaintiffs to sue terrorists and their supporters are to impair the functioning of terrorist groups, as well as to deter and prevent terrorism.[372] Section 4 of JVTA allows a civil action by citizens and permanent residents of Canada who are victims of terrorism, and if the action has a real and substantial connection to

368. 488 U.S. 428 (1989).

369. See *Samantar v. Yousuf*, 560 U.S. 305, 324–25 (2010), where the Supreme Court referred to the exception as an example of Congress's intent to distinguish "foreign states" and their officers, employees, and agents.

370. See *O'Neill v. Saudi Joint Relief Comm. (In re Terrorist Attacks on September 11, 2001 (Saudi Joint Relief Comm.))*, 714 F.3d 109, 113 (2d Cir. 2013), citing *Doe v. Bin Laden*, 663 F.3d 64, 70 (2d Cir. 2011).

371. Section 6.1(2) authorizes the Governor in Council to establish a list of States that are reasonably believed to be supporters of terrorism.

372. See Preamble and Section 3 of JVTA.

Canada. It creates a cause of action for victims of terrorism to sue individuals, organizations, and terrorist entities for loss or damage suffered, regardless of whether the loss or damage occurred inside or outside Canada, so far as the act or omission that caused the loss or damage "is, or had it been committed in Canada would be, punishable under Part II.1 of the Criminal Code," which contains terrorism-related offenses.[373] Under certain circumstances, victims can also sue foreign States that have supported the terrorist entities.

A foreign State supports terrorism if it commits an act or omission that is, or had it been committed in Canada would be, punishable under any of the sections 83.02 to 83.04 and 83.13 to 83.23 of the Criminal Code. Thus, if the foreign State, persons, organizations, or listed entities did not commit the act or omission, but merely did something to benefit the listed entity that committed the act or omission, they will be found liable only if they committed any of the offenses under sections 83.02 to 83.04 and 83.13 to 83.23 of the Criminal Code. The exception only applies to a foreign State that has been placed on a list established by the cabinet on the basis "that there are reasonable grounds to believe that the foreign state supported or supports terrorism."[374] Section 4(1) of JVTA has retroactive effect, but loss or damage must have occurred on or after January 1, 1985. Under Section 4(4) of JVTA, a court may refuse to hear a claim against a foreign State where the loss or damage to the plaintiff occurred in the foreign State and the plaintiff did not give that State a "reasonable opportunity to submit the dispute to arbitration in accordance with accepted international rules of arbitration."

In *Edward Tracy v. Iran*, the Ontario Superior Court of Justice held "that the *JVTA* was intended to provide a free-standing procedural and substantive mechanism for a plaintiff's recovery of losses caused by the acts of state sponsors of terrorism."[375] The plaintiffs in the case were American victims of eight different terrorist attacks who commenced proceedings in Canada to enforce the default judgments that they obtained against the defendants in American proceedings. The Canadian court noted that "[e]nforcment jurisdiction is different from jurisdictional immunity."[376] Nevertheless, the court ruled that "the *JVTA* operates independently of the *SIA* in respect of the plaintiffs' entitlement to commence proceedings against state sponsors of terrorism."[377] It also ruled that the

373. See Section 83 of the Criminal Code. As Section 4 of JVTA creates a civil cause of action, the applicable standard of proof is "balance of probabilities" as opposed to the "beyond a reasonable" standard used in criminal law.

374. Section 6.1(2) of SIA.

375. *Tracy v. Iran*, [2016] O.J. No. 3042, 2016 ONSC 3759, para. 69.

376. *Id.*, para. 120.

377. *Id.*, para. 66.

January 1, 1985, date in the JVTA relates to the date that the loss or damage from the terrorist attack was suffered by the victim, not the date of the terrorist attack.[378] It noted that there is a difference in the language of the JVTA and Section 6.1(1) of the SIA where the January 1, 1985 date relates to the date of the terrorist attack.[379]

Expropriation

Because expropriation by foreign States is considered a sovereign, as opposed to commercial, act, forum States generally do not exercise jurisdiction over expropriation cases. An expropriation exception to sovereign immunity is consequently controversial because it departs from the rule that immunizes *acta jure imperii*. It also departs from the general practice under the Act of State doctrine where a forum court will not question the validity of *acta jure imperii* performed by a foreign State within its own borders.[380]

The United States is the only State that has created an expropriation exception in its national legislation. It denies immunity to a foreign State in any case where

> rights in property taken in violation of international law are in issue and [1] that property or any property exchanged for such property is present in the United States in connection with commercial activity carried on in the United States by the foreign state; or [2] that property or any property exchanged for such property is owned or operated by an agency or instrumentality of the foreign state and that agency or instrumentality is engaged in a commercial activity in the United States.[381]

The legislative history states:

> The term "taken in violation of international law" would include the nationalization or expropriation of property without payment of prompt adequate

378. *Id.*, para. 76.

379. *Id.*

380. See *Underhill v. Hernandez*, 168 U.S. 250, 252 (1897). The legislative history of Section 1605(a)(3) of the FSIA, however, states that the expropriation exception to immunity "in no way affects existing law on the extent to which, if at all, the 'act of state' doctrine may be applicable." H.R. Rep. 94-1487 (1976), p. 6618.

381. 28 U.S.C. § 1605(a)(3) (1988).

> and effective compensation required by international law. It would also include takings which are arbitrary or discriminatory in nature. Since, however, this section deals solely with issues of immunity, it in no way affects existing law on the extent to which, if at all, the "act of state" doctrine may be applicable. See 22 U.S.C. 2370(e)(2).[382]

The exception applies in two categories of cases. The first category takes away immunity where (1) the taken property or any property exchanged for the taken property is (2) present in the United States (3) in connection with commercial activity carried on in the United States by a foreign State. Under the second category, the agency or instrumentality of a foreign State is not immune where (1) *either* the taken property *or* any property exchanged for the taken property is (2) owned or operated by the agency or instrumentality of the foreign State, and (3) the agency or instrumentality of the foreign State is engaged in a commercial activity in the United States. The second category requires that the agency or instrumentality of the foreign State be engaged in a commercial activity in the United States, but "the property need not be present in connection with the commercial activity of the agency or instrumentality."[383]

Thus, for the expropriation exception to apply the dispute must concern property "taken in violation of international law."[384] It also requires a connection between the taking and a commercial activity engaged in the United States, that is, it revolves on the character of the plaintiff's claims and the existence of one or two commercial activities by the defendant with a nexus to the United States.[385]

In *Arch Trading*, the Second Circuit Court of Appeals examined whether Ecuador or two of its instrumentalities engaged in the requisite "commercial activity" in the United States for the expropriation exception to apply. The plaintiffs, entities incorporated under the laws of the British Virgin Islands, sued for compensatory damages for seized companies against the Republic of Ecuador and two of its instrumentalities, namely CFN and Trust.[386] As plaintiffs did not allege that the expropriated property was present in the United States, the court was limited to considering whether the second prong of the exception was applicable against CFN and Trust as instrumentalities of Ecuador.

382. H.R. Rep. No. 94-1487 (1976), at 19–20.

383. *Id.* at 19.

384. See *Arch Trading Corp. v. Ecuador*, 839 F.3d 193, 196 (2d Cir. 2016).

385. See *Agudas Chasidei Chabad v. Russia*, 528 F.3d 934, 940 (D.C. Cir. 2008).

386. *Arch Trading*, 839 F.3d at 198.

The Second Circuit Court of Appeals applied the *Bancec* presumption[387] and considered whether to attribute to CFN and Trust any of the commercial activities in the United States that plaintiffs identified. It noted that the presumption is strong and is overcome only if "(1) the [entity] is so extensively controlled by its owner that a relationship of principal and agent is created, or (2) the recognition of an [entity's] separate legal status would work fraud or injustice."[388]

To the averment that CFN exercised some control over some entities that had activities in the United States, the Court of Appeals stated that "courts have consistently rejected the argument that the appointment and removal of an instrumentality's officer or directors, standing alone, overcomes the *Bancec* presumption . . . because the exercise of such powers is not synonymous with control over the instrumentality's day-to-day operations."[389] It conluded that "CFN's involvement in the operations of those companies are too threadbare, however, to rebut the *Bancec* presumption with respect to these companies."[390] Consequently, plaintiffs have not rebutted the *Bancec* presumption: "Accepting *arguendo* plaintiffs' argument that the Trust's legal status (as distinct from that of the entities whose stock it holds) rise or falls with CFN's parallel status as Trustee, they have not rebutted the *Bancec* presumption for the same reasons they have not rebutted it as between CFN and those entities."[391] CFN and Trust are legally separate from their American subsidiaries and, therefore, are not engaged in commercial activities in the United States within the meaning of the expropriation exception.[392]

The Ninth Circuit Court of Appeals has held that the expropriation exception "does not require that the foreign state against whom the suit is brought be the foreign state that took the property at issue in violation of international law."[393] In that case, an American citizen had sued the Kingdom of Spain and an instrumentality of Spain for the recovery of her grandmother's painting, which was allegedly

387. In *First National City Bank v. Banco Para El Comercio Exterior de Cuba*, 462 U.S. 611, 626–27 ("*Bancec*" (1983), the United States Supreme Court consecrated the principle that "government instrumentalities established as juridical entities distinct and independent from their sovereign should normally be treated as such."

388. *Arch Trading*, 839 F.3d at 201 [citation omitted].

389. *Id.* at 203 [citations and quotation marks omitted].

390. *Id.*

391. *Id.* at 205.

392. *Id.* at 208.

393. *Cassirer v. Kingdom of Spain*, 616 F. 3d 1019, 1032 (9th Cir. 2010).

confiscated in 1939 by an agent of the Nazi government of Germany because she was a Jew. The issues before the Court were whether the exception "covers a claim against Spain and the Foundation when neither was the foreign state that took the painting in violation of international law; whether the Foundation is engaged in sufficient commercial activity in the United States; and whether exhaustion of remedies is required as a prerequisite to jurisdiction."[394] The Court of Appeals noted that the text of Section 1605(a)(3) is written in the passive voice,[395] and then construed it to mean that the exception applies whenever the property had been taken in violation of international law and the instrumentality that claims to own the property engages in commercial activity in the United States, without any specificity that the taking must be by the foreign State being sued.[396] It distinguished the commercial activity exception from the expropriation exception. It stated that the latter does not require that "the lawsuit arise out of specific activity having to do with the property in the United States."[397] Thus, the expropriation exception restores jurisdiction against Spain and its instrumentality even though Germany was the foreign State that expropriated the property. It also held that the expropriation exception does not require exhaustion of local remedies as a prerequisite for the exercise of subject matter jurisdiction by the courts of the United States.[398]

In *Agudas Chasidei Chabad v. Russia*,[399] plaintiff, a nonprofit religious organization, brought a claim alleging that defendant, the Russian Federation as well as its Ministry of Culture and Mass Communication, had illegally seized its historic library collection and archive. Russia moved to dismiss the claims on the grounds of foreign sovereign immunity, *forum non conveniens*, and the Act of State doctrine. Russia had argued that as the first clause in § 1605(a)(3) requires that the property be present in the United States in connection with a commercial activity carried on in the United States, it would be quite anomalous if the second clause, requiring neither physical presence in the United States nor such a link (between property physically present and the commercial activity), could be satisfied unless the commercial activity had "substantial contact" with the United States. The District of Columbia Court of Appeals stated that Congress

394. *Id.* at 1027–28.

395. See *id.* at 1028.

396. See *id.* at 1031.

397. *Id.* at 1033.

398. *Id.* at 1037.

399. *Agudas Chasidei Chabad v. Russia*, 528 F.3d 934 (D.C. Cir. 2008).

differentiated between the two clauses and defined the "commercial activity" in the first clause. It stated:

> Moreover, we see no anomaly in applying the "commercial activity" definition set forth in *§ 1603(d)*. While the first clause of *§ 1605(a)(3)* and the definition in *§ 1603(e)* are quite demanding in some respects, the clause applies to activities "carried on *by the foreign state,*" whereas the second clause involves the commercial activities of the foreign state's agencies and instrumentalities. Congress might well have thought such entities' greater detachment from the state itself justified application of *§ 1603(d)*'s broad definition.[400]

It then held that the substantiality requirement of § 1603(e) is inapplicable in the second clause of § 1605(a)(3).[401] It found that the "agencies and instrumentalities" of the Russian Federation engaged in sufficient commercial activity in the United States to satisfy that element of the expropriation exception because they have entered transactions for joint publishing and sales in the United States.[402]

Does a plaintiff need to only plead some substantial and nonfrivolous facts to show an expropriation so as to survive a motion to dismiss for lack of jurisdiction, or must the complaint assert a claim that is legally sufficient to satisfy the substantive requirements of the expropriation exception? In *Venezuela v. Helmerich & Payne,* the Supreme Court, in a unanimous opinion, resolved the issue about the proper pleading standard for alleging an expropriation claim under the FSIA.[403]

An American (parent) company and its Venezuelan subsidiary brought a lawsuit against entities of the Venezuelan government, seeking compensation for the alleged unlawful expropriation of the subsidiary's oil rigs. Venezuela moved to dismiss the case because its sovereign immunity deprived the District Court of jurisdiction. The parties agreed that the District Court should then decide whether the expropriation exception applied, and the court decided that the exception did not apply to the subsidiary's claim because the subsidiary was a national of Venezuela. The court dismissed the subsidiary's claim on jurisdictional grounds because the court concluded that Venezuela possessed sovereign

400. *Id.* at 947.

401. *Id.*

402. *Id.* at 948.

403. *Venezuela v. Helmerich & Payne,* 137 S. Ct. 1312, 581 U.S.__ (2017). Justice Gorsuch, who had just arrived at the Court, did not participate in the decision.

immunity. It, however, rejected Venezuela's argument that the parent had no rights in property in the subsidiary. The subsidiary appealed the dismissal of its expropriation claim, and Venezuela appealed the refusal to dismiss the parent's claim to the Court of Appeals for the District of Columbia Circuit. The Court of Appeals decided that both the subsidiary's and the parent's claims fell within the exception, and that the legal standard that it would apply in deciding whether the expropriation exception applies is "wholly insubstantial or frivolous."

The Supreme Court framed the issue before it as follows: Does the phrase "case . . . in which rights in property taken in violation of international law are in issue" mean that, to defeat sovereign immunity, a party need only make a "nonfrivolous" argument that the case falls within the scope of the expropriation exception? "What happens in a case where the party seeking to rely on the expropriation exception makes a nonfrivolous, but ultimately incorrect, claim that his property was taken in violation of international law?" It held that the nonfrivolous-argument standard, adopted by the Court of Appeals, is not consistent with the FSIA, and the where the facts are not in dispute, the expropriation exception applies only if those facts "show (and not just arguably show) a taking of property in violation of international law."[404] It recognized that merits and jurisdiction may be intertwined sometimes and ruled that "rights in 'property taken in violation of international law,' is a jurisdictional matter that the court must typically decide at the outset of the case, or as close to the outset as is reasonably possible."[405] It found precedent for its interpretation in *Permanent Mission of India to the United Nations v. City of New York*, 551 U.S. 193 (2007), where it had interpreted the immovable property exception to FSIA and held that there was jurisdiction because the claim to enforce a tax lien directly implicated the property rights.[406] The Supreme Court reversed the Court of Appeals and clarified the pleading standard.

WAIVER

A foreign State may waive its immunity and, by so doing, consent to the exercise of jurisdiction by a court of the forum State. A waiver is, therefore, a voluntary submission to the exercise of jurisdiction. Waiver is often characterized as an exception to immunity, but it is not so because a waiver would be nugatory where an exception to immunity exists ab initio. "Questions of waiver only arise where

404. *Id.* at 1323.

405. *Id.* at 1319.

406. *Id.*

the impleaded State *does* qualify for jurisdictional immunity in the forum State, or else there is nothing to waive."[407] The consideration of waiver as an exception to immunity may be a relic of the doctrine of absolute State immunity under which no suit could be brought against a State without its consent.[408] A waiver is, therefore, a consent to jurisdiction and renunciation of a right to immunity, whereas exception is a denial of a right to immunity. At any rate, "all roads lead to Rome" as both waiver and exception have the same effect of submission to jurisdiction.

Waiver of immunity is concerned primarily with the conduct of a foreign State, whereas exception to immunity is focused on the nature of activity that is the subject matter of the dispute. Exception to and waiver of immunity might be at issue in the same case. For example, in *Joseph v. Consulate of Nigeria*, the Ninth Circuit Court of Appeals, after determining that the lease agreement in the case implicitly waived sovereign immunity, stated: "Nevertheless, because of the vagueness of the waiver provision at issue, and because the waiver exception should be narrowly construed, we deem it advisable to refer to other FSIA exceptions to immunity to support our finding of jurisdiction."[409]

A waiver can be express or implied. A clear intent to waive must be discernible from actions or words. Express waivers are not ambiguous. Ordinarily, a waiver of immunity from jurisdiction does not extend to immunity from execution or enforcement for which an additional or separate waiver is required except that an agreement to arbitrate is often construed to constitute a complete waiver of both immunities from jurisdiction and from execution.[410]

Immunity may be waived under Section 1605(a)(1) of FSIA, and once waived cannot be reasserted: "A foreign state shall not be immune from the jurisdiction of courts of the United States or of the States in any case in which the foreign state has waived its immunity either explicitly or by implication, notwithstanding any withdrawal of the waiver which the foreign state may purport to effect except in accordance with the terms of the waiver."[411] Under the FSIA, a waiver is to be "narrowly construed."[412] A foreign State may waive its immunity and that of

407. *Democratic Republic of Congo v. FG Hemisphere Associates*, [2011] 4 HKC 151, para. 392.

408. Even the classical theory of absolute immunity is subject to waiver or submission to the forum State's jurisdiction.

409. *Joseph v. Consulate of Nigeria*, 830 F.2d 1018, 1023 (9th Cir. 1987).

410. See MIXED INTERNATIONAL ARBITRATION: STUDIES IN ARBITRATION BETWEEN STATES AND PRIVATE PERSONS 146–50 (1990).

411. Section 1605(a)(1).

412. See *Siderman de Blake v. Republic of Argentina*, 965 F.2d 699, 720 (9th Cir. 1992), cert. denied, 507 U.S. 1017 (1993).

any organ or instrumentality that benefits from its immunity, but an instrumentality can only waive its own immunity, not that of another instrumentality of the State.[413]

Under the common law in the United Kingdom, immunity can only be waived before the court, that is, a State can consent to the jurisdiction of a court only at the time when the court is asked to exercise its jurisdiction over the State,[414] but it is now accepted that "a waiver of state immunity can be made either before the court or at an earlier stage."[415]

Express Waiver

A State may waive its immunity "by expressly submitting to the jurisdiction of the court before which it is sued, either by express consent given in the context of the particular dispute which has already arisen, or by consent given in advance in a contract or international agreement."[416] State immunity can be explicitly waived by a written agreement, such as treaty or contract. Article 2 of the Basle Convention provides that a Contracting State is not immune where it has undertaken to submit to the jurisdiction of a forum State: (1) by international agreement, (2) by express term contained in contract in writing, or (3) express consent given after a dispute has arisen. An express waiver means that the foreign sovereign has consented to be sued. Thus, express waiver arises where there is a contract or agreement that explicitly states that sovereign immunity is waived. It may also arise from express language in an applicable international agreement.[417]

The United States Supreme Court has held that: "we [do not] see how a foreign state can waive its immunity under § 1605(a)(1) by signing an international agreement that contains no mention of a waiver of immunity to suit in United States courts or even the availability of a course of action in the United States."[418] The Ninth Circuit Court of Appeals has held: "An express waiver under section

413. See *First Nat'l City Bank v. Banco Para El Comercio Exterior de Cuba (Bancec)*, 462 U.S. 611 (1983); *Chuidian v. Philippine Nat'l Bank*, 912 F.2d 1095, 1104–05 (9th Cir. 1990).

414. *Duff Development v. Kelantan*, [1924] AC 797, [1924] All ER 1.

415. See *Democratic Republic of Congo v. FG Hemisphere Associates*, [2011] 4 HKC 151 (Bohkary PJ).

416. 1 Oppenheim's International Law 351–52 (9th ed. 2008).

417. See *Harris Corp. v. Nat'l Iranian Radio & Television*, 691 F.2d 1344 (11th Cir. 1982).

418. *Argentina Republic v. Amerada Hess Shipping Corp.*, 488 U.S. 428, 442–43 (1989).

1605(a)(1) must give a clear, complete, unambiguous and unmistakable manifestation of the sovereign's intent to waive its immunity."[419]

In *World Wide v. Kazakhstan*, a Canadian corporation had entered several agreements with the Republic of Kazakhstan and two of its instrumentalities, and then sued Kazakhstan in the United States District Court for the District of Columbia alleging various wrongful acts. In the appeal, the Court of Appeals held that Kazakhstan had waived its immunity for some of World Wide claims but not for all of them. World Wide contended that the Pledge and Management agreements contained an explicit waiver of sovereign immunity.[420] The Court of Appeals disagreed with the District Court's holding "that the waiver in the Pledge Agreement indicated Kazakhstan's intention to waive immunity for World Wide's entire lawsuit."[421] It stated: "Neither the waiver in the Pledge Agreement, nor that in the Management Agreement, describes the kind of claims for which Kazakhstan waived immunity. And there is nothing 'clear and unambiguous' about either waiver other than that each extends to claims for breach of the agreement in which it is contained."[422] The Court of Appeals found support for its conclusion that the waiver did not extend to all of World Wide's claims in the respective limited scope of the various agreements.[423]

With respect to the Loan and Strategic Alliance agreements,[424] the Court of Appeals stated that they suggest that Kazakhstan did not contemplate that

419. See *Aquamar v. Del Monte*, 179 F.3d 1279, 1292 (11th Cir. 1999) [quotation marks omitted].

420. See *World Wide v. Kazakhstan*, 296 F.3d 1154, 1162, n.13 (D.C. Cir. 2002) ("The Management Agreement states: 'In respect of any arbitration or legal action or proceedings arising out of or in connection with this Agreement, . . . [the Kazakhstan State Committee] hereby irrevocably agrees not to claim and hereby irrevocably waives . . . immunity for itself and the assets of the Republic of Kazakhstan to the full extent permitted by the laws of such jurisdiction.' [] The Pledge Agreement states: 'The Grantor [defined as Kazakhstan and TGK] hereby irrevocably agrees not to claim and hereby irrevocably waives . . . immunity for themselves and their Assets to the full extent permitted by the laws of such jurisdiction with the intent inter alia that the foregoing waiver of immunity shall have irrevocable effect for the purposes of the [FSIA] in any legal action or proceedings to which such Act applies.' "

421. *Id.*

422. *Id.* at 1162–63.

423. See *id.* n.14.

424. See *id.* at 1163, n.15. ([The Strategic Alliance Agreement provides:] "If any dispute or difference arise out of or in connection with any matter in relation to this Strategic Alliance Agreement . . . , the same shall be arbitrated between the Parties and the arbitration shall be conducted . . . in Almaty, Kazakhstan." The Loan Agreement states: "If any default or dispute or difference . . . arises out of or in connection with any matter or thing in relation to the provisions of this Agreement, . . . any party may submit the Dispute to be settled by arbitration . . . conducted in Stockholm, Sweden."

disputes over them would be resolved in the U.S. courts, but rather by arbitration in Kazakhstan and Sweden.[425] It, therefore, concluded that Kazakhstan's waiver of immunity in the Management and Pledge agreements did not extend to claims under the Loan and Strategic Alliance agreements.[426]

Implied or Implicit Waiver

Although the FSIA provides for an implied waiver of immunity, it does not define it. According to the legislative history of the FSIA, "courts have found such waivers in cases where a foreign state has agreed to arbitration in another country or where a foreign state has agreed that the law of a particular country should govern a contract. An implicit waiver would also include a situation where a foreign state has filed a responsive pleading in an action without raising the defense of sovereign immunity."[427] This is, however, not an exhaustive list of circumstances where a waiver may be implied.[428] American courts may imply a waiver of immunity in a choice-of-law or governing law clause.[429] This is contrary to Article 7(2) of the United Nations Convention; Section 2(2) of the United Kingdom State Immunity Act; Section 4(2) of the Singapore State Immunity Act; and Section 10(2) of the Australia Foreign States Immunities Act, all of which provide that a choice-of-law or governing laws provision shall not be regarded as consent to jurisdiction. American courts may also imply a waiver of immunity by a foreign State from its participation in a lawsuit through filing responsive pleading without raising an immunity defense,[430] through an arbitration agreement and enforcement of award in the United States,[431] or through an international convention permitting enforcement of an arbitral award in the United States.[432]

425. *Id.*

426. *Id.* at 1164.

427. H.R. Rep. No. 1487, 94th Cong., 2d Sess. 18 (1976), reprinted in 1976 U.S.C.C.A.N. 6604, 6617.

428. See *Siderman v. Argentina*, 965 F.2d 699, 721 (9th Cir. 1992).

429. See *Marlowe v. Argentine Naval Comm'n*, 604 F. Supp. 703 (D.D.C. 1985). This is contrary to Article 7(2) of the United Nations Convention; Section 2(2) of the United Kingdom State Immunity Act; Section 4(2) of the Singapore State Immunity Act; and Section 10(2) of the Australia Foreign States Immunities Act, which provide that choice-of-law or governing laws provision shall not be regarded as consent to jurisdiction.

430. See *Drexel Burnham Lambert v. Comm. of Receivers*, 12 F.3d 317 (2d Cir. 1993).

431. See *Creighton v. Qatar*, 181 F.3d 118 (D.C. Cir. 1999).

432. See *Seetransport Wiking Trader v. Navimpex Centrala Navala*, 989 F.2d 572 (2d Cir. 1993).

In an employment dispute with an embassy, where the employment contract with the plaintiff expressly stated that it is subject to national law and legislation of the United States, the court held that the embassy has impliedly waived its immunity in connection with the dispute.[433] If a waiver is to be implied from a written agreement, then the essential inquiry is whether the foreign State contemplated the involvement of the courts of the forum State in the adjudication of the dispute.[434] In *Joseph v. Consulate of Nigeria*, the Ninth Circuit Court of Appeals stated that a foreign State does not waive its sovereign immunity by the mere act of entering a contract. However, a waiver of immunity is implied where the contract specifically states that it will be governed by the laws of the United States because the waiver "is premised on an agreement by the parties that the United States courts may become involved in disputes arising pursuant to the contract. Where an agreement contemplates adjudication of a dispute by the United States courts, the waiver exception should be applied, regardless of whether the governing law is explicitly identified."[435] The court concluded that sovereign immunity has been waived with respect to the breach-of-contract and tort claims: "Because the lease at issue provides for adjudication of landlord-tenant disputes in court, we conclude that the lease contemplates participation of the United States courts in disputes between Joseph and her tenants. In light of the wholly local nature of the transaction, it is virtually inconceivable that the Consulate contemplated that adjudication of disputes would occur in a court outside of the United States."[436]

In an action to confirm an ICSID arbitration award against Argentina in the United States, the Court of Appeals for the Second Circuit held that Argentina had implicitly waived its immunity under the FSIA.[437] The court noted that a waiver must be construed narrowly and recalled its decision in *Seetransport* where it held that when a State becomes a party to the New York Convention, by its provisions, the State must have contemplated enforcement actions in other Contracting States.[438] It stated that the provisions of ICSID require it to reach

433. See *Ashraf-Hassan v. Embassy of France*, 40 F. Supp. 3d 94, 101 (D.D.C. 2014).

434. See *Joseph v. Office of Consulate General of Nigeria*, 830 F.2d 1018, 1023 (9th Cir. 1987); *Frolova v. USSR*, 761 F.2d 370, 377 (7th Cir. 1985); *Argentina v. Amerada Hess*, 488 U.S. 428, 442–32 (1989).

435. *Joseph*, 830 F.2d at 1022–23 [citations omitted].

436. *Id.*

437. *Blue Ridge v. Argentina*, 735 F. 3d 72, 84 (2d Cir. 2013).

438. *Id.*

the same conclusion.[439] However, another court has held that as Qatar was not a signatory to the New York Convention, its agreement to arbitrate in a signatory country alone does not provide the requisite intent for its waiver of immunity in the United States.[440] The key or deciding factor, therefore, is whether the foreign State is a party to a convention on arbitration that contemplates an enforcement action against the Contracting State.

A foreign State impliedly waives its immunity through deep involvement in a proceeding without invoking its immunity: "If a sovereign files a responsive pleading without raising the defense of sovereign immunity, then the immunity defense is waived."[441] In that regard, where a plaintiff had claimed that a foreign State had waived its immunity by implication on account of filing an Answer to a Pleading without asserting the defense of *sovereign immunity*, the court disagreed.[442] The court stated that the foreign State "did not respond substantively to any of the averments in the complaint or pose any defenses to the claims; instead, [it] merely argued that the action should proceed in another forum, which it then did."[443] It also stated that the legislative history of the FSIA "demonstrates that Congress anticipated, at a minimum, that waiver would not be found absent a conscious decision to take part in the litigation and a failure to raise *sovereign immunity* despite the opportunity to do so."[444]

The involvement of the executive branch of the U.S. government in proceedings, such as through suggestions of immunity on behalf of a foreign State, does not constitute an implied waiver of immunity of the foreign State before the U.S. courts. To find implied waiver of sovereign immunity, courts require strong evidence of intent by the foreign State to be sued.[445] Waiver is not implied where there is no indication that the foreign State intended to avail itself of the privileges or protection of the courts of the United States[446] In a claim where India had

439. *Id.*

440. See *Creighton v. Qatar*, 181 F.3d 118, 118 (D.C. Cir. 1999).

441. *Haven v. Rzeczpospolita Polska*, 215 F.3d 727, 731 (7th Cir. 1999), cert. denied, 531 U.S. 1014 (2000).

442. *Foremost-McKesson v. Iran*, 905 F.2d 438 (D.C. Cir. 1990).

443. *Id.* at 443.

444. *Id.* at 443–44.

445. See *Rodriguez v. Transnave*, 8 F.3d 284, 287 (5th Cir. 1993); *Creighton*, 181 F.3d at 122; *In re Tamimi*, 176 F.3d 274, 278 (4th Cir. 1999).

446. See *Barapind v. India*, 844 F.3d 824, 831 (9th Cir. 2016).

exchanged diplomatic communications with the United States and reached an "Understanding" regarding a plaintiff, the court noted:

> Unlike in *Siderman de Blake*, the Indian government did not directly file documents in a court of the United States for the purposes of effecting Barapind's extradition. Instead, the Indian government used diplomatic channels to request Barapind's extradition from the United States, and the United States government "filed a complaint on India's behalf" in district court, seeking a certificate of extraditability.[447]

The Ninth Circuit Court of Appeals concluded that India did not impliedly waive its immunity because the Understanding did not expressly or implicitly indicate that India intended adjudication of disputes by United States courts.[448]

Submission to Jurisdiction

It admits of no contradiction or controversy that a foreign State cannot institute a proceeding and simultaneously claim immunity in the same proceeding. Under Article 1 of the Basle Convention, a State that institutes a proceeding or intervenes in one cannot subsequently invoke immunity. According to the Explanatory Report, such submission to jurisdiction extends to proceedings before an appeals court. However, a foreign State's intervention in proceedings, under this Article, "does not include cases of compulsory intervention provided for in the law of certain States, except where the State participates actively in the proceedings without invoking its immunity."[449]

A State also cannot claim immunity in a counterclaim where it could not have claimed immunity had the proceeding been instituted against it as a primary claim. Where immunity is unavailing because of submission to the jurisdiction of the courts of the forum State, it operates not only with respect to the counterclaim but also to the primary or principal claim. It is elementary but it bears reiteration that a foreign State who would not otherwise be subject to the jurisdiction of a forum court may by its own conduct confer on the court subject matter jurisdiction over it, which otherwise the court would not have. Submission to the jurisdiction of a forum State does not extend to proceedings regarding the enforcement of judgment against the foreign State.

447. *Id.* at 831.

448. *Id.*

449. Explanatory Report, Article 1, para. 16.

Article 8 of the United Nations Convention provides that a foreign State submits to jurisdiction in a proceeding before the courts of a forum State if it has "(a) itself instituted the proceedings; or (b) intervened in the proceeding or taken any other step relating to the merits." However, the State preserves its immunity if it "satisfied the court that it could not have acquired knowledge of the facts on which a claim to immunity can be based until after it took such a step . . . provided it does so at the earliest possible moment."[450] In the same vein, a State is not deemed to have submitted to jurisdiction "if it intervenes in a proceeding or takes any other step for the sole purpose of (a) invoking immunity; or (b) asserting a right or interest in property at issue in the proceeding."[451] Similarly, it is not considered a submission to jurisdiction when a representative of a foreign State appears before a forum court as a witness.[452] Furthermore, failure of a foreign State to enter an appearance in a forum court should not be construed as a submission to jurisdiction.[453]

Submission to jurisdiction is an expression of consent by conduct of the foreign State, which indicates "a willingness and readiness on the part of a sovereign State of its own free will to submit to the consequences of adjudication by the court of another State, up to but not including measures of constraint which require separate consent of that foreign State."[454] It follows that a foreign State submits to jurisdiction when it chooses to become a party to litigation in a forum State, and the appearance before the forum court is unconditional and unaccompanied by a plea of sovereign immunity.[455]

Under the United Nations Convention, failure of a foreign State to appear before a forum court does not automatically lead to a submission to jurisdiction or waiver of immunity.[456] By the same token, the Convention provides that a forum court shall determine on its own initiative to respect the immunity of the foreign State,[457] and that a default judgment shall not be rendered against a foreign State

450. Article 8(1), United Nations Convention.

451. Article 8(2), United Nations Convention.

452. See Article 8(3), United Nations Convention.

453. See Article 8(4), United Nations Convention.

454. Draft Articles and Commentaries, Article 8, Commentary (1).

455. *Id.* Commentary (2).

456. See Article 8(4), United Nations Convention ("Failure on the part of a State to enter an appearance in a proceeding before a court of another State shall not be interpreted as consent by the former State to the exercise of jurisdiction by the court.")

457. See Article 6(1) of United Nations Convention.

unless the forum court has found that the Convention does not preclude it from exercising jurisdiction.[458]

Section 2 of SIA provides: "(1) A State is not immune as respects proceedings in respect of which it has submitted to the jurisdiction of the courts of the United Kingdom. (2) A State may submit after the dispute giving rise to the proceedings has arisen or by prior written agreement." A State is deemed to have submitted to jurisdiction if it has instituted the proceedings, or intervened or taken any step in the proceedings.[459] However, a State is not deemed to have submitted to jurisdiction if the intervention or involvement in the proceedings is "for the purpose only of (a) claiming immunity or (b) asserting an interest in property in circumstances that the State would have been entitled to immunity if the proceedings had been brought against it."[460] It is also not a submission to jurisdiction if "any step taken by the State in ignorance of facts entitling it to immunity if those facts could not reasonably have been ascertained and immunity is claimed as soon as reasonably practicable."[461] A submission to jurisdiction under this Section 2 of SIA also extends to any appeal.[462]

Before the enactment of SIA, where solicitors were instructed by defendants to appear in a proceeding, and they had appeared unconditionally and participated in the proceedings long before defendants realized that they could avail themselves of the defense of sovereign immunity, the issue was whether they had submitted to the jurisdiction of the court and thereby waived their immunity.[463] In *Baccus S R L v. Servicio Nacional Del Trigo*, the majority of the Court of Appeal ruled that the instruction by the government official was done without the knowledge of his superiors and in ignorance of the right of immunity and without actual authority.[464] It ruled that there cannot be a submission to jurisdiction in a case "unless it is made by a person with knowledge of the right to be waived, with knowledge of the effect of our law of procedure, and with the authority of the foreign sovereign."[465] It held that there was no waiver in the case. Thus, it is

458. See Article 23(1)(c) of United Nations Convention.

459. Section 2(3), SIA.

460. Section 2(4), SIA.

461. Section 2(5), SIA.

462. Section 2(6), SIA. But the submission to jurisdiction does not extend to any counterclaim unless it arises out of the same legal relationship or facts as the claim. *Id.*

463. *Baccus S R L v. Servicio Nacional Del Trigo* [1957] QB 438, [1956] 3 All ER 715, 3 WLR 948, [1956] 2 Lloyd's Rep 448.

464. *Id.* (Jenkins LJ).

465. *Id.* (Parker LJ).

considered a submission to jurisdiction where the State does not have full knowledge of the right to raise immunity,[466] but an unreasonable delay in invoking immunity could be also prejudicial so as to support a submission to jurisdiction.

In *NML Capital v. Argentina*, one of the issues addressed by the Supreme Court of the United Kingdom was whether the bonds issued by Argentina, which expressly provided that they were governed by the law of New York, contained a submission to the jurisdiction of the English court in respect of proceedings for the enforcement of a New York court.[467] All five justices agreed that it did. In his judgment, Lord Phillips recalled *Mighell v. Sultan of Johore* [1894] 1 QB 149, where "the court held that the only way that a sovereign could waive immunity was by submitting to jurisdiction in the face of the court as, for example, by appearance to a writ."[468] He also recalled the cases of *Duff Development Co. v. Kelantan Government* [1924] AC 797 and *Kahan v. Pakistan Federation* [1951] 2 KB 1003, where the English courts held sovereign immunity could only be lost by submission to the jurisdiction when it was invoked, and not prior to the proceedings.[469] He then noted that Section 2(2) of the SIA varied the law as to what constitutes submission by a State to the jurisdiction of English court, and provides that a State "could submit to the jurisdiction by a written agreement prior to any dispute arising."[470] He further noted:

> If a state waives immunity it does no more than place itself on the same footing as any other person. A waiver of immunity does not confer jurisdiction where, in the case of another defendant, it would not exist. If, however, state immunity is the only bar to jurisdiction, an agreement to waive immunity is tantamount to a submission to the jurisdiction. In this case Argentina agreed that the New York judgment could be enforced by a suit upon the judgment in any court to the jurisdiction of which, absent immunity, Argentina would be subject. It was both an agreement to waive immunity and an express agreement that the New York judgment could be sued on in any country that, state immunity apart, would have jurisdiction.

Lord Mance, in his own judgment, agreed with Lord Phillips that the bonds contain a submission to the English jurisdiction.[471] In addition to agreeing with

466. See *Baccus v. Servicio Nacional del Trigo*.

467. See *NML Capital v. Republic of Argentina*, [2011] UKSC 32, para. 7.

468. *Id.*, para. 9.

469. *Id.*, para. 11.

470. *Id.*, para. 55.

471. See *id.*, paras. 83 and 98.

Lord Phillips, Lord Collins (with whom Lord Walker agrees in the judgment) elaborated on the position in English law prior to SIA with respect to submission to the jurisdiction. He noted that Section 2(2) of the SIA, which provides for submission to jurisdiction "by prior written agreement" is consistent with international practice.[472]

In *Schreiber v. Canada*,[473] the appellant, a Canadian citizen, brought a tort liability action against Germany arguing that pursuant to Section 4 of the State Immunity Act of Canada,[474] a foreign State cannot claim immunity from that suit after the extradition proceedings initiated by Canadian authorities at the request of the foreign State. The Supreme Court agreed with the submissions of the respondents that the foreign State did not initiate the prior extradition proceedings, and that proceedings and the present civil action for damages "are separate legal actions and any step taken in one does not amount to a step taken in the other."[475] Such a "waiver does not extend to fresh or distinct actions even if they are on the same or a related subject matter as the proceedings initiated by a foreign state."[476]

Arbitration

Arbitration is founded on the contractual principle of consent of the parties. It is an alternative dispute resolution mechanism, but it does not completely oust the jurisdiction of national courts, as there may still be need for judicial supervision of the arbitral process and judicial review of the arbitral award.[477] Between private parties, the undertaking to arbitrate is a contractual obligation to refer the dispute to arbitration for settlement and to honor the arbitral award.[478] However, where a State is a party to arbitration, the question arises as to whether the supervisory

472. *Id.*, para. 126, *citing* Section 1605(a)(1) of FSIA; Article 2(b) of Basle Convention; Article 7(1)(b) of the United Nations Convention.

473. *Schreiber v. Canada* (Attorney General), 2002 SCC 62, [2002] 3 S.C.R. 269 (Can).

474. Section 4(2)(b) of the Act provides: "In any proceedings before a court, a foreign state submits to the jurisdiction of the court where it initiates proceedings in the court."

475. *Schreiber*, paras. 21–22.

476. *Id.* at para. 23.

477. See, generally, Edward Chukwuemeke Okeke, *Judicial Review of Foreign Arbitral Awards: Bane, Boon or Boondoggle?*, 10 N.Y. INT'L L. REV. 29 (1997).

478. See Hazel Fox, *States and the Undertaking to Arbitrate*, 34 INT'L & COMPARATIVE L.Q. 1–29 (1988).

and enforcement powers of national courts should apply as would be the case between private parties.[479] The answer to the question depends on which doctrine of State immunity applies.

Under the doctrine of absolute immunity, there is no jurisdiction or enforcement measure against a State without its express consent: "Under such an absolute rule the consent to refer a dispute to commercial arbitration, even though made in writing and confined to an existing dispute, was insufficient to constitute consent to the local court's jurisdiction or waiver of the State's immunity."[480] Under the doctrine of restrictive immunity, whether a State's consent to arbitration is confined to only compliance with the arbitral process or also extends to the supervisory jurisdiction of the national courts over the arbitral process depends on the wording of the applicable legal instruments. Of course, if there is already an exception to immunity regarding the claim, then the issue of whether arbitration constitutes a waiver of immunity should not arise.

An arbitration agreement between a foreign State and a natural or legal person generally has the effect of an implied waiver of sovereign immunity in relation to proceedings regarding the arbitration. The justification for treating arbitration as a waiver of immunity is that "a state party to an arbitration agreement is precluded from asserting its immunity in order to frustrate the purpose of the agreement."[481] An arbitration agreement as a waiver of immunity does not operate to excuse arbitration and substitute litigation for it, but it allows the courts to exercise their ancillary role of aiding the arbitral process.

Article 17 of the United Nations Convention provides that a foreign State cannot invoke its immunity in proceedings relating to (1) the validity, interpretation, or application of the arbitration agreement; (2) the arbitration procedure; or (3) the confirmation or the setting aside of the award, unless the arbitration agreement states otherwise. Submission to arbitration, as expressed in an arbitration agreement, "constitutes an expression of consent to all the consequences of acceptance of the obligation to settle differences by the type of arbitration clearly specified in the arbitration agreement."[482] A foreign State's agreement to arbitrate is, therefore, consent by the foreign State to the exercise of supervisory jurisdiction by the forum State, which is competent to supervise the arbitration.

479. *Id.*

480. *Id.* at 5.

481. Sovereign Immunity and Transnational Arbitration, Georges R. Delaume in Contemporary Problems in International Arbitration 315 (Julian D.M. Lew ed., 1986) [Citation omitted].

482. Draft Articles and Commentaries, Article 17, Commentary (5).

Article 12 of the Basle Convention provides:

> Where a Contracting State has agreed in writing to submit to arbitration a dispute which has arisen or may arise out of a civil or commercial matter, that State may not claim immunity from the jurisdiction of a court of another Contracting State on the territory or according to the law of which the arbitration has taken or will take place in respect of any proceedings relating to (a) the validity or interpretation of the arbitration agreement; (b) the arbitration procedure; and the setting aside of the award, unless the arbitration agreement otherwise provides.[483]

FSIA provides that a foreign State is not immune from the jurisdiction of the courts of the United States:

> in which the action is brought, either to enforce an agreement made by the foreign state with or for the benefit of a private party to submit to arbitration all or any differences which have arisen or which may arise between the parties with respect to a defined legal relationship, whether contractual or not, concerning a subject matter capable of settlement by arbitration under the laws of the United States, or to confirm an award made pursuant to such an agreement to arbitrate, if (A) the arbitration takes place or is intended to take place in the United States, (B) the agreement or award is or may be governed by a treaty or other international agreement in force for the United States calling for recognition and enforcement of arbitral awards, (C) the underlying claim, save for the agreement to arbitrate, could have been brought in the United States court under this section [General Exceptions to the Jurisdictional Immunity of a Foreign State] or section 1607 [Counterclaim], or (D) paragraph (1) of this subsection [Express or Implied Waiver] is otherwise applicable.[484]

In *Creighton v. Qatar*, Creighton claimed that Qatar had implicitly waived its sovereign immunity in the United States when it agreed to arbitrate in France, because Qatar was on notice that an arbitral award rendered in France would

483. Proceedings for the enforcement of arbitral awards are outside the scope of the Basle Convention. See Explanatory Report on Article 12.

484. 28 U.S.C § 1605(a)(6) (1988). Section 1605(a) of the FSIA was amended in 1988 to include a new subsection (6) and create the arbitration exception for the purpose of denying immunity in actions seeking to enforce arbitration agreements or awards in a number of situations.

be enforceable in the United States under the New York Convention.[485] Qatar countered that the FSIA and judicial decisions interpreting and applying it make clear that an agreement to arbitrate in a State that is a party to the New York Convention does not operate as an implied waiver unless the foreign State is also a party to the Convention.[486] The District of Columbia Court of Appeals agreed with Qatar that because Qatar has not signed the New York Convention its agreement to arbitrate in a signatory country, without more, does not evince the requisite intent to waive sovereign immunity in the United States.[487]

A legal relationship may qualify for the arbitration exception under the FSIA even without the formality of a contractual arrangement.[488] In *Daig Human v. Czech Republic*, Daig Human, a medical technology and production company, had entered a Framework Agreement with the Ministry of Health of the Czech Republic. Following a dispute between the parties, Daig Human obtained an arbitral award against the Ministry which it sought to enforce in the district court of the District of Columbia, invoking the New York Convention. The district court dismissed the case but was reversed on appeal. The Court of Appeals analyzed the arbitration exception and noted that under the exception, two standards are at issue in the case: (1) whether the parties shared a "defined legal relationship, whether contractual or not"; and (2) whether the arbitration award "is or may be governed by a treaty or other international agreement in force for the United States." It concluded that the Framework agreement met the first standard: a relationship is legal where "the agreement defined a relationship between the parties, and given the subject matter of the reciprocal obligations and responsibilities."[489] With respect to the second standard, it noted that both the Czech Republic and the United States are signatories to the New York Convention, which has been codified in the Federal Arbitration Act (FAA), and concluded that the award may be governed by the Convention because the relationship between the parties was commercial in nature.[490] Although the New York Convention does not define "commercial," in international arbitration it refers to matters or relationships that

485. See United Nations Convention on the Recognition and Enforcement of Foreign Arbitral Awards, June 10, 1958, 330 U.N.T.S. 38; 21 U.S.T. 2517, T.I.A.S. No. 6997 ("New York Convention"). The treaty entered into force on June 7, 1959, and so far has 149 States parties.

486. *Creighton v. Qatar*, 181 F 3d. 118, 122 (D.C. Cir. 1999).

487. *Id.*

488. See *Daig Human v. Czech Republic*, 824 F.3d 131, 135 (D.C. Cir. 2016).

489. *Id.* at 135.

490. *Id.* at 136.

arise out of or in connection with commerce.[491] The Court of Appeals, therefore, held that the Czech Republic is not entitled to immunity under the arbitration exception of FSIA.[492]

At issue, sometimes, is whether an arbitration agreement is a general waiver of immunity in any jurisdiction or only in a particular jurisdiction. In *Ipitrade International, S.A. v. Federal Republic of Nigeria*,[493] the court held that an agreement to adjudicate all disputes arising under a contract in accordance with Swiss law and by arbitration under the International Chamber of Commerce (ICC) rules constituted a waiver of sovereign immunity under the FSIA because the award was subject to the New York Convention, and the United States, France, Nigeria, and Switzerland are all signatories to the Convention. Thus, the jurisdiction of the U.S. courts over the enforcement action was provided by a treaty to which both the United States and Nigeria were signatories, namely, the New York Convention, and none of its grounds for refusing recognition and enforcement were applicable.

Since the United States has ratified the New York Convention,[494] courts in the United States have held that it is the type of treaty or international agreement contemplated by Section 1605(a)(6)(B) of the FSIA.[495] In the United States, the law is more settled now around arbitration as a waiver of jurisdictional immunity after the early confusion caused by the House Report on implied waivers.[496]

The United States Federal Arbitration Act (FAA)[497] applies to both domestic and international arbitration, as well as implements the New York Convention and the Inter-American Convention on International Commercial Arbitration ("Panama Convention").[498] The FAA was also amended following the enactment

491. *Id.* at 136 [Citations omitted].

492. *Id.* at 137.

493. 465 F. Supp. 824, 826 (D.D.C. 1978).

494. United Nations Convention on the Recognition and Enforcement of Arbitral Awards, June 10, 1958, 21 U.S.T. 2517, 330 U.N.T.S. 3 ("New York Convention"), incorporated by FAA in 9 U.S.C. §§ 201–206 (1970).

495. See *Creighton Ltd. v. Qatar*, 181 F.3d 118, 123–24 (D.C. Cir. 1999); *TMR Energy Ltd. v. State Prop. Fund of Ukraine*, 411 F.3d 296, 305 (D.C. Cir. 2005). The bases for non-enforcement of an arbitral award are listed in Article V of the New York Convention.

496. H.R. Rep 94-1487 (1976), p. 6617 ("With respect to implicit waivers, the courts have found such waivers in cases where a foreign state has agreed to arbitration in another country or where a foreign state has agreed that the law of a particular country shall govern a contract.")

497. 9 U.S.C. §§ 1–16, 201–208, 301–307 (1990).

498. January 30, 1975, O.A.S.T.S. No. 42, 1438 U.N.T.S. 245, incorporated by FAA in 9 U.S.C. §§ 301–306 (1990).

of the FSIA's arbitration exception in 1988. The Convention on the Settlement of Investment Disputes between States and Nationals of Other States ("Washington Convention")[499] does not affect the FSIA,[500] but Article 26 of the Convention provides: "Consent of the parties to arbitration under this Convention shall, unless otherwise stated, be deemed consent to such arbitration to the exclusion of any other remedy."[501]

Where an entity, which qualified as an agency or instrumentality of a foreign State under Section 1603 of the FSIA, entered into a contract that provided for arbitration and then participated in the arbitration in which an arbitral award was issued against it, the court held that under Section 1605(a)(1), the State has implicitly waived sovereign immunity. Consequently, the court had subject matter jurisdiction in an action seeking recognition and enforcement of the ICC arbitral award pursuant to the New York Convention, which expressly permits such action in Contracting States.[502] The court distinguished the case from *Frolova v. USSR*, where the Seventh Circuit rejected the claim that the sovereign had impliedly waived its immunity merely because it was a signatory to the United Nations Charter and the Helsinki Accords.[503] The distinguishing factor, according to the court, is that the language, structure, or history of United Nations Charter or the Helsinki Accords did not imply a waiver of sovereign immunity, as opposed to the New York Convention that expressly permits recognition and enforcement actions in Contracting States.

In an action to enforce an International Centre for Settlement of Investment Disputes (ICSID) arbitral award against Argentina, it was held that Argentina waived its immunity under the arbitral award exception of the FSIA:

> To our knowledge, every court to consider whether awards issued pursuant to the ICSID Convention fall within the arbitral award exception to FSIA has concluded that they do.... Indeed, inasmuch as (1) the Award was issued pursuant to the ICSID Convention, which is a "treaty or other international agreement in force for the United States calling for recognition and enforcement of arbitral awards," and (2) the United States and Argentina

499. March 18, 1965, 17 U.S.T. 1270, 575 U.N.T.S. 159.

500. *Id.* Article 55: ICSID provisions on Recognition and Enforcement of the Award (Section 6) "shall [not] be construed as derogating from the law in force in any Contracting State relating to immunity of that State or of any foreign State from execution."

501. *Id.* Article 26.

502. See *Seetransport v. Navimpex*, 989 F. 2d 572, 578–79 (2d Cir. 1993).

503. *Id.* at 578.

> are both parties to the ICSID Convention, Argentina's agreement to submit its dispute to arbitration under the ICSID Convention constituted a waiver of immunity from suit.[504]

Section 9 of the SIA provides that "where a State has agreed in writing to submit a dispute which has arisen or which may arise in arbitration the State is not immune as respects proceedings in the courts of the United Kingdom which relate to the arbitration." It reverses the common law rule, whereby an agreement to arbitrate did not constitute a submission to the jurisdiction of the English courts in respect to that arbitration. The requirement of a written agreement conforms with Section 5 of the English Arbitration Act 1996.[505]

In *Svenska v. Lithuania*,[506] Svenska had attempted to enforce in England, pursuant to Section 101 of the Arbitration Act 1996, an arbitral award made in Denmark under the ICC Arbitration Rules. Although the government of Lithuania was not a party to the joint venture agreement (JVA), it signed the agreement and declared: "The Government of the Republic of Lithuania hereby approves the above agreement and acknowledges itself to be legally and contractually bound as if the Government were a signatory to the Agreement."[507] Article 9.2(b) of the JVA provided for "independent arbitration in Denmark, Copenhagen to be conducted in accordance with the International Chamber of Commerce Rules of Arbitration in the English language."[508] Article 35.1 of the

504. *Blue Ridge v. Argentina*, 735 F.3d 72, 84 (2d Cir. 2013) [citations omitted].

505. Section 5 (Agreement to be in writing) of Arbitration Act 1996 provides: (1) The provisions of this Part [Arbitration pursuant to an arbitration agreement] apply only where the arbitration agreement is in writing, and any other agreement between the parties as to any matter is effective for the purposes of this Part only if in writing. The expressions "agreement," "agree" and "agreed" shall be construed accordingly. (2) There is an agreement in writing—(a) if the agreement is made in writing (whether or not it is signed by the parties), (b) if the agreement is made by exchange of communications in writing, or (c) if the agreement is evidenced in writing. (3) Where parties agree otherwise than in writing by reference to terms which are in writing, they make an agreement in writing. (4) An agreement is evidenced in writing if an agreement made otherwise than in writing is recorded by one of the parties, or by a third party, with the authority of the parties to the agreement. (5) An exchange of written submissions in arbitral or legal proceedings in which the existence of an agreement otherwise than in writing is alleged by one party against another party and not denied by the other party in his response constitutes as between those parties an agreement in writing to the effect alleged. (6) References in this Part to anything being written or in writing include its being recorded by any means.

506. *Svenska Petroleum AB v. Republic of Lithuania*, [2006] EWCA Civ 1529, [2007] QB 886, [1 Lloyd's Rep 193.

507. *Id.*, para. 4.

508. *Id.*, para. 6.

JVA provided: "Government and EPG hereby irrevocably waives [sic] all rights to sovereign immunity."[509]

The Court of Appeal of England and Wales framed the issue as follows: "[D]id the Government agree in writing to submit the dispute in this case to arbitration, and if so, is Svenska's application for leave to enforce the award as a judgment under section 101 of the Arbitration Act 1996 to be regarded as 'proceedings which relate to the arbitration'?" With respect to the first question, the Court of Appeal established that Lithuania was a party to an agreement to arbitrate and that Section 9 of SIA was applicable. Regarding the second question, it noted:

> Arbitration is a consensual procedure and the principle underlying section 9 is that, if a state has agreed to submit to arbitration, it has rendered itself amenable to such process as may be necessary to render the arbitration effective.... The [SIA] itself draws a distinction between proceedings which relate to the arbitration (section 9) and the process in respect of property for the enforcement of an award (section 13). In our view, an application under section 101(2) of the Arbitration Act 1996 for leave to enforce an award as a judgment is, as subsection (1) recognises, one aspect of its recognition and as such is the final stage in rendering the arbitral procedure effective. Enforcement by execution on property belonging to the state is another matter, as section 13 makes clear.[510]

This ruling shows fidelity to the distinction between a court's adjudicatory jurisdiction (recognition of an arbitral award) and its enforcement jurisdiction (enforcement of an arbitral award). Recognition of an arbitral award is an enforcement proceeding to turn that award into an order of the court on which an execution could be levied.[511] The *Svenska* court discounted the argument that a wide interpretation of Section 9 to encompass proceedings to enforce a foreign arbitral award with no connection to the United Kingdom is contrary to the presumption of immunity in Section 1 of the SIA, as well as to the Basle Convention. It noted that although the SIA was enacted to give effect to the Basle Convention, it departed from the Convention in certain respects, particularly in Section 9 of the Act compared to Article 12 of the Convention. Section 9 of SIA is, therefore, not limited to awards made in the United Kingdom or according to its law, and,

509. *Id.*, para. 7.

510. *Id.*, para. 117.

511. See *id.*, para. 119.

as such, a foreign State has no immunity in respect of enforcement proceedings for any foreign arbitral award.[512]

The common law rule (in England), under the doctrine of absolute sovereign immunity, was articulated and applied in *Democratic Republic of the Congo v. FG Hemisphere*,[513] which was an action to enforce arbitral awards against the Democratic Republic of the Congo (DRC) in Hong Kong. "An application for the grant of leave to enforce the award, often referred to as the 'recognition phase of enforcement, therefore involves discretionary adjudicative proceedings in which the impleaded State may claim state immunity."[514] The case concerned credit agreements between Energoinvest, a Yugoslavian company, and DRC, which contained ICC Arbitration Rules clauses.[515] After DRC defaulted on its repayment obligation, Energoinvest pursued it in two arbitrations in France and Switzerland, both of which are signatories of the New York Convention, which also applied to Hong Kong. Energoinvest obtained two final awards against DRC, which did not challenge them. Energoinvest then assigned the benefits of the awards to FG Hemisphere, a New York company.

FG Hemisphere started proceedings in Hong Kong to enforce the arbitral awards, and obtained an ex parte order allowing it to enforce the arbitral awards as a judgment of the Hong Kong court. DRC applied to set aside the order on the basis of its sovereign immunity. Judge Reyes set aside the order and held that DRC's submission to arbitration did not constitute a waiver of its sovereign immunity. FG Hemisphere appealed to the Court of Appeal, which allowed it by a majority, and held that there was not only no immunity but also that there would have been no waiver if there had been immunity to waive.[516] The case was then appealed to the Court of Final Appeal in Hong Kong Special Administrative Region (HKSAR), which in a very comprehensive and magisterial opinion had to determine whether absolute or restrictive immunity was applicable in HKSAR. The court stated that prior to July 1, 1997, the Hong Kong courts applied the same theory of State immunity as England, which ceased with China's resumption

512. See *id.*, para. 121 ("It is quite clear that it was the intention of Parliament in formulating section 9 of the Act in unrestricted terms that application for leave to enforce arbitration awards should not attract sovereign immunity, whether the award was domestic or foreign.")

513. *DRC v. FG Hemisphere* [2011] 4 HKC 151.

514. *Id.*, para. 382.

515. Rule 28.6 of the 1998 version of the ICC Rules of Arbitration provides: "Every Award shall be binding on the parties. By submitting the dispute to arbitration under these Rules, the parties undertake to carry out any Award without delay and shall be deemed to have waived their right to any form of recourse insofar as such waiver can validly be made."

516. *FG Hemisphere v. Congo* [2010] 2 HKC 487.

of the exercise of sovereignty over Hong Kong, and that because of the status of Hong Kong as a special administrative region of the People's Republic of China (PRC), the doctrine of absolute immunity that applied in PRC also applies in HKSAR henceforth.[517] It also had to determine whether Congo had waived State immunity as a result of the arbitration. The Court of Final Appeal stated:

> A State which waives its immunity, does so by voluntarily submitting to the exercise of jurisdiction by the courts of the forum State over the waiving State's governmental entities or property. Obviously, when a State enters into an arbitration agreement with a private individual or company, that act does not constitute a submission to any other State's jurisdiction. It involves merely the assumption of contractual obligations *vis-à-vis* the other party to the agreement. So if a State fails to honour a promise made in the arbitration agreement to carry out the award and waive its immunity, it may put itself in breach of its contract but it will have done nothing to submit to the jurisdiction of any forum State.[518]

The Court of Final Appeal continued:

> Against that background, one should distinguish three situations in which a waiver may be relevant. First, by taking part in an arbitration, a State is obviously agreeing to submit to the contractual jurisdiction of the arbitrators. But that is obviously not the same thing as submitting to the jurisdiction of another State's court. Such conduct may however constitute an implicit submission to the jurisdiction of the courts—the French and Swiss courts in the present case—exercising a supervisory jurisdiction over the conduct of the arbitration.[519]

The Court of Final Appeal pointed out that a statute in a forum State, such as Section 9 of SIA, may "deem a submission to arbitration to be an implied waiver of state immunity in that State's courts," but HKSAR has no such legislation and, as such, the common law rules apply.[520]

517. See *id.*, paras. 225–226.

518. *DRC v. FG Hemisphere* [2011] 4 HKC 151, para. 377, citing *Duff Development Co. Ltd v. Government of Kelantan* [1924] AC 797, 810; *Kahan v. Pakistan Federation* [1952] 2 KB 1003, 1020.

519. *Id.*, para. 378 [citations omitted].

520. *Id.*, paras. 384–386.

The Court of Final Appeal noted the common law rule in England as to whether submission of a dispute to arbitration constituted an implied submission to the jurisdiction under the jurisprudence of *Duff Development Co Ltd v. Government of Kelantan*, [1924] AC 797, and *Mighell v. Sultan of Johore* [1894] 1 QBD 149. "Applying the common law rule to the present case [the Court concluded] that there is no basis for finding that the DRC has waived its state immunity before the HKSAR courts, either in respect of recognition or execution of the arbitral awards."[521]

The Court of Final Appeal was not persuaded to hold that an agreement to arbitrate constitutes an implied waiver of immunity in HKSAR courts:

> Whether or not a particular State accepts a commercial exception, the rationale of state immunity remains the *par in parem* principle. Mutual recognition as co-equal sovereign States leads each State to refrain from exercising jurisdiction over the foreign State concerned without the latter's consent. Questions of waiver only arise where the impleaded State *does* qualify for jurisdictional immunity in the forum State, or else there is nothing to waive. In such circumstances, the common law rule as to waiver is consonant with elementary good sense by requiring an unequivocal submission to the jurisdiction of the forum State at the time when the forum State's jurisdiction is invoked against the impleaded States. Courts would be ill-advised to attempt to deem an impleaded State to have submitted to their jurisdiction when it has not done so explicitly by its words or conduct and where its objection to such jurisdiction is made clear in the recognition proceedings.[522]

In any event, the majority or modern view is that an arbitration agreement may constitute a waiver of immunity.[523] Arbitration as a waiver of immunity has the same justice imperative that led to the development of restrictive immunity. A State that agrees to settle disputes through arbitration should not be allowed to renege on its promise and revoke the waiver when a dispute arises. Notwithstanding, for an arbitration agreement to amount to waiver of State immunity, it must be clear. Absence of ambiguity in an arbitral clause is key to the construction of an arbitration agreement as a waiver of State immunity. In the end, whether an arbitration agreement works as a waiver of State immunity comes down to the interpretation of the contract and any applicable legal instrument.

521. *Id.* at 390.

522. *DRC v. FG Hemisphere Associates*, [2011] 4 HKC 151, para. 392.

523. See Section 1605(a)(6) of the FSIA; Section 9 of SIA; Article 17 of the United Nations Convention; Article 12 of the Basle Convention, etc.

Counterclaim

A foreign State waives its immunity to a counterclaim when it voluntarily submits to the jurisdiction of the forum State by its participation in litigation as a claimant or plaintiff. The issue is whether such voluntary submission makes the foreign State amenable to all counterclaims or only those that involve the same subject matter, or as a setoff limited by the amount of the original claim.

Article 1 of the Basle Convention provides that when a foreign State submits to jurisdiction by instituting or intervening in proceedings in a forum court, it cannot claim immunity in respect of a counterclaim arising out of the legal relationship or the facts on which the principal claim is based if it would not have been entitled to immunity regarding the counterclaim in a separate proceeding.[524] Also, the denial of immunity in a counterclaim extends to the principal claim.[525]

Similarly, Article 9 of the United Nations Convention provides for denial of immunity for counterclaims where a foreign State has submitted to jurisdiction in a forum State in accordance with Article 8, and the State cannot also invoke immunity with respect to the principal claim. Obviously, a counterclaim presupposes the prior existence of an original or principal claim, but there would not be a counterclaim against a State that intervenes in a proceeding without also making a claim in connection with the proceedings.[526] An intervention, for example, as amicus curiae is not a submission to jurisdiction.[527] An independent counterclaim, that is, a counterclaim arising out of a different transaction or occurrence, or legal relationship, or separate facts from the principal claim is not considered a submission to jurisdiction, but it can be maintained against the State if and only if the subject matter of that independent counterclaim falls within an exception to immunity.[528] A State that brings a counterclaim in a proceeding is essentially treated as if it is instituting a new and separate proceeding and, as such, submits to jurisdiction.

Under the common law (in the United States), a foreign sovereign by voluntarily appearing as a plaintiff "abandons its immunity from suit and subjects itself to the procedure and rules of decision governing the forum which it has sought."[529] The FSIA codifies the common law rule: it provides that a foreign State shall not

524. See Article 1(2), Basle Convention.

525. See Article 1(3), Basle Convention.

526. See Draft Articles and Commentaries, Article 9, Commentary (3).

527. See *Id.*

528. See Draft Articles and Commentaries, Article 9, Commentary (4) and (5).

529. See *Guaranty Trust Co. v. United States*, 304 U.S. 126, 134, n.2 (1938).

be accorded immunity with respect to any counterclaim (1) for which a foreign State would not be entitled to immunity under [the enumerated exceptions to immunity under the FSIA] had such claim been brought in a separate action against the foreign State; or (2) arising out of the transaction or occurrence that is the subject matter of the claim of the foreign State; or (3) to the extent that the counterclaim does not seek relief exceeding in amount or differing in kind from that sought by the foreign State.[530]

The legislative history of Section 1607 of FSIA identified three situations where it would deny immunity in counterclaims against a foreign State that brings an action or intervenes in an action in a U.S. court. First, it would deny immunity in any counterclaim where the foreign State would not be entitled to immunity under the enumerated exceptions in Section 1605. Second, it would deny immunity in counterclaims "arising out of the transaction or occurrence that is the subject matter of the claim of the foreign state." It follows that a foreign State that institutes or intervenes in an action based on a particular transaction or occurrence should not benefit from litigation in U.S. courts while avoiding any liabilities claimed against it and arising from that transaction or occurrence. Third, a foreign State would not be immune from counterclaim for a setoff.[531]

530. 28 U.S.C. § 1607 (2010).

531. H.R. Rep 94-1487 (1976), p. 6622. Section 1607(c) codified the rule enunciated in *National Bank v. China*, 348 U.S. 356 (1955), where the Supreme Court reasoned: "The short of the matter is that we are not dealing with an attempt to bring a recognized foreign government into one of our courts as a defendant and subject it to the rule of law to which nongovernmental obligors must bow. We have a foreign government invoking our law but resisting a claim against it which fairly would curtail its recovery. It wants our law, like any other litigant, but it wants our law free from the claims of justice." It concluded: "It is recognized that a counterclaim based on the subject matter of a sovereign's suit is allowed to cut into the doctrine of immunity."

4

Competing or Conflicting Norms, and Related but Different Doctrine

The object of international law . . . is not to work injustice, nor to prevent the enforcement of just demand, but to substitute negotiations between governments, though they may be dilatory and the issue distant and uncertain, for the ordinary use of courts of justice in cases where such use would lessen the dignity or embarrass the functions of the representatives of a foreign state. . . . "[1]

The increasing recognition of the importance of ensuring that the perpetrators of serious international crimes do not go unpunished has had its impact on the immunities which State dignitaries enjoyed under traditional customary law.[2]

These trends reflect a balancing of interests. On the one scale, we find the interest of the community of mankind to prevent and stop impunity for perpetrators of grave crimes against its members; on the other, there is the interest of the community of States to allow them to act freely on the inter-State level without unwarranted interference. A balance therefore must be struck between two sets of functions which are both valued by the international community.[3]

1. *The Charkieh (6200)* [1873] L.R. 4 A. & E.59 at p. 97 (Sir Robert Phillimore).

2. Arrest Warrant of 11 April 2000 (Democratic Republic of the Congo v. Belgium) *("Arrest Warrant Case")*, Judgment, I.C.J. Rep. 2002, p. 3, Joint Separate Opinion of Judges Higgins, Kooijmans, and Buergenthal, para. 74.

3. *Id.*, para. 75.

COMPETING OR CONFLICTING NORMS OF INTERNATIONAL LAW

International law recognizes human rights and jus cogens norms, as well as the rule of State immunity. Human rights and jus cogens norms should hold their violators, usually high State officials, accountable and end impunity. But "immunities are granted to high State officials to guarantee the proper functioning of the network of mutual inter-State relations, which is of paramount importance for a well-ordered and harmonious international system."[4] State immunity is a prescriptive norm in the sense that it imposes an obligation of what should be done, whereas human rights is a proscriptive norm of what should not be done. Contemporary controversy centers on whether these conflicting or competing norms of international law can coexist or be reconciled. Is there, or should there be a human rights or jus cogens exception to State immunity?

Human Rights and Jus Cogens Norms

> Prior to the twentieth century, a virtually universal belief prevailed, namely, that the treatment of its citizenry by a state fell outside the province of international law since the individual, alone or collectively, was merely an object and not a subject of the law of nations.
>
> Since World War I, however, the community of nations has become increasingly aware of the need to safeguard minimal rights of the individual. In consequence, human rights have become a subject of vital and at times acrimonious concern to the traditional subjects of international law, and the individual has begun to emerge, to some extent at least, as a subject of that law.[5]

The Preamble of the Charter of the United Nations declares that the organization is determined "to reaffirm faith in fundamental human rights." In the same vein, Article 1 of the Charter proclaims, among the purposes of the organization, the "promoting and encouraging [of] respect for human rights." However, Article 2(7) of the same Charter makes it clear that it does not "authorize the United Nations to intervene in matters which are essentially within the domestic jurisdiction of any state." For the protection and exposition of the general and various human rights provision of the Charter, the General Assembly of the

4. *Id.*

5. Gerhad von Glahn, Law Among Nations: An Introduction to Public International Law 185 (4th ed. 1981).

United Nations adopted and proclaimed, on December 10, 1948, the Universal Declaration of Human Rights (UDHR).[6] Thus, was born international human rights law and the transformation of the individual from an object to a partial subject of international law.[7] International human rights law prohibits violation of human rights guarantees by States against individuals, including its nationals. "The way in which a state treated its own citizens within its own borders had become a matter of legitimate concern to the international community."[8] Human rights inhere to all human beings, and the principle of universality was first emphasized in the UDHR and subsequently reiterated in several international human rights conventions, declarations, and resolutions. Human rights abuses are normally handled in criminal proceedings. In Europe, alternative recourse may be had to the European Court of Human Rights (ECtHR) for human rights abuses by States.

Jus cogens (i.e., compelling law) is "a peremptory norm of general international law [that] is . . . accepted and recognized by the international community of States as a whole as a norm from which no derogation is permitted and which can be modified only by a subsequent norm of general international law having the same character."[9] Treaty law and customary international law form norms known as *jus dispositivum* (i.e., law subject to the dispensation of the parties), which are founded on the consent of States. Jus cogens, as opposed to *jus dispositivum*, are binding on all States, with or without consent. As a jus cogens norm is subject to derogation only by a subsequent jus cogens norm, the relationship between State immunity and jus cogens norms is one of the most contentious areas of contemporary international law. The determination of the actual content of the jus cogens norm is critical to a resolution of the quandary, as most courts have attempted to do.

6. See G.A. Res. 217A (III), U.N. Doc. A/810 at 71 (1948).

7. It is still debatable whether an individual is a subject of international law as an individual cannot assert his or her rights in the international plane, and must rely on the State for any such claim.

8. *R v Bow Street Metropolitan Stipendiary Magistrate and others, ex parte Pinochet Ugarte (Amnesty International and others intervening) (No 3)* [2000] 1 AC 147, [1999] 2 All ER 97, [1999] 2 WLR 827 ("*Ex Parte Pinochet 3*"), Lord Millett.

9. Article 53, Vienna Convention on the Law of Treaties ("Vienna Convention"), May 23, 1969, 1155 U.N.T.S. 332, 8 I.L.M. 679 ("Vienna Convention"); see Restatement (Third) of Foreign Relations Law of the United States ("Restatement Third"), Section 102, Comment K (Am. Law Inst. 1987).

Not all human rights norms are jus cogens. Torture is an international crime, and its prohibition is a jus cogens norm.[10] Article 14(1) of the Convention Against Torture provides:

> Each State Party shall ensure in its legal system that the victim of an act of torture obtains redress and has an enforceable right to fair and adequate compensation, including the means for as full rehabilitation as possible. In the event of the death of the victim as a result of an act of torture, his dependents shall be entitled to compensation.[11]

Courts have addressed whether there exists a human rights or jus cogens exception to State immunity under national laws or international law, and have applied what may be categorized into "competing norms" versus "conflicting norms" approaches. The competing norms approach is a conflict avoidance technique that does not see an antinomy between these norms of international law. Under this approach, the norms can coexist and be reconciled. It takes the position that jurisdictional immunity has intrinsic value: "International law seeks the accommodation of this value with the fight against impunity and not the triumph of one norm over the other."[12] The conflicting norms approach, on the other hand, sees a conflict between the norms that must be resolved in accordance with the hierarchy of norms under international law. Courts may consider several factors, and sometimes the consideration of the same factor yields a different outcome depending on the approach applied or on whether the defendant is an individual or a State. For example, a foreign State cannot be subject to criminal proceedings in a forum State under international law for jus cogens violations.

Competing Norms Approach

Application of National Law

A national court may look exclusively or primarily at the national law for its determination of whether there is an exception to immunity for violations of human rights and jus cogens norms.

10. See *Questions relating to the Obligation to Prosecute or Extradite (Belgium v. Senegal)*, Judgment, I.C.J. Reports 2012, p. 422, para. 99; *Jones v. Saudi Arabia*, [2006] UKHL 26, [2007] 1 A.C. 270, para. 43; *Al-Adsani v. United Kingdom*, (2001), 34 E.H.R.R. 273, para. 61.

11. Convention Against Torture and Other Cruel, Inhuman, or Degrading Treatment or Punishment ("Convention Against Torture" or "Torture Convention"), adopted by the General Assembly of the United Nations on December 10, 1984 (resolution 39/46). The Convention entered into force on June 26, 1987, after it had been ratified by 20 States. GA res. 39/46, annex, 39 UN GAOR Supp. (No. 51) at 197, UN Doc. A/39/51 (1984); 1465 UNTS 85.

12. *Arrest Warrant* Case (Joint Separate Opinion of Judges Higgins, Kooijmans, and Buergenthal), para. 79.

In the United States, the case of *Filartiga v. Pena-Irala*[13] heralded the idea of suing a private person for human rights violation. In *Filartiga*, the Second Circuit Court of Appeals found that the United States Alien Tort Statute of 1789 (ATS) established federal jurisdiction against an alien sued for a tort committed in violation of the laws of nations or a treaty of the United States.[14] The court held that there was jurisdiction in the claim by a Paraguayan citizen for torture by a Paraguayan police officer. The Paraguayan government was not joined as a defendant in the suit, and State immunity was not raised before the court. The case was a boon to plaintiffs who relied on it and the ATS to sue foreign officials for alleged violation of international law committed overseas.

The Torture Victim Protection Act (TVPA),[15] which was enacted in 1992, more than two hundred years after the ATS, provides another basis for human rights litigation in the United States. It provides for a cause of action for both U.S. nationals and aliens for extrajudicial killing and for torture, stating in relevant part that: "An individual who, under actual or apparent authority, or color of law, of any foreign nation—(1) subjects an individual to torture shall, in a civil action, be liable for damages to that individual; or (2) subjects an individual to extrajudicial killing shall, in a civil action, be liable for damages to the individual's legal representative, or to any person who may be a claimant in an action for wrongful death."[16] The TVPA was enacted as a note to ATS, to codify the cause of action recognized in *Filartiga* and to extend it as well to citizens of the United States.[17]

ATS and TVPA are distinct statutes with their own limitations. The TVPA contains a detailed definition of extrajudicial killing and torture, unlike ATS, which does not provide definitions for what constitutes "law of nations" or a "tort . . . committed in violation" of that law. Also, TVPA, unlike ATS, allows a civil action only against persons who acted under actual or apparent authority of a foreign State. A TVPA claimant must also exhaust all "adequate and available remedies in the place in which the conduct giving rise to the claim occurred."[18]

13. 630 F. 2d 876 (2d Cir. 1980).

14. See 28 U.S.C. § 1350 (2006). The ATS provides in its entirety: "The district courts shall have original jurisdiction of any civil action by an alien for a tort only, committed in violation of the law of nations or a treaty of the United States."

15. Torture Victim Protection Act of 1991, Pub. L. No. 102-256, 106 Stat. 73 (1992) (codified at 28 U.S.C. § 1350 note (1994)) ["TVPA"].

16. *Id.*

17. See 28 U.S.C § 1350 note (1994).

18. Section 2(b) of TVPA.

Suits have been filed under the TVPA and ATS, seeking redress against violations of human rights.

The U.S. Supreme Court addressed the scope of the ATS for the first time in *Sosa v. Alvarez-Machain* and held that the ATS granted federal courts jurisdiction over a narrow set of causes of action "based on the present-day law of nations [that] rest on a norm of international character accepted by the civilized world and defined with a specificity comparable to the features of the 18th–century paradigms recognized."[19] Alvarez had sought damages against Sosa, a Mexican citizen, under the ATS for his abduction in Mexico at the behest of the United States Drug Enforcement Administration, alleging a tort in violation of international law. The Court stated that "federal courts should not recognize private claims under federal common law for violations of any international law norm with less *definite content and acceptance among civilized nations* than the historical paradigms familiar when § 1350 was enacted."[20] It rejected the claim for arbitrary arrest and detention for want of the requisite definite content and acceptance as international law.[21]

The Supreme Court revisited ATS in *Kiobel v. Royal Dutch Petroleum*,[22] where it examined whether anyone can be sued under the ATS for violations of international law that occurred overseas. Plaintiffs, Nigerian nationals legally resident in the United States, sued certain Dutch, British, and Nigerian corporations in federal court under the ATS. They alleged that the corporations aided and abetted the Nigerian government in committing violations of the law of nations in Nigeria, namely, extrajudicial killings; crimes against humanity; torture and cruel treatment; arbitrary arrest and detention; violations of the rights to life, liberty, security, and association; forced exile; and property destruction. The Supreme Court framed the issue to be whether a claim under the ATS may reach conduct occurring in the territory of a foreign State.[23] It noted that "there is no indication that the ATS was passed to make the United States a uniquely hospitable forum for the enforcement of international norms.[24] It then held that the presumption against extraterritoriality applies to claims under the ATS, and that the plaintiffs' case is barred as all the relevant conduct took place outside the United States.[25]

19. *Sosa v. Alvarez-Machain*, 542 U.S. 692, 725 (2004).

20. *Id.* at 732 [emphasis added].

21. *Id.*

22. *Kiobel v. Royal Dutch Petroleum*, 133 S. Ct. 1659 (2013).

23. *Id.* at 1664.

24. *Id.* at 1668.

25. *Id.* at 1669.

Moreover, "even where claims touch and concern the United States, they must do so with sufficient force to displace the presumption against application."[26]

It is noteworthy that both the ATS and TVPA do not mention State immunity, and there is nothing in the legislative history of the TVPA regarding a relationship with FSIA. Most important, the Supreme Court has ruled the ATS does not affect State immunity under the FSIA as the ATS "by its terms does not distinguish among classes of defendants, and it of course has the same effect after the passage of the FSIA as before with respect to defendants other than foreign states."[27] Even where the Supreme Court had held that the FSIA did not apply to a (former) foreign official who was sued under the ATS and the TVPA, it did not base its holding on any ATS or TVPA exception to FSIA.[28]

Siderman v. Argentina[29] is a United States case that had squarely examined whether there is a torture exception to FSIA. In the case, the plaintiff had alleged that he was tortured by Argentina, and had argued that when a State violates a jus cogens norm it forfeits its immunity and becomes amenable to suit. The Ninth Circuit Court of Appeals of the United States held:

> Unfortunately, we do not write on a clean slate. We deal not only with customary international law, but with an affirmative Act of Congress, the FSIA. We must interpret the FSIA through the prism of the *Amerada Hess*. Nothing in the text or legislative history of the FSIA explicitly addresses the effect violations of jus cogens might have on the FSIA's cloak on immunity.[30]

The court, therefore, concluded that "if violations of *jus cogens* committed outside the United States are to be exceptions to immunity, Congress must make them so. The fact that there has been a violation of *jus cogens* does not confer jurisdiction under the FSIA."[31] The court, however, concluded that Argentina had impliedly waived its immunity to the claim of torture by deliberately seeking and engaging the United States in the persecution of the plaintiff in the very course

26. *Id.*

27. *Argentina v. Amerada Hess*, 488 U.S. 428, 438 (1989).

28. See *Samantar v. Yousuf*, 560 U.S. 305, 308 (2010) ("The narrow question we must decide is whether the Foreign Sovereign Immunities Act of 1976 (FSIA or Act), 28 U.S.C. §§ 1330, 1602 et seq., provides petitioner with immunity from suit based on actions taken in his official capacity. We hold that the FSIA does not govern the determination of petitioner's immunity from suit.").

29. *Siderman v. Argentina*, 965 F.2d 699 (9th Cir. 1992).

30. *Id.* at 718.

31. *Id.* at 719.

of activity for which the plaintiff seeks redress.[32] In sum, the outcome of the case revolved on a waiver of, instead of an exception to, immunity.

The Canadian Supreme Court has held that the State Immunity Act of Canada does not withdraw immunity for alleged torture abroad, and that this policy choice by the Parliament of Canada is not contrary to international law.[33] In *Kazemi Estate v. Iran*, the plaintiff brought civil proceedings on behalf of himself and the estate of his mother, a Canadian citizen, who had visited Iran as a free-lance photographer and journalist, and was arrested, detained, and interrogated by Iranian authorities. She was tortured during her detention and later died from the injury she sustained while in the custody of Iranian officials. At issue was whether the Islamic Republic of Iran, its head of State, and the officials who allegedly detained, tortured, and killed the plaintiff's mother in Iran are entitled to immunity under the Canadian State Immunity Act. The Court addressed "whether international law has created a mandatory universal jurisdiction in respect of claims of torture which would require states to open national courts to the claims of victims of acts of torture that were committed outside their national boundaries."[34] The Court stated that "the issue . . . is not whether torture is abhorrent or illegal . . . but whether one can sue a foreign state in [forum] courts for torture committed abroad."[35]

The Canadian Supreme Court concluded that the State Immunity Act "is a complete codification of Canadian law as it relates to state immunity from civil proceedings. In particular, s. 3(1) of the Act exhaustively establishes the parameters for state immunity and its exceptions."[36] Therefore, "reliance need not, and indeed cannot, be placed on the common law, *jus cogens* norms or international law to carve out additional exceptions to immunity granted to foreign states pursuant to s. 3(1) of the SIA. The SIA, in its present form, does not provide for an exception to foreign state immunity from civil suits alleging acts of torture occurring outside Canada."[37] The Court ruled that where a statute exhaustively lists the exceptions to State immunity, international law cannot be utilized to find new exceptions to immunity.[38] It concluded that based on the decisions of

32. *Id.* at 722. Section 1605(a)(1) of FSIA permits an implied waiver of immunity.

33. Kazemi Estate v. Islamic Republic of Iran, 2014 SCC 62 ¶ 2, [2014] 3 S.C.R. 176 (Can.) ("*Kazemi Estate*").

34. *Id.*, para. 32.

35. *Id.*, para. 53.

36. *Id.*, para. 54.

37. *Id.*, para. 56.

38. See *id.*, paras. 60–63.

several national courts and international tribunals, "customary international law does not extend the prohibition of torture so far as to require a civil remedy for torture committed in a foreign state."[39]

The European Court of Human Rights (ECtHR) addressed the issue of torture vis-à-vis State immunity in *Al-Adsani*.[40] The applicant, a dual British/Kuwaiti national had instituted civil proceedings in England against a Kuwaiti sheik and the State of Kuwait for "injury to his physical and mental health caused by torture in Kuwait . . . and threats against his physical and mental health caused by torture in Kuwait . . . and threats against his life and well-being made after his return to the United Kingdom."[41] The High Court struck down the proceedings on the ground that Kuwait was entitled to State immunity and that the exception provided for by section 5 of the State Immunity Act (SIA) of the United Kingdom did not apply.[42] "The clear language of the 1978 Act bestowed immunity upon sovereign States for acts committed outside the jurisdiction and, by making express provisions for exceptions, it excluded as a matter of construction implied constructions. As a result, there was no room for an implied execution for acts of torture in section I (1) of the 1978 Act."[43] The Court of Appeal dismissed the applicant's appeal, and the leave to appeal to the House of Lords was refused. It noted that events in Kuwait did not fall within the tort exception of Section 5 of the SIA. It also was not persuaded by the argument that "international law against torture is so fundamental that it is a *jus cogens*, or compelling law, which overrides all other principles of international law, including the well-established principles of sovereign immunity."[44]

Before the ECtHR, the applicant alleged, inter alia, that by granting Kuwait immunity the United Kingdom has failed to secure his right not to be tortured, in violation of Article 3 of the Torture Convention.[45] The ECtHR noted that the

39. *Id.*, para. 153.

40. *Al-Adsani v. United Kingdom* [GC], no. 35763/97, ECHR 2001-XI.

41. *Id.*, para. 14.

42. State Immunity Act, Section I(1) provides: "A State is immune from the jurisdiction of the courts of the United Kingdom except as provided in the following provisions of this Part of the Act. . . ." Section 5 provides: "A State is not immune as respects proceedings in respect of (a) death or personal injury . . . caused by an act or omission in the United Kingdom."

43. *Al-Adsani*, para. 17.

44. *Id.*, para. 18.

45. Article 3(1) provides: "No State Party shall expel, return ('refouler') or extradite a person to another State where there are substantial grounds for believing that he would be in danger of being subjected to torture."

alleged torture did not take place in the United Kingdom and that its authorities had no causal connection with the torture. It held that the United Kingdom did not violate Article 3 because it was not under a duty to provide a civil remedy to the applicant under the circumstances of the case.[46] The ECtHR ruled:

> While the Court accepts . . . that the prohibition of torture has achieved the status of a peremptory norm in international law, it observes that the present case concerns not, as in . . . *Pinochet*, the criminal liability of an individual for alleged acts of torture, but the immunity of a State in a civil suit for damages in respect of acts of torture within the territory of that State. Notwithstanding the special character of the prohibition of torture in international law, the Court is unable to discern in the international instruments, judicial authorities or other materials before it any firm basis for concluding that, as a matter of international law, a State no longer enjoys immunity from civil suit in the courts of another State where acts of torture are alleged. In particular, the Court observes that none of the primary international instruments referred to (Article 5 of the Universal Declaration of Human Rights, Article 7 of the International Covenant on Civil and Political Rights and Articles 2 and 4 of the UN Convention [Against Torture]) relates to civil proceedings or to State immunity.[47]

The ECtHR reaffirmed State immunity for acts of torture in *Jones v. United Kingdom*.[48] Applicants had sued Saudi Arabia and its officials in the United Kingdom claiming damages inter alia for torture, and alleged, in particular, that the grant of immunity in civil proceedings to Saudi Arabia and to the individual defendants violated their right of access to court under Article 6 of ECHR. The ECtHR determined that the sole question before it was whether a customary international law has developed to create a torture exception to State immunity since the ECtHR's earlier judgment in *Al-Adsani*.

After a comprehensive and magisterial review of the decisions of national courts and international tribunals both before and after the House of Lords judgment in *Jones v. Saudi Arabia*, the ECtHR concluded:

> In recent years, both prior to and following the House of Lords judgment in the present case, a number of national jurisdictions have considered

46. *Al-Adsani*, paras. 40–41.

47. *Id.*, para. 61.

48. *Jones v. United Kingdom* [2014] ECHR 34356/06.

> whether there is now a *jus cogens* exception to State immunity in civil claims against the State. . . . "[49]
>
> However, it is not necessary for the Court to examine all of these developments in detail since the recent judgment of the International Court of Justice in *Germany v. Italy* . . . which must be considered by this Court as authoritative as regards the content of customary international law—clearly establishes that, by February 2012, no *jus cogens* exception to State immunity had yet crystallised. The application by the English courts of the provisions of the 1978 Act to uphold the Kingdom of Saudi Arabia's claim to immunity in 2006 cannot therefore be said to have amounted to an unjustified restriction on the applicant's access to a court. It follows that there has been no violation of Article 6 § 1 of the Convention as regards the striking out of [the] complaint against the Kingdom of Saudi Arabia.[50]

With respect to the claims against the State officials, the Court noted that their immunity belongs to the State who can invoke or waive it. "Where, as in the present case, the grant of immunity *ratione materiae* to officials was intended to comply with international law on State immunity, then as in the case where immunity is granted to the State itself, the aim of the limitation on access to court is legitimate."[51] It noted the argument that immunity of State officials has been abrogated by the Torture Convention, which, it is claimed, provides in its Article 14 for universal civil jurisdiction, but it found the matter far from settled.[52] It found highly persuasive the lengthy and comprehensive judgment of the House of Lords and its conclusion "that customary international law did not admit of any exception—regarding allegations of conduct amounting to torture—to the general rule of immunity *ratione materiae* for State officials in the sphere of civil claims where immunity is enjoyed by the State itself."[53] It, therefore, held that the grant of immunity to the State officials under the UK SIA did not violate Article 6(1) of the Convention.[54]

Application of Treaty Law

Courts may consider treaty law in their determination of immunity vis-à-vis claims of violation of human rights or jus cogens norms. In *Holland v. Lampen-Wolfe*, the

49. *Id.*, para. 197.

50. *Id.*, para. 198.

51. *Id.*, para. 200.

52. *Id.*, para. 208.

53. *Id.*, para. 214.

54. *Id.*, para. 215.

House of Lords noted that the doctrine of State immunity is not inconsistent with Article 6 of the European Convention because it only "forbids a contracting state from denying individuals the benefits of its powers of adjudication; it does not extend the scope of those powers."[55] Furthermore, "[i]t presupposes that the contracting states have the powers of adjudication necessary to resolve the issues in dispute. But it does not confer on contracting states adjudicative powers which they do not possess. State immunity . . . is a creature of customary international law and derives from the equality of sovereign states. It is not a self-imposed restriction on the jurisdiction of its courts which the United Kingdom has chosen to adopt. It is a limitation imposed from without upon the sovereignty of the United Kingdom itself."[56]

It continued: "The Convention derives its binding force from the consent of the contracting states. The United Kingdom cannot, by its own act of acceding to the Convention and without the consent of the United States, obtain a power of adjudication over the United States which international law denies it."[57]

The ECtHR has examined the issue of State immunity vis-à-vis the right of access to court as enshrined in Article 6 § 1 in various contexts and has developed a consistent jurisprudence:

> The . . . right to a fair hearing, as guaranteed by Article 6 § 1 of the Convention, must be construed in light of the principle of the rule of law, which requires that all litigants should have an effective judicial remedy enabling them to assert their civil rights. . . . Article 6 § 1 embodies the "right to a court", of which the right of access, that is, the right to institute proceedings before courts in civil matters, constitutes one aspect only.
>
> However, the right of access to a court secured by Article 6 § 1 of the Convention is not absolute, but may be subject to limitations; these are permitted by implication since the right of access by its very nature calls for regulation by the State. In this respect, the Contracting States enjoy a certain margin of appreciation, although the final decision as to the observance of the Convention's requirements rests with the Court. . . .
>
> The Convention, including Article 6, cannot be interpreted in a vacuum. The Court must therefore be mindful of the Convention's special character as a human rights treaty, and it must also take the relevant rules of international law into account, including those relating to the grant of State immunity.

55. *Holland v. Lampen-Wolfe*, [2000] 1 WLR 1573, para. 49 (Judgment of Lord Millett).

56. *Id.*, para. 50.

57. *Id.*, para. 51.

> It follows that measures taken by a High Contracting Party which reflect generally recognised rules of public international law on State immunity cannot in principle be regarded as imposing a disproportionate restriction on the right to access to court as embodied in Article 6 § 1. Just as the right of access to a court is an inherent part of the fair trial guarantee in that Article, so some restrictions on access must likewise be regarded as inherent, an example being those limitations generally accepted by the community of nations as part of the doctrine of State immunity.
>
> Therefore, in cases where the application of the principle of State immunity from jurisdiction restricts the exercise of the right of access to a court, the Court must ascertain whether the circumstances of the case justify such restriction.
>
> The Court further reiterates that such limitation must pursue a legitimate aim and that State immunity was developed in international law out of the principle *par in parem non habet imperium*, by virtue of which one State could not be subject to the jurisdiction of another. It has taken the view that the grant of immunity to a State in civil proceedings pursues the legitimate aim of complying with international law to promote comity and good relations between States through the respect of another State's sovereignty.
>
> In addition, the impugned restriction must also be proportionate to the aim pursued.[58]

In *Ex Parte Pinochet 3*,[59] the House of Lords interpreted a treaty in its determination of whether a violation of jus cogens norms operated as an exception to immunity. The Court based its jurisdiction in the case on the Torture Convention, although Lords Browne-Wilkinson, Hope, Hutton, Saville, Millett, and Phillips considered that torture, as jus cogens violation, cannot be an official act for purposes of immunity *ratione materiae*. The dates on which Chile, Spain, and the United Kingdom respectively ratified the Torture Convention were critical to when Senator Augusto Pinochet Ugarte lost immunity for the alleged torture. Six of the seven judges agreed that he was not immune, but differed on when he lost the immunity.

Pinochet, the former head of State of Chile, was arrested, pursuant to an international arrest warrant issued by Spain, during a private visit to England for medical treatment. He challenged his extradition, and at issue during the extradition

58. *Sabel El Leil v.* France, App No. 34869/52 [2011] ECHR 1055, paras. 46–53 [citations omitted].

59. *R v Bow Street Metropolitan Stipendiary Magistrate and others, ex parte Pinochet Ugarte (Amnesty International and others intervening) (No 3)*, [2000] 1 AC 147, [1999] 2 All ER 97, [1999] 2 WLR 827.

proceedings was whether his immunity *ratione materiae* has been excluded under the Torture Convention to which the three States involved in the proceedings are all signatories. The law lords took disparate positions on the issue, and their judgments ended up raising more issues than they resolved. In the end, they variously took the view that the Torture Convention did not alter the immunity *ratione personae* of a head of State but that the immunity *ratione materiae* of a head of State should be limited, even though they differed on the scope of the limitation. The case did not address the immunity of a foreign State itself from the civil jurisdiction for acts of torture.

Lord Goff of Chieveley, in his judgment, noted that "the mere fact that the conduct is criminal does not of itself exclude the immunity, otherwise there would be little point in the immunity from criminal process; and this is so even where the crime is of a serious nature. It follows, in my opinion, that the mere fact that the crime in question is torture does not exclude state immunity."[60] He concluded that the Convention did not abrogate the immunity, and adopted the reasoning of Lord Slynn of Hadley in the first Appellate Committee:

> It does not seem to me that it has been shown that there is any state practice or general consensus let alone a widely supported convention that all crimes against international law should be justiciable in national courts on the basis of the universality of jurisdiction. Nor is there any *jus cogens* in respect of such breaches of international law which require that a claim of state or head of state immunity, itself a well-established principle of international law, should be overridden.[61]

Lord Hope of Craighead in his judgment stated that "even in the field of . . . high crimes as have achieved the status of *jus cogens* under customary international law there is as yet no general agreement that they are outside the immunity to which former heads of state are entitled from the jurisdiction of foreign national courts."[62] He declined to "accept that it was an implied term of the Torture Convention that former heads of state were to be deprived of their immunity *ratione materiae* with respect to all acts of torture as defined [in the Convention]."[63]

Lord Saville of Newdigate in his own judgment stated that there was no exception or qualification of immunity *ratione materiae* for torture before the coming

60. *Ex Parte Pinochet* 3.

61. *Id.* (Judgment of Lord Goff), citing [1998] 4 ALL ER 897 at 913, [1998] 3 WLR 1456 at 1473.

62. *Id.* (Judgment of Lord Hope).

63. *Id.*

into force of the Torture Convention, but concluded that the Convention expressly and unequivocally waived State immunity:

> So far as the states that are parties to the convention are concerned, I cannot see how, so far as torture is concerned, this immunity can exist consistently with the terms of that convention. Each state party has agreed that the other state parties can exercise jurisdiction over alleged official tortures found within their territories, by extraditing them or referring them to their own appropriate authorities for prosecution; and thus, to my mind, can hardly simultaneously claim an immunity from extradition or prosecution that is necessarily based on the official nature of the alleged torture.[64]

Lord Phillips of Worth Matravers in his own judgment ruled:

> The convention is . . . incompatible with the applicability of immunity *ratione materiae*. There are only two possibilities. One is that the state parties to the convention proceeded on the premise that no immunity could exist *ratione materiae* in respect of torture, a crime contrary to international law. The other is that the state parties to the convention expressly agreed that immunity *ratione materiae* should not apply in the case of torture. I believe that the first of these alternatives is the correct.[65]

Lord Millett in his (dissenting) judgment held:

> The definition of torture . . . in the [Torture] convention . . . is in my opinion entirely inconsistent with the existence of a plea of immunity *ratione materiae*. The offence can be committed only by or at the instigation of, or with the consent or acquiescence of, a public official or other person acting in an official capacity. The official or governmental nature of the act, which forms the basis of the immunity, is an essential ingredient of the offence. No rational system of criminal justice can allow an immunity which is co-extensive with the offence.[66]

He reasoned:

> The international community had created an offence for which immunity ratione materiae could not possibly be available. International law cannot

64. *Id.* (Judgment of Lord Saville).

65. *Id.* (Judgment of Lord Phillips).

66. *Id.* (Judgment of Lord Millett).

> be supposed to have established a crime having the character of a jus cogens and at the same time to have provided an immunity which is co-extensive with the obligation it seeks to impose.[67]

In the *Arrest Warrant Case,* the ICJ noted "although various international conventions on the prevention and punishment of certain serious crimes impose on States obligations of prosecution or extraclition, thereby requiring them to extend their criminal jurisdiction, such extension of jurisdiction in no way affects immunities under customary international law, including those of Ministers for Foreign Affairs. These remain opposable before the courts of a foreign State, even where those courts exercise such a jurisdiction under these conventions."[68]

Official versus Private Nature of Act

Courts may decide on the application of immunity based on the nature of the impugned act. The House of Lords returned to the issue of torture and State immunity in *Jones v. Saudi Arabia* in a claim against a foreign State and its officials for allegedly torturing the claimants in the territory of the foreign State.[69] The House of Lords framed the issue as follows:

> The issue turns on the relationship, in these circumstances, between two principles of international law. One principle, historically the older of the two, is that one sovereign state will not, save in certain specified instances, assert its judicial authority over another. The second principle, of more recent vintage but of the highest authority among principles of international law, is one that condemns and criminalises the official practice of torture, requires states to suppress the practice and provides for the trial and punishment of officials found to be guilty of it.[70]

It stated that it "must consider the balance currently struck in international law 'between the condemnation of torture as an international crime against humanity and the principle that states must treat each other as equals not to be subjected to each other's jurisdiction.' "[71] The argument by claimants is that the proscription of torture by international law is a jus cogens norm that "precludes

67. *Id.*

68. *Arrest Warrant Case,* para. 59.

69. *Jones v. Saudi Arabia* [2006] UKHL 26, [2007] 1 All ER 113, [2006] BHRC 621.

70. *Id.*, para. 1, Judgment of Lord Bingham of Cornhill.

71. *Id.*

the grant of immunity to states or individuals sued for committing acts of torture, since such cannot be governmental acts or exercises of state authority entitled to protection of state immunity *ratione materiae*."[72] Lord Bingham, in his judgment, disagreed "that torture cannot be a governmental or official act, since under art 1 of the Torture Convention torture must, to qualify as such, be inflicted by or with connivance of a public official or other person acting in an official capacity."[73] It construed Article 14 of the Torture Convention as not providing for universal jurisdiction.[74] It noted:

> [T]here is no evidence that states have recognised or given effect to an international law obligation to exercise universal jurisdiction over claims arising from alleged breaches of peremptory norms of international law, nor is there any consensus of judicial and learned opinion that they should. This is significant, since these are sources of international law. But this lack of evidence is not neutral: since the rule on immunity is well-understood and established, and no relevant exception is generally accepted, the rule prevails.[75]

Lord Hoffmann, in his judgment, noted that no rule of national or international law justifies torture, but that the issue is whether the prohibition against torture conflicts with State immunity.[76] He stated:

> To produce a conflict with state immunity, it is therefore necessary to show that the prohibition on torture has generated an ancillary procedural rule which, by way of exception to state immunity, entitles or perhaps requires states to assume civil jurisdiction over other states in cases in which torture is alleged. Such a rule may be desirable and, since international law changes, may have developed.[77]

He concluded that an act of torture must be official to come within the Torture Convention, and "would reject the argument that torture or some other

72. *Id.*, para. 17.

73. *Id.*, para. 19.

74. See *id.*, para. 25.

75. *Id.*, para. 27.

76. *Id.*, para. 43, Judgment of Lord Hoffmann.

77. *Id.*, para. 45.

contravention of a *jus cogens* cannot attract immunity *ratione materiae* because it cannot be an official act."[78]

The House of Lords unanimously dismissed Jones's appeal and allowed Saudi Arabia's appeal The *Jones* case is distinct from the *Pinochet* case where the jus cogens violation was not considered an official act in a criminal proceeding, and the Torture Convention was not at issue in the former, where torture was considered an official act attracting immunity in civil proceedings.

The conundrum is whether torture, although conceded as abhorrent, can be an official function for purposes of State immunity under the same international law that prohibits torture.[79] The Canadian Supreme Court stated that the heinous nature of torture does not transform the act of officials into a private act but "it is the state-sanctioned or official nature of torture that makes it such a despicable crime."[80] It concluded that the respondents in Kazemi Estate were public officials acting in their official capacity when carrying out the torture and, therefore, immune from the jurisdiction of Canadian courts under the Canadian SIA.[81] It noted that others have questioned "how can torture be an official function for purpose of immunity under international law when international law itself universally prohibits torture"[82] but Canada, in conjunction with the United States, has taken the position that the Torture Convention does not require the provision of civil remedies for torture in a foreign State.[83] "While the prohibition of torture is certainly a *jus cogens* norm from which Canada cannot derogate (and is also very likely a principle of fundamental justice), the question . . . is whether this norm extends in such a way as to require each state to provide a civil remedy for torture committed abroad by a foreign state."[84]

The heinousness of torture does not denude the act of its officialness. Torture is carried out by the State and it is the officialness of it that brings it within the contemplation of the legal instruments that prohibit it. Dwelling on whether torture can be an official act conflates a moral question with a legal question. Torture is an opprobrious act and even more so when it is perpetrated at the instigation of the State and with the coercive powers of the State. "An international crime is as offensive, if not more offensive, to the international community when committed

78. *Id.*, para. 85.

79. See *Kazemi Estate*, para. 173 (Dissent of Justice Abella).

80. *Id.*, para. 95.

81. *Id.*, para. 98.

82. *Id.*, para. 173 [citation omitted], (Dissent of Justice Abella).

83. *Id.*, para. 141.

84. *Id.*, para. 152.

under the colour of office."[85] Illegal and unlawful acts are often done officially. Therefore, to deny immunity on the basis of whether a violation of jus cogens norm is an official act is both logically and legally unpersuasive. An oppressive government, by contemporary human rights standards, still performs functions of State and its officials still act officially. The official and private acts dichotomy in the context of criminal proceedings is an unavailing attempt at adopting the *jure imperii* and *jure gestionis* distinction from civil proceedings in the determination of State immunity.

Nature of the Immunity

The distinction between immunity *ratione personae* and immunity *ratione materiae* may have a bearing on the determination of the applicability of any exception to immunity. Immunity *ratione personae* attaches to all public or private acts. Under customary international law, incumbent head of State and high-ranking State officials, such as foreign ministers, have immunity *ratione personae* in criminal proceedings for even jus cogens violations. However, this immunity is *ratione temporis* and does not survive when the head of State or official ceases to be in office. Immunity *ratione materiae,* on the other hand, is not as coextensive because it protects the beneficiaries only for what is considered official acts. In *Pinochet* 3, Lord Browne-Wilkinson ruled that Senator Pinochet as a former head of State enjoyed immunity *ratione materiae* for acts done in his official functions as head of State. Lord Hope expressed similar views: "The principle of immunity *ratione materiae* protects all acts which the head of state has performed in the exercise of the functions of government." He also stated that this principle admits of only two exceptions under customary international law: (1) criminal acts under color of authority but actually for the pleasure or benefit of the head of State, and (2) acts that have acquired jus cogens status. He, however, noted that for acts that violate jus cogens norms, "there is as yet no general agreement that they are outside the immunity to which former heads of state are entitled from the jurisdiction of foreign national courts."[86]

Lord Goff stated: "There can be no doubt that the immunity of a head of state, whether *ratione personae* or *ratione materiae,* applies to both civil and criminal proceedings."[87] Similarly, Lord Saville noted:

> In general, under customary international law, serving heads of state enjoy immunity from criminal proceedings in other countries by virtue of holding

85. *Ex Parte Pinochet* 3, Judgment of Lord Phillips of Worth Matravers.

86. *Id.*, Judgment of Lord Browne-Wilkinson.

87. *Id.*, Judgment of Lord Goff.

> that office. This form of immunity is known as immunity *ratione personae*. It covers all conduct of the head of state while the person concerned holds that office and this draws no distinction between what the head of state does in his official capacity (ie what he does as head of state for state purpose) and what he does in his private capacity.

Lord Saville also noted that a former head of State does not enjoy immunity *ratione personae* but enjoys immunity *ratione materiae* generally under customary international law "from criminal proceedings in other countries in respect of what he did in his official capacity as head of state."[88] He was of the view that the immunity *ratione personae* of a serving head of State attaches to the office and not to any particular conduct of the office holder and, as such, it does not follow that the immunity is removed in cases of torture. With respect to a former head of State, he was of the view that the immunity attaches to that person's conduct in office and revolves around what he did in his official capacity.

Lord Phillips put it this way: "While a head of state is serving, his status ensures him immunity. Once he is out of office, he is in the same position as any other state official and any immunity will be based upon the nature of the subject matter of the litigation."[89]

Lord Millett distinguished between immunity *ratione personae* and immunity *ratione materiae* and noted that the former was not in issue in the case as Pinochet was not a serving head of State. Lord Millett was of the view that the alleged acts by Pinochet were public and official, and that "immunity is available whether the acts in question are illegal or unconstitutional or otherwise unauthorized under the internal law of the state, since the whole purpose of state immunity is to prevent the legality of such acts from being adjudicated upon in the municipal courts of a foreign state."[90] He, however, opined that "crimes prohibited by international law attract universal jurisdiction under customary international law if two criteria are satisfied. First, they must be contrary to a peremptory norm of international law so as to infringe a *jus cogens*. Secondly, they must be so serious and on such a scale that they can justly be regarded as an attack on the international legal order."[91] He concluded that there was a jus cogens exception to immunity *ratione materiae*: "International law cannot be supposed to have established

88. *Id.*

89. *Id.*, Judgment of Lord Phillips.

90. *Id.*, Judgment of Lord Millett (Dissent).

91. *Id.*

a crime having the character of a *jus cogens* and at the same time to have provided an immunity which is co-extensive with the obligation it seeks to impose."[92]

Procedural versus Substantive Rules or Norms

The ICJ's latest pronouncement on the relationship between jus cogens and State immunity was in *Jurisdictional Immunities of the State (Germany v. Italy: Greece Intervening)*,[93] where Germany instituted proceedings against Italy for allegedly violating its obligation under international law by failing to respect Germany's jurisdictional immunity under international law and allowing civil claims against Germany in Italian courts based on violation of international humanitarian law during World War II. The Court stated that the question for it to decide was not the uncontested illegality of the acts perpetrated by the German armed forces and other organs of the German Reich during the war, but "whether or not, in proceedings regarding claims for compensation arising out of these acts, the Italian courts were obliged to accord Germany immunity."[94] It also noted that Germany and Italy agreed that immunity is not a mere matter of comity but is governed by international law, and in this case by customary international law rather than treaty.

Regarding the relationship between jus cogens and State immunity, the ICJ stated that the issue is whether there is a conflict between the two rules of international law. It opined that no such conflict exists, as both rules address different matters:

> The rules of State immunity are procedural in character and are confined to determining whether or not the courts of one State may exercise jurisdiction in respect of another State. They do not bear upon the question of whether or not the conduct in respect of which the proceedings are brought was lawful or unlawful.[95]

The ICJ observed:

> A *jus cogens* rule is one from which no derogation is permitted but the rules which determine the scope and extent of jurisdiction and when jurisdiction

92. *Id.*

93. Jurisdictional Immunities of the State (*Germany v. Italy: Greece Intervening*), Judgment, 2012 I.C.J. Rep. 99 ("*Jurisdictional Immunities of the State*").

94. *Id.*, para. 53.

95. *Id.*, para. 93

> may be exercised do not derogate from those substantive rules which possess jus cogens status, nor is there anything inherent in the concept of jus cogens which would require their modification or would displace their application.[96]

Finally, the ICJ noted that it was not alone in rejecting the argument that jus cogens rules trump those of State immunity, as several national courts have done so, and none of the national legislation it examined has restricted immunity for alleged violations of jus cogens.[97] It, therefore, held that the decision by the Italian courts denying Germany immunity to which it is entitled under customary international law constitutes a breach of international obligation of Italy to Germany.[98]

Nature of the Proceedings

Courts may distinguish between civil and criminal proceedings in the determination of State immunity.[99] In this regard, the Canadian Supreme Court has stated that "[w]hile an exception to immunity for *jus cogens* violations exists in the criminal context, no such exception has developed in the civil context."[100] It also stated:

> Whether or not these distinctions are convincing as a matter of policy is of secondary importance. The fact of the matter is that Canada has expressly created an exception to immunity for criminal proceedings, and has stopped short of doing so for civil suits involving *jus cogens* violations (*SIA*, s. 18; a similar exception also exists in the United Kingdom's *State Immunity Act 1978*, c. 33, s. 16(4)).[101]

In *Gaddafi*, the French Court of Cassation held that there was no jus cogens exception to the immunity *ratione personae* of an incumbent head of State of a foreign State from criminal proceedings in the courts of a forum State under customary international law.[102] In this case, criminal proceedings had been brought

96. *Id.*, para. 95.

97. *Id.*, para. 96.

98. *Id.*, para. 107.

99. See, e.g., *Jones v. United Kingdom*, ECtHR, para. 212.

100. See *Kazemi Estate*, para. 103.

101. *Id.*, para. 104.

102. *Gaddafi*, Court of Cassation, Paris, France, 13 March 2001, 125 ILR 490 (2004).

in French courts against the Libyan leader in connection with a terrorist attack that blew up an airline, killing 170 passengers including a number of French citizens. At the proceedings, it was examined whether there existed a jus cogens norm for international crimes superior to the rule of immunity of heads of State under customary international law. The Court of Appeal of Paris concluded that although head of State immunity was recognized under international law, no immunity could cover complicity in the terrorist attack. The Court of Cassation, however, reversed the Court of Appeal and ruled that under the current state of international law the alleged crime, no matter how serious, did not constitute an exception to head of State immunity, and terminated the proceedings.

States acts through their officials. Though a State can be held liable in civil proceedings, it cannot be subjected to criminal proceedings because the criminal conduct can be committed only by the officials. In *Pinochet (3)*, four of the six law lords in the majority considered the criminal nature of the proceeding. In the *Arrest Warrant Case*, where the Democratic Republic of Congo had instituted proceedings against Belgium in respect of the arrest warrant issued by Belgium against the minister for foreign affairs of Congo for alleged war crimes and crimes against humanity, the ICJ noted that under international law, high-ranking officials of a foreign State, such as head of State, head of government, and minister of foreign affairs, enjoy immunity in both civil and criminal jurisdiction of forum States.[103] The ICJ concluded that a minister of foreign affairs enjoys full immunity from criminal jurisdiction while in office.[104]

The ICJ stated that its examination of State practice, including national legislation and judicial decisions, did not reveal any exception, under customary international law, for such crimes to the immunity from criminal jurisdiction for ministers of foreign affairs.[105] It distinguished the immunity from criminal jurisdiction and individual criminal responsibility: "While jurisdictional immunity is procedural in nature, criminal responsibility is a question of substantive law."[106] The ICJ then concluded that the issue of the arrest warrant by Belgium violated the immunity of the minister of foreign affairs from criminal jurisdiction under international law.[107] Thus, according to the ICJ, there is no exception to the immunity of the minister of foreign affairs from criminal prosecution.

103. See *Arrest Warrant Case*, para. 51.

104. See *id.*, paras. 54–55.

105. See *id.*, para. 58.

106. See *id.*, para. 60.

107. See *id.*, para. 70.

The question is whether considering the principle of *aut dedere aut judicare,*[108] a forum State has an obligation erga omnes under international law to adjudicate the civil or criminal responsibility of a foreign official who is properly within its territorial jurisdiction. The Torture Convention does not provide for universal jurisdiction as it requires one of the traditional basis for jurisdiction, namely territorial or nationality. The "extradite or prosecute" obligation in treaties does not confer jurisdiction but is an exhortation to exercise an extant jurisdiction. "By the loose use of language [the obligation] has come to be referred to as 'universal jurisdiction', though this is really an obligatory territorial jurisdiction over persons, albeit in relation to acts committed elsewhere."[109]

The prohibition of torture is a question of prescriptive jurisdiction as opposed to adjudicative jurisdiction. The prohibition imposes an obligation on a State to criminalize the conduct under its national law. Traditionally, territory, nationality, protection, or passive personality form the basis for jurisdiction as each evinces a kind of link to the forum State. A treaty may provide independent and separate grounds for jurisdiction. Criminal jurisdiction is normally *ratione loci,*[110] except in the case of extraterritorial offenses.[111] Universal jurisdiction is justified where a matter is of a universal concern and legal interest to the international community.[112] "Some of the corresponding rights to protection have entered into the body of general international law . . . ; others are conferred by international instruments of a universal or quasi-universal character."[113] Justification for the existence of universal jurisdiction does not equate justification for the exercise of the jurisdiction. In its pure form, universal jurisdiction does not require a nexus to the forum State. Obviously, universal jurisdiction is controversial and unsettled. Universal jurisdiction exists for piracy and aircraft hijacking as these crimes occur normally outside the territorial jurisdiction of any particular State. Where there is universal jurisdiction for an international crime, then the question whether

108. Latin for either "extradite" or "prosecute."

109. *Arrest WarrantCase,* Joint Separate Opinion of Judges Higgins, Kooijmans, and Buergenthal, para. 41.

110. Latin for "by reason of the place." An alternative term is *ratione territoriae,* which is Latin for "by reason of the territory."

111. See *Lotus Case (France v. Turkey),* P.C.I.J. 1927 (Series A) No. 10, p. 19 ("The territoriality of criminal law . . . is not an absolute principle of international law and by no means coincides with territorial sovereignty.").

112. See Barcelona Traction, Light and Power Company, Limited, Judgment, 1970 I.C.J. Rep. p. 3, para. 33. ("*Barcelona Traction*") ("In view of the importance of the rights involved, all States can be held to have a legal interest in their protection; they are obligations *erga omnes.*")

113. *Id.,* para. 34.

there is immunity is redundant because the essence of the jurisdiction is to not permit the plea of immunity for such acts. This approach has led to the argument that immunity is inapplicable for jus cogens violations because acts that violate the norm cannot be official acts as to benefit from immunity *ratione materiae*. Another argument deriving from this approach is that these acts, without going into whether they are official or private, are excluded from the benefit of immunity as an exception. The argument about the existence of universal jurisdiction and the absence of immunity ab initio accords with the judgment of Lord Millett in *Pinochet (3)*:

> In my opinion there was no immunity to be waived. The offence is one which could only be committed in circumstances which would normally give rise to the immunity. The international community had created an offence for which immunity ratione materiae could not possibly be available. International law cannot be supposed to have established a crime having the character of a jus cogens and at the same time to have provided an immunity which is co-extensive with the obligation it seeks to impose.[114]

Lord Millett opined that "acts which attract state immunity in civil proceedings because they are characterised as acts of sovereign power may, for the very same reason, attract individual criminal liability."[115]

The prohibition of an international crime, such as torture, does not necessarily imply the presence of universal jurisdiction. However, as noted by the ICJ, State parties to the Convention Against Torture "have committed themselves to prosecuting suspects in particular on the basis of universal jurisdiction."[116] Where Belgium had brought proceedings against Senegal over a dispute as to whether Senegal complied with its obligation under the Convention Against Torture to prosecute or extradite the former president of Chad, ICJ held that the purpose of the treaty "is to prevent alleged perpetrators of acts of torture from going unpunished [and that the] State in whose territory the suspect is present does indeed have the option of extraditing him to . . . a State which has jurisdiction in some capacity, pursuant to Article 5 of the Convention, to prosecute and try him."[117]

114. *Ex Parte Pinochet* 3, Lord Millett, para. 651.

115. *Id.*

116. *Questions relating to the Obligation to Prosecute or Extradite (Belgium v. Senegal), Judgment, I.C.J. Reports 2012*, p. 422, para. 75.

117. *Id.*, para. 120.

Conflicting Norms Approach

Judge Al-Khaswneh in his dissent in the *Arrest Warrant Case* made a credible case for a jus cogens exception to immunity:

> The effective combating of grave crimes has arguably assumed a *jus cogens* character reflecting recognition by the international community of the vital community interests and values it seeks to protect and enhance. Therefore when this hierarchically higher norm comes into conflict with the rules on immunity, it should prevail. Even if we are to speak in terms of reconciliation of the two sets of rules, this would suggest to me a much more restrictive interpretation of the immunities of high-ranking officials than the Judgment portrays. Incidentally, such a restrictive approach would be much more in consonance with the now firmly established move towards a restrictive concept of State immunity, a move that has removed the bar regarding the submission of States to jurisdiction of other States often expressed in the maxim *par in parem non habet imperium*. It is difficult to see why States would accept that their conduct with regard to important areas of their development be open to foreign judicial proceedings but not the criminal conduct of their officials.[118]

A U.S. court has asserted that "under international and domestic law, officials from other countries are not entitled to foreign official immunity for *jus cogens* violations, even if the acts were performed in the defendant's official capacity."[119] In a civil action under the Alien Tort Statute (ATS) and the Torture Victim Protection Act (TVPA), the plaintiffs had alleged "torture, arbitrary detention and extrajudicial killings" by the government of Somalia at the instigation of Samantar when he was variously minister of defense and then prime minister before the government fell and he fled to the United States and became a permanent legal resident. Samantar had claimed that he was entitled to head of State immunity because he was prime minister when the alleged wrongdoings occurred, as well as foreign official immunity because the actions were taken in the course and scope of his official functions. The Court noted that a head of State recognized by the United States is immune from jurisdiction unless that immunity is waived by statute or by a recognized foreign government, and then gave absolute deference to that State Department's position that it recognized neither Samantar as head of State of Somalia nor any government of Somalia from which the immunity of Samantar would derive.

The plaintiffs had argued that Samantar cannot invoke immunity for acts that violate jus cogens norm. The Court noted that "as a matter of international

118. *Arrest Warrant Case*, Dissent of Judge Al-Khaswneh, para. 7.

119. *Yousuf v. Samantar*, 699 F.3d 763, 777 (4th Cir. 2012).

and domestic law, jus cogens violations are, by definition, acts that are not officially authorized by the Sovereign."[120] It also noted that allegations of jus cogens violations do not abrogate status-based immunity, such as head of State immunity, citing the *Arrest Warrant* Case.[121] It further noted: "American courts have generally followed the . . . trend, concluding that *jus cogens* violations are not legitimate official acts and therefore do not merit foreign official immunity but still recognize that head-of-state immunity, based on status, is of an absolute nature and applies even against jus cogens claims."[122] It, therefore, held that there is no "foreign official immunity for jus cogens violations, even if the acts were performed in the defendant's official capacity."[123]

Proponents and paladins of a human rights or jus cogens exception to immunity posit that there is a vertical international legal order with human rights at its apex and, as such, when human rights norms conflict with other international law norms, such as sovereign immunity, then the human rights obligation should trump all other obligations. Some have argued that a violation of jus cogens norms waives an otherwise applicable immunity. The argument confuses waiver with exception and does not resolve the fundamental question about whether there is a jus cogens exception to State immunity. An exception abrogates immunity ab initio but a waiver restores jurisdiction where an immunity already existed. Moreover, if the violation of jus cogens norms operates as a waiver, then it means the norm is not superior to State immunity in the hierarchy of norms, but if it is an exception, on the other hand, then it means that it trumps State immunity. In sum, judicial decisions reveal that no customary international law of jus cogens exception to State immunity exists, considering that the requisite elements, that is, State practice and *opinio juris*, for the development of such a customary international law have not yet crystallized. Thus, the current debate is mostly about what the law should be, not what the law is.

RELATED BUT DIFFERENT DOCTRINE

Act of State Doctrine

Jurisprudence

The Act of State doctrine is both related to and different from the rule of State immunity. It has developed doctrinally in the domestic law of States out of respect for sovereign equality and international comity. But unlike State immunity, the

120. *Id.* at 776.

121. *Id.* at 777, n.6.

122. *Id.* at 777 [citations omitted].

123. *Id.* at 777.

doctrine is neither based upon nor required by international law. The question usually is whether a court should decide a case involving the acts of a foreign State, after the court has determined that it has jurisdiction to hear the case and immunity is not available to the foreign State. The Act of State doctrine restrains courts in the forum State from adjudicating certain transactions of foreign States.[124] Although the Act of State doctrine exists to a varying extent in various countries, it is primarily a creature and feature of Anglo-American common law tradition, with cross-fertilization across the Atlantic between the United States and the United Kingdom. In *Buttes Gas (No. 3)*, Lord Wilberforce, in a unanimous judgment, opined that "there is, and for long has been, such a general principle, starting in English law, adopted and generalized in the law of the United States of America which is effective and compelling in English courts. This principle is not one of discretion, but is inherent in the very nature of the judicial process."[125] He stated that "the ultimate question what issues are capable, and what are incapable, of judicial determination must be answered in closely similar terms in whatever country they arise, depending, as they must, upon any appreciation of the nature and limits of the judicial function."[126]

However, in *Belhaj v. Straw, and Rahmatullah (No 1) v. Ministry of Defence*, Lord Mance noted: "The reasoning and nuances of United States law have not been constant and are not necessarily transposable to English law."[127] Lord Neuberger, for his part, cautioned:

> [The] decisions of courts of the United States, which have purported to adopt the Doctrine as initially developed in this jurisdiction, appears to me to be of very limited assistance. This is for three reasons. First, the constitutional arrangements and conventions in the USA are very different from those in the United Kingdom. Secondly, much of the reasoning in the cases where act of state was first referred to as principle (*Hatch v Baez* (1876) 7 Hun 596 and *Underhill v Hernandez* 168 US 250 (1897)) was really directed to the different doctrine of state immunity. And thirdly, the justification for the doctrine of act of state has been cast by the US Supreme Court . . . which ties in very well with the first reason.[128]

124. See *Buttes Gas and Oil Co. v. Hammer (No. 3)*, [1982] AC 888, 931; 3 All ER 616 (Lord Wilberforce) ("*Buttes Gas and Oil Co.*").

125. *Id.* at 932.

126. *Id.* at 936.

127. *Belhaj v. Straw, and Rahmatullah (No 1) v. Ministry of Defence* [2017] UKSC 3, at 57 ("*Belhaj*").

128. *Id.* at 134.

England

The English origin of the doctrine is traced to *Blad v. Bamfield*,[129] and *Duke of Brunswick v. King of Hanover*.[130] In the former case, the court declined to entertain proceedings against a Dane for the seizure of the property of English subjects in Iceland, which was sanctioned by the Danish authority. Lord Chancellor Nottingham stated that to involve the court in judging the validity of the patent from the king of Denmark for trade in Iceland and to "try whether the English have a right to trade in Iceland, is monstrous and absurd."[131] In the latter case, the Duke of Brunswick had been deposed and the king of Hanover took possession of his property as guardian. When the Duke brought a bill in the Court of Chancery against the king of Hanover for an account, the court refused to entertain the case. Lord Chancellor Cottenham stated that the English courts "cannot sit in judgment upon an act of a Sovereign, effected by virtue of his Sovereign authority abroad, an act not done as a British subject, but supposed to be done in the exercise of his authority vested in him as Sovereign."[132]

The Act of State doctrine re-emerged in English law in *Luther v. Sagor*,[133] where it was applied so as to not inquire into the validity of the Russian expropriation decree declaring Russian sawmills to be the property of the Russian Soviet Republic. The British government had recognized the State. The recognition was given retrospective effect, and the nationalization by Russia was determined legal and valid. The court stated that it was not at liberty to ignore and override legislative and executive acts of Russia affecting title to property in its territory.[134] The doctrine became firmly established in English law with the decision of the House of Lords in *Buttes Gas and Oil Co. v. Hammer (No. 2 and 3)*, where Lord Wilberforce stated that the doctrine is applicable where there are "no judicial or manageable standards by which to judge the issues" or where "the court will be in a judicial no-man's land."[135]

English law differentiates the Act of State doctrine into two, three, or four rules.[136] The first rule, which accords with private international law or conflicts of

129. *Blad v. Bamfield*, (1674) 3 Swans 604 ("*Blad*").

130. *Duke of Brunswick v. King of Hanover*, (1848) 2 HL Cas 1 ("*Duke of Brunswick*").

131. *Blad* at 607.

132. *Duke of Brunswick* at xx.

133. *Luther v. Sagor* [1921] 3 K.B. 532.

134. *Id.* at 549.

135. *Buttes Gas and Oil Co.* at 938.

136. See *Belhaj*. Although Lords Sumption, Mance, and Neuberger agreed that the (foreign) Act of State doctrine was subject to a public policy exception in the case, they did not quite agree on the difference in numbers or names of the rules under the doctrine.

law principles, recognizes and treats as valid a foreign State's legislation or other laws affecting movable or immovable property within the foreign State's jurisdiction, or regarding any act that takes place or has an effect within the territory of that State.[137] The second rule is that a forum court will not normally question the validity of any sovereign act with respect to property within the foreign State's jurisdiction, at least during periods of civil disorder. This rule distinguishes between legislative and executive acts of a foreign State but still accords them the same treatment.[138] Under the third rule, a forum court will abstain or refrain from adjudicating certain acts of a foreign State even if they occur outside the foreign State's jurisdiction.[139] This rule, which has several components, considers it inappropriate for English courts to resolve issues involving a challenge of the lawfulness of certain acts of a foreign State, such as dealings between sovereign States, or to determine the legality of the acts of a foreign State in the conduct of foreign affairs.[140] A possible fourth rule is that "the courts will not investigate acts of a foreign state where such an investigation would embarrass the government of our country: but that this doctrine only arises as a result of a communication from our Foreign Office."[141]

These fissiparous rules have been further differentiated into the municipal law Act of State and international law Act of State: "This distinction is supported by the case-law extending over more than three centuries . . . It is possible to extract two related principles from it. The first is concerned with the application to a state of its own municipal law, and the second with the application of international law to that state's dealings with other states."[142]

> Doctrine amounts to this, that the courts of the United Kingdom will not readily adjudicate upon the lawfulness or validity of sovereign acts of foreign states, and it applies to claims which, while not made against the foreign state concerned, involve an allegation that a foreign state has acted unlawfully. . . . Doctrine is purely one of domestic common law, and it has all the advantages and disadvantages of a principle that has been developed on a case by case basis by judges over the centuries. Thus, while it is pragmatic

137. *Id.*, para. 121.

138. *Id.* at 122.

139. See *id.* (Lord Mance), paras. 11, 35–45.

140. *Id.* at 123.

141. *Id.* at 124 citing *Yukos Capital v. Rosneft (No 2)* [2014] QB 458, (Rix LJ) para. 65.

142. *Belhaj,* (Lord Sumption), para. 227.

> and adaptable to changing norms . . . it is a principle whose precise scope is not always easy to identify.[143]

United States

Hatch v. Baez[144] is the first case to deal with the Act of State doctrine in the United States. The plaintiff sued the defendant, who was the president of the Dominican Republic, in New York, for injuries the plaintiff had suffered in the Dominican Republic as result of acts by the defendant in his official capacity as president. The Supreme Court of New York held:

> We think that, by the universal comity of nations and the established rules of international law, the courts of one country are bound to abstain from sitting in judgment on the acts of another government done within its own territory. Each state is sovereign throughout its domain. The acts of the defendant for which he is sued were done by him in the exercise of that part of the sovereignty of St. Domingo which belongs to the executive department of that government. To make him amenable to a foreign jurisdiction for such acts, would be a direct assault upon the sovereignty and independence of his country. The only remedy for such wrongs must be sought through the intervention of the person injured.[145]

The classic formulation of the doctrine in American law came from *Underhill v. Hernandez*. Underhill, a U.S. citizen, sued Hernandez, a Venezuelan military governor, who was in charge of a revolutionary army in Venezuela, for, amongst other things, unlawful confinement and assault by his soldiers when Underhill was in Venezuela under a government contract. The court refused to adjudicate the case against Hernandez on the grounds that his acts were those of the government of Venezuela and not justiciable in the U.S. courts. Chief Justice Fuller stated:

> Every sovereign State is bound to respect the independence of every other sovereign State, and the Courts of one country will not sit in judgment on the acts of the government of another done within its own territory. Redress of grievances by reason of such acts must be obtained through the means open to be availed of by sovereign powers as between themselves.[146]

143. *Id.* (Lord Neuberger), para. 118.

144. *Hatch v. Baez*, 7 Hun 596 (1876), 14 N.Y. Sup. Ct. 596 (1876).

145. *Id.* at 599–600.

146. *Underhill v. Hernandez*, 168 U.S. 250, 252 (1897).

Another major reiteration of the doctrine was *Banco Nacional de Cuba v. Sabbatino*.[147] The case was decided at the height of the Cold War, in the aftermath of the Cuban revolution, and the Cuban Missile Crisis and the Bay of Pigs invasion, which were both causes and consequences in the deterioration of the political and economic relations between the United States and Cuba. Instead of deciding on the legality of Cuba's nationalization of its sugar industry and the consequent expropriation of sugar business concerns owned by some American, the Supreme Court held that the Act of State doctrine barred suit alleging unlawful expropriation by a State. The U.S. Congress was outraged by the decision and consequently enacted a statute to reverse the Supreme Court's decision. The statute, known as the Second Hickenlooper Amendment, made the doctrine inapplicable to takings of property in violation of international law, if the property or proceeds of the property have been brought within the United States.[148] A taking is a violation of international law if it is retaliatory, discriminatory, and without adequate compensation.[149]

In *Kirkpatrick*, the United States Supreme Court recapitulated its jurisprudence on the doctrine:

> This Court's description of the jurisprudential foundation for the act of state doctrine has undergone some evolution over the years. We once viewed the doctrine as an expression of international law, resting upon "the highest considerations of international comity and expediency," *Oetjen v. Central Leather Co.*, 246 U.S. 297, 303–304 (1918). We have more recently described it, however, as a consequence of domestic separation of powers, reflecting "the strong sense of the Judicial Branch that its engagement in the task of passing on the validity of foreign acts of state may hinder" the conduct of foreign affairs, *Banco Nacional de Cuba v. Sabbatino*, 376 U.S. 398, 423 (1964). Some Justices have suggested possible exceptions to application of the doctrine, where one or both of the foregoing policies would seemingly not be served: an exception, for example, for acts of state that consist of commercial transactions, since neither modern international comity nor the current position of our Executive Branch accorded sovereign immunity to such acts, see *Alfred Dunhill of London, Inc. v. Republic of Cuba*, 425 U.S. 682, 695–706 (1976) (opinion of WHITE, J.); or an exception for cases in which the Executive Branch has represented that it has no

147. 376 U.S. 398 (1964).

148. See 22 U.S.C. § 2370(e)(2) (2006).

149. See *First Nat'l City Bank v. Banco Nacional de Cuba*, 406 U.S. 759, 775 (1971).

> objection to denying validity to the foreign sovereign act, since then the courts would be impeding no foreign policy goals, see *First National City Bank v. Banco Nacional de Cuba*, 406 U.S. 759, 768–770 (1972) (opinion of REHQUIST, J.).[150]

Kirkpatrick involved the alleged payment and receipt of bribes in the award of government contracts. The Court determined that the factual predicate for the application of the doctrine did not exist as nothing in the case required the Court to declare invalid the official act of a foreign State.[151] It noted that "neither the claim nor any asserted defense requires a determination that Nigeria's contract with Kirkpatrick International was, or was not, effective."[152] The only issue was whether the alleged bribes had occurred, not whether bribery was illegal under Nigerian law, as it was common knowledge that Nigerian law prohibited bribery. "Act of state issues only arise when a court *must decide*—that is, when the outcome of the case turns upon—the effect of the official action by a foreign sovereign."[153] The Court unanimously held that the Act of State doctrine was inapplicable in the case and ultimately declared:

> The short of the matter is this: Courts in the United States have the power, and ordinarily the obligation to decide cases and controversies properly presented to them. The act of state doctrine does not establish an exception for cases and controversies that may embarrass foreign governments, but merely requires that, in the process of deciding, the acts of foreign sovereign taken within their own jurisdiction shall be deemed valid.[154]

Kirkpatrick, therefore, stands for the proposition that the Act of State doctrine does not apply where the only issue to decide is whether certain acts had occurred, not whether they were invalid or wrongful. A court's characterization or framing of the issue to be decided is, therefore, key to the determination of the applicability of the doctrine. What is the court asked to adjudicate? Put differently, what is the act of the foreign State for purposes of deciding whether it is subject to judicial review?

150. *W.S. Kirkpatrick v. Envtl.*, 493 U.S. 400, 404–05 (1990).

151. See *id.* at 405.

152. *Id.* at 406.

153. *Id.* [emphasis in original].

154. *Id.* at 409.

Over time, the Act of State doctrine in the United States has developed through judicial decisions, federal legislation, and executive branch actions. International comity, respect for the sovereignty of foreign States on their own territory, and the avoidance of embarrassment to the executive branch in its conduct of foreign relations are the policies underlying the Act of State doctrine in the United States. The Supreme Court has cautioned that the underlying policies are not a doctrine unto themselves.

Applicability and Rationale

> Whenever the foreign act of state doctrine is invoked, the court must decide whether it applies. If it cannot do it by reference to the pleadings or admissions, it must examine the evidence. This may involve examining what the state has done, for example where there is an issue as to its responsibility for the acts of its alleged agents. . . . The need to establish a factual foundation for the application of the doctrine must equally apply where the issue concerns not the character of the act but the availability of an exception.[155]
>
> In every case in which we have held the act of state doctrine applicable, the relief sought or the defense interposed would have required a court in the United States to declare invalid the official act of a foreign sovereign performed within its own territory. In *Underhill v. Hernandez,* 168 U.S. 250, 254 (1897), holding the defendant's detention of the plaintiff to be tortious would have required denying the legal effect to "acts of a military commander representing the authority of the revolutionary party as government, which afterwards succeeded and was recognized by the United States." In *Oetjen v. Central Leather Co., supra,* and in *Ricaud v. American Metal Co., supra,* denying title to the party who claimed through purchase from Mexico would have required declaring that government's prior seizure of the property, within its own territory, legally ineffective. See *Oetjen, supra,* at 304; *Ricaud, supra,* at 310. In *Sabbatino,* upholding the defendant's claim to the funds would have required a holding that Cuba's expropriation of goods located in Havana was null and void.[156]

The doctrine ordinarily requires a forum court to accept the validity of the public acts of a foreign State performed within its own territory. The core element of the

155. *Belhaj,* (Lord Sumption), para. 267.

156. *Kirkpatrick,* 493 U.S. at 405–06.

doctrine is territorial sovereignty, which means that a foreign State is sovereign within its borders and its acts within its territory may not be questioned in the courts of a forum State.[157]

For the doctrine to apply, the "act of State" must be the public act of those with authority to exercise sovereign power.[158] An act of State usually takes the form of a formal executive or legislative action. In that regard, a statute, decree, order, or resolution of the government of the foreign State could serve as proof of the act of State.[159]

The rationale for the Act of State doctrine in the United States, as expounded by the Supreme Court, has evolved over time.[160] In *Underhill v. Hernandez*, it was sovereign equality and independence. International comity was the rationale in *Oetjen v. Central Leather Co.*, which was a replevin action involving hides confiscated and sold during the Mexican civil war by a government recognized by the U.S. government, and later shipped to the United States. The U.S. Supreme Court held that the doctrine was applicable in a case involving the title to property brought within the custody of the U.S. court in which claims for damages were based on acts done in a foreign State. It reasoned: "To permit the validity of the acts of one sovereign state to be re-examined and perhaps condemned by the courts of another would very certainly 'imperil the amicable relations between governments and vex the peace of nations.' "[161]

In *Banco Nacional de Cuba v. Sabbatino*, the rationale was underpinned to the separation of powers under the Constitution among the different branches of government:

> It concerns the competency of dissimilar institutions to make and implement particular kinds of decisions in the area of international relations. The doctrine as formulated in past decisions expresses the strong sense of the Judicial Branch that its engagement in the task of passing on the validity of foreign acts of state may hinder rather than further this country's pursuit of goals both for itself and for the community of nations as a whole in the international sphere.[162]

157. See *Underhill v. Hernandez*, 168 U.S. 250, 252 (1897).

158. Cf. Alfred Dunhill v. Republic of Cuba, 425 U.S. 682, 694 (1976).

159. See *id.* at 695 and 718.

160. See *Kirkpatrick*, 493 U.S. at 404.

161. *Oetjen v. Central Leather Co.*, 246 U.S. 297, 304 (1918).

162. *Banco Nacional de Cuba v. Sabbatino*, 376 U.S. 398, 423 (1964).

The Act of State doctrine in its application in the United Kingdom is distinguished into two principles: municipal law and international law. The municipal law Act of State doctrine applies to sovereign acts done in the territory of the foreign State, such as legislative acts expropriating property.[163] Under the international law Act of State doctrine, "English courts will not adjudicate on the lawfulness of the extraterritorial acts of foreign states in their dealings with other states or the subjects of other states."[164] The rationale is:

> It is not for an English domestic court to apply international law to the relations between states, since it cannot give rise to private rights or obligations. Nor may it subject the sovereign acts of a foreign state to its own rules of municipal law or (by the same token) to the municipal law of a third country. . . . Once the acts alleged are such as to bring the issues into the "area of international dispute" the act of state doctrine is engaged.[165]

Exceptions or Limitations

The application of the Act of State doctrine is discretionary, and some courts have fashioned some exceptions or limitations to it.[166]

> [A]lthough the doctrine is often expressed in wide terms, it has limitations, founded in the very language of the doctrine and in its rationale. First, the act of state must, generally speaking, take place within the territory of the foreign state itself. A second limitation is that "the doctrine will not apply to foreign acts of state which are in breach of clearly established rules of international law, or are in contrary to English principles of public policy, as well as where there is a grave infringement of human rights" . . . (*Kuwait Airways Corpn v. Iraqi Airways Co. (Nos. 4 and 5)* [2002] 2 AC 883). A third limitation is that judicial acts will not be regarded as acts of state for the purposes of the act of state doctrine (*Altimo Holdings and Investment Ltd. v. Kyrgyz Mobil Tel Ltd.* [2012] 1 WLR 1804). A fourth limitation is that the doctrine does not apply where the conduct of the foreign state is of commercial as opposed to a sovereign character (*Empresa Exportadora de Azucar v. Industria Azucarera Nacional SA (The*

163. See *Belhaj*, para. 229.

164. *Id.*, para. 234.

165. *Id.*

166. See *Yukos Capital v. Rosneft*, [2012] EWCA Civ 855, paras. 68–115; *Belhaj*, paras. 153–165.

Playa Larga) [1983] 2 Lloyd's Rep 171; *Korea National Insurance Corpn v. Allianz Global Corporate & Specialty AG* [2008] 2 CLC 837). A fifth limitation is that the doctrine does not apply where the only issue is whether certain acts have occurred, as opposed to where the court is asked to enquire into them for the purpose of adjudicating upon their legal effectiveness (*Kirkpatrick & Co. Inc. v. Environmental Tectonics Corpn International* (1990) 493 US 400).[167]

International Law or Public Policy Exception

In *Kuwait Airways Corporation v. Iraqi Airways Co (Nos 4 and 5)*, the Court did not apply the Act of State doctrine because of exceptions based on international law and English public policy. The expropriation in the case followed the 1991 Iraqi invasion of Kuwait, a sovereign State, which was condemned internationally by way of the United Nations Security Council Resolution. It noted:

> Having forcibly invaded Kuwait, seized its assets, and taken KAC's aircraft from Kuwait to its own territory, Iraq adopted this decree [RCC Resolution 369] as part of its attempt to extinguish every vestige of Kuwait's existence as a separate state. An expropriatory decree made in these circumstances and for this purpose is simply not acceptable today.
>
> "A breach of international law of this seriousness is a matter of deep concern to the worldwide community of nations. . . . Such a fundamental breach of international law can properly cause the courts of this country to say that, like the confiscatory decree of the Nazi government of Germany in 1941, a new law depriving those whose property has been plundered of the ownership of their property in favour of the aggressor's own citizens will not be enforced or recognised in proceedings in this country. Enforcement or recognition of this law would be manifestly contrary to the public policy of English law. . . . International law, for its part, recognises that a national court may properly decline, to give effect to the legislative and other acts of foreign states which are in violation of international law.[168]

167. *Belhaj v. Straw, [2014] EWCA Civ 1394,,* para. 54, adopting the analysis and conclusions of *Yukos Capital v. Rosneft*, [2012] EWCA Civ 855.

168. *Kuwait Airways Corporation v. Iraqi Airways Co (Nos 4 and 5)* [2002] 2 AC 883, paras 28–29. (Lord Nicholls) [citations omitted].

The Court, however, cautioned about the public policy exception:

> The golden rule is that care must be taken not to expand its application beyond the true limits of the principle. These limits demand that, where there is any room for doubt, judicial restraint must be exercised. But restraint is what is needed, not abstention. And there is no need for restraint on grounds of public policy where it is plain beyond dispute that a clearly established norm of international law has been violated.[169]

The Court stated that "a legislative act by a foreign state which is in flagrant breach of clearly established rules of international law ought not to be recognised by the courts of this country as forming the *lex situs* of that state."[170] It, however, cautioned that not every breach of international law triggers the public policy exception.[171] The breach must be "so repugnant to British ideas of international and personal morality,"[172] a "gross violation of established rules of international law of fundamental importance,"[173] and "so grave an infringement of human rights that courts of this country ought to refuse to recognise it as a law at all."[174]

The speech of Lord Cross in *Oppenheimer v. Cattermole* envisioned an exception to the doctrine in the case of a grave violation of human rights:

> A judge should, of course, be very slow to refuse to give effect to the legislation of a foreign state in any sphere in which, the foreign state has jurisdiction. He may well have an inadequate understanding of the circumstances in which the legislation was passed and his refusal to recognise it may be embarrassing to the branch of the executive which is concerned to maintain friendly relations between this country and the foreign country in question. But I think... that it is part of the public policy of this country that our courts should give effect to the clearly established rules of international law. Of course on some points it may be by no means clear what the rule of

169. *Id.*, para. 140 (Lord Hope).

170. *Id.*, para. 148.

171. *Id.*, para. 114 (Lord Steyn).

172. *Empresa Exportadora De Azucar (CUBAZUCAR) v. Industria Azucarera Nacional SA (IANSA) (The Playa Larga and Marble Islands)* [1983] 2 Lloyd's Rep. 171, 190 (Ackner L.J.).

173. *Kuwait Airways* [2002] UKHL 19; [2002] 2 A.C. 883.

174. *Oppenheimer v. Cattermole* [1976] A.C. 249, 278 (Cross L.J.) The case was about the deprivation of Jews of their German nationality by the Nazi government of Germany in 1941 and confiscation of their property.

> international law is. Whether, for example, legislation of a particular type is contrary to international law because it is "confiscatory" is a question upon which there may well be wide differences of opinion between communist and capitalist countries. But what we are concerned with here is legislation which takes away without compensation from a section of the citizen body singled out on racial grounds all their property on which the state passing the legislation can lay its hands and, in addition, deprives them of their citizenship. To my mind a law of this sort constitutes so grave an infringement of human rights that the courts of this country ought to refuse to recognise it as law at all.[175]

The common thread in the *Oppenheimer* and *Kuwait Airways* cases is that the "violations of human rights and international law, respectively, were established beyond doubt. As a result, in neither case was it necessary for the courts . . . to conduct an investigation into the conduct of the foreign state concerned."[176] In *Belhaj*, in contrast to both *Oppenheimer* and *Kuwait Airways*, the facts were not established and would have to be investigated and determined by the court during trial. The claim in *Belhaj* concerned the role of the government and officials of the United Kingdom in the alleged torture and torts carried out by officials of China, Malaysia, Thailand, and Libya, committed under the U.S. program of "rendition" in the years after 9/11 against a Libyan national and his wife. At issue is whether the Act of State doctrine applied to the claim or was dis-applied by the public policy limitation on the doctrine.

The Court of Appeal in *Belhaj* had to decide whether it "should go beyond *Oppenheimer* and *Kuwait Airways* and apply the public policy limitation in a case where the court, if it exercised jurisdiction, would be required to conduct a legal and factual investigation into the validity of the conduct of a foreign state."[177] It ruled that the holding of *Kuwait Airways* extends also to cases where such an investigation may be necessary.[178] It considered the allegations of torture in the case as grave violations of human rights and international law, which would fall within the public policy limitation on the Act of State doctrine. Considering *Buttes Gas*, the Court of Appeal in *Belhaj* declared that "this is not a case in which there is a lack of judicial or manageable standards. On the contrary, the applicable

175. *Id.* at 277–278.

176. *Belhaj*, [2014] EWCA Civ 1394, at 88.

177. *Id.* at 114.

178. *Id.*

principles of international law and English law are clearly established. The court would not be in judicial no man's land."[179]

The United Kingdom Supreme Court upheld the judgment of the Court of Appeal and itself held that English public policy would not be consistent with the application of the Act of State doctrine to bar the court from determining the allegations of complicity by British authorities and officials in torture, unlawful detention, enforced rendition, and disappearance by foreign States.[180] "Act of state is and remains essentially a domestic law doctrine, and it is English law which sets its limits."[181]

In the United States, to varying degrees, there is an international law limitation to the Act of State doctrine. *Sabbatino* recognized that the justification for applying the doctrine may be weaker where the relevant rules of international law are clear. To that effect, it held that "rather than laying down or reaffirming an inflexible and all-encompassing rule in this case, we decide only that the Judicial Branch will not examine the validity of a taking or property within its own territory by a foreign sovereign government, extant and recognized by this country at the time of the suit, in the absence of a *treaty or other unambiguous agreement regarding controlling legal principles*, even if the complaint alleges that the taking violates international law."[182] The Court accepted the relevance of international law "when there is an appropriate degree of 'consensus concerning a particular area of international law, the more appropriate it is for the judiciary to render decisions regarding it, since the courts can then focus on the application of an agreed principle to circumstances of fact rather than on the sensitive task of establishing a principle not inconsistent with the national interest or with international justice.' "[183]

Extraterritoriality Exception

Another limitation on the Act of State doctrine is extraterritoriality, as the act in question must generally be confined within the territory of the foreign State.[184] For example, in *Agudas Chasidei Chabad v. Russia*, where the court determined that Russia had confiscated the documents in Poland, it held that the doctrine does not apply to expropriation outside the sovereign territory.[185]

179. *Id.* at 118.

180. See *Belhaj v. Straw*, [2017] UKSC 3.

181. *Belhaj v. Straw*, [2017] UKSC 3, para. 98.

182. *Sabbatino*, 376 U.S. at 428. [emphasis added].

183. *Id.* at 455.

184. See *Kirkpatrick*, 493 U.S. at 405.

185. *Agudas Chasidei Chabad v. Russia*, 528 F.3d 934, 952 (D.C. Cir. 2008).

Judicial Decisions Exception

Although judicial decisions are acts of State, they are not generally regarded as such for purposes of the doctrine.[186] Where a claimant had relied on the Act of State doctrine to submit that the court should not sit in judgment on the independence of a foreign judicial system, the Privy Council found that the doctrine did not apply where there was a risk that justice could not be obtained in a foreign legal system in general.[187] Whether judicial acts benefit from the doctrine was also at issue in *Yukos Capital v. Rosneft*.[188] The *Yukos* case arose out arbitral awards issued in Russia and then set aside in Russia. Yukos Capital, the claimant, first applied to the Dutch courts for enforcement of the awards. The Dutch courts enforced the awards and refused to recognize the annulment of the awards by the Russian courts because it was the product of a "partial and dependent judicial process." Yukos Capital then applied to the English High Court for the enforcement of the award under the 1996 English Arbitration Act but Rosneft, a Russian government-controlled entity, objected to the enforcement on several grounds, including the Act of State doctrine. Roseneft had contended that the allegations by Yukos Capital were prohibited by the Act of State doctrine:

> It is submitted that the essence of the allegations requires the English court to adjudicate upon and call into question the legitimacy and legality of the acts of a recognised (and friendly) foreign state or government within its own territory, including the legitimacy and legality of the decisions of its courts. The allegation made is that all the events relating to the Yukos matter (for example, the tax claims, their pursuit through the Russian courts, the resulting judgments of the Russian courts, the enforcement of those judgments under Russian law in Russia by the relevant arm of the executive, the decisions of the Russian courts upholding that enforcement process, the auction of the YNG shares effected by the Russian state, and even extending, so it is alleged, to the Russian decisions annulling the Awards in this case) are part of a governmental and political campaign involving, it is effectively alleged, the expropriation of assets from Yukos by illegitimate and illegal means, arranged and directed by the Russian state or government.[189]

186. See *Altimo Holdings and Investment Ltd. v. Kyrgyz Mobil Tel Ltd.* [2012] 1 WLR 1804.

187. *AK Investment v. Kyrgyz Mobil Tel* [2011] UKPC 7.

188. *Yukos Capital v. Rosneft,* [2012] EWCA Civ 855; [2013] 1 All ER 223; [2012] 2 Lloyd's Rep 208; [2014] 1 QB 458; [2013] 3 WLR 1329.

189. *Id.,* para. 37.

The Court of Appeal in its comprehensive and magisterial opinion upheld that judgment of Judge Hamblen that the court is not prohibited from adjudicating the issues raised in an arbitral award enforcement proceeding despite it having been set aside by the courts of the country where it was made. The Court of Appeal examined relevant authorities, most notably *AK Investment*, and found that the Act of State doctrine does not prevent an investigation of, or adjudication on the conduct of the judiciary of a foreign state, whether the conduct was in the past or future, and if such conduct in the past is relied on as the foundation for an assessment of risk as to its conduct in the future[190] Thus, no distinction is made between past and future conduct of the judiciary of a foreign state. The *Yukos* court disagreed with *Philippine National Bank v. U.S. District Court for the District of Hawaii*,[191] "that the doctrine applies to prevent adjudication on an otherwise appropriate challenge to foreign court decision."[192]

In *Philippine National Bank v. U.S. District Court for the District of Hawaii*, the Ninth Circuit Court of Appeals had decided that in the "unusual circumstances" of the case, the forfeiture judgment of the Philippine Supreme Court is an act of State and that the District Court's injunction violated the doctrine.[193] The court noted that the "doctrine is normally inapplicable to court judgments arising from private litigation."[194] It also noted that the doctrine is not an "inflexible rule preventing a judgment sought by a foreign government from qualifying as an act of state." However, the "forfeiture action was not a mere dispute between private parties; it was an action initiated by the Philippine government pursuant to its 'statutory mandate to recover property allegedly stolen from treasury.' "[195] Thus, the subject matter of the forfeiture action and the underlying governmental interest support the treatment of the judgment of the Philippine Supreme Court as an act of state.[196] Under the unusual circumstance of the case, it can be reconciled with *Yukos* and the proposition that ordinarily a foreign court decision is not an act of state for purposes of the doctrine.

The *Yukos* court held that "the act of state doctrine does not prevent an investigation of or adjudication upon the conduct of the judiciary of a foreign state, whether that conduct lies in the past, or in the future, and whether or not its

190. *Id.*, para 86.

191. *Philippine National Bank v. U.S. District Court for the District of Hawaii (In re Philippine Nat'l Bank)*, 397 F. 3d 768 (9th Cir. 2005).

192. *Id.*, para. 89.

193. *In re Phlippine Nat'l Bank* at 774.

194. *Id.* at 773 [citations omitted].

195. *Id.*

196. *Id.* at 773–74.

conduct in the past is relied upon as the foundation for the assessment of the risk as to its conduct in the future."[197] It differentiated judicial acts from the legislative or executive acts of a friendly State acting within its territory. For this, it relied on the classic statement of the Act of State doctrine, which refers only to legislative or executive acts. It also based the distinction on the fact that "the judicial acts of a foreign state are judged by judicial standards, including international standards regarding jurisdiction, in accordance with doctrines separate from the act of state doctrine, even if the dictates of comity still have an important role to play."[198] It concluded that "the act of state doctrine does not apply to allegations of impropriety against foreign court decisions, whether in the case of particular decisions or in the case of a systemic dependency on the dictates or interference of the domestic government."[199]

The Court of Appeal reckoned that the *Yukos* case goes beyond the situation in cases such as *Kirkpatrick*, as "Yukos does not merely seek to show that certain events occurred (and did so in Russia and as matter of state policy), but that such events are not to be regarded as valid or effective or lawful, but invalid, ineffective, wrongful, arbitrary, and directed by the hostile motive of a campaign of expropriation and wrongful imprisonment."[200] After all, the essence of the Yukos case is that the Russian annulment decision is ineffective to set aside and nullify the arbitration awards. In sum, the allegations in the case are not simply concerned with proving what occurred but with impugning what occurred as wrongful and consequently ineffective.[201] The Court of Appeal stated that "English courts will require cogent grounds for any allegation that a foreign court decision should not be recognised on the grounds of a failure of substantial justice. However, that is a matter of evidence and argument, not a matter of any immunity or doctrine of non-justiciability."[202] It concluded that the Act of State doctrine did not bar Yukos Capital's case as the judicial question raised in respect of judicial acts is whether the annulment of the arbitral award by the Russian court should be recognised by the English court in a claim by Yukos Capital to enforce the arbitration awards.[203]

197. *Yukos Capital*, para. 86.

198. *Id.*, para. 87.

199. *Id.*, para. 90.

200. *Id.*, para. 103.

201. *Id.*, para. 104.

202. *Id., para.* 125.

203. *Id.*, para. 133.

Commercial Activity Exception

The commercial activity exception to the Act of State doctrine is a function of the relatedness of the doctrine to State immunity.[204] In the *Playa Larga* case, the court stated that "if the Courts were being asked to sit in judgment on the conduct of the Cuban government, then that conduct was not immune from the jurisdiction of the English Courts since its activity was a trading rather than a governmental activity. What the Cuban government did was to induce breaches of contract by Cubazucar."[205] Cubazucar, a Cuban state trading enterprise, was the seller of sugar, and Iansa, a Chilean private company with majority share ownership by a Chilean state trading organization, was the buyer. The case was about the non-delivery of a cargo of sugar by Cubazucar to Iansa following the decision of the Cuban government after the 1973 coup d'état in Chile that toppled the Allende government that had a close diplomatic and commercial relationship with the Cuban government of Fidel Castro. The *Playa Larga* court also mentioned that the case of *Alfred Dunhill v. Cuba*[206] dealt with the Act of State doctrine and that the plurality decision was approved by Lord Wilberforce in *I Congreso*[207]where that court "decided that immunity should be granted only with respect to causes of action arising out of a foreign state's public or governmental action and not with respect of those arising out of its commercial or private action."[208]

In *Dunhill*, Cuba had nationalized the cigar business, and former owners of cigar plants brought an action against importers of cigars for the purchase price of the cigars that had been shipped to the importers from their nationalized cigar plants. A plurality of four justices of the United States Supreme Court held that "repudiation of a commercial debt is not an act of state."[209] It stated: "We decline to extend the act of state doctrine to acts committed by foreign sovereigns in the course of their purely commercial operations. Because the act relied upon by respondents in this case was an act arising out of the conduct by Cuba's agents in the operation of cigar businesses for profit, the act was not an act of state."[210] In creating a commercial activity exception to the Act of State doctrine, the Court conflates the doctrine with Restrictive State immunity: "Repudiation

204. See *Empresa Exportadora de Azucar v. Industria Azucarera Nacional SA (The "Playa Larga")* [1983] 2 Lloyd's Rep 171 (CA); *Korea National Insurance Corp. v. Allianz Global* [2008] 2 CLC 837.

205. *The Playa Larga*, at 194.

206. *Alfred Dunhill of London, Inc. v. Republic of Cuba*, 425 U.S. 682 (1976).

207. *I Congreso del Partido*, [1981] 2 Lloyd's Rep. 367; [1981] 3 W.L.R. 328.

208. *Id.*

209. *Dunhill*, 425 U.S. 682, 697 (White J, joined by Burger, Powell and Rehnquist JJ).

210. *Id.* at 706.

of a commercial debt cannot, consistent with this restrictive approach to sovereign immunity, be treated as an act of state; for if it were, foreign governments, by merely repudiating the debt before or after its adjudication, would enjoy an immunity which our Government would not extend them under prevailing sovereign immunity principles in this country."[211] However, the Sixth Circuit, in *Kalamazoo Spice Extraction Co. v. Provisional Military Government of Ethiopia*, did not see any precedential effect of the pluralist opinion of the Supreme Court.[212] The Eleventh Circuit, in *Honduras Aircraft Registry, Ltd. v. Honduras*, has rejected the commercial act exception to the doctrine.[213]

In *McKesson v. Iran*, the court after holding that it had subject matter jurisdiction under the commercial activities exception of the FSIA, had to decide whether the Act of State doctrine applied and shielded Iran from liability in the case.[214] Pak was a joint venture between McKesson and private Iranian citizens that was incorporated in 1960. McKesson's ownership interest of 50 percent was decreased after the Islamic Revolution, and the board of directors of Pak eventually froze out McKesson's stake in Pak and blocked McKesson's receipt of dividend payment.[215] The court decided that the facts of the case did not lend it to the application of the Act of State doctrine. It stated:

> Iran did not pass a law, issue and edict or decree, or engage in formal governmental action explicitly taking McKesson's property for the benefit of the Iranian public. Instead, it allegedly took control of Pak's board of directors and abused its position as a majority shareholder, making McKesson's claims "akin to a corporate dispute between majority and minority shareholders."[216]

The court used the occasion to give examples of its understanding of the "official action" requirement of the Act of State doctrine: denial of an export license for uranium from Kazakhstan, as well as the transfer of corporate shares to a State entity, where the "transfer and alleged conversion were accomplished pursuant to an official decree of the Republic of Kazakhstan."[217] The doctrine was equally

211. *Id.* at 698–99.

212. 729 F.2d 422, 425 n.3 (6th Cir. 1984).

213. 129 F.3d 543, 550 (11th Cir. 1997).

214. *McKesson v. Iran*, 672 F.3d 1066 (D.C. Cir. 2012).

215. *Id.* at 1070.

216. *Id.* at 1074 [citation omitted].

217. *Id.* [citation omitted]

applied in the case of an official order by a foreign government's finance minister for the payment of a tax to the foreign government.[218]

Absent the definitive ruling of the Supreme Court, the Circuit Courts are split on the commercial activity exception to the doctrine.

Bernstein Exception

There is (or was) the so-called *Bernstein* exception to the Act of State doctrine, which is named after the eponymous decision in the Second Circuit where the plaintiff obtained a declaration from the State Department that it is the policy of the executive branch that courts should not decline to decide cases of Nazi expropriation on the basis of the Act of State doctrine.[219] Thus, under this exception, the executive branch acting through the State Department may convey its views to the court on the application of the Act of State doctrine in a particular case. The status or significance of the *Bernstein* exception is unclear as it has never been applied by a majority of the Supreme Court. A plurality of the justices urged its adoption in *First National City Bank v. Banco Nacional de Cuba*, 406 U.S. 759 (1972), but six justices were not swayed by the idea of a dispositive deference to the executive branch in expropriation cases. Further calling into question the exception is the duty of federal courts under Article III of the U.S. Constitution to decide cases and controversies as stressed by the Supreme Court in *Kirkpatrick*.

Treaty Exception

Courts have extrapolated a treaty exception to the Act of State doctrine from *Sabbatino*:

> The Judicial Branch will not examine the validity of a taking of property within its own territory by a foreign government, extant and recognized by this country at the time of suit, *in the absence of a treaty* or other unambiguous agreement regarding controlling legal principles, even if the complaint alleges that the taking violates customary international law.[220]

In *Kalamazoo Spice*, the Sixth Circuit held that the 1953 Treaty of Amity between the United States and Ethiopia makes the Act of State doctrine inapplicable so as to preclude judicial inquiry into the validity of an expropriation by the Ethiopian government of shares in an Ethiopian business entity held by an

218. *Id.* [citations omitted].

219. *Bernstein v. N.V. Nederlandsche-Amerkaansche*, 210 F.2d 375 (2d Cir. 1954).

220. *Sabbatino*, 376 U.S. at 428 [emphasis added].

America corporation.[221] The Court of Appeals disagreed with the District Court that the treaty was too ambiguous to be susceptible to judicial interpretation, but determined instead that the treaty in the case may provide a basis for the plaintiff to receive compensation. It found support in *Sabbatino,* where the Supreme Court stated:

> It should be apparent that the greater the degree of codification or consensus concerning a particular area of international law, the more appropriate it is for the judiciary to render decisions regarding it, since the courts can then focus on the application of an agreed principle to circumstances of fact rather than on the sensitive task of establishing a principle not inconsistent with the national interest or with international justice.[222]

Statutory Exceptions

Although the Act of State doctrine is judge-made, there are statutory exceptions to it in the United States. Congress passed the so-called Second Hickenlooper Amendment in response to the *Sabbatino,* where the Supreme Court held that the Act of State doctrine barred U.S. courts from invalidating an official act of expropriation by a foreign State within its own territory. The *Hickenlooper* exception provides that U.S. courts may not apply the doctrine in cases of expropriation in violation of international law.[223] The exception can be overcome by the express representation of the executive branch that the doctrine should apply in a particular case. The United States enacted an arbitration exception to the doctrine in 1988, which applies mostly in arbitration involving States under foreign investment agreements.[224] There is also the Helms Burton Act passed by the Congress in 1996, which provides: "No court of the United States shall decline, based upon the act of state doctrine, to make a determination on the merits in an action brought" against anyone who traffics in property confiscated by the Cuban government after January 1, 1959.[225]

221. *Kalamazoo Spice v. Ethiopia,* 729 F. 2d 422 (6th Cir. 1984).

222. *Id.* at 427 (citing *Sabbatino,* 376 U.S. at 423).

223. See 22 U.S.C. § 2370(e)(2) (1964).

224. See Federal Arbitration Act, 9 U.S.C. § 15 (1988), which provides that "enforcement of arbitral agreements, confirmation of arbitral awards, and the execution upon judgments based on orders confirming such awards shall not be refused on the basis of the Act of State doctrine."

225. See Cuban Liberty and Democratic Solidarity (LIBERTAD) Act [Helms Burton Act], 22 U.S.C. § 6082 (1996).

ANALOGY BETWEEN STATE IMMUNITY AND ACT OF STATE DOCTRINE

The Act of State doctrine, which is sometimes conflated with State immunity, is a matter of justiciability, not jurisdiction. Jurisdiction and justiciability are related but different principles. Immunity is a procedural bar that ousts the jurisdiction of a court. Immunity is not concerned with justiciability. Where a court's jurisdiction is not ousted by immunity, the case may still not be justiciable. Justiciability deals with whether a court should exercise its jurisdiction.

The Act of State doctrine is discretionary and deals with the appropriateness of judicial determination or review of a particular issue. "Properly speaking, the term non-justiciability refers . . . to a case where an issue is said to be inherently unsuitable for judicial determination by reason only of its subject matter."[226] The Act of State doctrine has the same effect as immunity *ratione materiae* in that it leads to the same disposition of a case:

> It is true, of course, that a particular litigant's claim may be effectively defeated by application of the act of state doctrine as by a foreign government's invocation of sovereign immunity. But the doctrines of sovereign immunity and act of state, while related, differ fundamentally in their focus and in their operation. Sovereign immunity accords a defendant exemption from suit by virtue of its status. By contrast, the act of state doctrine exempts no one from the process of the court. Equally applicable whether a sovereign nation is a party or not, the act of state doctrine merely tells a court what law to apply to a case; it "concerns the limits for determining the validity of an otherwise applicable rule of law." In the absence of "unambiguous agreement regarding controlling . . . principles' of international law, the act of state doctrine commands that the acts of a sovereign nation committed in its own territory be accorded presumptive validity.[227]

In *Pinochet (No 3)*, Lord Millett noted the closeness of the Act of State doctrine and immunity *ratione materiae*:

> Given its scope and rationale, [immunity *ratione materiae*] is similar to and may be indistinguishable from aspects of the Anglo-American act of state doctrine. As I understand the difference between them, state immunity is a

226. *Shergill v. Khaira* [2014] UKSC 33; [2014] 3 WLR 1, para 41.

227. *Dunhill*, 425 U.S. at 725–26 (Marshall J. dissenting, joined by Brennan, Stewart and Blackmun JJ).

> creature of international law and operates as a bar to the jurisdiction of the national court, whereas the act of state doctrine is a rule of domestic law which holds the national court incompetent to adjudicate upon the lawfulness of the sovereign act of a foreign state.[228]

For his part, Lord Phillips of Worth Matravers described the relationship between State immunity and Act of State doctrine as follows:

> The second explanation for the immunity [*ratione materiae*] is the principle that it is contrary to international law for one state to adjudicate upon the internal affairs of another state. Where a state or a state official is impleaded, this principle applies as part of the explanation for immunity. Where a state is not directly or indirectly impleaded in the litigation, so that no issue of state immunity as such arises, the English and American courts have nonetheless, as a matter of judicial restraint, held themselves not competent to entertain litigation that turns on the validity of the public acts of a foreign state, applying what has become known as the act of state doctrine.[229]

State immunity and Act of State doctrine both have roots in the principles of comity of nations and territorial sovereignty. "Act of state is not to be confused with state immunity. It is a very limited defence and requires strong proof."[230] The Act of State doctrine is so related to State immunity that they are sometimes confused for each other or their principles are used interchangeably:

> As a member of the family of nations, the Government of the United Kingdom (of which this court forms part of the judicial branch) observes the rules of comity, *videlicet*, the accepted rules of mutual conduct between state and state which each state adopts in relation to other states and expects other states to adopt in relation to itself. One of those rules is that it does not purport to exercise jurisdiction over the internal affairs of any other independent state, or to apply measures of coercion to it or its property, except in accordance with the rules of public international law. One of the commonest applications of this rule by the judicial branch of the United Kingdom government is the well-known doctrine of sovereign immunity. . . . For the English court to pronounce upon the validity of a law of a foreign sovereign state within its own territory, so that the validity of that

228. *Ex Parte Pinochet 3*, para. 269.

229. *Id.* at 286 B-C.

230. *I Congreso*, [1983] 1 A.C. 244, 250.

> law became the *res* of the *res judicata* in the suit, would be to assert jurisdiction over the internal affairs of that state. That would be a breach of the rules of comity. In my view, this court has no jurisdiction so to do.[231]

The Act of State doctrine provides a substantive defense on the merits, as opposed to State immunity, which is a jurisdictional defense, and the party asserting the applicability of the doctrine bears the burden of proof.[232] "As a substantive rather than a jurisdictional defense, the Act of State doctrine is more appropriately raised in a motion for summary judgment than in a motion to dismiss."[233] Under the United States Federal Rules of Civil Procedure, the Act of State doctrine does not operate to dismiss a claim for lack of subject matter jurisdiction[234] but instead for failure to state a claim upon which relief could be granted.[235] The Act of State doctrine does not arise if State immunity is applicable and, as such, a court must address sovereign immunity as a threshold matter because it deals with the subject matter jurisdiction of the court.[236] Unlike immunity, the Act of State doctrine cannot be waived, and the consent of the parties is nugatory.

In sum, the rule of State immunity and the Act of State doctrine are related but operate differently. The Act of State doctrine is nebulous with uncertain contours: "a common law principle of uncertain application which prevents the [forum] court from examining the legality of certain acts performed in the exercise of sovereign authority within a foreign country or, occasionally, outside it."[237] Notwithstanding, at the core it applies to necessary, not ancillary, challenges to the validity of the acts of foreign States. State immunity operates by reference to the identity of the parties, whereas the Act of State doctrine operates by reference to the subject-matter of the claim.[238] "This is inevitably reflected in the different detailed rules which have developed in relation to the scope and operation of the two principles." State immunity and its exceptions are codified in the United Kingdom and the United States, but the Act of State doctrine and its limitations or exceptions remain governed by mostly common law.

231. *Buck v. Attorney General*, [1965] 1 Ch 745, 770 (CA) (Diplock, LJ).

232. See *Liu v. Republic of China*, 892 F.2d 1419, 1432 (9th Cir. 1989).

233. *Daventree Ltd. v. Republic of Azerbaijan*, 349 F. Supp. 2d 736, 755 (S.D.N.Y. 2004).

234. See Fed. R. Civ. P. 12(b)(1) for dismissal for want of jurisdiction.

235. See Fed. R. Civ. P. 12(b)(6) for dismissal on the merits.

236. See *Siderman v. Argentina*, 965 F.2d 699, 706 (9th Cir. 1992).

237. *Ex Parte Pinochet* 3, para.106.

238. See *Belhaj v. Straw*, [2014] EWCA Civ 1394, para 48.

PART TWO

Immunity of International Organizations

5

Nature of International Organizations and Purpose of Their Immunity

DEFINITION AND CREATION OF INTERNATIONAL ORGANIZATION

Generally, "international organization"[1] refers to an organization established by treaty or other legal instruments governed by international law and possessing its own international personality.[2] Various international conventions use the term "intergovernmental organization" to denote "international organization," which emphasizes that it is an organization composed mostly of States and that it differs from nongovernmental organizations.[3] Intergovernmental organizations are also

1. The expressions "international organization," "intergovernmental organization," and "public international organization" as used interchangeably in this book have the same meaning, unless the context explicitly indicates otherwise.

2. See Article 2 of the Draft Articles on the Responsibility of International Organizations.

3. See Article 2(1)(i), 1969 Vienna Convention on the Law of Treaties, 1155 UNTS 331; Article 1(1)(1), 1975 Vienna Convention on the Representation of States in Their Relations with International Organizations of a Universal Character, A/CONF.67/16; Article 2(1)(i), 1986 Vienna Convention on the Law of Treaties between States and International Organizations or between International Organizations, A/CONF.129/15.

known as public international organizations.[4] As a distinguishing feature from private international organizations or nongovernmental organizations (NGOs), public international organizations are established by international agreements by States. International agreements are concluded under international law, unless otherwise stated in the particular agreement. International agreements subject public international organizations to international law. A convention or treaty is, however, not always necessary for the establishment or existence of an international organization. For example, the Organization for Security and Co-operation in Europe (OSCE) was established without a treaty.[5] At any rate, "*on définira l'organisation international comme un groupement à vocation permanente, essentiellement compose d'États, constitué par eux sur la base d'une convention, géneralement multilatérale, dote d'organes propres, et disposant de compétences d'attribution*."[6] An international organization can also include one or more international organizations.

An international organization can be created by the legal act of an already existing international organization. For example, the International Bank for Reconstruction and Development (IBRD) was the mother-organization of the International Finance Corporation (IFC). Nevertheless, IFC was still established based on a separate international agreement.[7] In the same vein, the United Nations International Development Organization (UNIDO) was first set up as an organ of the United Nations General Assembly (UNGA) before it became a separate international organization and a specialized agency of the United Nations.[8]

4. See Article 34 of the Statute of the International Court of Justice. International organizations are sometimes classified into intergovernmental organizations and nongovernmental organizations, but nongovernmental organizations are not the subject of this study. Nongovernmental organizations (NGOs) are also known as private international organizations, as they are not subject of international law. Although NGOs play active and important roles in the international arena, they lack international legal capacity, and their legal personality is governed by applicable domestic, national, or municipal law, usually the law of the State of establishment. A very important NGO is the International Committee of the Red Cross (ICRC), which performs an equally important function under the Geneva Convention on the Laws of War. Another very important NGO is Amnesty International, which plays a very important role in human rights.

5. See Helsinki Final Act signed on August 1, 1975, which is an "agreement" signed by 35 nations that concluded the Conference on Security and Cooperation in Europe held in Helsinki, Finland.

6. Jean Combacau & Serge Sur, Droit international public 706 (5e edition Montchrestien). Author's translation: "the international organization will be defined as a group with permanent vocation, composed essentially of States, constituted by them on the basis of a convention, generally multilateral, endowed with its own organs, and having powers of attribution."

7. Articles of Agreement of the International Finance Corporation.

8. General Assembly Resolution 2152 (XXI) of 17 November 1966 provided that "the United Nations Industrial Development Organization . . . established as an organ of the General Assembly, shall function as an autonomous organization within the United Nations." The General Assembly,

Ordinarily, international organizations have States as members, but some include other entities. The World Tourism Organization (UNWTO) is one such organization that has non-State actors in its membership. Presently, UNWTO's membership includes 157 countries, 6 Associate Members, and 500 Affiliate Members representing the private sector, educational institutions, tourism associations, and local tourism authorities.[9] Another international organization whose membership is not made up entirely of States is the Joint Vienna Institute (JVI), which was established in 1992 as a cooperative venture of six international organizations and Austria. Each of these entities is a party to the Agreement for the Establishment of the JVI, as amended on May 1, 2003, either as a Primary Member or as a Contributing Member. The original sponsoring organizations were the Bank for International Settlements (until 2004), the European Bank for Reconstruction and Development (EBRD), the IRBD, the International Monetary Fund (IMF), and the Organisation for Economic Co-operation and Development (OECD). The World Trade Organization (WTO) became a sponsoring organization in 1998, the European Investment Bank (EIB) joined as a Contributing Member in 2013, and the European Commission has had observer status since 2007.

Some international organizations are closed and have their requirements for membership. For instance, Article I, Section I(b), of the Articles of Agreement of the World Bank provides that membership in the World Bank "shall be open to other members of the [International Monetary] Fund, at such times and in accordance with such terms as may be prescribed by the Bank."[10]

Geographically, international organizations may be either universal, such as the United Nations (UN) and its specialized agencies, or regional, such as the European Union (EU), the Organization of American States (OAS), and the African Union (AU), which limit their membership to States within a defined geographical region.

in Resolution 3362 (S-VII), endorsed the recommendation that UNIDO be converted into a specialized agency, and the organization became one in 1985.

9. Article 4 of the Statute of UNWTO provides that Membership of the Organization shall be open to: (a) Full Members, (b) Associate Members, and (c) Affiliate Members, and Article 5 extends Full Membership of the Organization to all sovereign States. Article 7(1) provides: "Affiliate membership of the Organization shall be open to international bodies, both intergovernmental and non-governmental, concerned with specialized interests in tourism and to commercial bodies and associations whose activities are related to the aims of the Organization or fall within its competence." Article 7(6) provides: "Affiliate Members may participate in the activities of the Organization individually or grouped in the Committee of Affiliate Members."

10. See Article II, Section 1, of the Articles of Agreement of the International Bank for Reconstruction and Development.

International organizations are established by their members to achieve common objectives and, as such, the members define the mission of the organization. They serve many and varied functions, and play very important roles in world politics, global economy, and the international legal order. They also provide platforms for the discussion and resolution of common issues and significant problems. In the case of the United Nations, its primary goals include reaffirmation of "faith in fundamental rights" and establishment of "conditions under which justice and respect for the obligations arising from treaties and other sources of international law can be maintained."[11] Its purposes are principally to maintain international peace and security, to develop friendly relations among nations, to achieve international cooperation in solving international problems, and to promote and encourage respect for human rights and for fundamental freedoms for all.[12] For UNESCO, its purpose "is to contribute to peace and security by promoting collaboration among nations through education, science and culture in order to further respect for justice, for the rule of law and human rights and fundamental freedoms which are affirmed for the peoples of the world, without distinction of race, sex, language or religion, by the Charter of the United Nations."[13] Some international organizations provide technical cooperation, whereas others are responsible for standard-setting. The International Labour Organization (ILO) brings together governments, employers, and workers' representatives of its member States to set labor standards, develop policies, and devise programs promoting decent work for all women and men.[14] International organizations have enormous normative powers as most treaties in that regard are concluded under their auspices. Some international organizations, such as ILO, have supervising mechanism to ensure adherence to its conventions.[15]

International organizations differ in their missions but also have a lot in common. They share the basic characteristics of being established by treaty or international agreements, with a few exceptions; exclusively or primarily composed of States, except, for example, in the case of the European Union, which has become a member of international organizations such as the Food and Agriculture Organization (FAO), whose constitution was amended in 1991 to

11. Preamble, Charter of the United Nations.

12. Article 1, Charter of the United Nations.

13. Article I, Constitution of UNESCO.

14. ILO has the distinction of being the only tripartite organization within the United Nations system that brings together representatives of governments, employers, and workers in its executive bodies.

15. See Articles 24–34 of ILO Constitution.

allow the admission of regional economic integration organizations. A State or an entity becomes a member of an international organization by becoming a party to the constituent instrument establishing the organization, or by admission through the rules or procedure of the organization.

Another important feature or requirement of an international organization is the existence of a plenary organ in which all member States are represented. In the United Nations, the organ is the General Assembly. In some of the specialized agencies of the United Nations, the plenary organ goes by the moniker "General Conference."[16] In the international financial institutions, it is the board of governors.[17] International organizations also have other organs formed by delegates of representatives of some member States, which are charged with some functions within the organization. An example is the board of executive directors of some of the specialized agencies.[18]

In sum, an international organization is neither a super-State nor the sum of its member States, but a separate entity with a "personality" apart from that of the States that created it.[19] "International organizations are subjects of international law and, as such, are bound by any obligations incumbent upon them under general rules of international law, under their constitutions or under international agreements to which they are parties."[20]

HISTORY OF INTERNATIONAL ORGANIZATIONS

International organizations, as we know them today, came into existence during the Concert of Europe[21] from the end of the Napoleonic Wars in 1815 to the outbreak of World War I in 1914. This system of cooperation between governments in the form of either diplomatic conference or administrative bureau started with the Congress of Vienna in 1815 as the first such conference and the Commission for the Navigation of the Rhine as the first permanent administrative body set up by governments. The International Telegraphic Union (ITU) was established

16. See Article IV of the Constitution of UNESCO.

17. See, e.g., Article V, Section 2, of the Articles of Agreement of the World Bank.

18. See, e.g., Article V of the Constitution of UNESCO.

19. See *Reparation for Injuries Suffered in the Service of the United Nations*, Advisory Opinion, I.C.J. Reports 1949, p. 179.

20. *Interpretation of the Agreement of 25 March 1951 between the WHO and Egypt*, Advisory Opinion, I.C.J. Reports 1980, p. 73, para. 37.

21. Concert of Europe was the period following the Napoleonic Wars when major European powers met in a system of consultation to preserve and protect their governments.

in 1865,[22] followed by the Universal Postal Union (UPU) in 1874.[23] These permanent international bodies had enduring common objectives, and permanent structure with membership. "The smooth and successful functioning of these agencies gave rise to speculation about the possibility of more far-reaching institutions to facilitate transnational relations. Such speculations were based on actual experiences, not only the experiences of the 'permanent' regulatory agencies but also those resulting from the multilateral treaty-making process. The international legislative process had, by the end of the nineteenth century, proved effective for resolving some aspects of the problems besetting states in their relations with one another. Especially successful were conferences drafting laws covering behavior in war, communications, and health."[24]

The Treaty of Versailles at the end of World War I gave birth to the modern or contemporary international organization with the establishment in 1920 of both the League of Nations for cooperation among governments in the political arena, and the ILO for the international improvement and maintenance of labor standards and conditions. "The creation of the League of Nations was attended by great optimism [but increasing] conflict in the world, rising tensions, and political maneuvering began to undermine the League's ability to play a significant and meaningful role in the world. . . . Although the League had failed, the idea that there should be a world organization was very much alive."[25] The League of Nations was the forerunner of the United Nations, which was created in 1945 at the United Nations Conference on International Organization in San Francisco.[26] The ILO, on the other hand, with the promise of the usefulness of organizations dealing with specialized areas of concerns, was the impetus for the idea of specialized agencies, which became an integral part of the United Nations system as provided for in Articles 57 to 59 of the Charter of the United Nations.

22. ITU was founded in Paris in 1865 as the International Telegraph Union and took its present name in 1934. It became a specialized agency of the United Nations in 1947. An organization based on public-private partnership since its inception, ITU currently has a membership of 193 countries and almost 800 private-sector entities and academic institutions. ITU is the United Nations specialized agency for information and communication technologies.

23. UPU, with its headquarters in Berne, Switzerland, is the second oldest international organization worldwide. It has a membership of 192 countries and is the primary forum for cooperation between postal sector players.

24. Alexine L. Atherton, International Organizations: A Guide to Information Sources, at xix (Gale Information Guide Library 1976).

25. *Id.* at xx.

26. The Charter of the United Nations was signed on June 26, 1945, and came into force on October 24, 1945. 1 UNTS XVI.

International organizations emerged on the international scene to enable States to collectively tackle common problems, as well as to promote, preserve, or protect common interests. Since the creation of the United Nations, international organizations have proliferated and may outnumber States. Undoubtedly, they have not only grown in number but also in the nature of activities that fall within their remit. International organizations are ever present in the lives of people all over the world in one way or another. The proliferation of international organizations and the expansion in their activities have resulted in a concomitant enormous increase in the number of officials that they employ to carry out their functions.

PURPOSE OF IMMUNITY OF INTERNATIONAL ORGANIZATIONS

As a matter of necessity, States opted for international cooperation through the establishment of and participation in international organizations. International organizations are, therefore, created by the constituent member States to discharge vital functions and responsibilities on their behalf, and in some cases on behalf of the world community. They are established to offer cooperative and concerted approaches to common challenges and myriad problems that have the best chance of being alleviated or arrested through multilateral actions. Consequently, international organizations were invested with functions that may require them to act independently or autonomously of the member States. The price for this international cooperation is the partial abdication of the sovereignty of the member States of these international organizations.

To achieve their objectives, international organizations are invested with certain privileges and immunities by their member States. Article 105 of the Charter of the United Nations is a quintessential statement of the justification of the immunity of international organizations: "The Organization shall enjoy in the territory of each of its Members such privileges and immunities as are necessary for the fulfilment of its purposes."[27]

The Canadian Supreme Court had this to say about the immunities of international organizations:

> International organizations are active and necessary actors on the international stage. Although they are subjects of international law, they have to

27. Another example of a statement about the purpose of privileges and immunities is Article VII, Section 1, of the Articles of Agreement of the World Bank: "To enable the Bank to fulfill the functions with which it is entrusted, the status, immunities and privileges set forth in this Articles shall be accorded to the Bank in the territories of each member."

> operate on the territories of sovereign states and with political and legal systems of their own. To avoid undue interference in the operations of an international organization, the treaty that establishes it will recognize certain privileges and immunities. If not, the host state will promise to do so. In this regard, some form of immunity from legal process in domestic courts is critical, and commonly granted.[28]

Also, in the context of explaining the of immunity of the World Bank, the Canadian Supreme Court had noted:

> It must be remembered that when a state agrees to become a member of the World Bank Group, it makes a deliberate decision to accept the terms and conditions of the organization, which include archival and personnel immunities. It is part of the original agreement that in exchange for admission to the international organization, every member state agrees to accept the concept of collective governance. As a result, no single member can attempt to control the institution, which may occur if domestic courts apply local and variegated conceptions of implied and constructive waiver. Requiring express waiver avoids these problems.[29]

Jurisdictional immunity serves to ensure that member States through their national courts do not interfere in the administration, management, and operation of the international organization. In this regard, the District of Columbia Court of Appeals in *Broadbent v. Organization of American States (OAS)* noted:

> The United States has accepted without qualification the principle that international organizations must be free to perform their functions and that no member state may take action to hinder the organization. The unique nature of the international civil service is relevant. International officials should be as free as possible, within the mandate granted by the member states, to perform their duties free from the peculiarities of national politics. The OAS charter, for example, imposes constraints on the organization's employment practices. Such constraints may not coincide with the employment policies pursued by various member states. It would seem singularly inappropriate for the international organization to bind itself to the employment law of any particular member, and we have

28. *Amaratunga v. Northwest Atlantic Fisheries Organization*, 2013 SCC 66, [2013] 3. S.C.R. 866 (Can.), at para. 1.

29. *World Bank Group v. Wallace*, 2016 SCC 15, para. 93.

> no reason to think that either the President or Congress intended this result. An attempt by the courts of one nation to adjudicate the personnel claims of international civil servants would entangle those courts in the internal administration of those organizations. Denial of immunity opens the door to divided decisions of the courts of different member states passing judgment on the rules, regulations, and decisions of the international bodies. Undercutting uniformity in the application of staff rules or regulations would undermine the ability of the organizations to function effectively.[30]

In addition to courts, legal luminaries have formulated justifications for the immunity of international organizations.[31] Hugh McKinnon Wood of the defunct League of Nations had proposed:

> Jurisdictional immunity is for several reasons essential for an organisation like the League. The least important in relation to a country like Switzerland is the danger of prejudice or bad faith in the national courts. The second reason is the need for protection against baseless actions brought from improper motives or by the numerous cranks, fanatics or cantankerous persons who may conceive that they have a duty to compel the organisation to take some particular step or that they have suffered wrong at its hand. The third is the undesirability of allowing the courts of particular members to determine, quite possibly in different senses, the legal effects of acts performed in the exercise of the organisation's functions.[32]

30. *Broadbent v. Organization of American States (OAS)*, 628 F.2d 27, 34–35 (D.C. Cir. 1980).

31. See, e.g., Kuljit Ahluwalia, The Legal Status, Privileges and Immunities of the Specialized Agencies of the United Nations and Certain Other International Organizations (Martinus Nijhoff 1964); Jean Duffar, Contribution A L'Étude Des Privilèges Et Immunités Des Organisations Internationales (1962); Jean-Luc Fagnart, L'Immunité De Juridiction Des Organisations Internationales (2004); Jean-Flavien Lalive, L'Immunité De Juridiction Des États Et Des Organisations Internationales (Hague Académie De Droit International 1953); Josef L. Kunz, *Privileges and Immunities of International Organizations*, 41 Am. J. Int'l L. (828 (1947); Peter H.F. Bekker, The Legal Position of Intergovernmental Organizations: A Functional Necessity Analysis of Their Legal Status and Immunities (Martinus Nijhoff (1994); Christian Dominicé, L'immunité de juridiction et d'exécution des organisations internationales, Académie de droit international, Recueil des cours, Tome 187 de la collection, 1984.

32. H. McKinnon Wood, *Legal Relations Between Individuals and a World Organization of States*, in 30 Transactions of the Grotius Society for 1944, at 143–44 (1945), *cited in* C. Wilfred Jenks, International Immunities 40 (1961). Wood was counselor and legal adviser at the League of Nations.

C. Wilfred Jenks stated:

> The basic function of . . . immunities is to bridle the sovereignty of States in their treatment of international organisations. This bridling of sovereignty is as much in the interest of States as in that of international organisations. While it debars each State from illicit interference, it also protects it from such interference by other States. It represents, indeed, an indispensable guarantee to each member State that the organization will not become, by means of pressure and constraint which are not fully apparent and over which there is therefore no possibility of control, an instrument of the policy of other States directed against its own policy and interests, but will serve legally the common interest as determined by the recognized constitutional processes of the organisation. States, have, moreover, an interest when creating international organisations in equipping these organisations to discharge their functions efficiently and economically. It is for these reasons that States have made a practice of making provision for appropriate immunities in the constituent instruments of international organisation."[33]

When a member State of the United Nations proposed to accede to the General Convention subject to reservation denying privileges and immunities to any official of that State's nationality, the Secretary-General responded and articulated the nature and purpose of the immunity of the United Nations:

> 3. Numerous privileges and immunities specified in article V [of the Convention] are not ordinarily understood to have practical application as between an official of the United Nations and his Government of nationality. Such an official will have no occasion, unless in rare circumstances, to require immunity from immigration restrictions in his own country, or privileges in respect of exchange facilities, or repatriation facilities in time of international crisis; he cannot by definition require immunity from alien registration, and it would be exceptional for him to have reason to claim duty-free entry for his personal effects on taking up his post in the country.

33. Jenks, International Immunities, at 166. Clarence Wilfred Jenks joined the ILO in 1931 as a member of its Legal Division and then served successively as Legal Adviser, Assistant Director-General, Deputy Director-General, principal Deputy Director-General, and Director-General. Jenks participated in the drafting of the Declaration of Philadelphia in 1944, which became part of the ILO Constitution, and was a member of the ILO delegation to the San Francisco conference that established the United Nations in 1945.

4. The situation is quite otherwise in the matter of his official acts, and it is here that the reservation cannot be reconciled with the Charter. Section *18(a)* in article V [of the Convention] requires that officials of the United Nations be "immune from legal process in respect of words spoken or written and all acts performed by them in *their official capacity*." (Underscoring supplied.) It follows that your country, in proposing the reservation quoted above, has (no doubt unintentionally) reserved the right to prosecute United Nations officials of its nationality for words spoken or written or for any acts performed by them in their official capacity, indeed for actions which are in effect the acts of the Organization itself. It would equally be the consequence of the reservation that your country would be reserving jurisdiction to its national courts to entertain private lawsuits against its citizens for acts performed by them as officials of the United Nations.
5. Article 105 of the Charter provides in its second paragraph that officials of the Organization shall "enjoy such privileges and immunities as are necessary for the independent exercise of their functions in connexion with the Organization." Likewise, by the second paragraph of Article 100 each Member of the United Nations "undertakes to respect the exclusively international character of the responsibilities of the Secretary-General and the staff". It needs no argument to demonstrate that the reservation by a Member of the right, even in the abstract, to exercise jurisdiction over the official acts of United Nations staff, either through its courts or through other organs or authorities of the State, would be incompatible with the independent exercise and the exclusively international character of the responsibilities of such officials of the Organization. This derogation from the clear terms of the Charter would in no way be affected by the common nationality of the international official and the prosecuting authority. . . .
6. The situation is similar with regard to article VI of the Convention. Experts of your country's nationality would not normally perform their missions for the United Nations on national territory. On the other hand, the inevitable consequence of reserving article VI would be to permit the exercise over nationals of your country, who have performed or are performing official United Nations missions, of jurisdiction in respect of words spoken or written and acts done by them in the course of the performance of their mission. For example, an officer who might be seconded by your Government for service abroad as a United Nations Military Observer would technically be subject on his return to inculpation or sanction for some aspect of his activity on behalf of the Organization. This is particularly evident from

> the fact that one of the provisions reserved states (in section 22*(b)* of the Convention): "This immunity from legal process shall continue to be accorded notwithstanding that the persons concerned are no longer employed on missions for the United Nations." Papers and documents of the United Nations in his possession could likewise be deprived of their inviolability, while the confidential character of his communications with the United Nations could equally be overridden. In such circumstances the Organization itself could not be said to enjoy in the territory of the Member in question the privileges and immunities necessary for the fulfillment of its purposes, as required by Article 105, paragraph 1 of the Charter.[34]

In sum, international organizations generally enjoy such privileges and immunities from the jurisdictions of their member States as are necessary for the fulfillment of the functions and purposes for which they were established.[35] To carry out their functions, international organizations act through their officials. As they are "without any sovereign territory of their own, international organizations are vulnerable to state interference. In light of this, member states often agree to grant international organizations various immunities and privileges to preserve their orderly, independent operation. Commonly . . . its personnel are made immune from legal process."[36] These "immunities are extended to international organizations to protect them from intrusions into their operations and agenda by a member state or a member state's courts."[37] Thus, if international organizations immunity may be bifurcated, the immunities of the organization qua organization are necessary for the fulfillment of their purposes, whereas the immunity of their officials are necessary for the independent exercise of their functions for the organization.

34. United Nations Juridical Yearbook 1963, pp. 188–89.

35. See Restatement Third of Foreign Relations § 467 (Am. Law. Inst. 1987)

36. *World Bank Group v. Wallace*, 2016 SCC 15, para. 2.

37. *Id.*, para. 71.

6

Legal Status of International Organizations

LEGAL STATUS

The legal status of international organizations matters because issues of their jurisdictional immunity would not arise, a priori, if they did not have personality in both international and national laws. The legal instruments that provide for the legal status of international organizations also normally provide for their privileges and immunities. In this regard, the Charter of the United Nations[1] provides for its "legal capacity" in Article 104.

> "It is apparent that an organization like the United Nations which will have offices and employees, will purchase supplies, and presumably rent or purchase office space, must have the legal capacity to enter into contracts, to take title to real and personal property and to appear in court (although its position as a defendant is protected by Article 105). The purpose of Article 104 is to make clear that the Organization has that legal capacity. No such provision was included in the Covenant but the capacity was recognized in practice as in the relations between the League of Nations and the Swiss Government. A provision similar to that stated in this article

1. Charter of the United Nations, June 26, 1945, 59 Stat. 1031, T.S. 993.

Jurisdictional Immunities of States and International Organizations. Edward Chukwuemeke Okeke.

was included in the agreements relative to the following United Nations organizations: Food and Agriculture Organization; UNRRA; International Monetary Fund; International Bank for Reconstruction and Development; Provisional International Civil Aviation Organization. . . . It is the national law of each country which determines whether a particular body or organization which is not set up as a corporation under the law of that country will have legal capacity. National laws vary greatly on this matter; in some instances Article 104 may be unnecessary, in some cases it may need to be supplemented by legislation, and in others it may operate of its own force to confer the necessary status."[2]

Article 105 provides that the organization, its officials and representatives of its member States shall have the necessary privileges and immunities to carry out their functions. Regarding the immunity of the United Nations at its founding the United States delegation had this to say about the immunity of the United Nations:

> "The United Nations, being an organization of all of the member states, is clearly not subject to the jurisdiction or control of any one of them and the same will be true for the officials of the Organization. The problem will be particularly important in connection with the relationship between the United Nations and the country in which it has its seat. The problem will also exist, however, in any country in which the officials of the United Nations are called upon from time to time to perform official duties. The United States shares the interest of all Members in seeing that no state hampers the work of the Organization through the imposition of unnecessary local burdens."[3]

The Convention on Privileges and Immunities of the United Nations adopted by the General Assembly on February 13, 1946 ("General Convention"), also provides for the legal capacity of the United Nations in Article 1 and for its jurisdictional immunity in Article II, Section 2. Article V, Section 18, of the General Convention establishes the immunity of the Organization's officials from legal process in connection with acts performed by them in their official

2. 1 Charter of the United Nations. Report to the President on the Results of the San Francisco Conference by the Chairman of the United States Delegation, the Secretary of State, June 26, 1945, Department of State Publication 2349, Conference Series 71 ("Report to the President of United States"), p. 157.

3. Report to the President of United States, p. 159.

capacity.[4] Absent such a legal status, an international organization would be devoid of the legal basis and "capacity to participate meaningfully in international and national life."[5]

The legal status of an international organization concerns its international personality under international law, as well as its legal personality or capacity under national laws. The distinction in both personalities is evident in, for example, Article 2 of the headquarters agreement between the Swiss Federal Council and the International Labour Organization, which provides: "The Swiss Federal Council recognizes the international personality and legal capacity in Switzerland of the International Labour Organization."[6] Although "legal personality" and "legal capacity" are used interchangeably, legal capacity and legal personality are distinct. Capacity and personality do not necessarily mean the same thing. Sometimes, "juridical" is substituted for "legal" in legal personality and legal capacity, or for "international" in international personality. "Whereas juridical personality of an international organization is neither derived from nor limited by the laws of any one State, it is the national laws of each State which determine the extent to which such an organization shall enjoy legal capacity."[7]

Legal capacity derives from legal personality. Personality is the status of an entity within a legal system, and capacity is the scope of rights and obligations that inure to that person or entity within a legal system. Thus, in law there exists the concepts of natural person and legal person. A natural person is a human being, whereas a legal person is an entity that is allowed by law to take certain legal actions, such as the legal capacity to sue or be sued, own property, enter into contracts, function legally, and make decisions regarding its existence. Under national laws, legal persons are, therefore, not natural but fictitious persons, such as corporations, companies, and other groups of natural persons that act as distinct entities.

To function, international organizations possess the legal capacity, at a minimum, to contract, to acquire and dispose of property, and to initiate legal

4. Convention on the Privileges and Immunities of the United Nations, February 13, 1946, 1 U.N.T.S. 15.

5. See Henry G. Schermers & Neils M. Blokker, International Institutional Law § 1559 (2003).

6. See Jean-Flavien Lalive, *L'Immunité de Juridiction des États et des Organisations Internationales, Recueil Des Cours* 348, Hague Académie de Droit International (1953) ("Les deux types de personnalités sont nettement distingues; une pratique déjà ancienne permet d'utiliser les termes propres et une technique juridique correcte.")

7. See, e.g., Kuljit Ahluwalia, The Legal Status, Privileges and Immunities of the Specialized Agencies of the United Nations and certain other International Organizations 60 (The Hague: Martinus Nijhoff, 1964).

proceedings under the national laws of its member States, as well as the international personality with the attributes of rights and duties under international law. As a function of their legal status, international organizations can enter into legal relationships with their member States; their staff, nonmember States, other international organizations, nongovernmental organizations, and other private parties. With international personality and legal personality, the legal relations of an international organization are separate and independent from those of its member States. An international organization is an autonomous and different legal person from its member States. "When international organizations acquired legal personality by international agreement, they also acquired privileges and immunities in their own right."[8]

The constituent or other legal instruments of most international organizations regarding their legal status do provide explicitly for their legal personality but rarely do they provide also for their international personality. For example, Article 104 of the Charter of the United Nations provides only for its legal capacity.[9] Article XII of the Constitution of UNESCO provides: "The provisions of Articles 104 and 105 of the Charter of the United Nations Organization concerning the legal status of that Organization, its privileges and immunities, shall apply in the same way to this Organization." Article VII, Section 2, of the Articles of Agreement of the International Bank for Reconstruction and Development provides: "The Bank shall possess full juridical personality, and in particular, the capacity: (i) to contract; (ii) to acquire and dispose of immovable and movable property; (iii) to institute legal proceedings." Article I, Section 1, Convention on the Privileges and Immunities of the United Nations provides that the Organization shall possess juridical personality: "It shall have the capacity: (a) to contract; (b) to acquire and dispose of immovable and movable property; (c) to institute legal proceedings."

Unlike the constituent text of most international organizations, Article 50 of the Articles of Agreement of the African Development Bank provides explicitly for its international personality: "To enable it to fulfil its purpose and functions

8. Restatement (Third) of Foreign Relations Law (Am. Law Inst. 1987) Introductory Note, Subchapter B, Immunities of International Organizations.

9. "Article [104] does not deal with what is called the 'international personality' of the Organization. The Committee which discussed this matter was anxious to avoid any implication that the United Nations will be in any sense a 'super-state'. So far as the power to enter into agreements with states is concerned, the answer is given by Article 43 which provides that the Security Council is to be a party to the agreements concerning the availability of armed forces. International practice, while limited, supports the idea of such a body being a party to agreements. No other issue of 'international personality' requires mention in the Charter. Practice will bring about the evolution of appropriate rules so far as necessary." Report to the President of United States, pp. 157–58.

with which it is entrusted, the Bank shall possess full international personality. To those ends, it may enter into agreements with members, non-member States and other international organizations." Although the Covenant of the defunct League of Nations did not provide explicitly for its international personality, the 1926 modus vivendi between the League of Nations and Switzerland provided that the organization had international personality and legal capacity.

The possession of international personality may not necessarily or automatically translate into the possession of privileges and immunities by an international organization. At the same time, an organization does not have to possess international personality in order to be accorded privileges and immunities by a State.[10]

International Personality

The question of the international personality of the United Nations had to be addressed on October 7, 1948, when the Secretary-General of the United Nations, compelled by the death or serious injury of United Nations agents and the assassination of the United Nations Mediator in Palestine, submitted a memorandum on the reparation of injuries incurred in the service of the United Nations for the consideration of the third session of the General Assembly. Consequently, by Resolution 258 (III) the General Assembly requested the advisory opinion of the ICJ on two legal questions:

> I. In the event of an agent of the United Nations in the performance of his duties suffering injury in circumstances involving the responsibility of a State, has the United Nations, as an organization, the capacity to bring an international claim against the responsible *de jure* or *de facto* Government with a view to obtaining the reparation due in respect of the damage caused (a) to the United Nations, (b) to the victim or to persons entitled through him?
>
> II. In the event of an affirmative reply on point I (b), how is action by the United Nations to be reconciled with such rights as may be possessed by the State of which the victim is a national?[11]

10. Although the Global Fund to Fight AIDS, Tuberculosis, and Malaria ("Global Fund") is not an international organization, privileges and immunities have been accorded to the Global Fund by the United States in 2006, under the International Organizations Immunities Act of the United States of America (22 U.S.C.§§ 288 and 288f–6), and by Switzerland in 2004, through the Headquarters Agreement between the Global Fund and the Swiss Federal Council.

11. Resolution of the General Assembly dated December 3, 1948.

In its advisory opinion dated April 11, 1949,[12] the International Court of Justice (ICJ) concluded that the United Nations is an international person, which means that it is a subject of international law and capable of possessing international rights and duties, and that it has the capacity to maintain its rights by bringing international claims. To reach its conclusion, the Court had to first define what is meant by the "capacity to bring an international claim," as well as to consider the characteristics of the United Nations.[13] It noted that a State, as a subject of international law, possessed such a capacity to bring international claims. To answer the question of whether the United Nations has such a capacity, the Court had to enquire whether the Charter gave the Organization such a capacity vis-à-vis its Members, that is, whether the Organization possesses international personality.[14] Because the actual terms of the Charter are silent on the question, the Court considered the characteristics that the Charter gave to the United Nations:

> [The Charter] has defined the position of the Members in relation to the Organization by requiring them to give every assistance in any action undertaken by it (Article 2, para. 5), and to accept and carry out the decisions of the Security Council; by authorizing the General Assembly to make recommendations to the Members; by giving the Organization legal capacity and privileges and immunities in the territory of each of its Members; and by providing for the conclusion of agreements between the Organization and its Members . . . The "Convention on the Privileges and Immunities of the United Nations" of 1946 creates rights and duties between each of the signatories and the Organization (see, in particular, Section 35). It is difficult to see how such a convention could operate except upon the international plane and as between parties possessing international personality.[15]

The Court reasoned:

> [T]he Organization was intended to exercise and enjoy, and is in fact exercising and enjoying, functions and rights which can only be explained on the basis of the possession of a large measure of international personality and the capacity to operate upon an international plane. It is at the present the supreme type of international organization, and it could not

12. *Reparation for Injuries Suffered in the Service of the United Nations*, Advisory Opinion: I.C.J. Rep. 1949, p. 174.

13. See *id.* 177.

14. *Id.* at 178.

15. *Id.* at 178–79.

> carry out the intentions of its founders if it was devoid of international personality. It must be acknowledged that its members, by entrusting certain functions to it, with the attendant duties and responsibilities, have clothed it with the competence required to enable those functions to be effectively discharged.[16]

Consequently, the Court concluded that the United Nations is an international person but clarified that this "is not the same thing as saying that it is a State, which it certainly is not, or that its legal personality and rights and duties are the same as those of a State. Still less is it the same thing as saying that it is 'a super-State,' whatever that expression may mean."[17] The Court also clarified: "Whereas a State possesses the totality of international rights and duties recognized by international law, the rights and duties of an entity such as the Organization must depend upon its purposes and functions as specified or implied in its constituent documents and developed in practice."[18]

In response to the specific questions posed by the General Assembly, the Court by unanimous vote answered Question I (a) in the affirmative on the ground that, as the claim was based on the breach of an international obligation on the part of the State held responsible by the Organization, the State could not contend that this obligation was governed by national law, and the Organization was justified in giving its claim the character of an international claim. By 11 votes to 4, the Court gave an affirmative answer to Question I (b), stating: "Under international law, the Organization must be deemed to have those powers which, though not expressly provided in the Charter, were conferred upon it by necessary implication as being essential to the performance of its duties."[19]

The Court opined that the member States of the United Nations, "representing the vast majority of the members of the international community, had the power, in conformity with international law, to bring into being an entity possessing *objective international personality*, and not merely personality recognized by them alone, together with the capacity to bring international claims."[20] The answer of the Court to Question I, therefore, applied not only to members of the United Nations, but also to nonmember States held responsible by the Organization.[21]

16. *Id.* at 179.

17. *Id.*

18. *Id.* at 180.

19. *Id.* at 182.

20. *Id.* at 185 [emphasis added].

21. *Id.*

Although the *Reparation for Injuries* opinion provided definitive legal authority that international organizations have international personality, the scope of that personality remains nebulous. Even though an international organization is an international person, its capacities, rights, and responsibilities are not the same or coextensive as those of a State. A State possesses the totality of rights and duties recognized by international law, which is not the case with international organizations. The rights and responsibilities of international organizations, on the other hand, are defined and circumscribed by their constituent documents.

Considering that a State is the prototypical international person, some international law scholars and courts have struggled with the subject of international organizations as international persons. This struggle is often reflected in the borrowed terminology of Statehood, such as sovereignty, that is employed in the description of acts of international organizations. The misuse of terminology sometimes obfuscates the concept of international personality. Nevertheless, it is now well-settled that international organizations are (also) subjects of international law: "International organizations are subjects of international law and, as such, are bound by any obligations incumbent upon them under general rules of international law, under their constitutions or under international agreements to which they are parties."[22] For instance, they can enter into agreements with States and other international organizations. With this recognition of international organizations as international persons, that is, subjects of international law, international law is no longer merely the law of nations.

As a result of the *Reparation for Injuries* opinion, the question of the international legal personality should be settled, not only for the United Nations but also for major international organizations. "By analogy, the reasoning of the Court can also be applied to other international organizations. Most arguments supporting the Court's conclusion that the UN has international personality are true for other international organizations."[23] However, the doctrinal debate on the international personality of international organizations has not abated, despite or because of the *Reparation for Injuries* case.[24] The debate centers on whether the international personality of an international organization is objective in the

22. *Interpretation of the Agreement of 25 March 1951 between the WHO and Egypt*, Advisory Opinion, I.C.J. Reports 1908, p. 73, para. 37, pp. 89–90.

23. Henry G. Schermers & Neils M. Blokker, § 1568, Fourth Revised Edition.

24. See C.F. Amerasinghe, Principles of the Law of International Organizations 81 (2d ed. Cambridge University Press 2015); Jan Klabbers, An Introduction to International Organizations Law 46 (3d ed. Cambridge University Press 2015).

sense that it is also valid against nonmember States.[25] Critics of the *Reparation for Injuries* opinion argue that international personality of an international organization depends not only on the constituent instrument establishing the international organization but also "that recognition (or acquiescence) is necessary on the part of non-member States, since these are not parties to the constitution of the Organization."[26] The argument "is based upon the assumption (1) that an intergovernmental organization has international personality only if and to the extent that this follows from its constitution and the intention of its drafters, and (2) that the constitution of an intergovernmental organization, like any other treaty is not binding upon States which have not acceded to it."[27] Another school of thought is that international personality, whether expressed or implied in its constitution, confers upon the international organization certain rights, duties and powers under international law.

No matter whether international personality is constitutive or declaratory, an organization will lack international personality without the criteria of an international organization notwithstanding the expressed will of its members. "Thus, the establishment of international personality for an international organization does not appear to be as simple an exercise as identifying certain objective criteria which confer personality in general international law."[28]

What is the legal effect of objective international personality? "In the case of intergovernmental organizations, as well as in the case of States, objective international personality merely means that the State or Organization is subject to the rights and duties of international law by any other subject of international law which has relations with it."[29] In other words, "Objective international personality for a State or an intergovernmental organization means that third parties must treat the State or Organization as a subject of international law in any relations that they have with it, but it does not imply an obligation to enter into such

25. See Finn Seyersted, Objective International Personality of Intergovernmental Organization: Do Their Capacity Really Depend upon Their Constitution? (Copenhagen 1963). Seidl-Hohenveldern takes the opposite view that international organizations do not have an objective international personality.

26. See *id.* at 9–10.

27. *Id.* at 9–10; see P. Sands & P. Klein, Bowett's Law of International Institutions 479 (6th ed.) (2009) ("Whether it flows directly from the constituent instrument or other multilateral agreements, or whether it arises by implication from such instruments, the international legal personality of international organizations is based upon the will of the founders.")

28. Amerasinghe, Principles of the Law of International Organizations 81 (2d ed. Cambridge University Press 2015.

29. Seyertsed, [citation omitted], at 98.

relations. A confusion of these two aspects should not be allowed to confuse the law of international personality and recognition, neither of States nor of intergovernmental organizations."[30]

By analogy, the argument for objective international personality is that an international organization does not need the recognition of nonmember States to come into existence, just as a State does not need the recognition of (all) other States to come into existence, provided the elements of Statehood are satisfied. The undeniable effect of (objective) international personality for international organizations is that they have rights and duties under international law, but because international organizations do not have the full panoply of rights and duties like States as a subject of international law, it is still debatable whether whatever attributes of the objective international personality are opposable to nonmember States. With respect to member States of an international organization, it is settled that the international legal personality is opposable to them as they are bound by the legal instrument that created the international organization and gave its international personality. It is worth noting that the *Reparation for Injuries* opinion involved a dispute between the United Nations and a (then) nonmember of the international organization, and that the notion of objective international personality valid erga omnes may conflict with the principle that a treaty is a *res inter alios acta* for the nonparties. Ordinarily, international personality *erga tertios* will apply only after the recognition of an international organization by nonmember States. The ICJ addressed this point in a rather conclusory fashion: "Court's opinion is that fifty States, representing the vast majority of the members of the international community, has the power, in conformity with international law, to bring into being an entity possessing objective international personality, and *not merely personality recognised by them alone. . . .*"[31]

The reasoning of the ICJ in *Reparation for Injuries* may have been circular, but the ruling is clear about the distinct (international) legal personality of an international organization from those of its members—a distinctiveness that has ramifications for an international organization's privileges and immunities. Despite any criticism of the reasoning, the ICJ ruling did affirmatively establish the concept of international personality for international organizations, as opposed to the timid approach of the Permanent Court of International Justice in the *European Commission on the Danube* case.[32]

30. *Id.* at 102.

31. *Reparation for Injuries Suffered in the Service of the United Nations*, ICJ Rep. 1949, 174, 185 [emphasis added].

32. See PCIJ Series B. No. 14. P.64 ("As the European Commission is not a State, but an international institution with a special purpose, it only has the functions bestowed upon it by the Definitive

In the *Reparation* case, it was necessary for the ICJ to determine whether the United Nations has international personality because of the attributes of such a personality. The attributes of international personality are that the international organization has a personality distinct from that of its member States, as well as the capacity to conclude treaties, and enter diplomatic or international legal relations. The Court also affirmed the international personality of the United Nations by referring, inter alia, to its treaty-making capacity.[33]

The *Reparation* case may, therefore, lend support to the proposition that the objective international personality of an international organization means that its rights and duties are enforceable against nonmember States, with or without their recognition of the international organization. Although the *Reparation* case concerned the capacity of the United Nations to bring an international claim in respect of injury to the organization itself and to its personnel, it follows that the international personality of an international organization implicates its legal status, privileges, and immunities. Put differently, the privileges and immunities of an international organization derive from its legal status as an international person.

The debate about objective international personality is often a proxy for the debate about whether there is a customary international law on the status, privileges, and immunities of international organizations.[34] The status, privileges and immunities are mostly treaty-based and, as such, if there are also based on customary international law, then it would mean that nonmember States of international organizations have an international obligation to accord them privileges and immunities.[35] Where questions of customary international law arise, it

Statute with a view to the fulfilment of that purpose, but it has power to exercise these functions to their full extent, in so far as the Statute does not impose restrictions upon it.")

33. 1949 I.C.J. Reports, p. 174.

34. See Singer at 99 ("Although customary law on the jurisdictional immunity of the United Nations is relatively well developed, there is little persuasive evidence of customary norms delimiting the jurisdictional immunities of other specific international organizations, or of international organizations in generals."); August Reinisch, *Privileges and Immunities*, *in* Research Handbooks in International Law: Research Handbook on the Law of International Organizations 135 (Jan Klabbers & Asa Wallendahl eds., Edward Elgars Publishing 2015) [citations omitted] ("Whether there is a customary international law on privileges and immunities of international organizations and, if so, the precise content of such customary law has remained controversial and led to divergent answers by different courts."); Jean-Luc Fagnart, L'immunité de juridiction des organisations internationales, Mélanges Jacques van Compernolle. 2004, p. 184 ("*Existe-t-il une coutume internationale en vertu de laquelle l'immunité de juridiction devrait être reconnue à toute organisation internationale? La réponse est incertaine et la jurisprudence divisée.*").

35. See Restatement (Third) of Foreign Relations Law § 467, Reporters' Note (Am. Law Inst. 1987) (Immunities of international organizations under customary law): "Since membership

would be in connection with nonmember States, as the status, privileges, and immunities of international organizations with respect to the member States are largely covered by treaties and similar agreements.[36]

It has been persuasively posited:

> Where no agreement concerning immunities has been negotiated with a third State the organization will not be able to rely in relation to that State on any general provisions of its own Constitution providing for appropriate immunities as an international obligation of that State. It does not follow that the organization has no legal rights in such a situation. The rights which it is entitled to claim may be less extensive than those which it is entitled to claim in relation to its own members, but the organization cannot reasonably be regarded in relation to third States as a group of private persons with no legal status of any kind; at the lowest it is a group of States acting collectively; it appears to follow from *Reparation for Injuries* . . . that a group of governments so acting can create an international entity with an objective legal personality which will be recognized by international law; it is only one stage further in the argument to recognize that they can vest such an entity with the immunities recognized to be appropriate for such an entity by general international agreements. A third State has, of course, no obligation to allow such an entity to operate on its territory, but if it allows it to do so it must, it is suggested, respect the immunities appropriate to such an entity. This general line of reasoning is supported by the analogy of the recognition in third States of the immunities of diplomatic agents.[37]

It has been stated that from the viewpoint of international law, the notion of international personality "seemed less problematic if it was confined to international organizations of a universal character" such as the United Nations and its specialized agencies, because third states "might be loath to grant privileges and immunities to [regional] bodies in which it did not participate."[38] On the other

in the principal international organizations enjoy privileges and immunities in virtually every state under the charters of the organization, which are international agreements, as well as under general conventions on the immunities of international organizations. For the view that the United Nations now enjoys those privileges and immunities under customary law, see the statement of the legal counsel of the United Nations in Annual Report of the Secretary-General, 23 U.N. GAOR., Supp. No. 1 at 208–209 (1968)."

36. See [1992] 2(2) Y.B. Int'l Law Comm'n, para.360.

37. C. Wilfred Jenks, International Immunities 34, Preface (1961).

38. See [1987] 1 Y.B. Int'l Law Comm'n 196, para. 29, in A/CN.4/SER.A/1987.

hand, it has been asserted that there exists an obligation in international law to grant immunity to international organizations. In this regard, the Geneva Labor Court has held that "international organizations, whether universal or regional, enjoy absolute jurisdictional immunity."[39] Similarly, the Netherlands Supreme Court has held that "even in case where there is no treaty . . . it follows from unwritten international law that an international organization is entitled to the privilege of immunity from jurisdiction on the same footing as generally provided for in the treaties . . . in any event in the State in whose territory the organization has its seat, with the consent of the host State."[40] The Belgian Court of Cassation has taken the position that the immunity of international organizations is granted either by a general principle of international law or by special agreements.[41] For its part, the Supreme Court of the Philippines has decided: "One of the basic immunities of an international organization is immunity from local jurisdiction, i.e., that it is immune from the legal writs and processes issued by the tribunal of the country where it is found."[42]

It has been argued that with the possession of international personality, international organizations perform some functions that are analogous to those of States, which require certain privileges and immunities from States for their effective exercise.[43] It follows that with the recognition of this objective international personality, member States and nonmember States have an obligation under international law to accord the international organization the privileges and immunities necessary for it to function. "An international organization with substantial membership is a person in international law even in relation to states not members of the organization. However, a state does not have to recognize the legal personality of an organization of which it is not a member, which has few members, or which is regional in scope in a region to which the state does not belong."[44]

The Italian Court of Cassation addressed the correlation between international personality and immunity in a case involving the Italian Latin-American Institute

39. *Z.M. v. Permanent Delegation of the League of Arab States to the United Nations* (Switzerland, November 17, 1993) 116 I.L.R. 643, 646.

40. *Iran-United States Claims Tribunal v. AS*, Judgment of December 20, 1985, ILR, vol. 94, pp. 327–29.

41. *T.M. v. Ligue des Etats Arabes*, Judgment of December 3, 2001, available at www.cass.be.

42. *South-east Asian Fisheries Development Center v. Acosta*, Judgment of September 2, 1993, available at www.lawphil.net.

43. See SANDS & KLEIN, at 490.

44. See RESTATEMENT (THIRD) OF FOREIGN RELATIONS LAW § 223, Comment (e) (AM. LAW. INST. 1987).

("IILA"), which was established as an international organization by a convention concluded between Italy and 20 Latin American States. The Court stated: "The traditional theory, which our jurisprudence has consistently followed, maintains that immunity depends on international personality and applies to international organizations the principle commonly recognized in relation to States, of *par in parem non habet jurisdictionem*."[45]

Legal Personality

With respect to international organizations, "legal personality" is often used interchangeably with "international personality," but such usage is imprecise. International personality is what distinguishes an international organization from other entities that can operate in one or more national legal orders but not on the international legal plane. To carry out their functions, international organizations must have legal personality under national laws. Legal personality enables international organizations to perform their functions on the national plane and to do so independently of their member States. Thus, just like international personality confers rights and responsibilities on the international plane, legal personality invests an entity with both rights and responsibilities within a domestic or national legal order. Domestic or national law confers legal personality to an international organization, already existing in international law and possessing international personality, in order for that international organization to function within the framework of the municipal law. An organization cannot have international personality without also having legal personality, but it can have the latter without having the former. Legal personality may be conferred expressly by the charter or other constituent instrument of an international organization, or it may be inferred or implied from the organization's object and purpose.

The legal personality of the United Nations, which represents the norm for international organizations, encompasses its *capacity* to contract, to acquire and dispose of both movable and immovable property, to institute legal proceedings.[46] Capacity is a facet of legal personality.[47] With respect to legal personality,

45. *Cristiani v. Italian Latin-American Institute*, Case No. 5819, Court of Cassation, Plenary Session (Italy, November 25, 1985), 87 I.L.R. 21, 24.

46. See Article I, Section 1, Convention on the Privileges and Immunities of the United Nations, adopted by the General Assembly on February 13, 1946; Article II, Section 3, Convention on the Privileges and Immunities of the Specialized Agencies, Approved by the General Assembly of the United Nations on 21 November 1947; and Article VII, Section 2, Articles of Agreement, International Bank for Reconstruction and Development.

47. *Rayner (J.H.) (Mincing Lane) Ltd. v. United Kingdom (Department of Trade and Industry)* ("*Tin Case*"), [1989] House of Lords, para. 65 ("[T]o have legal personality is also to have 'in particular'

the constituent instrument of most international organizations follows either the provisions of either the privileges and immunities conventions or that of the Articles of Agreement of the World Bank, or a slight variation of them incorporating the wording of Article 104 of the Charter of the United Nations, which makes clear that the organization has legal personality.

The legal instrument creating most international organizations provides for their legal personality in their member States. Legal personality of an international organization may be recognized in national law or a special agreement such as the Headquarters Agreement. For some States, the implementation of an international legal obligation would need to be given effect in national legislation so as to be also enforceable in their national legal systems. Even nonmember States of an international organization may recognize the legal personality of the organization in its territory. This was the case with Switzerland, which was the European headquarters of the United Nations before it became a member of the United Nations in 2002.

The concept of legal personality of international organizations could be a tricky subject, as evinced by the decision of the House of Lords in *Arab Monetary Fund v. Hashim (3)*.[48] Although international organizations are created by treaty, and constituent legal instruments may provide that the organization shall have legal personality in its member States, the law and practice of States in recognizing or giving effect to the legal personality are varied. For instance, in the United Kingdom, the situation with the legal personality of international organizations is as follows:

> There is no uniform practice with regard to international organisations in this country. In some cases, as in the *Tin* case, the organisation is given corporate capacity by means of an Order in Council issued under the International Organisations Act 1968 or its predecessors. In other cases provisions of the treaty agreeing to the establishment of the international organisation are declared by Parliament to have the force of law. This was done, for example, by the Bretton Woods Agreements Act 1945 and the Bretton Woods Agreement Order in Council 1946, SR & O 1946/36. In other cases, principally, but not exclusively, cases where the United Kingdom is not a party to the treaty, no legislative steps are taken in the United Kingdom but this does not debar Her Majesty's government from recognizing the international organisation and does not debar the courts

the capacity to contract, to acquire and dispose of movable and immovable property and to institute legal proceedings, which are thus described merely as facets of legal personality.")

48. [1991] 2 AC 114, [1991] 1 All ER 871, [1991] 2 WLR 729.

> of the United Kingdom from recognizing the international organisation as a separate entity by comity provided that the separate entity is created not by treaty but by one or more of the member states. This is the position of the fund.[49]

The Arab Monetary Fund ("AMF or Fund") is an international organization established by treaty signed in 1976 by 20 Arab States including the United Arab Emirates (UAE) where the headquarters is situated. UAE ratified the AMF Agreement in Federal Decree No. 35 of 1997 in accordance with its domestic laws. Article 2 of the Articles of Agreement (AMF Agreement) provides that the Fund shall have an independent juridical personality and shall, in particular, the right to own, contract, and litigate. AMF sued Hashim, its former Director-General, in England where he was domiciled, for embezzlement. Hashim applied to strike out the statement of claim on the ground that the AMF lacked the capacity to sue in an English court. The High Court dismissed the application by Hashim, but the Court of Appeal reversed the High Court, and AMF appealed to the House of Lords.

At the High Court, Judge Hoffmann considered two grounds advanced by AMF for the recognition of its legal existence under English law.[50] The first was that English conflict of laws recognizes the legal personality of an international organization as it recognizes the existence of legal entities constituted under systems of domestic laws. The second was that AMF should be recognized as an ordinary foreign juridical entity as it had been constituted under the domestic law of UAE. He was inclined to adopt the first ground but it became untenable, in his view, following the judgment of the House of Lords in *J.H. Rayner (Mincing Lane) Ltd v. Department of Trade and Industry* ("*Tin Case*").[51] He found the extension of English conflicts-of-law rule to international organizations "sensible and practical" as "[t]they are invariably recognised as juridical entities by the domestic systems of the parties to the treaty as well as by many other countries." He wondered why an international organization should be less entitled to recognition than an entity created under the law of one foreign State.[52]

49. *Arab Monetary Fund v. Hashim* (No. 3) [1991] 2 AC 114, [1991] 1 All ER 871, [1991] 2 WLR 729 (Lord Tempelman).

50. *Id.*, 83 ILR 247.

51. [1989] 3 W.L.R. 969.

52. 83 ILR 248.

Despite noting the difference between the International Tin Council, which was the subject of the *Tin Case*, and the AMF,[53] he felt compelled by the *Tin Case*[54] to disregard the treaty that created AMF as an international organization and to regard it "as constituted under Abu Dhabi law as separate *persona ficta*."[55] He found that AMF existed in English law because it exists under the law of one of its member States, UAE, noting: "I accept that a logical consequence is the existence of other emanations of the fund under the laws of other member states. This raises questions of Trinitarian subtlety into which I am grateful that I need not enter."[56]

At the Court of Appeal, Lord Donaldson of Lymington, Master of the Rolls, saw the issue of AMF legal existence as follows:

> What is in issue is whether the law of this country permits the courts to recognise its existence to the extent necessary to enable it to enforce such rights as it may have against, *inter alios*, the principal defendant who is resident in this country. If it does not, the law is in urgent need of revision, for the A.M.F. is not unique.[57]

He noted that the United Kingdom is not a member State of AMF and that the organization does not propose to maintain an establishment in the United Kingdom, which would have enabled Her Majesty by Order in Council to "confer on the organisation the legal capacities of a body corporate" in accordance with the International Organisations Act 1968.[58] He also noted:

> The *Tin* case itself was concerned with the extent to which such an Order in Council invested the organisation with a separate personality distinct

53. 83 ILR 250. ("The International Tin Council was created by a treaty to which the United Kingdom was a party, had its headquarters in London and was accorded the legal capacities of a body corporate in English domestic law by statutory instrument. The A.M.F., on the other hand, was created by a treaty to which the United Kingdom was not a party and is not the subject of a statutory instrument or any other United Kingdom legislation.")

54. In *Tin Case*, Lord Oliver of Aylmerton, with the agreement of his brethren, ruled: "Whilst it is, of course, not accurate to describe article 4 of the Order [in Council] as one which 'recognises' the I.T.C. as an international organisation, such 'recognition' is of no consequence in domestic law unless and until it is accompanied by the *creation* of a legal persona. Without the Order in Council the I.T.C. had no legal existence in the law of the United Kingdom and no significance save as the name of an international body created by treaty between sovereign states which was not justiciable by municipal courts." [citation omitted] 83 ILR 251.

55. *Id.* at 251–52.

56. *Id.*

57. *Id.* at 255.

58. *Id.* at 259.

> from its constituent members and, if so, to what extent (if at all) liability, whether primary or secondary, for its obligations attached to its constituent members. The House of Lords answered the first question "Yes" and the second question "Not at all." Neither question arises directly on this appeal, but the discussion of the nature of an international organisation upon which the legal capacities of a body corporate have been conferred casts some light on how English law would or should regard an international organisation upon which an Abu Dhabi or U.A.E. decree has conferred similar capacities.[59]

Lord Donaldson thought that Lord Hoffmann (at the High Court) had misconstrued the opinion of Lord Oliver in the *Tin Case* regarding the treatment of treaties:

> It seems to me to be wholly consistent with Lord Oliver's approach to have regard to the A.M.F. agreement, not as creating rights and obligations enforceable by English courts, but as casting light on, and indeed determining, the true nature of the independent juridical personality which exists under the laws of the signatory states including Abu Dhabi and the U.A.E. and under the laws of any other states which adopt the same approach as Swiss law.[60]

He, therefore, did not see why English courts should treat AMF as a juridical person because of its recognition under the laws of UAE.

Lord Nourse felt that English law would not recognize AMF as a legal person and that it was up to the government to legislate to fill the lacuna created by Sections 1 and 4 of the International Organisations Act 1968 so as to confer legal personality on international organizations in which the United Kingdom is not a member, or which maintain or want to maintain an establishment in the United Kingdom.[61] For his part, Lord Bingham did not think that the *Tin Case* required the disregard of the AMF treaty altogether because "the A.M.F. treaty

59. *Id.*

60. *Id.* at 263. As evidence of Swiss law, Professors Pierre Lalive and Christian Dominсé provided the following affidavit: "23. [The founding states] have specifically established that A.M.F. enjoys legal capacity of domestic law including that of being able to sue or be sued. 24. For the abovementioned reasons, this state of affairs of such capacity is recognised (automatically or '*de plano*') by Swiss courts without any need for a process of incorporation or ratification. 25. *A fortiori*, the fact that in some foreign states (whether or not they are members of A.M.F.) some process of ratification or incorporation has taken place is totally irrelevant from the Swiss point of view." *Id.* at 258.

61. *Id.* at 266.

was . . . incorporated in the law of the U.A.E., and one can as readily look at it as at a treaty expressly incorporated into our own municipal law."[62]

The House of Lords struggled with the legal personality of AMF in the United Kingdom, and ended up rendering the correct decision but for the wrong reason. It held that the "status of an organization incorporated by a foreign state is recognised by the courts of the United Kingdom. The status of an international organisation incorporated by at least one state should be recognised by the courts of the United Kingdom." The AMF Agreement, as a treaty, created an international organization in international law and obligated its member States to accord it legal personality in the national systems. The House of Lords resorted to conflicts-of-law rules to recognise the legal personality of the AMF. It construed the AMF as owing its existence to the law of UAE as the AMF Agreement had been made part of UAE law and, as such, the English courts can recognise the AMF as a foreign corporate body.

The expedience of English law is to confer the status of a body corporate on an international organization. However, an international organization is not a foreign corporation, and is not created under the law of any of its member States, but by international law. To be sure, the legal personality of an international organisation in a State may not be automatic and may require national legislation to give it effect. However, any national legislation according legal personality to an international organization does not mean that the organization is created under the law of that State. The quirk of English law is revealed in the dissent by Lord Lowry:

> At common law, with due respect to learned writers who have sought to maintain a different view, international organisations set up by treaty are not recognised as having legal status in our courts. Parliament's response to the emergence of such organisations was to pass a series of Acts starting with the Diplomatic Privileges (Extension) Act 1944. Statute law now recognises international organisations as having juridical personality in three instances. The International Organisations Act 1968, in regard to an organisation of which the United Kingdom and any other sovereign power are members, and also in regard to an organisation of which two or more sovereign powers (but not the United Kingdom are members and which maintains or proposes to maintain an establishment in the United Kingdom, gives power to Her Majesty by Order in Council to "confer on the organisation the legal capacity of a body corporate" and also to confer certain privileges and immunities. . . . A third recognised class consists of

62. *Id.* at 267.

> those international organisations which have been the subject of special Acts such as the Bretton Woods Agreements Act 1945 and the International Sugar Organisation Act 1973. Viewed as an international organisation, the fund belongs to a fourth class, which continues to have no legal standing.[63]

Lord Lowry continued his dissent:

> My Lords, I think it is clear that both the ITC and the fund, having started as international organisations created by agreements made under international law, continue as such with the addition of legal personality and capacity which have been conferred on them by one or more member states. Like the ITC, the fund is not a new creation under the law of the headquarter state it is still an international organisation with a conferred capacity in that state.
>
> [T]here is only one fund (and one ITC), an international organisation which may have juridical personality conferred on it in more than one state.[64]

The issue in AMF was the legal capacity or standing of an international organization to sue in a nonmember State, not whether the international organization has immunity in a nonmember State. The question of legal personality precedes that of jurisdictional immunity, even in member States, but it is generally not disputed, nor even explicitly considered, in domestic legal proceedings. The issue of an international organization's legal personality in a nonmember State is less straightforward as evidenced by the AMF case. Legal personality is concerned with the recognition of the status of an international organization within the legal system of the State in which the organization operates or with whom it relates. An international organization comes into existence upon acts of its member States alone, typically through the conclusion of a treaty among them, although it is argued that such a treaty creates no obligation for any nonparty unless it consents.

The AMF saga continued in *In re Hashim and Others*, where the United States Bankruptcy Court, District of Arizona, addressed the issue of whether an organization of which the forum State is not a member and that is not designated as an international organization under the national legislation (International Organizations Immunities Act or IOIA) has capacity and standing to participate

63. *Arab Monetary Fund v. Hashim (No.3)* [1991] 2 AC 114, [1991] 1 All ER 871, [1991] 2 WLR 729, [1991] BCC 180 (Lord Lowry's dissent).

64. *Id.*

in legal proceedings in the United States.[65] The AMF had instituted proceedings against Hashim in England, and the House of Lord had ruled in 1991 that AMF had capacity to bring proceedings against Hashim in English courts on the basis that the English courts should give comity to UAE law, under which AMF was a corporate body. The English courts awarded AMF monetary damages against Hashim.

Subsequently, AMF instituted proceedings to enforce the judgment in Arizona where Hashim and his family had resettled after fleeing England. Hashim had filed for bankruptcy before the case could progress, and had also challenged AMF's legal capacity to participate in the bankruptcy proceedings. Hashim argued that AMF lacked legal capacity in the United States because it was not an international organization designated as such under the IOIA. AMF countered that the IOIA was not the sole source of legal capacity and maintained that it had capacity as a creditor and also a corporate or similar entity under UAE law. The Bankruptcy Court denied Hashim's motion, and stated that the IOIA neither denied nor granted AMF legal capacity. It noted that the legal personality of an international organization could derive from its status under the national laws of its member States, and that as the English House of Lords recognized the legal personality of AMF by giving comity to the laws of UAE, it was proper for the Bankruptcy Court to do the same:

> The issue to which comity will be given effect is whether the AMF is a juridical person (a corporation, a *persona ficta,* an entity capable of legal battle) under UAE law, not whether this means the AMF has capacity under English law. Once this has been decided, capacity follows under American law as a matter of "customary law."[66]

In sum, the legal status of an international organization encompasses both its international and legal personality, which is distinct in law and fact from that of its member States. It is critical that an international organization be endowed with legal personality, otherwise its conduct would be attributable to its members. "[I]t is elementary that the only persons liable and entitled under a contract, in the absence of trust or agency, are the parties to the contract."[67] In this regard, the main issue before the courts in the International Tin Council (ITC) case

65. *In re Hashim and Others,* United States Bankruptcy Court, District of Arizona, 15 August 1995, reported in 107 ILR 405.

66. *Id.*

67. *Tin Case,* para. 72.

was whether the member States were liable for the debts of ITC.[68] The treaty establishing the ITC showed that its member States had established an international organization with a legal personality distinct from those of its Members.[69] The International Tin Council (Immunities and Privileges) Order 1972 SI 1972 No. 120 ("1972 Order") merely gave effect in English law to that international personality. In a dualist state, such as the United Kingdom, a treaty will have to be incorporated into national law to give it effect. In a monist state, on the other hand, such as the United States, treaties are usually self-executing and given automatic effect in national law. No matter the constitutional law or practice of a member State with respect to giving effect to treaties, it has an international legal obligation to recognize the legal personality of the international organization even where the constituent instrument does not expressly so provide. In consideration of the different approaches, for instance, Article VII (Status, Immunities and Privileges), Section 10 (Application of Article), of the Articles of Agreement of the World Bank provides: "Each member shall take such action as is necessary in its own territories for the purposes of making effective in terms of its own law the principles set forth in this Article and shall inform the Bank of the detailed action which it has taken."

68. Article 16, paragraph 1, of the Sixth International Tin Agreement typically provided: "The Council shall have legal personality. It shall in particular have the capacity to contract, to acquire and dispose of movable and immovable property and to institute legal proceedings."

69. See Sixth International Tin Agreement (New York, 30 April 1982).

7

Sources of the Law of Immunity of International Organizations

INTERNATIONAL LAW

International law is the corpus of norms that inform and of rules that conform the conduct of States and of international organizations in their relations and interrelationships. States in their mutual relations create international organizations and agree to norms and rules that regulate their behavior toward each other and toward the international organizations. International law is, therefore, central to the determination of the jurisdictional immunity of international organizations.

Article 38(1) of the Statute of the International Court of Justice is generally regarded as an authoritative statement of sources of international law: international conventions, whether general or particular, establishing rules expressly recognized by the contesting states; international custom, as evidence of a general practice accepted as law; and general principles of law recognized by civilized nations. Article 38(1)(a) is generally referred to as treaty law, and Article 38(1)(b) as customary international law.[1] Article 38(1)(d) provides for recourse to

1. Restatement (Third) § 102 has similar provisions for the sources of international law: "A rule of international law is one that has been accepted as such by the international community of states (a) in the form of customary law; (b) by international agreement; or (c) by derivation from general principles common to the major legal systems of the world."

"judicial decisions and the teachings of the most highly qualified publicists of the various nations, as subsidiary means for the determination of rules of law."

Treaty

A treaty is an international agreement between two or more subjects of international law, which is governed by international law.[2] The distinguishing factor between a treaty and an ordinary contract is that the former is governed by international law.[3] The agreement must manifest an intent by the parties to create a relationship governed by international law. Thus, a treaty is an international agreement between States, or between States and international organizations, or between international organizations inter se.[4] Treaties also serve the purpose of formulating new principles and rules of immunities of international organization where rules of customary international law are nonexistent. Treaties are the main, or some will argue the only, source of the international law of the immunity of international organizations.

The privileges and immunities of international organizations are determined by reference to their constituent and other treaties. These treaties may be multilateral, which are concluded for the organizations by their members, or bilateral, which are concluded by the organization itself with a State. It is axiomatic that a treaty applies only to the parties to it: *pacta tertiis nec nocent nec prosunt.* In other words, a treaty cannot bind a third party without its consent.[5] In the determination of the immunity of international organizations, reference must be had first to the treaty provision.[6] The paramountcy of treaties in the determination of the immunities of international organizations accords with the maxim *lex specialis derogate legi generali,* that is, the specific prevails over the general. The provisions of a treaty create less doubt and more certainty than ascertaining the existence and content of customary international law.

The constituent instrument by which member States establish an international organization usually provide for the organization's privileges and immunities. For example, Article 105 of the Charter of the United Nations provides that the

2. Such an international agreement has various appellations, such as convention, charter, covenant, and protocol.

3. See Article 2(1)(a), VCLT.

4. See Article 1, VCLT; and Article 1, Vienna Convention on the Law of Treaties between States and International Organizations or between International Organizations, done at Vienna on 21 March 1986, but not yet in force.

5. See Article 34, VCLT.

6. Recourse to customary international law is only had in the absence of a treaty provision.

"Organization shall enjoy in the territory of each of its Members, such privileges and immunities as are necessary for the fulfillment of its purposes." The Article also instructed the General Assembly of the United Nations to take measures that eventually led to the birth of the Convention on the Privileges and Immunities of the United Nations ("General Convention"), as well as the related Convention on the Privileges and Immunities of the Specialized Agencies ("Specialized Agencies Convention").

Article II, Section 2, of the General Convention provides: "United Nations, its property and assets, wherever located and by whomsoever held, shall enjoy immunity from every form of legal process, except in so far as in any particular case it has expressly waived its immunity." It specifies that "it is, however, understood that no waiver of immunity shall extend to any measure of execution."[7] For the specialized agencies of the United Nations, there is the Specialized Agencies Convention, which lays out the standard privileges and immunities that are applicable to all these international organizations, with annexes that are specific to each specialized agency and take account of its specialized functions and purposes.[8] International organizations are not parties to the multilateral treaties on their privileges and immunities, such as the General Convention and the Specialized Agencies Convention, but are beneficiaries of these conventions. Thus, international organizations may be said to be third parties to these treaties that offer them rights that are enforceable by them.[9] Section 39 of the Specialized Agencies Convention permits its State parties to enter host or supplemental agreements with any specialized agency regarding the privileges and immunities granted by the convention.[10]

7. The United States did not accede to the General Convention until April 29, 1970.

8. International Labour Organization (Annex I), Food and Agriculture Organization of the United Nations (Annex II), International Civil Aviation Organization (Annex III), United Nations Educational, Scientific and Cultural Organization (Annex IV), International Monetary Fund (Annex V), International Bank for Reconstruction and Development (Annex VI), World Health Organization (Annex VII), Universal Postal Union (Annex VIII), International Telecommunication Union (Annex IX), International Refugee Organization (Annex X) before the organization was liquidated pursuant to a resolution adopted by its General Council in 1952, World Meteorological Organization (Annex XI), International Maritime Organization (Annex XII), International Finance Corporation (Annex XIII), International Development Association (Annex XIV), World Intellectual Property Organization (Annex XV), International Fund for Agricultural Development (Annex XVI), and United Nations Industrial Development Organization (Annex XVII), including any other agencies that may enter into a relationship with the United Nations pursuant to Articles 57 and 63 of the Charter.

9. See Article 36, VCLT.

10. See *Interpretation of the Agreement of 25 March 1951 between the WHO and Egypt, Advisory Opinion, I. C.J. Reports 1980*, pp. 73, 85 ("These provisions [of the host agreement] are on the

Provisions on privileges and immunities are also found in bilateral treaties, such as headquarters or host agreements.[11] Most host agreements replicate or refer to the provisions of the Specialized Agencies Convention. In its 1988 Advisory Opinion on the Applicability of the Obligation to Arbitrate under Section 21 of the 1947 United Nations Headquarters Agreement, the International Court of Justice ruled: "There is no question but that the Headquarters Agreement is a treaty in force binding the parties thereto."[12] Headquarters agreements are particularly important because problems regarding privileges and immunities are more likely to arise in those States where an international organization has its headquarters or offices. The United Nations Headquarters Agreement with the United States, however, does not address the jurisdictional immunity of the United Nations in the United States, which is provided for in the General Convention.[13] Bilateral agreements may be concluded between an international organization and a nonmember State, as was the case with the 1946 Interim Arrangement on Privileges and Immunities of the United Nations concluded between the Secretary-General of the United Nations and the Swiss Federal Council.[14]

In sum, treaties are the main source of international law with respect to the immunities of international organizations. Most treaties contain clauses that provide for a dispute resolution mechanism concerning disputes about interpretation

lines of the Convention of 21 November 1947 on the Privileges and Immunities of the Specialized Agencies, to which Egypt became a party on 28 September 1954. Under Section 39 of that Convention, however, the Agreement of 25 March 1951 continued to be the instrument defining the legal status of the Regional Office in Alexandria as between the WHO and Egypt.")

11. The agreements are variously known as the Headquarters Agreement, Establishment Agreement, Accord de siege, or Host State Agreement. The agreements also govern the status of the international organization in the host State as a matter of national law.

12. 1988 ICJ Reports 15, para. 7.

13. Section 26 of the Headquarters Agreement provides: "The provisions of this agreement shall be complementary to the provisions of the General Convention. In so far as any provision of this agreement and any provisions of the General Convention relate to the same subject matter, the two provisions shall, wherever possible, be treated as complementary, so that both provisions shall be applicable and neither shall narrow the effect of the other; but in any case of absolute conflict, the provisions of this agreement shall prevail." The General Assembly stated, in its Resolution 259 (III), that the Agreement was complementary to the General Convention "since these instruments taken together are intended to define the status of the United Nations in the country where these headquarters are located." The United States acceded to the General Convention on April 29, 1970.

14. 1 U.N.T.S. 163. Switzerland, which is the host of the United Nations Office in Geneva, and other international organizations, finally joined the United Nations on September 10, 2002.

or application of the treaty.[15] Regarding the interpretation of treaties, Article 31(1) of VCLT provides: "A treaty shall be interpreted in good faith in accordance with the ordinary meaning to be given to the terms of the treaty in their context and in the light of its object and purpose." Interpretation, however, must proceed with an analysis of the text of the treaty, but recourse may be had to supplementary means, in accordance to Article 32 of VCLT, when the interpretation under Article 31: "*(a)* Leaves the meaning ambiguous or obscure; or *(b)* Leads to a result which is manifestly absurd or unreasonable." Conversely, in the case of customary international law, the primary task is ascertainment ab initio of the existence and content of the rule.

Customary International Law

Presently, it is unsettled whether international organizations enjoy immunity on the basis of customary international law in addition to treaties. Considering the preeminence of treaties in the law of immunity of international organizations, the question in determining customary international law is whether nonmember States have an international law obligation to grant privileges and immunities to international organizations. In other words, the issue is whether international organizations are entitled to immunity absent a treaty to that effect. Customary international law is understood as general and consistent practice of States observed by them out of a sense of legal obligation. The *North Sea Continental Shelf* judgment provides an encapsulation of the ascertainment of customary international law:

> Not only must the acts concerned amount to a settled practice, but they must also be such, or be carried out in such a way, as to be evidence of a belief that this practice is rendered obligatory by the existence of a rule requiring it. The need for such a belief, i.e., the existence of a subjective or psychological element, is implicit in the very notion of the *opinio juris sive necessitates.* The States concerned must therefore feel that they are conforming to what amounts to a legal obligation.[16]

15. See, e.g., Article VIII, Section 30, Convention on the Privileges and Immunities of the United Nations; Article IX, Section 32, Convention on the Privileges and Immunities of the Specialized Agencies of the United Nations; Article IX, Articles of Agreement of the World Bank.

16. North Sea Continental Shelf, Judgment, 1969 I.C.J. Rep., p.3, at pp. 43–44, paras. 74 and 77. See also Military and Paramilitary Activities in and against Nicaragua (Nicaragua v. United States of America), 1986 I.C.J. Rep., p.14, at p. 108-9, para. 207; Jurisdictional Immunities of the States (*Germany v. Italy: Greece Intervening*), 2012 I.C.J. Rep., p. 99, at p. 122, para. 55.

The practice, which is the objective or material element, must be accompanied by a belief about the practice, which is the subjective or psychological element, which in turn manifests itself in the practice.[17] Sometimes, *opinio juris* is conceded or established prior to the assessment of the practice: "The Court must satisfy itself that the existence of the rule in the opinio juris of States is confirmed by practice. . . . It is therefore in the light of this 'subjective element'—the expression used by the Court in its 1969 Judgment in the North Sea Continental Shelf cases (I.C.J. Reports 1969, p. 44)—that the Court has to appraise the relevant practice."[18] The challenge lies with evidence of each element, which must be separately ascertained. For an act to constitute practice for purposes of customary international law, it must be general in the sense that it possesses consistency, duration, and generality.[19] General practice has both temporal and spatial elements. General practice is settled practice, but general practice is not universal practice. Inaction may also be evidence of practice. Consequently, context is critical in the ascertainment of practice.

As international persons, international organizations have rights and duties under international law. It is widely accepted that international organizations have come of age as full subjects of international law. It is equally argued that as they are subject to international law, including customary international law, they should "also take part in the formation of the relevant customary international law, in the specific fields in which each organization operates."[20] The argument is that if international organizations are to be bound by customary international law, then they must contribute to its formation. To be sure, international organizations are parties to some treaties that govern their activities. However, it must be also recognized that the fact that an entity is bound by a particular law does not necessarily entail that the entity is entitled to partake in the formation of that law. For example, legal or juridical persons, such as corporations, are subject to municipal or national laws, but they do not take part in the formation of the relevant laws, at least not directly in the lawmaking process. In the area of jurisdictional immunity of international organizations, the question is whether

17. For varied views of the relationship between the two constituent elements of customary international law, see Third Report on Identification of Customary International Law, A/CN.4/682 (March 27, 2015).

18. See Case Concerning Military and Paramilitary Activities in and against Nicaragua (Nicaragua v. United States), 1986 I.C.J. Rep. p.14, at p. 98, paras. 185-6.

19. For a discussion of these elements of general practice, see MARK. E. VILLIGER, A MODERN THEORY OF CUSTOMARY INTERNATIONAL LAW 42–47 (Kluwer 1997).

20. Niels Blokker, *International Organizations and Customary International Law: Is the International Law Commission Taking International Organizations Seriously?*, 14 INT'L ORGS. L. REV. 1, 10 (2017).

the practice of international organizations is relevant for the identification of customary international law.

When Article 38 of the ICJ Statute was drafted, States were the only recognized subject of international law. Although Article 38(1)(b) does not explicitly refer to the practice of States, the ILC has stated that "[t]he requirement, as a constituent element of customary international law, of a general practice means that it is primarily the practice of States that contributes to the formation, or expression, of rules of customary law."[21] However, in "certain cases, the practice of international organizations contributes to the formation, or expression, of rules of customary international law."[22] For example, the practice of an international organization, such as the European Union, where the member States have transferred certain competence to it, is relevant as it is construed to represent the practice of its member States.[23] Although international organizations are autonomous and independent actors under international law, the relevance of their practice to the formation of customary international law may be limited to their practice being an expression of the collective will of their member States. Thus, even though the practice of international organizations may contribute to the development of customary international law, it still does not change the requirement that the requisite practice is that of States. Unless the practice of international organizations alone, with the accompanying opinio juris, can contribute to the formation of customary international law, it is inaccurate to state or claim that the practice of international organizations may contribute to the development of customary international law if the requisite practice remains primarily that of States.

As immunity of international organizations is a derogation from the jurisdiction of States, it is the practice of States that can contribute to the formation of customary international law in that regard. This is so because it is only States that can accord immunity to international organizations. "States remain the primary subjects of international law and . . . it is primarily their practice that contributes to the formation, and the expression, of the rules of customary international law."[24] International organizations cannot and do not give each other jurisdictional immunities before national courts.[25] Consequently, the pertinent

21. Report of the International Law Commission (ILC) on its Sixty-Eight Session, Identification of Customary International Law, United Nations Document A/71/10, Conclusion 4 (19 August 2016).

22. *Id.*

23. *Id.* at Commentary (5).

24. A/CN.4/682, p. 47, para. 70; A/CN.4/672, para. 43.

25. Jurisdictional immunity is not implicated in proceedings before the administrative tribunals of international organizations.

question, for purposes of customary international law, is whether States have a practice of granting immunity to international organizations out of a sense of legal obligation, not whether international organizations have a practice of claiming immunity out of a sense of legal right. Although the practice of international organizations may influence the practice of States, the practice of consequence remains that of States.

Customary international law on the immunity of international organizations may be developed through the relations between international organizations and States, especially the relations between international organizations and third States, that is, States that are not members of the particular international organization. The practice of (third) States with respect to the privileges and immunities of international organizations may contribute to the development of customary international law in that realm. This practice may crystalize a customary international law rule in *statu nascendi* or constitute evidence of existence of a customary international law rule.

In assessing the emergence or existence of customary international law, the content, context, and circumstances of the particular rules must also be examined.[26] The pertinent question is whether all States, that is, both member and nonmember States, are under a customary international law obligation to accord jurisdictional immunity to all international organizations as subjects of international law. In other words, is jurisdictional immunity an attribute of the international personality of an international organization under customary international law, that is, can international organizations claim immunity, as an attribute of their international personality? In this regard, it must be noted that the fact that international organizations have rights and duties under international law, just like States, does not mean that international organizations have the same or equal rights and duties as States under international law.

Interrelationship between Treaty and Customary International Law

A treaty may create a new customary international law if it has engendered a general practice that is accepted as law.[27] Over the years, the International Law Commission in its works has recognized the relationship of customary

26. See Jurisdictional Immunities of the State (*Germany v. Italy: Greece Intervening*), Judgment, 2012 I.C.J. Rep., p. 123, para. 55.

27. See RESTATEMENT (THIRD) FOREIGN RELATIONS LAW (AM. LAW INST. 1987) ("RESTATEMENT (THIRD)"), § 102(3) ("International agreements create law for the states parties thereto and may lead to the creation of customary international law when such agreements are intended for adherence by states generally and are in fact widely accepted.")

international law with treaties. It has observed that a treaty may codify existing rules of customary international law or contribute to the crystallization or development of a rule of customary international law, even though it does not itself bind third parties. Thus, in the commentary to the draft Article 34 of what substantially and subsequently became Article 38 of the 1969 Vienna Convention on the Law of Treaties, it was observed:

> A treaty concluded between certain States may formulate a rule . . . which afterwards comes to be generally accepted by other States and becomes binding upon other States by way of custom. . . . So too a codifying convention purporting to state existing rules of customary law may come to be regarded as the generally accepted formulation of the customary rules in question even by States not parties to the convention.
>
> In none of these cases, however, can it properly be said that the treaty itself has legal effects for third States. They are cases where, without establishing any treaty relation between themselves and the parties to the treaty, other States recognize rules formulated in a treaty as binding customary law. In short, for these States the source of the binding force of the rules is custom, not the treaty.[28]

No customary international law on the immunity of international organizations existed when the United Nations and its specialized agencies were created and the applicable treaties or conventions on their immunities were drafted. International law recognizes the interaction and interrelation between treaties and customary international law.[29] A treaty may codify an existing rule of customary international law or may develop a new rule of customary law.[30] As stated by the International Law Commission:

> A principle or rule of customary international law may be embodied in a bipartite or multipartite agreement so as to have, within the stated limits, conventional force for the State parties to the agreement so long as it is in force; yet it would continue to be binding as a principle or rule of customary international law for other States. Indeed, not infrequently conventional formulation by certain States of a practice also followed by other States is relied upon in efforts to establish the existence of a rule of customary

28. [1966] 2 Y.B. Int'l Law Comm'n 230–31.

29. See Mark E. Villiger, A Modern Theory of Customary International Law 15, para. 13 (rev. 2d ed. 1997).

30. See A/CN.4/682, p. 15, para. 28.

> international law. Even multipartite conventions signed but not brought into force are frequently regarded as having value as evidence of customary international law.[31]

To be sure, the General Convention and the Specialized Agencies Convention did not codify any customary international law on the jurisdictional immunity of international organizations. However, these treaties or conventions may be relevant in the formation of customary international law of immunities of international organizations.[32]

> "The provisions of treaties do not in and of themselves constitute rules of customary international law, but such provisions, as "an explicit expression of the will of states", may offer valuable evidence of the existence (or otherwise) and content of such rules. In particular, they may contain relatively precise formulations of possible customary rules, and reflect the views of States as to their nature (at least as of the time when the relevant treaty is concluded). Treaties may thus allow a preliminary consideration of "whether a customary rule applicable to the case had already been identified before finding it necessary to examine the primary evidence of custom de novo"; the International Court of Justice has indeed said that it "can and must take them into account in ascertaining the content of the customary international law.[33]

As international organizations are not parties to, but beneficiaries of, the General Convention and the Specialized Agencies Convention, what would count as evidence of State practice is whether States accord the same treatment under the conventions to international organizations that are not designated beneficiaries to the treaties. "[W]hen States act in conformity with a treaty by which they are not bound, or apply conventional obligations in their relations with non-parties to the treaty, this may evidence the existence of acceptance as law in the absence of any explanation to the contrary."[34]

31. 2 Y.B. INT'L LAW COMM'N 268, para. 19 (1950); Third report on identification of customary international law, by Michael Wood, Special Rapporteur, International Law Commission, United Nations Document No. A/CN.4/682, pp. 16–17, para. 32.

32. See *North Sea Continental Shelf* Case, ICJ Reports 1969, p. 3.

33. A/CN.4/682, p. 17, para. 33 [citations omitted].

34. United Nations Document No. A/71/10, Identification of customary international law, Conclusion 9, Commentary (4), p. 98.

The practice by a great number of States to generally accord privileges and immunities to the United Nations and its specialized agencies, regardless of treaties, has led some to infer the existence of a rule of customary international law. It is assumed that this practice is borne out of a sense of legal obligation. Thus, although these multilateral treaties did not codify any existing law, they may have over time contributed to the development of customary international law.[35]

There is no denying that host States of international organizations are "States whose interest are specifically affected" by the immunity of those organizations. "State practice, including that of States whose interests are specifically affected, should [be] both extensive and virtually uniform in the sense of the provision invoked; -- and should moreover [occur] in such a way as to show a general recognition that a rule of law or legal obligation is involved."[36] The proposition that the various multilateral and bilateral treaties on privileges and immunities of international organizations may contribute to the development of customary international law accords with the draft Conclusion 11 adopted by the International Law Commission:

> 1. A rule set forth in a treaty may reflect a rule of customary international law if it is established that the treaty rule: (a) codified a rule of customary international law existing at the time when the treaty was concluded; (b) has led to the crystallization of a rule of customary international law that had started to emerge prior to the conclusion of the treaty; or (c) has given rise to a general practice that is accepted as law (opinio juris), thus generating a new rule of customary international law.
> 2. The fact that a rule is set forth in a number of treaties may, but does not necessarily, indicate that the treaty rule reflects a rule of customary international law.[37]

An argument against treaties on privileges and immunities as evidence of customary international law is that the continued practice of both States and international organizations "to address the issue of immunity in bilateral and multilateral treaties perhaps indicates a lack of conviction that the matter is covered by customary international law."[38]

35. See C. Dominice, *L'immunite de jurisdiction et d'execution des organizations internationals,* 187 Recueil des Cours 145–238, at pp. 174–77 and 219–25.

36. North Sea Continental Shelf, 1969 I.C.J. Rep. 3, at p. 43, para. 74.

37. United Nations Document No. A/71/10, p. 102.

38. Michael Wood, *Do International Organizations Enjoy Immunity Under Customary International Law?,* 10 Int'l Orgs. L. Rev. 287, 313 (2014).

Judicial Decisions

Decisions of national courts play a role in both the development and determination of customary international law.[39] The decisions may serve as evidence of a practice accepted as law, as well as subsidiary means for the determination of the existence and content of the customary international law.[40] "Decisions of courts and tribunals on questions of international law, in particular those decisions in which the existence of rules of customary international law is considered and such rules are identified and applied, may offer valuable guidance for determining the existence or otherwise of rules of customary international law. The value of such decisions varies greatly, however, depending both on the quality of the reasoning of each decision (including the extent to which it is founded upon a close examination of an alleged practice accepted as law) and on the reception of the decision by States and by other courts."[41]

With respect to the immunity of international organizations, different courts have reached different conclusions on the existence of customary international law. The question of customary international law when it does arise is usually in the context of nonmember States of international organizations. For example, the Court of Appeal of Paris rejected an international organization's claim to immunity because France was not a party to the treaty establishing that organization, and it was not shown that France was obligated to accord it immunity as a matter of customary international law.[42] The court discounted the organization's argument that as an international organization with objective international personality opposable to nonmember States, it was entitled to immunity.

Even where the host State is a member of the international organization, the Malaysian High Court denied the claim to immunity because the "relevant international agreements as a result of which ITC was established specifically provided for ITC to enjoy certain immunities in the United Kingdom. Provisions were made in respect of the position of ITC in the other member countries and immunity from suit was not one of them. The parties to the agreements appear to have treated the host country (i.e., the United Kingdom) in a different way from other member countries. Immunity from suits in the other member countries does not appear to have

39. See United Nations Document No. A/71/10, Conclusion 13 (2), p.109.

40. *Id.* Conclusion 13, Commentary (1), p. 109.

41. *Id.* Commentary (3), Conclusion 13.

42. *CEDAO v. Bank of Credit and Commerce*, French Court of Appeals, Paris (January 13, 1993), [1993] 120 Clunet 353.

been sought or given."[43] It must be noted that in this case, the decision of the court did not revolve on the existence of customary international law on immunity but on the court's interpretation of a treaty establishing the international organization.

Where a host State is a member of the international organization, even in the absence of a treaty, some courts have upheld the immunity of the international organization as a matter of customary international law. For example, the Italian Court of Cassation has held that once international (legal) personality has been ascertained, then the international organization "is also entitled to jurisdictional immunity (irrespective of the presence or absence of treaty provisions explicitly granting that right) pursuant to the rule of customary international law *par in parem non habet jurisdictionem*."[44] Similarly, the Dutch Supreme Court upheld the immunity of the Iran–US Claims Tribunal on the ground that it was customary for a host State to accord immunity to organizations on its territory:

> It must be assumed that even in cases where there is no treaty . . . it follows from unwritten international law that an international organization is entitled to the privileges of immunity from jurisdiction on the same footing as generally provided for in the treaties . . . in any event in the State in whose territory the organization has its seat, with the consent of the government of the State.
>
> This means that, according to unwritten international law, as it stands at present, an international organization is in principle not subject to the jurisdiction of the courts of the host State in respect of all disputes which are immediately connected with the performance of the tasks entrusted to the organization in question.[45]

Other courts have taken a contrary view to those of the Italian and Dutch courts. For instance, where the host State is a member of the international organization, the Canadian Supreme Court was of the view: "In the case of international organizations, unlike that of states, the prevailing view at present is that no rule of customary international law confers immunity on them. International organizations derive their existence from treaties, and the same holds true for their rights to immunities."[46]

43. *Bank Bumiputra Malaysia Bhd. v. International Tin Council and Another*, High Court of Malaysia (January 13, 1987), [1989] 80 ILR 24, 29.

44. *Cristiani v. Italian Latin-American Institute*, Italian Court of Cassation (November 25, 1985), [1992] 87 ILR 21, 26.

45. *Iran-US Claims Tribunal v. AS*, Supreme Court of Netherlands (December 20, 1985) [1994] 94 ILR 321, 329.

46. *Amaratunga v. Northwest Atlantic Fisheries Organization*, 2013 SCC 66, para. 29 (Can.) [citation omitted].

It is not clear whether any State practice of according jurisdictional immunity to international organizations, absent a treaty provision, is accompanied by the requisite *opinio juris* to form customary international law. Most of the pronouncements of courts and commentators are ex cathedra and lack rigorous analysis of the formation or existence of customary international law of the jurisdictional immunities of international organizations. "While one still comes across assertions, by writers, governments or courts, that international organizations enjoy immunity under customary law, the authorities relied upon are largely unconvincing."[47]

"[D]omestic judges are not necessarily experts or even trained in public international law; and domestic courts may be influenced by their own State's view of whether or not a particular rule of customary international law exists, and are anyway likely to (and perhaps should) adopt a cautious approach to developing the law."[48] It is apparent that the case law of the various national courts on whether international organizations enjoy jurisdictional immunity under customary international law is inconclusive, inconsistent, and sometimes incoherent, and the ICJ has not weighed in to date as it has done with respect to State immunity.[49] With the divergent decisions by different courts on whether there is a customary international law on privileges and immunities of international organizations, it is, therefore, unsettled whether jurisdictional immunity is an attribute of international organizations under customary international law that all States, not just member States of an international organization, are obliged to recognize. "Where the existence of a general practice accepted as law cannot be established, the conclusion will be that the alleged rule of customary international law does not exist."[50]

The debate about the source of the law of the immunity of international organizations matters because rules of customary international law, with obligations erga omnes, "by their very nature, must have equal force for all members of the international community."[51] Therefore, under customary international law, States cannot disavow their obligation as they would under treaty law.

47. Wood at 316–17. The author takes the definitive position that there is not sufficient State practice and *opinio juris* to conclude that there is a customary international law on the privileges and immunities of international organizations.

48. United Nations Document No. A/CN.4/663, First report on formation and evidence of customary international law by Michael Wood, Special Rapporteur, International Law Commission, p. 37, para. 84 (May 17, 2013) [citation omitted].

49. See, generally, Wood at 287–318.

50. United Nations Document No. A/71/10, Conclusion 2, Commentary (3), p. 83.

51. North Sea Continental Shelf, 1969 I.C.J. Rep. 38, para. 63.

NATIONAL LAWS

Some States have enacted legislation concerning the legal status, privileges, and immunities of international organizations. Two prominent examples of national laws on privileges and immunities are the United States International Organizations Immunities Act (IOIA)[52] and the United Kingdom International Organizations Act (IOA)[53] respectively.

The IOIA confers legal status and extends certain privileges and immunities to international organizations "in which the United States participates pursuant to any treaty or under the authority of any Act of Congress authorizing such participation or making an appropriation for such participation, and which shall have been designated by the President through appropriate Executive order as being entitled to enjoy the privileges . . . and immunities . . . provided [in the Act]."[54] The officers and employees of the organizations also benefit from the organizations' privileges and immunities. The Act authorizes the president to withhold or withdraw from an organization or its officers or employees any of the privileges and immunities provided under the Act, as well as to condition or limit the enjoyment of the privileges and immunities.[55] Additionally, the Act authorizes the president to revoke the designation of any international organization as a beneficiary of the privileges and immunities under the Act for abuse of the privileges and immunities as determined by the president.[56]

Section 2(b) of IOIA provides: "International organizations, their property and their assets, wherever located, and by whomsoever held, *shall enjoy the same immunity from suit and every form of judicial process as is enjoyed by foreign governments*, except to the extent that such organization may expressly waive their immunity for the purpose of any proceedings or by terms of any contract."[57] Immunity under this subsection is subject to two limitations: (1) waiver by the international organization, or (2) authority of the president under the Act. IOIA has many flaws, such as the discretionary authority of the president under the Act and the reference nature of the statute. With codification of the doctrine of restrictive State immunity in the Foreign Sovereign Immunities Act (FSIA), the

52. 22 U.S.C. 288 (1945).

53. International Organisations Act 1968 ("IOA"), modifying International Organisations Act (Immunities and Privileges) Act 1950, United Nations Juridical Yearbook 1968, 20–33.

54. Section 1 of IOIA.

55. *Id.*

56. *Id.*

57. [emphasis added].

IOIA provision on the jurisdictional immunity of international organizations has become a thorny problem. It has ineluctably led to the following syllogism: IOIA grants international organizations the same immunity enjoyed by foreign governments; FSIA grants foreign governments restrictive immunity; therefore, IOIA grants international organizations restrictive immunity. The logic is flawed. FSIA does not address the immunity of international organizations, which does not come within the definition of foreign States under the statute. To be sure, the jurisdictional immunity of States has changed significantly since the enactment of IOIA in 1945, but the change from absolute State immunity in 1945 to restrictive State immunity in 1976 does not mean that the immunity of international organizations from legal process under U.S. law also changed with that of States with the enactment of FSIA.

Section 1(1) of the IOA[58] applies the Act "to any organisation declared by Order in Council to be an organisation of which *(a)* the United Kingdom, or Her Majesty's Government in the United Kingdom, and *(b)* one or more foreign sovereign Powers, or the Government or Governments of one or more such Powers, are members." Thus, it applies to organizations of which the United Kingdom is a member,[59] specialized agencies of the United Nations,[60] Commission of the European Communities,[61] other organizations of which the United Kingdom is not a member,[62] international judicial and other proceedings,[63] and representatives at international conferences in the United Kingdom.[64] Article 1(2) of IOA confers on international organizations of which the United Kingdom is a member the legal capacities of a body corporate, and provides that the organizations shall have the privileges and immunities in Schedule 1 of the Act. Part I of Schedule 1 provides for, inter alia, immunity from suit and legal process of the organization. Part II of Schedule 1 provides for, amongst other things, immunity from suit and legal process of representatives, members of subordinate bodies, high officers, experts, and persons on missions of the organizations. Part III of

58. The long title of the Act is: "An Act to make new provision (in substitution for the International Organisations (Immunities and Privileges) Act 1950 and the European Coal and Steel Community Act 1955) as to privileges, immunities and facilities to be accorded in respect of certain international organisations and in respect of persons connected with such organisations and other persons; and for purposes connected with the matters aforesaid."

59. Article 1 of IOA.

60. Article 2 of IOA.

61. Article 3 of IOA.

62. Article 4 of IOA.

63. Article 5 of IOA.

64. Article 6 of IOA.

Schedule 1 provides pertinently for immunity from suit and legal process in respect of things done or omitted to be done by officers and servants of the organization in the course of the performance of official duties.

National laws providing for the privileges and immunities of international organizations do not derogate from the treaty obligations of the member States of the organizations. For the most part, the national laws serve the purpose of giving effect to the treaty obligation of the member State under its national law.

RELATIONSHIP BETWEEN INTERNATIONAL LAW AND NATIONAL LAW

International law and national have a symbiotic relationship, and do influence each other. Under the Monist approach, international law and national law automatically form the same legal system in a State. The Dualist approach, on the other hand, considers international law and national law as separate and distinct legal systems, which requires international law to be incorporated into national law so as to be effective and enforceable in the State. National laws on privileges and immunities are more a feature of the common law tradition Dualist approach, which requires international law to be transformed into national law in order to be effective and enforceable on the domestic plane. In recognition of this approach, Article VII, Section 10, of the Articles of Agreement of the International Bank for Reconstruction and Development provides explicitly for member States of the organization to take the necessary steps for the implementation of the treaty provisions on its privileges and immunities in the national laws of the member States.

Ideally, international and national laws should operate harmoniously to govern the privileges and immunities of international organizations. However, the reality is that international law and national law are not always in sync and can give rise to controversy. The judicious judicial task is for courts to reconcile them. To this effect, the United States Supreme Court has held:

> International law is part of our law, and must be ascertained and administered by the courts of justice of appropriate jurisdiction as often as questions of right depending upon it are duly presented for their determination. For this purpose, where there is no treaty and no controlling executive or legislative act of judicial decision, resort must be had to usages of civilized nations; and, as evidence of these, to the works of jurists and commentators, not for the speculations of their authors concerning what the law ought to be, but for trustworthy evidence of what the law really is.[65]

65. *Paquete Habana*, 175 U.S. 677, 700 (1900).

The United States Supreme Court has also exhorted courts to construe federal statutes, wherever possible, as not to violate international law, in what is known as the *Charming Betsy* canon from the eponymous case.[66] Courts have struggled with the application of the IOIA in the United States.

Some courts are not clear about what law to apply to cases implicating the privileges and immunities of an international organization. International law is the binding character of norms (pacta sunt servanda), which is codified in Article 26 of the Vienna Convention on the Law of Treaties (VCLT): "Every treaty in force is binding upon the parties to it and must be performed by them in good faith." To underscore the international obligation under a treaty, Article 27 of VCLT provides: "A party may not invoke the provisions of its internal law as justification for its failure to perform a treaty."[67] Thus, a State is not relieved of its international obligation for breach of international rules if its courts deny an international organization of privileges and immunities of which it is entitled under international law.

The debate about the source of the law of the immunity of international organizations matters because rules of customary international law, with obligations erga omnes, "by their very nature, must have equal force for all members of the international community."[68] Even when courts are clear about what law to apply with respect to the privileges and immunities of international organizations, their interpretation of international law is not always consistent or coherent. Thus, the sources of the law are very critical to the determination of the jurisdictional immunity of international organizations, which may revolve around the interpretation of international or national law or both, and should be construed in *pari materia*, as applicable.

66. See *Murray v. Schooner Charming Betsy*, 6 U.S. (2 Cranch) 64, 118 (1804).

67. However, Article 27 is without prejudice to Article 46, which allows for a invalidity of a treaty on certain grounds.

68. North Sea Continental Shelf, 1969 I.C.J. Rep. 38, para. 63.

8

Determination and Scope of Immunity of International Organizations

DETERMINATION OF IMMUNITY

In the determination of the jurisdictional immunity of international organizations and their officials, questions remain: What are the functions of an international organization? What are official activities? Who decides these questions? Legal instruments on privileges and immunities of international organizations generally provide that their officials shall be immune from legal process in respect of words spoken or written and all acts performed by them in their official capacity, but with no statement as to who determines what constitutes an official act.[1]

The United States case of *County of Westchester v. William Ranollo*[2] was the first judicial attempt at determination of the jurisdictional immunity of staff of

1. See, e.g., Articles V, Section 18(a) and IV, Section 11, of the Convention on the Privileges and Immunities of the United Nations ("General Convention"); Articles VI, Section 19(a) and V, Section 13, of the Convention on the Privileges and Immunities of the Specialized Agencies of the United Nations ("Specialized Agencies Convention").

2. 67 N.Y.S.2d 31 (1946).

Jurisdictional Immunities of States and International Organizations. Edward Chukwuemeke Okeke.

the United Nations.[3] The defendant was employed by the United Nations as the chauffeur of the Secretary-General, and was charged with speeding while driving the Secretary-General to an official business event. At the court hearing, the Legal Counsel of the United Nations appeared for the defendant and invoked the immunity of the United Nations, claiming that defendant was performing an official function at the time of the alleged offense.

The trial judge recognized that for international organizations "to function properly within the borders of the particular nation that may be housing their activities, a certain amount of immunity, exemption and privilege is *necessary* to insure their *necessary personnel* against harassment by way of court proceedings, civil or criminal."[4] However, the judge did not consider the defendant to fall under the category of such necessary personnel.[5] According to him, necessary personnel are those "whose activities are such as to be necessary to the actual execution of the purposes and deliberations of the United Nations as distinguished from those household servants and personnel who merely serve the personal comfort, convenience or luxury of the delegates and Secretariat who actually perform the true functions of the organization."[6] He "fel[t] strongly that the question of immunity under these circumstances should be entrusted not to the whim or caprice of any individual or committee that might speak for the United Nations Organization, but rather that such immunity should be available only when it is truly necessary to assure the proper deliberations of the organization."[7]

By distinguishing between those personnels whose activities were such as to be necessary to the actual execution of the purposes and deliberations of the United Nations, Judge Rubin held that the defendant driver was not entitled to immunity as a matter of law without a trial of the issue of fact. Following the ruling, the Legal Counsel of the United Nations wrote to the trial judge:

> It will be noted that the legal adviser of the Department of State has expressed the opinion that the defendant, William Ranollo, is entitled to the immunity provided in Section 7(b) of the Immunities Act under the facts of this case. The opinion thus covers the issue of principle presented. However, the Secretary-General has no desire to press the principle of

3. For a thorough and contemporaneous analysis of the case and its surrounding circumstances, see Lawrence Preuss, *Immunity of Officers and Employees of the United Nations for Official Acts: The* Ranollo *Case*, 41 AM. J. INT'L L. 555 (1947).

4. 67 N.Y.S.2d 31, 34 [emphasis added].

5. 67 N.Y.S.2d 31, 34.

6. *Id.* at 35.

7. *Id.*

> immunity in the instant case, and he has, therefore, requested me to inform the Court that he is prepared, on behalf of the defendant, to pay such fine as the Court may levy.[8]

The surrounding circumstance of the *Ranollo* case detracted from any jurisprudential relevance that it may have had: "Although the waiver of immunity by the Secretary-General left the principal issue unsettled the reasoning of Judge Rubin's opinion has thereby lost little of interest and importance since it touches upon problems which will be recurrent and possibly adumbrate the judicial attitude which will be assumed in future cases presenting similar or analogous circumstances."[9] The ruling of the trial judge has been roundly criticized as demonstrating that national courts are ill-equipped to determine what constitutes official acts of staff of international organizations.[10]

The determination of the immunity of the United Nations was the subject of a binding Advisory Opinion[11] on the *Difference Relating to the Immunity from Legal Process of a Special Rapporteur of the Commission on Human Rights*

8. United Nations, Press Release M/78 (Nov. 29, 1946), p. 1. (cited in Preuss, at 557).

9. See Preuss, at 558–59 ("It may be surmised, however, that the decision not to press the claim of immunity in this case, while reserving the principle at stake, may have been influenced also by a desire to avoid a controversial issue which would endanger the successful conclusion of negotiations on larger issues involving the legal position of the United Nations and its personnel in the United States.")

10. See Kuljit Ahluwalia, The Legal Status, Privileges and Immunities of the Specialized Agencies of the United Nations and Certain Other International Organizations (Martinus Nijhoff 1964) at 111 ("In this regard we can say that if the court assumes jurisdiction to determine the issue of fact, nothing remains of such immunity. Any requirement of that nature would make a mockery of the whole principle of immunity from suit. Moreover, it is the court or the international organization in question which should determine whether the function performed was necessary or proper for the organization or not? To draw a line between 'necessary' and 'unnecessary' functions is as complex as drawing a distinction between 'official' and 'unofficial' acts can sometimes be.") [citation omitted].

11. Section 30 of the General Convention provides: "All differences arising out of the interpretation or application of the present convention shall be referred to the International Court of Justice, unless in any case it is agreed by the parties to have recourse to another mode of settlement. If a difference arises between the United Nations on the one hand and a Member on the other hand, a request shall be made for an advisory opinion on any legal question involved in accordance with Article 96 of the Charter and Article 65 of the Statute of the Court. The opinion given by the Court shall be accepted as decisive by the parties." The power of the Court to give an advisory opinion derives from Article 96, paragraph 2, of the Charter, and Article 65 of the Statute, which both require that the subject matter of the request should be a "legal question."

(*"Cumaraswamy"*) issued by the International Court of Justice (ICJ).[12] The *Cumaraswamy* case required the ICJ to determine whether Article VI, Section 22, of the Convention on the Privileges and Immunities of the United Nations ("General Convention") was "applicable" to a Malaysian jurist who was appointed a Special Rapporteur by the United Nations, particularly, whether he was entitled to immunity from legal process for the words spoken by him during an interview as published in a magazine. The ICJ was also required to determine whether the government of Malaysia had the obligation to inform the Malaysian court of the Secretary-General's finding as to the Special Rapporteur's entitlement to immunity from legal process.[13]

Regarding the applicability of Section 22 of the General Convention to the Special Rapporteur, the ICJ considered its earlier opinion in the *Mazilu* case[14] and examined the mandate of the Special Rapporteur before concluding that he must be regarded as an expert on mission within the meaning of this provision of the General Convention.[15] According to the ICJ, "Malaysia has acknowledged that Mr. Cumaraswamy, as Special Rapporteur of the Commission, is an expert on mission and that such experts enjoy the privileges and immunities provided for under the General Convention in their relations with States parties, including those of which they are nationals or on the territory of which they reside. Malaysia and the United Nations are in full agreement on these points, as are other States participating in the proceedings."[16]

The ICJ next considered whether the words used by the Special Rapporteur during the interview with the magazine were spoken in the course of the performance of his mission so as to be immune from legal process. It noted that in "the process of determining whether a particular expert on mission is entitled, in the prevailing circumstances, to the immunity provided for in Section 22(b),

12. *Difference Relating to Immunity from Legal Process of a Special Rapporteur of the Commission on Human Rights*, Advisory Opinion, 29 April 1999, I.C.J. Reports 1999, p. 62.

13. It must be noted that various participants in the proceedings, including Malaysia, differed in their views as to what was the legal question to be answered by the Court, but the Court maintained that it will answer the question as formulated by the Economic and Social Council (ECOSOC).

14. In its Advisory Opinion of 14 December 1989 on the *Applicability of Article VI, Section 22, of the General Convention (Mazilu case)*, the Court examined the applicability of Section 22 *ratione personae, ratione temporis,* and *ratione loci,* and stated: "The Purpose of Section 22 is . . . evident, namely, to enable the United Nations to entrust missions to persons who do not have the status of an official of the Organization, and to guarantee them 'such privileges and immunities as are necessary for the independent exercise of their functions'. . . . The essence of the matter lies not in their administrative position but in the nature of their mission." I.C.J. Reports 1989, p. 194, para. 47.

15. See I.C.J. Reports 1999, p. 62, paras. 42–45.

16. *Id.*, para. 46.

the Secretary-General of the United Nations has a pivotal role to play."[17] Furthermore, the "determination whether an agent of the Organization has acted in the course of the performance of his mission depends upon the facts of a particular case."[18] The ICJ concluded that "in view of the circumstances of this case . . . the Secretary-General correctly found that Mr. Cumaraswamy, in speaking the words quoted in the article . . . was acting in the course of the performance of his mission."[19]

In a separate opinion, Vice President Weeramantry underscored the importance of the conclusiveness of the Secretary-General's determination:

> The Secretary-General is better informed than any external authority regarding such questions as the limits of a given agent's functions, the purpose or purposes the appointment was intended to serve, and the needs of the United Nations in relation to any particular enquiry. He is better informed than any other authority of the practice relating to and the factual background surrounding the particular matter. With his unique overview of the entire scheme of the United Nations operations, he, more than any other authority, can assess a given agent's functions within the overall context of the rationale, traditions and operational framework of the United Nations activities as a whole.[20]

The second part of the question posed by the United Nations Economic and Social Council (ECOSOC) to the ICJ concerned the legal obligations of the government of Malaysia in the case. The ICJ noted that the difference between the United Nations and Malaysia arose out of "the failure of the Government of Malaysia to inform the competent Malaysian judicial authorities of the Secretary-General's finding that Mr. Cumaraswamy had spoken the words at issue in the course of the performance of his mission and was, therefore, entitled to immunity from legal process."[21] The ICJ further noted that the Secretary-General's "finding, and its documentary expression, creates a presumption which can only be set aside for the most compelling reasons and is thus to be given the greatest weight by national courts."[22] The ICJ concluded that under both the Charter of the United Nations and the General Convention, the government of Malaysia

17. *Id.*, para. 50.

18. *Id.*, para. 52.

19. *Id.* at 56.

20. *Id.* Separate Opinion of Vice-President Weeramantry, p. 96.

21. *Id.*, para. 59.

22. *Id.*, para. 61.

had the obligation to apprise its courts of the finding of the Secretary-General, and that the conduct of any organ of a State must be regarded as an act of that State according to the well established rule of international law.[23] It ruled: "By necessary implication, questions of immunity are therefore preliminary issues which must be expeditiously decided *in limine litis*. This is a generally recognized principle of procedural law, and Malaysia was under an obligation to respect it."[24]

"[S]ometimes domestic courts lack knowledge of immunities of international organizations, as such cases rarely arise, and fall outside the ambit of what national courts—especially lower courts—are used to dealing with. They may tend to confuse legal concepts and be simply wrong."[25] A recent example of the ignorance of the nature of immunities of international organizations by a national court is *Kevin Wallace v. World Bank Group* in the Superior Court of Justice, Toronto, Ontario, Canada.[26] The *Wallace* case arose out of the anti-corruption policy of the World Bank. The World Bank Group Integrity Vice Presidency unit (INT) unit has the institutional mandate to investigate allegations of fraud and corruption in connection with World Bank financed projects and activities. One such project was the Padma Bridge project in Bangladesh. INT had received information that representatives of a Canadian company were planning to bribe Bangladeshi officials to obtain a contract for the construction of the bridge.

INT conducted its investigation, after which it shared some of the information from the investigation with the Royal Canadian Mounted Police (RCMP). The RCMP carried out its own independent investigation, interviewed some of the four confidential informants, and made disclosure of all of the information it had received from the World Bank as well as all the investigative information it had researched and developed on its own, including all the information it had put before a judge to obtain the wiretap authorization against the suspects.

In every transmission and communication to the RCMP, the World Bank expressly reserved all its immunities. As part of its investigative procedures, INT keeps certain information it collects confidential for the following reasons:

23. See *id.*, para. 62.

24. *Id.*, para. 63.

25. Cedric Ryngaert, The Immunity of International Organizations Before Domestic Courts: Recent Trends, Working Paper No. 143 – December 2009, Institute for International Law, K.U. Leuven.

26. *Kevin Wallace v. World Bank Group*, 2014 ONSC 7449. "Given the particular wording of the provisions that govern the World Bank Group, there is no basis for a conclusion that the World Bank Group can be found to have waived its immunity if it has done so expressly. Rather, the World Bank Group is in the same category of a person who enjoys a privilege. Privileges may be expressly or impliedly waived and, I conclude, on the plain wording of s. 8 of Article VII, so can the immunity enjoyed by the World Bank Group." *Id.*, para. 47.

(1) to preserve the integrity of an investigation and prevent interference with the investigation or destruction of evidence, (2) to protect informants and witnesses who might otherwise face retaliation, and (3) to reassure potential witnesses, complainants, and whistleblowers that they can come forward, confident that their identities will be kept confidential.

The defendants, who were charged with an offence under Canada's Foreign Corruption of Public Officials Act (CFPOA), challenged the wiretap authorization and applied for a third-party production order to compel INT investigators to appear before the Ontario Superior Court and produce World Bank documents. The trial judge granted the defendants' application. He concluded that the World Bank enjoyed immunity from the jurisdiction, but that the immunity had been "impliedly" waived by the "benefit/burden" exception to Crown immunity under Canadian law. His reasoning, based on Canadian law, is that "if the World Bank wishes to take the benefits of causing a criminal prosecution to be instituted in [Canada], it must accept the burden of so doing, that is, it must accept that it will be required to comply with the procedural rules, and the attendant obligations, of such a prosecution, including the possible result that third party records will be ordered to be disclosed."[27]

According to the trial judge, the Articles of Agreement of the World Bank do not explicitly require an express waiver of immunities. He ruled that the different sections of Article VII of the Articles of Agreement are not distinct and separate, and a waiver is for all purposes. In other words, according to the trial judge, the immunities of officials and archives of the World Bank should be construed holistically and, therefore, a waiver of one entails a waiver of the other.

The order by the trial judge was appealed by the World Bank to the Supreme Court of Canada, which allowed the appeal and set aside the trial judge's order.[28] The Supreme Court disagreed with the trial judge and held that the archival immunity of the World Bank shields the organization's entire collection of stored documents from both search and seizure and from compelled production. It reasoned: "Shielding an organization's entire collection of stored documents, including official records and correspondence, is integral to ensuring their proper, independent functioning."[29] It held: "Further, we are of the view that partial voluntary disclosure of some documents by the World Bank Group does not amount to a waiver of this immunity. Indeed, on our reading, the archival immunity is not subject to waiver."[30]

27. *Kevin Wallace v. H.M.Q.*, 2014 ONSC 7449, para. 36.

28. *World Bank Group v. Wallace*, 2016 SCC 15.

29. *Id.*, para. 71.

30. *Id.*, para. 82.

With respect to the immunity of officials of the World Bank under its Articles of Agreement, the Supreme Court was of the view that "the object and purpose of the treaty favour an express waiver requirement."[31] According to the Court:

> The application of the IBRD's and IDA's immunity provisions are not subject to a case-by-case determination. To read "waiver" as including forms of implied or constructive waiver would subject immunities to case-by-case determination. Representatives of the World Bank Group would be required to appear in national courts to argue whether their conduct amounted to waiver, or whether for other reasons they should be deemed to have waived their immunity. Such a conclusion would be inconsistent with our view that the IBRD's and IDA's immunities apply without further justification.[32]

The Supreme Court recounted its jurisprudence that "the purpose for according immunity to international organizations and their personnel is to shield these organizations from interference by member states."[33] It reasoned that if the immunity of officials were subject to implied or constructive waiver, which are varied concepts globally, "then inconsistencies from jurisdiction to jurisdiction could cause considerable confusion and interfere with IBRD's and IDA's orderly operations."[34] It concluded that the requirement of express waiver avoids the problem of individual member States attempting to control the organization "which may occur if domestic courts apply local and variegated conceptions of implied and constructive waiver."[35]

Notwithstanding the oddity of the opinions of the trial judges in the *Ranollo* and *Wallace* cases, there is no gainsaying that it is the province of the national courts to decide questions of immunity. Perhaps the trial judge's opinion in *Wallace* was unduly influenced by his perception that the World Bank disrespected his court by not appearing before it,[36] or his lack of knowledge about international organizations and information about the World Bank in particular. The

31. *Id.*, para. 90.

32. *Id.*

33. *Id.*, para. 91, citing *Amaratunga*.

34. *Id.*, para. 92.

35. *Id.*, para. 93.

36. See *Kevin Wallace v. H.M.Q.*, 2014 ONSC 7449, para. 26 ("Putting aside the measure of disrespect that the World Bank Group demonstrates to this court by absenting themselves from this application, it remains the fact that it becomes more difficult for this court to fully understand and assess the claim for immunity, in these circumstances, given the dearth of evidence from the World Bank Group on the various issues that would be helpful to the analysis.")

way an international organization asserts its jurisdictional immunity depends on the procedural law of the municipal court, as well as on diplomatic practice and protocol in the particular country.[37] An international organization may make a limited appearance before the court to assert its immunity or it may request the ministry of external affairs to intervene through the ministry of justice to assert its immunity.

A court may, *sua sponte*, dismiss a suit based on the organization's jurisdictional immunity without the organization appearing before the court. The Danish Court of Second Instance for the Eastern Circuit addressed this issue in a suit for alleged failure to pay for goods. The plaintiff had filed the case on June 28, 1999, and duly served a writ of summons upon UNICEF at its address in Copenhagen on July 26, 1999. The writ of summons directed UNICEF to file its defense with the court no later than August 13, 1999, but UNICEF neither filed a defense nor responded to the court in any other way. As a result, the plaintiff requested a default judgment against UNICEF. The court had to decide whether to follow its normal procedure to render a default judgment when a defendant does not file a proper defense or to decide on its own whether UNICEF was entitled to immunity. The court considered that the Danish Government Notice no. 37 of 10 July 1948 incorporated the General Convention, and that the Danish Government Notice no. 94 of 22 September 1983 incorporated the 1983 Agreement between the Government of Denmark and the United Nations Relating to the Headquarters in Copenhagen of the Integrated Supply Centre of UNICEF ("Headquarters Agreement"). The Preamble of the Headquarters Agreement provides that the General Convention applied to the Integrated Supply Centre of UNICEF and that the Headquarters Agreement regulates questions not envisaged in the General Convention that may arise as a result of the establishment of the Centre. The court determined that UNICEF was immune from the lawsuit and dismissed the case summarily ex officio.[38]

In the United States, federal courts have an obligation to inquire into subject-matter jurisdiction, even if the parties do not contest this threshold issue.[39] The court must then dismiss a case if it "determines at any time that it lacks

37. See Anthony Miller, *Privileges and Immunities of the United Nations*, 6 INT'L ORG. L. REV. 41 (2009), for the practice of the United Nations with respect to the assertions of its jurisdictional immunity.

38. *The Investment & Finance Company of 11 January 1984 Ltd. v. UNICEF*, U. 2000.478 Ø; ILDC 64 (DK 1999), available on ildc.oxfordlawreports.com. Jon Stockton's commentary on the case, dated August 31, 2006, notes that the Court's reference to Article VIII, Section 29(a) of the General Convention may suggest that the Court felt that the company should have recourse against UNICEF through the alternative dispute resolution mechanism mandated for the UN by the Convention.

39. *D'Amico Dry Ltd. v. Primera Maritime (Hellas) Ltd.*, 756 F.3d 151, 161 (2d Cir. 2014).

subject-matter jurisdiction."[40] The party asserting subject-matter jurisdiction bears the burden of proving jurisdiction by a preponderance of the evidence.[41]

A determination of the immunity is a procedural matter that does not turn on the validity of the underlying suit. Clearly a court must have subject-matter jurisdiction so as to have the authority to make determinations of jurisdictional immunity.[42] In some cases, it is a matter of competence, not immunity, as noted by some French writers whose position is that national courts are not competent to adjudicate employment cases between international organizations and their employees.[43]

According to the principle espoused by Chief Justice Marshall in *Marbury v. Madison*, "It is, emphatically, the province and duty of the judicial department to say what the law is."[44] Although this principle, as a constitutional norm in the United States, is concerned with the judicial review of legislative action, it has been extended to other realms such as judicial review of administrative action. Other common law jurisdictions have accepted and followed this principle as axiomatic. This principle is the bedrock of the rule of law. Until international tribunals are established with the competence to adjudicate disputes between international organizations and private parties, it will remain the province of national courts to make judicial determinations of the immunity of international organizations. As of now, the only such international tribunals are administrative tribunals whose jurisdiction is limited to the adjudication of disputes between international organizations and their personnel. Thus, consistent with the *Cumaraswamy* opinion, it is the proper role of courts to determine questions of jurisdictional immunity, with due regard to the opinion of the international organization on its functions and the acts of its personnel.

40. FED. R. CIV. P. 12(h)(3).

41. See *Makarova v. United States*, 201 F.3d 110, 113 (2d Cir. 2000).

42. See Christian Dominicé, L'immunité de juridiction et d'exécution des organisations internationales, Académie de droit international, Recueil des cours, Tome 187 de la collection, 1984 (*« L'incompétence d'attribution est nettement distincte de l'immunité de juridiction. Nous verrons cependant que les tribunaux n'ont pas toujours une juste vision des questions à résoudre.»*).

43. Jean-Flavien Lalive, L'Immunité De Juridiction Des États Et Des Organisations Internationales (Hague Académie De Droit International 1953, p. 352 (*« Nous avons constaté qu'en bonne doctrine les différends entre l'Organisations et ses fonctionnaires échappent ou devraient échapper é l'emprise des lois territoriales pertinentes, non point par application de la notion d'immunité juridictionnelle, mais parce que nous nous trouvons dans un secteur juridique différent: les rapports de service entre une organisation et ses fonctionnaires sont régis par le droit administratif international. Le contentieux interne de l'organisation sera donc réglé par application de ce droit. Si un tribunal territorial était saisi d'un litige de cet ordre, il y aurait donc ici une irrecevabilité absolue, sans qu'il soit besoin de faire appel à la notion l'immunité juridictionnelle. »*).

44. 5 U.S. 137, 177 (1803).

SCOPE OF IMMUNITY

The scope of immunity of international organizations deals with the fundamental question of who and what are covered by the immunity. "There are very significant differences among international organizations with regard to their powers and functions, size of membership, relations between the organizations and their members, procedures for deliberation, structure and facilities, as well as the primary rules including treaty obligations by which they are bound."[45] As international organizations vary in their functions and size, the scope of their immunities are equally varied.[46] Generally, under international law, international organizations enjoy such privileges and immunities as are necessary for the fulfillment of their functions.[47] This concept of functional necessity or functionalism is to be found in, for instance, Article 105, paragraph 3, of the Charter of the United Nations, which provides that the organization shall enjoy such privileges and immunities "as are necessary for the fulfillment of its purposes." This Charter provision is implemented and fleshed out in the General Convention. The purpose of the General Convention, as expressed by the Sixth Committee of the General Assembly during the drafting of the Convention, is as follows:

> It is important that in setting up this great new international Organization we should not ask for it to possess privileges and immunities which are greater than those required for its efficient organization. That would lead to unnecessary conflicts with the national sovereignty of particular Member States. On the other hand, equally important is to ensure that it has adequate privileges and immunities. To give too few would fetter the United Nations Organization in the discharge of its tasks. The Charter provides that the immunities and privileges to be granted should be such as are necessary for the fulfillment of its purposes, and that is exactly what this important and historic document does. Within the scope and ambit of the Charter this Convention will give the United Nations Organization, in every Member State, a sufficient degree of sovereignty in regard to its own affairs to enable it to carry out its functions independently, impartially and efficiently.[48]

45. United Nations Document A/71/10, p. 88, n.274 (Official Records of the General Assembly, Sixty-sixth Session, Supplement No. 10 (A/66/10).

46. See *Amaratunga v. Northwest Atlantic Fisheries Organization*, 2013 SCC 66, [2013] 3. S.C.R. 866 (Can.), para. 30.

47. See Restatement (Third) of the Foreign Relations Law of the United States § 467(1) (Am. Law. Inst. 1987).

48. Verbatim Records of February 13, 1946, at 452, First Session of the General Assembly, Plenary Meetings of the General Assembly, GAOR.

With respect to the United Nations and its specialized agencies, the General Assembly Resolution 179 (II) of 21 November 1947 (Co-ordination of the privileges and immunities of the United Nations and of the specialized agencies) noted its Resolution 22(I) D, of 13 February 1946, "contemplating the unification as far as possible of the privileges and immunities enjoyed by the United Nations and by the specialized agencies." The General Assembly also considered it desirable that the specialized agencies derive their privileges and immunities from the Convention on the Privileges and Immunities of the Specialized Agencies "with such modifications as may be necessary to meet the particular requirements of that agency to be contained in an annex."[49]

As international organizations are creations of treaty, the determination of the scope of their immunity is usually a task that entails the interpretation and application of the relevant treaty provision. "A treaty shall be interpreted in good faith in accordance with the ordinary meaning to be given to the terms of the treaty in their context and in the light of its object and purpose."[50] With respect to the United Nations, "Any interpretation of the provisions of the General Convention must be carried out within the spirit of the underlying principles of the United Nations Charter, and in particular Article 105 thereof, which provides that the Organization shall enjoy such privileges and immunities as are necessary for the fulfilment of its purposes. Moreover, in accordance with article 26 of the Vienna Convention on the Law of Treaties, 1969 . . . every treaty in force is binding upon the parties to it and must be performed by them in good faith."[51]

Immunity of international organizations from "every form of legal process" has been broadly interpreted to include all legal proceedings before national (administrative, judicial, or executive) authorities. It applies regardless of whether the international organization is a defendant or witness. The immunity does not preclude the organization, in its own determination, from participating in such proceedings. However, the initiation of court proceedings by an international organization may be construed as a waiver of its jurisdictional immunity in that particular case.

The scope of the immunity of international organizations specializing in financial transactions and economic development lending, such as the World Bank, is in sharp contrast with that of other international organizations that are immune from suit unless they expressly waive their immunity. The constituent instrument of these international financial institutions (IFIs) or multilateral development banks (MDBs) contains provisions permitting suits by bondholders and related

49. General Assembly Resolution 179(II)(B) of 21 November 1947.

50. Article 31(1), Vienna Convention on the Law of Treaties.

51. United Nations Juridical Yearbook 2012, Chapter VI, p. 461 (November 20, 2012).

creditors. This limitation on immunity is impelled by the consideration that inability to sue in national courts might render securities issued by these international organizations less attractive to potential lenders.[52]

The Articles of Agreement of the Inter-American Development Bank (IADB), which came into effect in 1959, contain a provision that closely follows Article VII, Section of the IBRD Articles, but more recent multilateral development banks, such as the African Development Bank (AfDB)[53] and the Asian Development Bank (AsDB),[54] have expressly limited the right to bring action to purely financial transactions of the organizations, such as those arising out of borrowings, guarantees given, or sales of securities made by these international organizations. It appears that the charters of the AfDB and the AsDB were in response to the apparent ambiguity in the Articles of Agreement of the World Bank as to the scope of its jurisdictional immunity.[55]

The *Lutcher* case[56] addressed the scope of immunity of the IADB. In that case, the plaintiff, a Brazilian corporation engaged in lumbering operations and the

52. The immunity from execution of international financial institutions, such as IBRD, is influenced by the same functional considerations limiting the immunity from jurisdiction. It would be self-contradictory to be able to bring an action against an organization without being able to enforce a judgment against that organization. Investors and creditors of these organizations must be assured not only that they could sue the organization but also that if they prevail they would not be prevented from enforcing the judgment. Consequently, the charter of these organizations recognizes the rational link between immunity from suit and immunity from execution.

53. Article 52 of the Articles of Agreement of AfDB provides: "The Bank shall enjoy immunity from every form of legal process except in cases arising out of the exercise of its borrowing powers when it may be sued only in a court of competent jurisdiction in the territory of a member in which the Bank has its principal office, or in the territory of a member or non-member State where it has appointed an agent for the purpose of accepting service or notice of process or has issued or guaranteed securities. No action shall, however be brought by members or persons acting for or deriving claims from members" [emphasis added].

54. Article 50 of the Articles of Agreement of AsDB provides: "The Bank shall enjoy immunity from every form of legal process, except in cases arising out of or in connection with the exercise of its powers to borrow money, to guarantee obligations, or to buy and sell or underwrite securities, in which cases action may be brought against the Bank in a court of competent jurisdiction in the territory of a country in which the Bank has its principal or a branch office, or has appointed an agent for the purpose of accepting service or notice of process, or has issued or guaranteed securities. [emphasis added].

55. See Report of the Preparatory Committee on the AsDB, Economic Commission for Asia and the Far East, Report of the Second Ministerial Conference on Asian Economic Cooperation, Final Act of the Conference of Plenipotentiaries on the Asian Development Bank and Report of the Preparatory Committee on the Asian Development Bank, United Nations Document No. E/CN. 11/716 Rev. 1. page 61.

56. *Lutcher S. A. Cellulose e Papel v. Inter-American Development Bank*, 382 F. 2d 454 (C.A.D.C. 1967).

processing of paper pulp, sued the IADB in the United States, alleging that the organization had violated its earlier commitments under a loan agreement with the plaintiff by making loans to certain of its competitors. IADB moved to dismiss the suit on two grounds: (1) jurisdictional immunity, and (2) failure to state a claim upon which relief could be granted. IADB argued that, although its Articles of Agreement provide in effect that any person could bring an action against it in a court of competent jurisdiction in a member country in which it had an office, had issued securities, or had appointed an agent for the purpose of accepting service of process, such provision meant that submission to jurisdiction of the relevant court should be limited to suits brought by "bondholders, and other like creditors and beneficiaries of its guarantees." The IADB argued that its Articles of Agreement are "similar" to those of AsDB, which limit suits against AsDB to "cases arising out of, or in connection with, the exercise of [the Bank's] power to borrow money, to guarantee obligations, to buy and sell or underwrite the sale of securities." However, the court countered that "similar" did not mean "identical," and that if the Articles of Agreement of AsDB expressively and effectively limit the right to sue it to specific classes of creditors, no such limitation could be read in the Articles of Agreement of IADB.[57]

Looking at the *scope* of immunity of international organizations through only the prism of functionalism would avoid the unhelpful dichotomy or distinction between "absolute" versus "restrictive" immunities. Borrowing from sovereign immunity, absolute or restrictive, is often, but erroneously, used to describe the scope of immunity of international organizations. Thus, "functional" immunity is sometimes equated with restrictive immunity. However, functional immunity is not the opposite of absolute immunity. Even the so-called absolute immunity that international organizations, such as the United Nations, are said to have, is founded on functional necessity.[58] Similarly, the so-called limited or restrictive immunity of IFIs, such as the World Bank, is based on functional necessity. In common parlance, where there is no express exception to immunity in the constituent text of international organizations or legal instrument on privileges and immunities, the international organization is said to have absolute immunity, notwithstanding the functional necessity basis of the immunity.

57. See 382 F.2d at 459.

58. Considering the principle of functional necessity, as international organizations are rarely found to have acted ultra vires because of the implied powers doctrine, their functional immunity is de facto absolute immunity. The argument is that any and all acts of international organizations are deemed in furtherance of their functions.

Beneficiaries of Immunities

Under Article 105 of the Charter of the United Nation, the organization, representatives of its member States, and its officials benefit from the organization's privileges and immunities. In the case of the World Bank and IMF, their respective Articles of Agreement provide for the privileges and immunities of the following persons: governors, executive directors, alternates, officers, and employees. The General Convention provides that the United Nations, its property, assets, and funds shall be immune from legal process except when expressly waived.[59] It also provides for the immunity of (1) officials of the organization, (2) representatives of member States of the Organization, and (3) experts performing missions for the Organization. The Specialized Agencies Convention has similar provisions as the General Convention, except that it does not contain any provision on "experts."[60] The immunity of an international organization does not generally extend to independent contractors engaged by the organization.[61] The archives and documents of an international organization also benefit from the jurisdictional immunity of which they are complementary.

With respect to "officials" of the United Nations, the General Assembly by Resolution 76(I) of 7 December 1946 defined them to include staff except those "recruited locally and paid hourly rates." In a statement to the 59th meeting of the Fifth Committee of the General Assembly on 1 December 1981, the Legal Counsel of the United Nations addressed the suggestion "by some delegations that locally recruited staff members were not officials of the United Nations and specialized agencies for the purpose of privileges and immunities and that they were first and foremost nationals of the country concerned and, as such, were subject to its laws." He clarified:

> [T]he meaning of the term "officials" as it was used in the Conventions. Section 17 of the Convention on the Privileges and Immunities of the United Nations stated that the Secretary-General would specify the categories of officials to which articles V and VII of the Convention should apply. The Convention on the Privileges and Immunities of the Specialized Agencies and the IAEA Agreement contained similar provisions. In 1946, the General Assembly had adopted resolution 76 (I), in which it had approved the granting of the privileges and immunities referred to in articles V and VII

59. See Article II, Section 2, General Convention.

60. See Article VI of General Convention.

61. See *Herbert Harvey, Inc. v. NLRB*, 424 F.2d 770 (D.C. Cir.1969) (independent contractor providing maintenance and operating services for World Bank is not so related to the functions of the Bank as to warrant exemption from National Labor Relations Act and jurisdiction of NLRB).

> of the Convention on the Privileges and Immunities of the United Nations to all members of Staff of the United Nations, apart from those who were recruited locally and were assigned to hourly rates. The specialized agencies and the IAEA had taken similar actions. Consequently, all staff members regardless of rank, nationality or place of recruitment, whether Professional or General Service were considered officials of the organizations for the purposes of privileges and immunities except for those who were both locally recruited and employed at hourly rates. United Nations locally recruited staff such as clerks, secretaries and drivers were in nearly every case paid according to established salary or wage scales and not at hourly rates and they were, therefore, covered by the terms of General Assembly resolution 76 (I).[62]

Article VI, Section 22, of the General Convention provides: "Experts . . . performing missions for the United Nations shall be accorded such privileges and immunities as are necessary for the independent exercise of their functions during the period of their mission, including the time spent on journeys in connection with their mission." This provision on "experts" was the subject of differences between the United Nations and Romania. By its resolution 1985/12 of 29 August 1985, the Sub-Commission on the Prevention of Discrimination and Protection of Minorities, a subsidiary organ of the United Nations Commission on Human Rights, requested Dumitru Mazilu, a Romanian national, to "prepare a report on human rights and youth analyzing the efforts and measures for securing the implementation and enjoyment by youth of human rights, particularly, the right to life, education and work."[63]

The Secretary-General, on October 26, 1988, addressed a note verbale to the Permanent Representative of Romania to the United Nations in New York, pursuant to resolution 1988/37 of 1 September 1988, in which he invoked the General Convention in respect of Mr. Mazilu and requested the Romanian government to accord him the necessary facilities to enable him to complete his assigned task.

By its resolution 1989/37 of 6 March 1989, the Commission recommended that the Economic and Social Council of the United Nations (ECOSOC) request an advisory opinion from the ICJ on the applicability of the relevant provisions of the General Convention to Mr. Mazilu. On May 24, 1989, ECOSOC adopted

62. Statement made by the Legal Counsel at the 59th meeting of the Fifth Committee of the General Assembly on 1 December 1981, United Nations Juridical Yearbook, 1981, 161–62.

63. *Applicability of Article VI, Section 22, of the Convention on the Privileges and Immunities of the United Nations*, Advisory Opinion, I.C.J. Reports 1989, paras. 23–24.

resolution 1989/75, which concluded that a difference had arisen between the United Nations and Romania as to the applicability of the General Convention to Mr. Mazilu as Special Rapporteur of the Sub-Commission, and requested an advisory opinion from the Court on the legal question of the applicability of Article VI, Section 22, of the General Convention in the case of Mr. Mazilu as Special Rapporteur of the Sub-Commission.

Romania had disagreed that the General Convention was applicable to Mr. Mazilu. It argued that the General Convention "does not equate rapporteurs, whose activities are only occasional, with experts on mission for the United Nations" and that "even if rapporteurs are given some of the status of experts, they can enjoy only functional immunities and privileges." Romania also opposed the request of an advisory opinion from the ICJ regarding the case. Notwithstanding, on December 15, 1989, the ICJ delivered its advisory opinion, and considered what was meant by "experts on missions" for the purposes of Section 22 of the General Convention.

Although the General Convention does not define "experts on mission" nor indicate what is a "mission," the ICJ found that the purpose of Section 22 was undeniably to enable the United Nations to entrust missions to persons who do not have the status of an official of the Organization and to guarantee them such privileges and immunities as are necessary for the independent exercise of their functions. The experts thus appointed or elected may or may not be remunerated, may or may not have a contract, and may be given a task requiring work over a lengthy period or short time. The crux of the matter lay not in their administrative position but in the nature of their mission. The Court noted that the practice of the United Nations showed that such experts had been entrusted with various missions, including, inter alia, mediation, preparing studies, conducting investigations, or finding and establishing facts and participating in peacekeeping forces. In addition, many committees, commissions, or similar bodies whose members serve, not as representatives of States, but in a personal capacity, have been set up within the Organization. The Court concluded that the practice of the United Nations shows that the persons so appointed, and in particular the members of those committees and commissions, have been regarded as experts on missions within the meaning of Section 22.

To determine whether experts on mission were covered by Section 22 "only during missions requiring travel or whether they were also covered when there was no such travel or apart from such travel," the Court had to interpret the meaning of the phrase "during the period of their missions" in Section 22. The Court noted that Section 22, in its reference to experts performing missions for the United Nations, uses the word "mission" in a general sense "of the tasks entrusted to a person, whether or not those tasks involve travel." The Court reasoned that the intent of Section 22 was to ensure the independence of such experts in the interest of the Organization by according them the privileges and immunities necessary for the purpose. The Court, therefore, concluded that Section 22 "is applicable to every expert on mission, whether or not he travels."

The Court next addressed whether the privileges and immunities provided for in Section 22 could be invoked against the State of which an expert is a national or on the territory of which he or she resides. It found that the privileges and immunities under Article VI of the General Convention—like those conferred on officials in Article V of the General Convention—were conferred to ensure the independence of experts in the interests of the Organization. Consequently, this independence must be respected by all States, including the State of nationality and of residence of the expert. The Court noted that some State Parties to the General Convention had entered reservations to certain provisions of Article VI as regards their nationals or persons habitually resident in their territory. The Court stated that for those States to find it necessary to make such reservations confirmed the conclusion that "in the absence of such reservations, experts on missions enjoy the privileges and immunities provided for under the Convention in their relations with the States of which they are nationals or on the territory of which they reside."

In conclusion, the Court stated:

> [Section 22 of the General Convention] is applicable to persons (other than United Nations officials) to whom a mission has been entrusted by the Organization and who are therefore entitled to enjoy the privileges and immunities provided for in this Section with a view to the independent exercise of their functions. During the whole period of such missions, experts enjoy these functional privileges whether or not they travel. They may be invoked as against the State of nationality or of residence unless a reservation to section 22 of the General Convention has been validly made by that State.

In its disposition of the actual case before it, the Court concluded that Mr. Mazilu was an expert on mission within the meaning of Section 22 of the General Convention.

Functions, Activities or Acts of an International Organization

Functions or missions of international organizations are provided for in their constituent instruments. International organizations undertake certain activities in furtherance or fulfilment of those functions and are invested with certain privileges and immunities, including jurisdictional immunity, to that effect. To perform these functions, international organizations employ officials who act on behalf of the organization.

International organizations may undertake activities or perform acts that are not explicitly provided for in their constituent documents. The doctrine of implied powers is often applied to justify the exercise of powers that are implied from a treaty language and an organization's functional objectives. The doctrine of implied powers, which exists in the national context,[64] have been applied by international courts and tribunals.

The powers conferred on international organizations are normally the subject of an express statement in their constituent instruments. Nevertheless, the necessities of international life may point to the need for organizations, in order to achieve their objectives, to possess subsidiary powers which are not expressly provided for in the basic instruments which govern their activities. It is generally accepted that international organizations can exercise such powers, known as "implied" powers.[65] In 1926, the Permanent Court of International Justice (PCIJ) applied the doctrine in an advisory opinion addressing the question "whether it is within the competence . . . of the International Labour Organization 'to draw up and propose labour legislation which, in order to protect certain classes of workers, also regulates incidentally the same work when performed by the employer himself.' "[66] The Court noted that the answer to the question put to it "depends upon the terms of Part XIII of the Peace Treaty of Versailles of June 28th, 1919, by which the competence of the International Labour Organization is defined."[67] It noted: "Not only does the entire framework of Part XIII justify the inference that the International Labour Organization is not excluded from proposing measures for the protection of wage-earners because they may incidentally regulate the personal work of the employers, but there are specific provisions of the Treaty, in the application of which, as they are generally understood, it may be assumed that

64. In *McCulloch v. Maryland*, 17 U.S. 316 (1819), the United States Supreme Court applied the doctrine when it held that, despite the absence of an express provision in the Constitution of the United States, Congress was empowered to charter the Second Bank of the United States under the necessary and proper clause in Article I § 8 of the Constitution. According to this interpretation, Congress may take any action that is rationally related to its objectives under the broadly enumerated powers in Article I, provided the action is not prohibited by the Constitution.

65. *Legality of the Use by a State of Nuclear Weapons in Armed Conflict*, Advisory Opinion, 1996 I. C. J. Reports, p. 66, 79.

66. *Competence of the Int'l Labor Org. to regulate, incidentally, the personal work of the employer*, Advisory Opinion of July 23, 1926, P.C.I.J. Publications, Series B, No. 13 at 12.

67. *Id.* at 14.

the incidental regulation of the personal work of the employers is potentially involved."[68] After examining the ILO's broad mandate, the Court answered the question put to it in the affirmative and concluded that the organization had the competence.[69]

The ICJ reaffirmed the PCIJ's approach in the *Reparation for Injuries* advisory opinion.[70] At issue pertinently in the case was whether the United Nations has the capacity to bring international claims against a State for injuries to UN agents.[71] To answer the question, the Court noted:

> "The Charter does not expressly confer upon the Organization the capacity to include, in its claim for reparation, damage caused to the victim or to persons entitled through him. The Court must therefore begin by enquiring whether the provisions of the Charter concerning the functions of the Organization, and the part played by its agents in the performance of those functions, imply for the Organization power to afford its agents the limited protection that would consist in the bringing of a claim on their behalf for reparation for damage suffered in such circumstances. Under international law, the Organization must be deemed to have those powers which, though not expressly provided in the Charter, are conferred upon it by necessary implication as being essential to the performance of its duties. This principle of law was applied by the Permanent Court of International Justice to the International Labour Organization in its Advisory Opinion No. 13 of July 23rd, 1926 (Series B., No. 13, p. 18), and must be applied to the United Nations."[72]

The Court concluded that the United Nations impliedly possesses the power to bring international claims for reparations "[b]oth to ensure the efficient and independent performance of [its] missions and to afford effective support to its agents."[73] Subsequent ICJ opinions have reaffirmed the implied powers doctrines.

68. *Id.* at 18.

69. *Id.* at 24.

70. *Reparation for Injuries Suffered in the Service of the United Nations*, Advisory Opinion, 1949 I.C.J. Reports 1949, p.174.

71. *Id.* at 175. The Court first concluded that the United Nations possesses personality and the capacity to bring international claims. *Id.* at 178–79.

72. *Id.* at 182–3.

73. *Id.* at 183–84.

In the *Effect of Awards* advisory opinion, some member States had challenged the power of the General Assembly of the United Nations to establish an administrative tribunal to adjudicate employment disputes between the United Nations and its staff, and render binding judgments against the organization. The ICJ stated:

> "Accordingly, it is necessary to consider whether the General Assembly has been given this power by the Charter. There is no express provision for the establishment of judicial bodies or organs and no indication to the contrary.... The Court must therefore begin by enquiring whether the provisions of the Charter concerning the relations between the staff members and the Organization imply for the Organization the power to establish a judicial tribunal to adjudicate upon disputes arising out of the contracts of service."[74]

In concluding that there is implied power to establish the tribunal, the ICJ observed:

> It was inevitable that there would be disputes between the Organization and staff members as to their rights and duties. The Charter contains no provision which authorizes any of the principal organs of the United Nations to adjudicate upon these disputes, and Article 105 secures for the United Nations jurisdictional immunities in national courts. It would, in the opinion of the Court, hardly be consistent with the expressed aim of the Charter to promote freedom and justice for individuals and with the constant preoccupation of the United Nations Organization to promote this aim that it should afford no judicial or arbitral remedy to its own staff for the settlement of any disputes which may arise between it and them.[75]

Implied powers doctrine is not without limitations. International courts and tribunals apply a presumption that actions taken by an international organization to fulfill a purpose stated in the constituent instrument are not ultra vires.[76] But a mandate or mission stipulated in a constituent instrument can be interpreted to limit the scope of an organization's powers. In the *Legality of Nuclear Weapons*

74. *Effect of Awards of Compensation Made by the U.N. Administrative Tribunal*, Advisory Opinion, 1954 I.C.J. Reports, pp. 47, 57.

75. *Id. See also Certain Expenses of the UN*, Advisory Opinion, 1962 I.C.J. Report 151, 168 ("But when the Organization takes action which warrants the assertion that it was appropriate for the fulfilment of one of the stated purposes of the United Nations, the presumption is that such action is not *ultra vires* the Organization.")

76. Id.

advisory opinion, the ICJ held that the World Health Organization (WHO) could not request an advisory opinion on the legality of using or threatening to use nuclear weapons because the WHO's mandate does not depend on the legal status of nuclear weapons.[77] The Court concluded:

> The question put to the Court in the present case relates, however, *not to the effects* of the use of nuclear weapons on health, but to the *legality* of the use of such weapons *in view of their health and environmental effects.* Whatever those effects might be, the competence of the WHO to deal with them is not dependent on the legality of the acts that caused them. Accordingly, it does not seem to the Court that the provisions of Article 2 of the WHO Constitution, interpreted in accordance with the criteria referred to above, can be understood as conferring upon the Organization a competence to address the legality of the use of nuclear weapons, and thus in turn a competence to ask the Court about that.[78]
>
> In the opinion of the Court, to ascribe to the WHO the competence to address the legality of the use of nuclear weapons—even in view of their health and environmental effects—would be tantamount to disregarding the principle of speciality; for such competence could not be deemed a necessary implication of the Constitution of the Organization in the light of the purposes assigned to it by its member States.[79]

Since the raison d'etre of the jurisdictional immunity of international organizations is functional necessity, the implied powers doctrine may be relevant in the determination of whether an international organization is entitled to immunity for certain activities or acts. It is unquestionable that officials of international organizations enjoy immunity for their official acts or activities. Sometimes in the determination of the scope of immunity of an international organization, courts and tribunals examine whether an impugned act or activity is official so as to fall within the ambit of the functions of the organization. In other words, examination of whether an act or activity is official, as to benefit from immunity, applies to both the organization and its officials. The immunity for official acts is granted *ratione materiae.* Officials benefit from the immunity of the organization and, as such, their acts are imputed to the organization. At issue is what constitutes an official activity or act.

77. *Legality of the Use by a State of Nuclear Weapons in Armed Conflict,* Advisory Opinion, 1996 I.C.J. Reports, p. 66.

78. *Id.* at 76.

79. *Id.* at 79.

Although not directly concerned with jurisdictional immunity of international organizations, but with tax immunity, the European Molecular Biology Laboratory (EMBL) arbitration case construed what constitutes official activity under the applicable legal instruments.[80] The arbitral tribunal had to decide whether the EMBL's guest house, canteen, and cafeteria fell within certain provisions in the Headquarters Agreement between EMBL and Germany that exempted the EMBL from specific taxes when it acted within the scope of its "official activities." The tribunal determined that an "official activity" of the organization must be "strictly necessary" to the exercise of the organization's functions. Consequently, it held that EMBL's official activities included supplying meals and accommodation free of charge to conference participants, because it would otherwise be more difficult to organize such activities. However, the EMBL's sale of meals in a staff canteen was beyond its official activities as it was not strictly necessary for EMBL to function.

Like the EMBL case, an international organization, with headquarters in Russia, did not pay taxes levied in Russia, and had initiated a suit against the State Tax Service, claiming that it was exempt from all taxes pursuant to Article 7 of the Convention on the Legal Status, Privileges, and Immunities of Intergovernmental Economic Organizations Acting in Certain Areas of Cooperation, Budapest, 5 December 1980. The Convention was ratified by the Soviet Union in 1981, and Russia became a party to the Convention as a successor of the Soviet Union. The Russian court held that the international organization generally enjoyed functional immunity, but because it also engaged in other types of activities, such as renting out rooms and rendering household services, not provided for in the organization's charter, any sums derived from these non-charter activities of the Organization should be subject to domestic taxation, as they were not covered by the immunity.[81]

Another case interpreting the official activities of an international organization was *Mukoro v. European Bank for Reconstruction and Development* (EBRD), where the applicant brought a claim of racial discrimination against the EBRD, which had rejected his application for employment.[82] Before the Industrial Tribunal in England, the complaint was dismissed because EBRD was immune from legal

80. *European Molecular Biology Laboratory (EMBL) v. Federal Republic of Germany*, Award of 29 June 1990, 105 ILR 1.

81. Information Letter No. 58 of the Presidium of the Supreme Arbitrazh Court, January 18, 2001; ILDC 26 (RU 2001), available on ildc.oxfordlawreports.com. ("Information Letters of the Presidium of the Supreme Arbitrazh Court contain summaries of otherwise unreported decisions of arbitrazh courts on particular topics and are meant to give guidance as to Russian judicial practice on such topics.")

82. *Mukoro v. European Bank for Reconstruction and Development and Another*, Employment Appeal Tribunal, England, 19 May 1994, reported in 107 ILR 604.

process. The applicant appealed to the Employment Appeal Tribunal, claiming that the immunity that was conferred by the 1991 Order in Council did not extend to legal proceedings arising from unlawful acts of racial discrimination, which could not be regarded as official activities of the EBRD and which were inconsistent with the commitment to the rule of law and respect for human rights expressed in the agreement establishing the EBRD. The appeal was dismissed, with the conclusion that the Industrial Tribunal had no choice than to dismiss the complaint for want of jurisdiction. The Appeal Tribunal reasoned:

> (1) The Bank and its employees were granted immunity from suit and legal process for acts done "within the scope of its official activities."
> (2) "Official activities" include all activities undertaken pursuant to the agreement establishing the bank "including its administrative activities." The selection of staff for employment by the Bank is an administrative activity undertaken pursuant to the agreement and appropriate to fulfill the bank's purpose and functions. The relevant activity is the selection of staff for employment. The applicant's complaint is about the alleged unlawfulness of the manner in which the activity of selecting staff for employment was carried out. In our view, it is not correct to argue that the relevant activity is that of unlawful discrimination and that that was not an official activity. The correct question to pose under the Order of 1991 and the headquarters agreement is whether the selection of staff for employment was within the "official activities" of the bank. To pose the question in the form: "Is unlawful racial discrimination within the official activities of the bank?" confuse, on the one hand, the activity of selecting staff for employment with, on the other hand, the mode of performance of the activities and the consequences of performance. If [applicant's] interpretation of the Order of 1991 were correct, the immunity from suit and legal process conferred by article 5(2) would be meaningless. It would only apply where, after an industrial tribunal had exercised jurisdiction and conducted an investigation into the complaint, it concluded that no unlawful act had been committed by the bank, in which case it would be unnecessary to confer or claim immunity. The purpose of conferring immunity is to protect the relevant organization from having legal proceedings brought against it for alleged wrongs, whether those wrongs have actually been committed by the organization or not.[83]

83. *Id.* The Appeal Tribunal noted that as jurisdictional immunity "may produce severe disabilities for individuals in respect of fundamental rights, it can only be justified by an overriding public

Some claimants have asked courts to construe some activities of international organizations as "commercial activities" so as to not benefit from immunity, as is the case with the doctrine of restrictive State immunity. For instance, in *Broadbent v. Organization of American States (OAS)*, former staff members of OAS had filed complaints against OAS before its Administrative Tribunal, which ordered their reinstatement, but the Secretary-General opted, as is permissible under OAS rules, to compensate them with an indemnity fixed by the Tribunal. The former employees brought a suit against OAS in the District Court in the United States for breach of their employment contract, and OAS asserted its immunity. In dismissing the action for lack of subject-matter jurisdiction, the court determined that the doctrine of restrictive State immunity did not apply to international organizations. The Court of Appeals for the District of Columbia Circuit upheld the District Court's decision, ruling that the employment relationships between international organizations and their staff are not commercial activities.[84]

As was the case in *Broadbent*, most courts recognize the jurisdictional immunity of international organizations in employment-related cases. In *Mendaro*, the same Court of Appeals in *Broadbent* upheld the immunity of the World Bank in a case brought by a former staff member alleging discrimination and harassment. The Court stated that the broad international and national policy considerations calling for immunity for international organizations from employee lawsuits applied to the World Bank notwithstanding the provision in its Articles of Agreement that actions against the Bank may be brought where the Bank has an office or has issued securities.[85] The Court noted:

> That "the purpose of immunity from employee actions is rooted in the need to protect international organizations from unilateral control by a member nation over the activities of the international organization within its territory. The sheer difficulty of administering multiple employment practices in each area in which an organization operates suggests that the purposes of an organization could be greatly hampered if it could be subjected to suit by its employees worldwide. But beyond economies of administration, the very structure of an international organization, which ordinarily consists of an administrative body created by the joint action of several participating

policy or interest. In the case of an international organization, such as the bank, immunity from suit and legal process may be justified on the ground that it is necessary for the independence and neutrality from control by or interference from the host state and for the effective and uninterrupted exercise of its multinational functions through its representatives."

84. *Broadbent v. OAS*, 625 F.2d 27 (D.C. Cir. 1980).

85. *Mendaro v. World Bank*, 717 F.2d 610 (D.C. Cir. 1983).

nations, requires that the organization remain independent from the intranational policies of its individual members."[86]

In *Spaans v. Netherlands*,[87] the applicant's employment with the Iran–United States Claims Tribunal in The Hague had been terminated, and he brought an action in the Dutch courts claiming that his termination was unlawful. At the District Court (*Kantongerecht*) in The Hague, the applicant claimed that the Claims Tribunal must pay his salary up until when his employment was terminated in accordance with Dutch law. The Claims Tribunal pled jurisdictional immunity and requested the District Court to declare itself incompetent to hear the case, but the request was denied. The decision of the District Court was appealed by the Claims Tribunal to the Regional Court (*Arrondissementsrechtbank*) in The Hague, which annulled the decision and declared that it had no jurisdiction to hear the case. The Supreme Court (*Hoge Raad*) of The Netherlands confirmed the decision of the Regional Court, and held that the Claims Tribunal, as an international organization, was immune from the jurisdiction of the Dutch courts in respect of the applicant's claim. It concluded that under international law, an international organization is, in principle, not subject to the jurisdiction of the courts in the host State concerning disputes that have a direct connection with the organization's tasks.[88] Consequently, the applicant brought The Netherlands before the European Commission of Human Rights,[89] claiming, inter alia, that the Netherlands had violated his rights to an independent and impartial tribunal, in accordance with Article 6(1) of the European Convention on Human Rights (ECHR).[90] The Commission held that the application was inadmissible because the immunity enjoyed by the Claims Tribunal under the law of The Netherlands excluded the administrative decisions of the Claims Tribunal from the jurisdiction of The Netherlands within the intendment of Article 1 of ECHR.[91] The Commission reasoned that the functional

86. *Id.*

87. *Spaans v. Netherlands* (Application No. 12516/86) decided on 12 December 1988; in 107 ILR 1.

88. The decisions of the Dutch courts are reported in 94 ILR 321 (*Iran-United States Claims Tribunal v. AS*).

89. From 1954 to 1998 when Protocol 11 of the European Convention on Human Rights came into force, individuals did not having standing to brings claims before the European Court of Human Rights but had to petition the European Commission on Human Rights which decided on the admissibility of an individual's claim before it could be heard by the Court.

90. Article 6(1) provides: "In the determination of his civil rights and obligations . . . everyone is entitled to a fair and public hearing within a reasonable time by an independent and impartial tribunal established by law. . . ."

91. Article 1 provides: "The High Contracting Parties shall secure to everyone within their jurisdiction the rights and freedom defined in Section I of this Convention."

immunity granted to international organizations, which is a restriction on national sovereignty, did not raise an issue under the Convention.

In an employment dispute brought by Paolo Pistelli, an Italian citizen, against the European University Institute of Florence, the Italian Court of Cassation upheld the decision of the Florence Court of Appeal that confirmed the decision of the Florence Tribunal that recognized the immunity of the international organization. The Court of Appeal had held that in employment disputes, an international organization enjoyed immunity for the official acts of its employees. The Court of Cassation reasoned that the existence and scope of immunity of an international organization depends on the applicable legal instrument, such as the constituent treaty or the headquarters agreement. It noted that Article 4 of the convention establishing the Institute provides that the Institute and its staff shall enjoy such privileges and immunities as are necessary for the performance of their task. In the same vein, Article 1 of the annexed Protocol grants the Institute immunity from enforcement measures in the exercise of its official activities. Similarly, Article 9 of the Protocol provides for immunity from legal process of the Principal, Secretary, and staff. It also noted that although immunity from execution and immunity from jurisdiction are different concepts, the formulation of Article 1 presupposed that the Institute also enjoyed immunity from jurisdiction whenever it engaged in official activities. It further noted that as an alternative judicial remedy, staff can address claims to the commission established under Article 6(5) of the Convention setting up the Institute, and that the jurisdictional immunity of international organizations will be respected when its internal rules respect the same rights and interests before an independent and impartial judicial tribunal.[92]

Because immunity for official acts is *ratione materiae*, it survives the employment of the official in the international organization. A 1952 Note by the Office of Legal Affairs of the United Nations had addressed whether the functional immunity of an official survived the termination of that function, and opined that officials should be immune for official acts even after ceasing to be officials. It noted that Section 18 of the General Convention is not specific on the point, unlike Section 12, which deals with the immunity of representatives of member States of the United Nations. It also noted paragraph 22 of the Rapporteur's Final Report on the work of Sub-Committee 7 to the Sixth Committee during the preparation of the Specialized Agencies Convention, which had declared:

> In connexion with Section 19 *(a)* [of the Specialized Agencies Convention] which (following the General Convention) prescribes that officials shall be

92. *Pistelli v. European University Institute*, Court of Cassation, all civil sections, 28 October 2005, no 20995, Guida al diritto 40 (3/2006) (in Italian); ILDC 297 (IT 2005), available at ildc.oxfordlawreports.com.

> immune from legal process in respect of words spoken or written and all acts performed by them in their official capacity, it was agreed that, to fulfil the purpose of the provision (namely that officials should pursue their official duties, feeling confident that they are protected from all personal liability in regard thereto before municipal tribunals unless immunity is waived), it was necessary that this immunity should continue after the officials had ceased to be officials.[93]

With respect to representatives of member States of the United Nations and its specialized agencies, Section 11 of the General Convention and Section 13 of the Specialized Agencies Convention respectively provide that they shall enjoy the privileges and immunities listed in those provisions "while exercising their functions and during their journey to and from the place of meeting." To a query by one of the specialized agencies as to the interpretation to be given the phrase "while exercising their functions," the Legal Counsel of the United Nations in 1961 gave an interpretation that suggests that the privileges and immunities granted representatives under the conventions become operative when the representatives leave their country or duty station en route to a meeting of the international organization:

> You inquire whether the words "while exercising their functions" should be given a narrow or broad interpretation. By the former, the words could mean only the "the period of time during which the representative concerned is actually doing something as part of his functions as representative", "e.g., is present in the room or building where the meeting . . . is being held".
>
> We have not been confronted with such a question here in the United Nations, and the preparatory work on neither of the two privileges and immunities conventions throws any specific light on the point you raise. Nevertheless, I have no hesitation in believing that it was the "broad" interpretation that was intended by the authors of the Convention. This must follow from the fact that the expression "while exercising their function" is contained in the opening paragraph and qualified each and all of the privileges and immunities provided in the subparagraphs, (a) through (g), that follow.
>
> A glance at those paragraphs will clearly show that the privileges and immunities provided by any of them would become meaningless if it is applicable only when the representative is actually doing something as part of his function, "e.g., is present in the room or building where the meeting . . . is being held." Such an interpretation would lead to the absurd conclusion

93. [1967] 2 Y.B. Int'l Law Comm'n 269–70.

> that, a representative, immediately after having performed an official function, or after having left the meeting room may, under paragraph (a) for example, be arrested, or detained, or have his personal baggage seized. By the same narrow interpretation, he may, the moment he left the meeting room, have his papers confiscated, or his right to use codes suspended, or his courier seized, or be conscripted into national service, etc. Should such a narrow interpretation prevail, the basic purpose of the Convention, which is to assure the representatives the independent exercise of their functions, would clearly be totally defeated.
>
> The broader interpretation is also borne out of the fact that the phrase "while exercising their function" is immediately accompanied and complemented by the phrase "and during their journey to and from the place of meeting". In other words, "while exercising" means during the entire period of presence in the State (not city) for reasons of the conference in question. This is logical because the "journey" necessarily is that to and from the State, not the conference hall. Only this interpretation avoids absurdity and only this is consistent with the immediately following reference in subsection (a) to "personal baggage". Therefore, in accordance with the general principle that a treaty must be interpreted to effectuate its purpose and not to lead to absurdity, it seems to me, without reference to other criteria of interpretation, that only the "broad interpretation" should have been intended by the phrase in question.[94]

In a June 24, 1949, press release, Secretary-General Trygve Lie elucidated on the nature of immunity of officials of the United Nations:

> I should like to explain . . . the situation with respect to immunities. United Nations Secretariat personnel enjoy immunity from arrest or question in connexion with any of their official duties or acts written or spoken.
>
> United Nations personnel do not enjoy immunity from arrest or interrogation for alleged acts unrelated to their official duties which are unlawful in the Member State where they are committed, or alleged to have been committed.
>
> There has been some confusion about the immunities of United Nations personnel.
>
> Under the Agreement between the United Nations and the United States of America regarding the Headquarters of the United Nations, in Section 15, a limited number of persons are granted the same diplomatic privileges

94. *Id.* at 176.

> and immunities as are granted to diplomats accredited to the United States Government.
>
> These persons have the official status of ambassadors or ministers in their country for the main part, except for those persons who are put on the diplomatic list because they have been agreed upon by the United States Government, the United Nations and the member country concerned as entitled to such a status because they are resident members of staff and need such immunities in order to carry on necessary work for their own countries in connexion with the United Nations. These diplomatic functionaries are not put on the diplomatic list unless they hold a status at least as high as diplomatic secretary of delegation.
>
> The privileges and immunities granted to this small number of persons are exactly similar to those granted in Washington to diplomatic representative of foreign governments there. The same privileges are granted to American diplomats serving in foreign countries.
>
> They were not invented especially for the United Nations since, for at least three centuries in every civilized country, ambassadors and ministers serving abroad have enjoyed diplomatic privileges and immunities under international law as a necessary facility for their work.
>
> The Secretary-General and the eight assistant Secretaries-General have diplomatic immunity in those countries which have acceded to the Convention on Privileges and Immunities. Other Secretariat members do not have diplomatic immunity outside of performance of their official duties.[95]

On May 17, 2000, the Austrian Supreme Court decided whether the wife of a high-ranking UN official can invoke (diplomatic) immunity in divorce proceedings brought by her husband, and held that because the wife's immunity derived from that of her husband's functions, which had ceased, she could no longer invoke it to be exempt from domestic jurisdiction.[96] The focus of this decision is primarily on the scope and duration of the derived (diplomatic) immunity of a family member of a staff member of an international organization.

95. *Id.*, Relations between States and inter-governmental organizations, at 265–66. Ordinarily, most staff members of international organizations do not have diplomatic immunity, and would therefore not be immune from administrative, civil, or criminal jurisdiction for nonofficial acts. But a few officials of international organizations have diplomatic immunity, which extends beyond their official acts.

96. *K v. K*, 2 Ob 166/98 w; ILDC 356 (AT 2000), available at ildc.oxfordlawreports.com.

Waiver and Exception

Waiver

Waiver of immunity is the consent or voluntary submission by an international organization to the jurisdiction of a national court. The norm is that an international organization is immune from the jurisdiction of national courts unless it expressly waives its immunity. As legal instruments regarding jurisdictional immunity do not normally define waiver, it is open to dispute what constitutes a waiver of jurisdictional immunity. This has led some courts to imply a waiver in some circumstances.

Some legal instruments on the privileges and immunities of international organizations provide that the organization "shall enjoy immunity from every form of legal process except insofar as in any particular case it has expressly waived its immunity."[97] Others provide that the organization "shall enjoy immunity from every form of judicial process except to the extent that it expressly waives its immunity for the purpose of any proceedings or by the terms of any contract."[98] These provisions have raised the following questions: When can an international organization waive its immunity? Is a waiver of immunity only in relation to a particular proceeding or could it be waived in advance in a contractual provision? Does a choice-of-law or governing law clause in a contract constitute a waiver of immunity?

Although the jurisdictional immunity of international organizations implies the right to decline to submit to proceedings in municipal courts ab initio, it is sometimes the practice that international organizations make a limited appearance to plead their immunity, which they always stress should not be construed as a waiver of their immunity. Whether an appearance to contest jurisdiction constitutes a waiver of immunity was addressed by the Philippines' Intermediate Appellate Court in *United States Lines Inc. v. World Health Organization.*[99] WHO had appeared before the Court of First Instance of Manila for the sole purpose of pleading immunity and had stipulated that the appearance did not constitute a submission to the jurisdiction. The lower court dismissed the complaint against WHO on the ground that WHO was immune from suit as a specialized agency of the United Nations and under the terms of its 1951 Headquarters Agreement with the Philippines. The plaintiff had argued that the Headquarters Agreement was not binding because it had not been ratified by the Philippines Senate as required

97. See Section 2, General Convention.

98. See, e.g., Article IX, Section 3, Articles of Agreement of the International Monetary Fund.

99. *United States Lines Inc. v. World Health Organization*, Intermediate Appellate Court, Fourth Civil Cases Division, 30 September 1983, 107 ILR 182.

under the Constitution of the Philippines in force at the time the Agreement was entered. The Appellate Court dismissed the appeal and held that the lack of ratification of the Headquarters Agreement by the Senate did not deprive WHO of immunity because it was immune, not only under the Headquarters Agreement, but also under the Specialized Agencies Convention, which had been ratified by the Philippines. The court also pointed out that Article III of the Convention provided for the WHO's immunity from process in the absence of an express waiver of immunity.

A limited appearance or a response by an international organization solely for the purpose of asserting immunity is not considered a waiver. However, if an organization takes an action that is inconsistent with its immunity, such as institution of a lawsuit in a national court, such act would constitute a waiver of immunity and would make the organization liable to a counterclaim or a defense in the suit. Some courts have given effect to prospective waiver provision in a contract.[100] Some courts have also construed a governing law or choice-of-law provision in a contract as an implied waiver. In a decision involving the International Tin Council, the English High Court held that a clause in a loan agreement designating that court as a forum for adjudicating any controversies that might arise was a specific waiver of immunity within the meaning of the immunity provision in the Headquarters Agreement modeled on the conventions.[101] It is now common for contracts with organizations to provide for arbitration, but there is no consensus as to whether the agreement to arbitrate constitutes a waiver of the organization's jurisdictional immunity. The Swiss Federal Tribunal held that the immunity of the European Council for Nuclear Research ("Conseil Européen pour la Recherche Nucléaire or CERN") prevented the intervention of a national court in arbitral proceedings without an express waiver of immunity.[102] The French Court of Appeal in Paris took a contrary position in *Boulois v. UNESCO* by not upholding the organization's jurisdictional immunity in a dispute between the parties concerning the constitution of an arbitral tribunal.[103] Similarly, in *International Tin Council v. Amalgamet*, a court in the United States

100. See *Standard Chartered Bank v. International Tin Council*, England and Wales High Court of Justice, Queen's Bench Division, 17 April 1986, [1986] 3 ALL ER 257, 25 Int'l Leg. Mat. 650 (1986).

101. See *Maida v. Administration for International Assistance* (Italian Court of Cassation), 27 May 1955, [1955] 23 ILR 510; *International Institute of Refrigeration v. Elkaim*, French Court of Appeals, Paris, 7 February 1984, [1988] 77 ILR 498.

102. *Groupement d'Enterprises Fougerolle v. CERN*, Swiss Federal Tribunal, 21 December 1992, [1996] 102 ILR 209.

103. French Court of Appeal, Paris, 19 June 1998, [1999] Revue de l'Arbitrage 343.

held that whatever immunity ITC may have had, it is deemed waived by the arbitration clause in the contract between the parties.[104]

For the avoidance of doubt, some international organizations such as the United Nations and its specialized agencies, even when they enter into an arbitration agreement, stress that such an agreement shall not be construed as a waiver of the organization's immunity. They also avoid choice-of-law or governing law provisions in their contracts so as to ensure that the provision is not construed as a waiver of immunity.[105]

The Second Circuit Court of Appeals in the United States has rejected the argument, in a case against the United Nations, that an international organization's participation in its own internal dispute resolution mechanism constitutes a waiver of immunity.[106] The suit arose from an employment dispute, with claims of sexual harassment and retaliation. Plaintiff sought review of the "administrative decisions" through the Organization's internal justice system, but withdrew her appeal before the Joint Appeals Board before her case was reviewed, and elected instead to seek administrative and judicial redress in the United States courts. Plaintiff filed suit against the Organization, the Secretary-General, and other officials of the United Nations in the United States District Court for the Southern District of New York. The United Nations moved to dismiss the complaint for lack of subject matter jurisdiction, invoking its immunity and that of its officials. The District Court granted the Organization's motion, and dismissed the complaint in its entirety. Plaintiff appealed this decision to the Second Circuit Court of Appeals, which held that the United Nations enjoys immunity under the General Convention and that it had not expressly waived that immunity. The court rejected plaintiff's argument that the "purported inadequacies with the United Nations' internal dispute resolution mechanism indicate a waiver of immunity," reasoning that "crediting this argument would read the word 'expressly' out of" the General Convention.[107]

An international organization is under no obligation to waive its own immunity but *may* have a legal duty to waive the immunity of its officials, according to most legal instruments on the privileges and immunities of international organizations. For example, the General Convention provides: "The Secretary-General

104. *International Tin Council v. Amalgamet*, 138 Misc. 2d 383; 524 N.Y.S. 2d 971 (Supreme Court of New York 1988).

105. See United Nations Juridical Yearbook, 1994, p. 449; United Nations Juridical Yearbook, 2012, p. 494 ("an express choice of national law in a contract is not accepted because it could imply or result in the waiver of the Organization's privileges and immunities.")

106. *Brzak v. United Nations*, 597 F.3d 107, 112–13 (2d Cir. 2010).

107. *Id.*

shall have the right and the duty to waive the immunity of any official in any case where, in his opinion, the immunity would impede the course of justice and can be waived without prejudice to the interests of the United Nations. In the case of the Secretary-General, the Security Council shall have the right to waive immunity."[108] In the same vein, the Specialized Agencies Convention provides: "Each specialized agency shall have the right and the duty to waive the immunity of any official in any case where, in its opinion, the immunity would impede the course of justice and can be waived, without prejudice to the interests of the specialized agency."[109] For the most part, immunity of the organization may be waived by the appropriate organ, whereas the immunity of officials may be waived by the Administrative Head of the organization as the case may be.[110]

The waiver of immunity of officials presents an anomaly, as it would mean that although the official acted in an official capacity for the act to attract immunity, the immunity may still be waived so as to not impede the course of justice. Another essential requirement is for the waiver not to prejudice the interests of the organization. The intuitive question is why the immunity of an official acting in official capacity should ever be waived with the consequence that the official forfeits the benefits of the immunity for official acts on behalf of the organization. To be sure, the immunity is granted to the official in the interest of the organization and not for the personal benefit of the official.[111] However, absent an abuse of privileges and immunities, it may never be appropriate or fair to waive the immunity of an official for an official act as such a waiver would be tantamount to the proverbial "throwing a person under the bus." The essence of immunity is to absolve an official from personal liability for acts performed within the ambit of (official) functions of the organization.

The General Convention, for example, does not specifically provide a mechanism to deal with claims brought against officials who have acted in an official capacity, and whose immunity has not been waived, but it does state in Article VIII, Section 29 that the UN will make provisions for appropriate forms of settlement. In the same vein, Article V, Section 21, states that the United Nations will

108. Article IV, Section 20, Convention on the Privileges and Immunities of the United Nations.

109. Article VI, Section 22, Convention on the Privileges and Immunities of the Specialized Agencies of the United Nations.

110. See Restatement Third Foreign Relations § 467, Comment e (Waiver of Immunity) (Am. Law. Inst. 1987), ("Immunity may be waived by an appropriate organ of the organization, usually the secretary-general or other chief executive officer, by authority implied in the office or delegated by the general assembly of the organization. Waiver must be express.")

111. See, e.g., Article VI, Section 22, Convention on the Privileges and Immunities of the Specialized Agencies of the United Nations.

"cooperate at all times with appropriate authorities of Members to facilitate the proper administration of justice, secure the observance of police regulations and prevent the occurrence of any abuse in connection with the privileges, immunities and facilities set out in Article V." The UN carries insurance for liability for personal injury or property damage and asserts no immunity for purposes of suit on such claims. The specialized agencies generally follow the same practice.

An exposition or encapsulation on waiver was provided by the Canadian Supreme Court in *World Bank Group v. Wallace* where it interpreted the Article of Agreement of the World Bank and determined that the "only reference to 'waiver' in Article VII is in the text of [Section] 8, which confers immunity from legal process to the personnel of the IBRD or the IDA 'except when the [IBRD or IDA] waives this immunity.' The term 'waiver' is not qualified, leaving open the question whether waiver means 'express' waiver, or whether implied waiver or constructive forms of waiver are recognized."[112] The Court reasoned:

> In our view, the object and purpose of the treaty favour an express waiver requirement. The application of the IBRD's and IDA's immunity provisions are not subject to a case-by-case determination. To read "waiver" as including forms of implied or constructive waiver would subject immunities to case-by-case determination. Representatives of the World Bank Group would be required to appear in national courts to argue whether their conduct amounted to waiver, or whether for other reasons they should be deemed to have waived their immunity. Such a conclusion would be inconsistent with our view that the IBRD's and IDA's immunity apply without further justification.[113]

The Court expounded:

> If "waiver" is limited to express waiver, then the IBRD and IDA will be firmly in control of when their personnel may be subjected to domestic legal processes. This is essential for a large international organization which, in this case, comprises 188 member states. If [Section] 8 were to include forms of implied and constructive waiver—concepts that are liable to vary significantly across the globe—then inconsistencies from jurisdiction to jurisdiction could cause considerable confusion and interfere with IBRD's and IDA's orderly operations.[114]

112. *Wallace*, para. 89.

113. *Id.*, para. 90.

114. *Id.*, para. 92.

It is well-settled that a waiver of immunity from jurisdiction does not also constitute a waiver of immunity from execution. However, in the case of MDBs such as the World Bank with limited immunity from suit, the scope of their immunity from execution is impelled by functional considerations. To protect the World Bank from harassment, the Articles of Agreement provide that its assets and property shall be immune from all forms of seizure, attachment, or execution, but the immunity ends after delivery of a final judgment against the World Bank.[115] To provide otherwise would have been self-contradictory and counterproductive to the idea of allowing creditors to bring an action against the Bank without giving those creditors the means to enforce or execute the judgment against the Bank. As the basic objective of the Bank's limited immunity from suit was to give investors and creditors alike the incentive to do business with the Bank, it was equally necessary to give assurance, through this provision, to these private investors that they would not be powerless with respect to enforcing judgments against the Bank in the limited instances where the Bank is amenable to suit. Thus, there is a rational link between the Bank's immunity from suit and its immunity from execution, in that investors needed assurance that not only could they sue the Bank but also that if they prevail in their suit, they would not be prevented from enforcing their judgment against the Bank's property and assets.

Exception

An exception to immunity is different from a waiver of immunity. A waiver subsumes the existence of immunity ab initio, whereas an exception is about the absence of immunity in the first place. An exception to immunity arises from the constituent instrument of an international organization, whereas a waiver derives from a provision in a contract or a similar legal instrument.[116] Despite widespread usage, "a limitation of jurisdictional immunity made in the moment of an international organization's creation is not a waiver in any normal sense [and the] sole justification for describing such a provision as a waiver is that the

115. Article VII, Section 3, Articles of Agreement of the World Bank ("The property and assets of the Bank shall, wheresoever located and by whomsoever held, be immune from all forms of seizure, attachment or execution before delivery of final judgment against the Bank.")

116. See Jean-Luc Fagnart, L'Immunité De Juridiction Des Organisations Internationales (2004) p. 188. (« *Dans d'autres organisations internationales, l'acte constitutive ou le protocole sur les privilèges et immunités dispose expressément que l'immunité de juridiction ne peut être invoquée par ces organisations à propos des activités commerciales qu'elles peuvent entreprendre. La compétence des juridictions nationales résulte parfois non de l'acte constitutif de l'organisation concernée, mais d'une clause d'attribution de compétence insérée dans le contrat de droit prive ou de droit public conclus par l'organisation internationale. Il va de soi que la clause par laquelle une organisation accepte de se soumettre à la juridiction des tribunaux nationaux pour le règlement des litiges relatifs à un contrat déterminé, emporte renonciation de la part de celle-ci à l'immunité de juridiction dont elle bénéficie en principe.* »)

courts have uniformly used this terminology, so that it is now well established."[117] Despite the misuse of terms, "all roads lead to Rome" as both exception and waiver have the same negating effect on immunity.

Determining whether an exception to immunity exists requires interpretation of the constituent instrument of the international organization. The provisions of the Charter or Articles of Agreement of MDBs, such as the World Bank and the IADB, with respect to jurisdictional immunity are in sharp contrast with those of other international organizations such as the United Nations and its specialized agencies. Most international organizations, especially those in the United Nations system, are immune from legal process, unless they expressly waive their immunity. In the case of these MDBs, their Articles contain the so-called charter-based waiver, which is essentially an exception to the general rule of immunity. The jurisdictional immunity of MDBs is limited through the creation of exception for their external financial activities in their constituent instrument. Claimants against these MDBs have often argued that the so-called charter-based waiver should be read so broadly as to establish a blanket exception to immunity for claims. For instance, Article VII, Section 3 (Position of the Bank with regard to Judicial Process) of the Articles of Agreement of the World Bank provide:

> Actions may be brought against the Bank only in a court of competent jurisdiction in the territories of a member in which the Bank has an office, has appointed an agent for the purpose of accepting service or notice of process, or has issued or guaranteed securities. . . .[118]

The charter-based waiver was the subject of the seminal case of *Mendaro v. World Bank*,[119] where the question presented to the court was whether the World Bank had immunity from a suit by a former staff member for sexual harassment and discrimination. The court noted that the Articles of Agreement of the World Bank "expressly waive immunity, but the scope of its limitation on immunity is

117. See Michael Singer, Jurisdictional Immunity of International Organizations: Human Rights and Functional Necessity Concerns, 36 Virginia Journal of International Law 53, 81 (1995).

118. Articles of Agreement of the International Bank for Reconstruction and Development, 2 UNTS 134. Article VII, Section 3, of the Articles of Agreement of the World Bank is dissimilar to Article III, Section 4, of the Specialized Agencies Convention, which provides: "The specialized agencies, their property and assets, wherever located and by whomsoever held, shall enjoy immunity from every form of legal process except in so far as in a particular case they have expressly waived their immunity. It is, however, understood that no waiver of immunity shall extend to any measure of execution."

119. *Mendaro v. World Bank*, 717 F.2d 610 (D.C. Cir. 1983).

unclear."[120] It, therefore, applied the "corresponding benefit" analysis or test and stated that it "cannot construe the vague language of Article VII, section 3 more broadly than necessary to enable the Bank to fulfill its functions."[121]

According to the court, the choice of language in the provision "suggests that the Bank's immunity is limited only to the extent necessary to further its objectives [and the] exceptions to its immunity were designed primarily to enhance the marketability of its securities and the credibility of its activities in the lending markets."[122] It reasoned that the intent of member States is to waive the Bank's immunity from suits by its debtors, creditors, bondholders, and those other potential plaintiffs to whom the Bank would have to subject itself to suit in order to achieve its chartered objectives. Thus, the charter-based waiver is only applicable to actions arising out of the Bank's external contracts and activities. It held that the World Bank had not waived its immunity from employment disputes because the potential benefit of attracting qualified staff was offset by the Bank's employee grievance process and outweighed by the disruption to its employment practices.

The court was also persuaded in its reasoning by a comparison of the Bank's Articles of Agreement with those of the International Monetary Fund ("Fund"),[123] which was also established by the 1944 Bretton Woods Conference. Considering that the Fund was not designed to issue securities or to duplicate the Bank's active role in commercial capital markets, the Fund's Articles of Agreement provide for "absolute" immunity from suit. In contrast, the Bank's Articles expressly limited its immunity, making it amenable to suits relating to its external activities and contracts, but not to the Bank's internal operations, such as its employment relationship with its staff.

The jurisprudence of *Mendaro* was followed in *Chiriboga v. International Bank for Reconstruction and Development et al.*,[124] where the plaintiff sued the World Bank to recover benefits under an accident insurance policy held by a deceased staff member of the World Bank. The World Bank contended that the case arose from an employment relationship and, as such, it was immune from the suit. The plaintiff argued that "they should be viewed as creditors, not employees of the Bank, and that in this capacity the denial of insurance benefits constitutes

120. *Id.* at 617.

121. *Id.*

122. *Id.* at 618.

123. Articles of Agreement of the International Monetary Fund, adopted at the United Nations Monetary and Financial Conference in Bretton Woods, 22 July 1944, entered into force on 27 December 1945, 2 UNTS 3.

124. *Chiriboga v. Int'l Bank for Reconstruction & Dev.*, 616 F. Supp. 963 (D.C. Cir. 1985).

commercial activity for which the Bank is not immune."[125] The court dismissed plaintiff's argument and ruled that the World Bank had no commercial dealings with the plaintiff and that the suit arose out of an alleged breach of contract between the Bank and its employee. Following the reasoning of *Mendaro*, the court did not see any corresponding benefit to the Bank of allowing employees and third-party beneficiaries to sue the Bank in employment dispute matters. The court noted that were the plaintiff alive, the only action that she could have brought regarding insurance benefits would have been a breach of contract action as an employee against the Bank.

In *Morgan v. International Bank for Reconstruction and Development*, a temporary worker at the World Bank had sued the organization for damages for various torts. The plaintiff had argued that the Bank's decision to hire him from a temporary employment agency is like hiring a contractor for repairs and construction, and consequently that the "charter-based waiver" applied to his suit.[126] The court did not buy the plaintiff's argument, and ruled that plaintiff's claim arose directly from the Bank's employment practices, which do not constitute commercial activities. The court held: "Accordingly, the fact that Morgan is not in all respects formally an employee of the Bank but serves on detail from his agency is of no legal consequence. Morgan's suit, if allowed to proceed, would force the Bank to defend internal employment practices traditionally shielded by immunity. That the conduct of Bank officials may have been improper is irrelevant."[127]

In a suit by a former staff member of the World Bank who had purchased the Bank's bonds and had invoked her status as a holder of the Bank's bonds in her wrongful termination claim, the court ruled that it "cannot permit Plaintiff to use her status as a bondholder to circumvent the Bank's immunity from employment-related suits. Such an outcome would render the Bank's immunity meaningless; would-be plaintiffs would merely need to purchase the Bank's bonds in order to file suit. This cannot be what the Bank's members intended in crafting its Articles of Agreement."[128]

In *Osseiran v. IFC*, the court followed *Mendaro* and held that as the International Finance Corporation (IFC) is in the business of selling its investments to private parties, and because sales agreements result from negotiations, the exception to IFC's immunity in the plaintiff's promissory estoppels and confidentiality claims "might help attract prospective investors by reinforcing expectations of

125. *Id.* at 968, n.3.

126. *Morgan v. Int'l Bank for Reconstruction & Dev.*, 752 F. Supp. 492 (D.C. Cir. 1990).

127. *Id.* at 494.

128. *Hudes v. Aetna Life Ins.*, 806 F. Supp. 2d 180, 189 (D.C. Cir. 2011).

fair play."[129] Similarly, in *Vila v. IIC*, the United States Court of Appeals for the District of Columbia Circuit affirmed the denial of the immunity of the Inter-American Investment Corporation (IIC) in an unjust enrichment suit and ruled:

> By waiving immunity from unjust enrichment claims of independent consultants whom IIC solicits to help negotiate the commercial lending agreement that are central to its function, the IIC gains a corresponding benefit that furthers its objectives. Consultants would be more willing to negotiate the commercial lending agreements that are central to its function, the IIC gains a corresponding benefit that furthers its objectives. Consultants would be more willing to negotiate with the IIC and to enter contracts with it if they had the reassurance that should their agreement or formal contract fail for whatever reason, they would be fairly compensated for any benefit they have provided that IIC has unjustly retained. Such a benefit affords the IIC flexibility in using independent consultants, allowing it, for instance, to establish and maintain relationships with consultants whom it may engage without a formal written agreement. Furthermore, underlying an unjust enrichment claim are the same contract principles as the promissory estoppels claim held not to be barred by immunity in *Osseiran v. Int'l Fin. Corp.*, 552 F.3d 836 (D.C. Cir. 2009).[130]

In *Jam v. IFC*, the United States Court of Appeals for the District of Columbia Circuit revisited its jurisprudence on "charter-based waiver," applying the "corresponding benefits" test of *Mendaro*.[131] The appeal arose from the District Court's decision dismissing the complaint by a group of Indian nationals against IFC on the grounds of immunity. The appellants brought several tort claims against IFC, alleging that a power plant that had been financed by IFC had caused damage to their surrounding communities and destroyed their way of life. They also claimed to be third-party beneficiaries of the social and environmental terms of the loan agreement between IFC and an Indian company for the construction and operation of the power plant. The appellants argued that IFC is not immune to these claims and that even if it were, it had waived the immunity under its charter. The Court of Appeals considered the appellant's argument to "run counter to our long-held precedent concerning the scope of international organization immunity and charter-document immunity waivers."[132]

129. *Osseiran v. Int'l Fin. Corp.*, 552 F.3d 836 (D.C. Cir. 2009).

130. *Vila v. Inter-Am. Invest. Corp.*, 570 F.3d 274, 276 (D.C. Cir. 2009).

131. *Jam v. IFC*, 860 F. 3d 703 (D.C. Cir. 2017).

132. *Id.* at 705.

The Court of Appeals noted:

> Ironically, the line of cases applying *Mendaro* ended up tying waiver to commercial transactions, so there is superficial similarity to the commercial activities test that appellants would urge us to accept. But whatever the scope of the commercial activities exception to sovereign immunity, that standard is necessarily broader than the *Mendaro* test; if that exception applied to the IFC, the organization would *never* retain immunity since its operations are *solely* "commercial," i.e., the IFC does not undertake any "sovereign" activities.[133]
>
> The *Mendaro* test instead focused on identifying those transactions where the other party would not enter into negotiations or contract with the organization absent waiver. *See* 717 F.2d at 617 (inferring waiver only insofar as "necessary to enable the [organization] to fulfill its functions"). *Mendaro* provided examples: suits by debtors, creditors, bondholders, and "those other potential plaintiffs to whom the [organization] would have to subject itself to suit in order to achieve its chartered objectives." *Id.* at 615.
>
> We have stretched that concept to include a claim of promissory estoppel, *see Osseiran*, 552 F.3d at 840–41, and a quasi-contract claim of unjust enrichment, *see Vila v. Inter-Am. Invest. Corp.*, 570 F.3d 274, 278–80 (D.C. Cir. 2009). But all the claims we have accepted have grown out of business relations with outside companies (or an outside individual engaged directly in negotiations with the organization). Compare *Lutcher S.A. Celulose e Papel v. Inter-Am. Dev. Bank*, 382 F.2d 454 (D.C. Cir. 1967) (finding waiver in debtors' suit to enforce loan agreement) with *Mendaro*, 717 F.2d at 611 (rejecting employee sexual harassment and discrimination claim); *Atkinson*, 156 F.3d at 1336 (rejecting garnishment proceeding against organization employee).[134]

The Court of Appeals concluded that appellant's claim failed the *Mendaro* test because IFC would not "benefit" if it could be subject to suit for every loan it makes to fund projects. The reasoning behind the *Mendaro* test has not been immune to criticism, even from within:

> Our cases seem to construe charter-document immunity waivers to allow suits only by commercial parties likely to be repeat players, or by parties with substantial bargaining power. But the opposite would make more sense: Entities doing regular business with international organizations can write waivers of immunity into their contracts with the organizations. *See*,

133. *Id.* at 707.

134. *Id.* [emphasis in original; footnote omitted].

> *e.g., OSS Nokalva*, 617 F.3d at 759 (contract clause authorizing software developer to sue European Space Agency in state and federal courts in New Jersey). Sophisticated commercial actors that fail to bargain for such terms are surely less entitled to benefit from broad immunity waivers than victims of torts or takings who lacked any bargaining opportunity, or unsophisticated parties unlikely to anticipate and bargain around an immunity bar.[135]

An exception to immunity of international organizations, which is widely recognized, is with respect to road accidents. In this regard, on the same day that the General Assembly approved the General Convention, it adopted Resolution 22E (I):

> It has been found that a frequent source of difficulty is road accidents in which motor cars, owned and driven by persons possessing immunity from legal process, are involved.
>
> It is the intention of the United Nations to prevent the occurrence of any abuse in connection with privileges, immunities and facilities granted to it under Articles 104 and 105 of the Charter and the general convention on privileges and immunities, which determines the details of the application of these articles.
>
> Therefore, the General Assembly instructs the Secretary-General to ensure that drivers of all official motor-cars of the United Nations and all members of the staff, who own or drive motor-cars, shall be properly insured against third party risks.

In the case of those officials of international organizations who have diplomatic immunity,[136] in addition to functional immunity, the narrow exceptions laid out in Article 31 of the Vienna Convention on Diplomatic Relations may apply to them:

> A diplomatic agent shall enjoy immunity from the criminal jurisdiction of the receiving State. He shall also enjoy immunity from its civil and

135. *Id.* at 711 (Pillard J. concurring).

136. For example, Article V, Section 19, of the Convention on the Privileges and Immunities of the United Nations provides that "the Secretary-General and all Assistant Secretaries-General [which include the Deputy Secretary-General and all Under-Secretaries-General] shall be accorded . . . the privileges and immunities, exemptions and facilities accorded to diplomatic envoys, in accordance with international law." The relevant international law is codified in the Vienna Convention on Diplomatic Relations, 18 April 1961.

administrative jurisdiction, except in the case of: (a) A real action relating to private immovable property situated in the territory of the receiving State, unless he holds it on behalf of the sending State for the purpose of the mission; (b) An action relating to succession in which the diplomatic agent is involved as executor, administrator, heir or legatee as a private person and not on behalf of the sending State; (c) An action relating to any professional or commercial activity exercised by the diplomatic agent in the receiving State outside his official functions.

Access to Court and Denial of Justice

Access to court is considered a human right. Human rights instruments, such as, the Universal Declaration of Human Rights (UDHR),[137] the International Covenant on Civil and Political Rights (ICPR),[138] and the European Convention on Human Rights (ECHR),[139] recognize specifically and respectively the right to a fair proceeding before an independent and impartial court or tribunal. This human rights principle may conflict or compete with jurisdictional immunity. Can the human rights principle of access to court coexist with the international law principle of jurisdictional immunity? The case for a limitation or restriction on the jurisdictional immunity of international organizations has often found a rampart on the need to provide access to court and avoid a denial of justice.

A compelling consideration for the jurisdictional immunity of international organizations is the need to protect them so that they can carry out their functions with independence and without interference. A competing (or even countervailing) consideration is that jurisdictional immunity should not undermine the imperatives of justice or lead to a denial of justice. International organizations do

137. G.A. Res. 217A (III), art. 10 (Dec. 10, 1948) "In the determination of his civil rights and obligations . . . everyone is entitled to a fair and public hearing within a reasonable time by an independent and impartial tribunal established by law."

138. *Id.* at Art. 14 (1), International Covenant on Civil and Political Rights. Adopted and opened for signature, ratification and accession by General Assembly resolution 2200A (XXI) of 16 December 1966, United Nations, Treaty Series, vol. 999, p. 171 ("In the determination of his . . . rights and obligations in a suit at law, everyone shall be entitled to fair and public hearing by a competent, independent, and impartial tribunal established by law.")

139. Article 6(1), European Convention for the Protection of Human Rights and Fundamental Freedoms ("ECHR"), adopted 4 November 1950, entered into force 3 September 1953, 213 UNTS 221 ("In the determination of his civil rights and obligations or of any criminal charge against him, everyone is entitled to a fair and public hearing within a reasonable time by an independent and impartial tribunal established by law.").

not have sovereign territories and do operate in the territories of their member States (and sometimes in nonmember States). In their operation, they also interact with third parties, and have legal relationships. Legal disputes may result from their operations and relationships with private parties. The problem with jurisdictional immunity is that it could deny these private parties recourse or remedy for legal wrongs.

In *Ranollo*, Judge Rubin stated:

> To recognize the existence of a general and unrestricted immunity from suit or prosecution on the part of the personnel of the United Nations, so long as the individual be performing in his official capacity, even though the individual's function has no relation to the importance or the success of the organization's deliberations, is carrying the principle of immunity completely out of bounds. To establish such a principle would in effect create a large preferred class within our borders who would be immune to punishment on identical facts for which the average American would be subject to punishment. Any such theory does violence and is repugnant to the American sense of fairness and justice and flouts the very basic principle of the United Nations itself, which in its preamble to its charter affirms that it is created to give substance to the principle that the rights of all men and women are equal.[140]

With respect to the jurisdictional immunity of the United Nations, it has been posited that Sections 20 and 23 of the General Convention were intended to prevent a denial of justice by requiring the Secretary-General to waive the immunity of officials whenever (1) the assertion of immunity would impede the course of justice, and (2) waiver may be accomplished without prejudice to the interests of the Organization. Most legal instruments on privileges and immunities oblige international organizations to provide an alternative or appropriate mode of resolution of disputes of contracts or other disputes of a private nature.[141]

140. 67 N.Y.S. 2d 31, 34 (1946).

141. Article VIII, Section 29 of the General Convention provides: "The United Nations shall make provision for appropriate modes of settlement of (a) Disputes arising out of contracts or other disputes of a private law character to which the United Nations is a party." Article IX, Section 31(a) of the Specialized Conventions similarly provides: "Each specialized agency shall make provision for appropriate modes of settlement of: (a) Disputes arising out of contracts or other disputes of private character to which the specialized agency is a party; (b) Disputes involving any official of a specialized agency who by reason of his official position enjoys immunity, if immunity has not been waived in accordance with the provisions of section 22."

Although the ICJ, in the *Cumaraswamy* case, raised the issue of the obligation of the United Nations under Section 29 of the General Convention to provide alternative modes of settlement of disputes, it did not address whether the organization's entitlement to immunity is conditioned on the availability of an alternative remedy. The ICJ noted: "However, as is clear from Article VIII, Section 29, of the General Convention, any such claims against the United Nations shall not be dealt with by national courts but shall be settled in accordance with the appropriate modes of settlement that '[t]he United Nations shall make provisions for' pursuant to Section 29."[142]

Considering Section 29 of the General Convention, it has been argued that a failure to meet the obligation to provide appropriate modes of settlement of third-party disputes may affect the availability of immunity for an international organization. The premise is that "immunity is not a franchise to break the law, but a guarantee of complete independence from interference by national authorities with the discharge of official international duties. In general, such immunity confers only exemption from legal process and not exemption from the obligation to obey the law."[143]

In *Georges v. United Nations,* the question presented before the United States Court of Appeals for the Second Circuit was whether the fulfillment by the United Nations of its obligation under Section 29 of the General Convention is a condition precedent for its immunity under Section 2 of the General Convention such that the United Nations' failure to make provisions for appropriate modes of settlement of certain disputes compels the conclusion that its immunity does not exist.[144] The Court held that the United Nations' fulfillment of its Section 29 obligation is not a condition precedent for its Section 2 immunity. Plaintiffs, who are citizens of the United States or Haiti, had sued the United Nations, the United Nations Stabilization Mission in Haiti ("MINUSTAH"), the Secretary-General, and the former Head of MINUSTAH. They claimed that they "have been or will be sickened, or have family members who have died or will die, as a direct result of the cholera" that was introduced by the Nepalese contingent of MINUSTAH and the epidemic that has ravaged Haiti since 2010.

In answering the question whether Section 29 is a condition precedent for Section 2, the Court noted that the interpretation of a treaty begins with the text, and where the language is plain, a court must construe it and refrain from

142. *Difference Relating to Immunity from Legal Process of a Special Rapporteur of the Commission on Human Rights,* Advisory Opinion, I. C. J. Reports 1999, p. 62 ("*Cumaraswamy Case*"), para. 66.

143. See ILO Memorandum, at 219, ILO Official Bulletin, Vol. XXVII, No. 2, December 10, 1945.

144. *Georges v. United Nations,* 834 F.3d 88 (2d Cir. 2016).

amending it. It also noted that a treaty is a contract between nations and must be interpreted upon the principles that govern the interpretation of contracts between individuals.[145] It, therefore, applied the negative-implication canon or the principle of *expressio unius est exclusio alterius*: as Section 2 expressly mentions express waiver as the only circumstance when the United Nations shall not enjoy immunity, by negative implication all other circumstances, including failure to fulfill its Section 29 obligation, are excluded. Thus, Section 29 is not a condition precedent for Section 2.[146] The Court buttressed its conclusion by the principle that condition precedents for contractual obligations are generally disfavored, and must be expressed in plain and unambiguous language—which is lacking regarding Sections 2 and 29 of the General Convention. The Court also agreed with the United States executive branch's interpretation that Section 29 is not a condition precedent for Section 2.[147]

A contrary position is that an international organization's jurisdictional immunity must be conditioned on the provision or availability of an alternative and adequate dispute resolution mechanism. This position has been championed or buoyed by the jurisprudence of the European Court of Human Rights (ECtHR).[148]

In judgments delivered on the same day in the cases of *Waite and Kennedy v. Germany*, and *Beer and Regan v. Germany*, the ECtHR unanimously held that the German courts in giving effect to the jurisdictional immunity of the European Space Agency (ESA) did not violate Article 6 § I of the ECHR. The applicants in *Waite and Kennedy*, British nationals resident in Germany, were employed by a company to provide services for ESA.[149] When the company informed the applicants that their employment would be terminated at the expiration of their contract, they instituted proceedings against ESA before the Darmstadt

145. *Id.* at 92–93.

146. *Id.* at 93–94.

147. *Id.* The Court did not reach the merits of plaintiffs' argument that the material breach by the United Nations of its obligation under Section 29 of the General Convention deprives it of the entitlement of immunity under Section 2 because they, as individuals, lack standing to raise the violation of international law.

148. *Waite and Kennedy v. Germany* (Application No. 26083/94), and *Beer and Regan v. Germany* (Application No. 28934/95), European Court of Human Rights (18 February 1999). The European Court of Human Rights was set up by the Council of Europe member States in 1959 to deal with allegations of violations of the 1950 European Convention on Human Rights.

149. European Space Agency is an international organization established under the Convention for the Establishment of a European Space Agency (ESA Convention) of 30 May 1975, UNTS 1983, vol. 1297, I no. 21524.

Labour Court, claiming that under the German Provision of Labor (Temporary Staff) Act, they had acquired the status of employees of the ESA. ESA invoked its immunity under Article XV(2) of the ESA Convention and Annex I, and the Darmstadt Labor Court declared the applicants' action inadmissible. The Frankfurt/Main Labor Appeals Court, as well as the Federal Labor Court, dismissed the applicants' appeal. The applicants then applied to the European Commission of Human Rights, complaining that they had been denied access to a court for a determination of their dispute with ESA regarding an issue under German labor law in violation of Article 6 § I of the ECHR. The Commission declared their application inadmissible and referred the case to the ECtHR.

The ECtHR declared that the right to institute proceedings before courts in civil matters is but one aspect of the "right to a court" as embodied in Article 6.[150] The ECtHR, however, noted that "the right of access to the courts secured by Article 6 § I of the Convention is not absolute, but may be subject to limitations; these are permitted by implication since the right of access by its very nature calls for regulation by the State."[151] Although States enjoy a certain margin of appreciation, it remains the province of the ECtHR to decide on whether the requirements of the Convention are met.

To ensure the essence of the right of access is not impaired, "a limitation will not be compatible with Article 6 § I if it does not pursue a legitimate aim and if there is not a reasonable relationship of proportionality between the means employed and the aim sought to be achieved."[152] The ECtHR then concluded that the jurisdictional immunity of international organizations had a legitimate objective because the attribution of privileges and immunities is essential to the proper functioning of international organizations, and to freedom from unilateral interference by individual governments.[153]

With respect to proportionality, the ECtHR noted "that the Convention is intended to guarantee not theoretical or illusory rights, but rights that are practical and effective."[154] Under the circumstances of the case, a material factor for the Court in determining whether granting ESA jurisdictional immunity in Germany is permissible was whether the applicants had available to them reasonable alternative means to protect effectively their rights under the Convention. The assessment of proportionality "cannot be applied in such a way as to compel

150. See *Waite and Kennedy*, para. 50.

151. *Id.*, para. 59.

152. *Id.*

153. *Id.*, para. 63.

154. *Id.*, para. 67.

an international organisation to submit itself to national litigation in relation to employment conditions prescribed under national labour law."[155] It, therefore, held: "Taking into account in particular the alternative means of legal process available to the applicants, it cannot be said that the limitation on their access to the German courts with regard to ESA impaired the essence of their 'right to a court' or was disproportionate for the purposes of Article 6 § I of the Convention."[156]

Under the ECtHR jurisprudence, it can safely be inferred that as long as an international organization provides an independent dispute resolution mechanism, its jurisdictional immunity would be respected by national courts. In the wake of *Waite and Kennedy*, Belgian and French courts have declined to give effect to the jurisdictional immunity of international organizations in three cases where they found the dispute resolution mechanism in those organizations deficient.

In *Lutchmaya v. General Secretariat of the African, Caribbean and Pacific Group of States* ("ACP"), an employee of ACP had successfully challenged the non-renewal of her fixed-term appointment before the Belgian Labor Tribunal, which awarded her retroactive salary, indemnity in lieu of notice, and other monetary allowances. When ACP failed to pay the award, the employee sought an order attaching the organization's bank accounts. ACP contested the attachment, relying on its immunity under its constituent instrument, and the Tribunal upheld the organization's immunity and vacated the attachment. The employee appealed to the Brussels Labor Court, which ruled that, if it is to be effective, the right to a hearing consistent with Article 6(1) of ECHR must include the enforcement of a final decision. The Court applied the rationale of *Waite and Kennedy*, and ruled that giving effect to immunity from enforcement would violate Article 6 because ACP did not provide an alternative dispute resolution mechanism for the employee to challenge ACP's refusal to abide by a decision rendered against the organization. It ordered attachment of the ACP account.[157]

In *Siedler v. Western European Union*,[158] an employee of Western European Union (WEU) challenged her termination before the organization's internal appeals mechanism, and was awarded damages. Dissatisfied with the disposition of her appeal, she took her case to the Belgian Labor Tribunal, arguing that her employment contract was subject to national labor law rather than the internal

155. *Id.*, para. 72.

156. *Id.*, para. 73.

157. *Lutchmaya v. General Secretariat of African, Caribbean and Pacific Group of States*, Brussels Labor Court, March 4, 2003, Journal des Tribunaux, 2003, pp. 684–87.

158. *Siedler v. Western European Union*, Belgian Labor Court of Appeals, Brussels, September 17, 2003, Journal des Tribunaux 2004, 617.

law of WEU. The Tribunal ruled in her favor, and WEU appealed the decision to the Belgian Labor Court, invoking its jurisdictional immunity. WEU also argued that Belgian law was inapplicable to the employment relationship between the organization and its staff. It invoked the test enunciated by ECtHR in *Waite and Kennedy* as to the legitimacy of purpose served by immunity and the proportionality to that purpose. In contrast, the employee contended that to give effect to the immunity would contravene Article 6(1) of the Convention.

At issue is whether the jurisdictional immunity of WEU could be reconciled with the right to a fair trial as guaranteed in Article 6(1) of ECHR. The Belgian Labor Court considered that, absent an independent dispute resolution mechanism within an international organization, Article 6(1) mandates that the organization be subject to the jurisdiction of national courts. It concluded that WEU's internal mechanism did not provide the necessary safeguards for an independent tribunal required under the Convention because the hearings were closed, the decisions were not published, the adjudicators were nominated by the organization for a two-year term, and there was no provision for adjudicators to recuse themselves, calling into question their independence. Consequently, it ruled that granting immunity to the international organization would result in a denial of justice and violate Article 6(1) of ECHR.[159]

In *Degboe v. African Development Bank*,[160] an employee of the African Development Bank (AfDB) was terminated following an administrative reorganization of AfDB. He appealed the decision to AfDB's appeals committee, which made a recommendation in his favor. When AfDB's president rejected the recommendation, the employee brought an action before the French Labor Tribunal, which ruled in his favor and ordered the payment of monetary awards and other damages. AfDB, which did not appear before the Labor Tribunal, appealed the decision of the Tribunal before the Paris Court of Appeal, invoking jurisdictional immunity. The employee countered that AfDB's immunity contravened Article 6(1) of ECHR, and that a dismissal of his application on that basis would result in a denial of justice. (It is noteworthy that a similar claim had been rejected by the national courts in Ivory Coast based on AfDB's immunity.) The Paris Court of Appeal applied the principle of *Waite and Kennedy*, and noted that the (then) dispute resolution mechanism within AfDB did not provide for a binding decision. The case arose before the establishment of the AfDB's Administrative Tribunal. As a result, the French Court concluded that respecting AfDB's immunity would deny its employees an adequate recourse to challenge its decisions and thereby negate their right under Article 6 of the Convention. It declined to

159. *Id.*

160. *Degboe v. African Development Bank*, Court of Appeal, Paris, October 7, 2003.

dismiss the case on jurisdictional grounds and ordered further proceedings before the national court.

In the case of *Stichting Mothers of Srebrenica and Others v. The Netherlands,*[161] the ECtHR clarified its decision in *Waite and Kennedy*, and restated its jurisprudence regarding Article 6 of ECHR vis-à-vis international organizations. The case arose out of the "Srebrenica Massacre" during the 1992–1995 war in Bosnia and Herzegovina, and the applicants were a foundation created under Dutch law to bring proceedings on behalf of relatives of the victims of the massacre, and 10 nationals of Bosnia and Herzegovina who were the surviving relatives of people killed in the massacre. The United Nations Security Council had set up the United Nations Protection Force (UNPROFOR) for the Yugoslav crisis, and the Netherlands was one of the troop-contributing nations. The Security Council had also adopted Resolution 819 (1993) declaring Srebrenica in eastern Bosnia a "safe area." In 1995, the Bosnian Serb Army overran the "safe area" and, despite the presence of a battalion of UNPROFOR, made up of lightly-armed Dutch soldiers ("Dutchbat"), massacred about 8,000 Bosniac men and boys.

The applicants first brought proceedings against The Netherlands and the United Nations before the Regional Court of The Hague, claiming that they failed to act appropriately and effectively defend Srebrenica. They argued that the immunity of the United Nations had been overridden by Article 6 of the Convention and the jus cogens prohibition of genocide. The Regional Court declined jurisdiction against the United Nations, noting that "the creation of the United Nations predated the entry into force of the Convention. Moreover, the United Nations was an organisation whose membership was well-nigh universal; this distinguished it from organisations such as the European Space Agency, the organisation in issue in *Waite and Kennedy* and *Beer and Regan,* which had been created only in 1980 and whose membership was limited to European States."[162] The applicants appealed to the Court of Appeal of The Hague, which upheld the judgment of the Regional Court. They lodged an appeal with the Supreme Court, which confirmed that, pursuant to the Charter of the United Nations and the Convention on the Privileges and Immunities of the United Nations, the organization could not be summoned before national courts of member States.

Following the proceedings in the Dutch courts, the applicants took their case to the ECtHR, complaining that the recognition of the immunity of the United

161. *Stichting Mothers of Srebrenica and Others v. the Netherlands,* Application No. 65542/12, European Court of Human Rights.

162. *Stichting Mothers of Srebrenica,* para. 70.

Nations by the Dutch courts violated their right of access to courts under Article 6 of the Convention. In assessing the scope of the case before it, the Court noted:

> [T]he attribution of responsibility for the Srebrenica massacre or its consequences, whether to the United Nations, to the Netherlands State or to any other legal or natural person, is not a matter falling within the scope of the present application. Nor can the Court consider whether the Secretary-General of the United Nations was under any moral or legal obligation to waive the United Nations' immunity. It has only to decide whether the Netherlands violated the applicants' right of "access to a court", as guaranteed by Article 6 of the Convention, by granting the United Nations immunity from domestic jurisdiction.[163]

ECtHR then restated its jurisprudence:

> (a) Article 6 § 1 secures to everyone the right to have any claim relating to his civil rights and obligations brought before a court or tribunal. In this way the Article embodies the "right to a court", of which the right of access, that is, the right to institute proceedings before courts in civil matters, constitutes one aspect only. . . .
>
> (b) The right of access to the courts secured by Article 6 § 1 of the Convention is not absolute, but may be subject to limitations; these are permitted by implication since the right of access by its very nature calls for regulation by the State. In this respect, the Contracting States enjoy a certain margin of appreciation, although the final decision as to the observance of the Convention's requirements rests with the Court. It must be satisfied that the limitations applied do not restrict or reduce the access left to the individual in such a way or to such an extent that the very essence of the right is impaired. Furthermore, a limitation will not be compatible with Article 6 § 1 if it does not pursue a legitimate aim and if there is not a reasonable relationship of proportionality between the means employed and the aim sought to be achieved. . . .
>
> (c) The attribution of privileges and immunities to international organisations is an essential means of ensuring the proper functioning of such organisations free from unilateral interference by individual governments. The immunity from jurisdiction commonly accorded

163. *Id.*, para. 137.

by States to international organisations under the organisations' constituent instruments or supplementary agreements is a long-standing practice established in the interest of the good working of these organisations. The importance of this practice is enhanced by a trend towards extending and strengthening international cooperation in all domains of modern society. Against this background, the immunity from domestic jurisdiction afforded to international organisations has a legitimate objective. . . .

(d) Where States establish international organisations in order to pursue or strengthen their cooperation in certain fields of activities, and where they attribute to these organisations certain competences and accord them immunities, there may be implications as to the protection of fundamental rights. It would be incompatible with the purpose and object of the Convention, however, if the Contracting States were thereby absolved from their responsibility under the Convention in relation to the field of activity covered by such attribution. It should be recalled that the Convention is intended to guarantee not theoretical or illusory rights, but rights that are practical and effective. This is particularly true for the right of access to the courts in view of the prominent place held in a democratic society by the right to a fair trial . . . It would not be consistent with the rule of law in a democratic society or with the basic principle underlying Article 6 § 1—namely that civil claims must be capable of being submitted to a judge for adjudication—if a State could, without restraint or control by the Convention enforcement bodies, remove from the jurisdiction of the courts a whole range of civil claims or confer immunities from civil liability on categories of persons. . . .

(e) The Convention, including Article 6, cannot be interpreted in a vacuum. The Court must be mindful of the Convention's special character as a human rights treaty, and it must also take the relevant rules of international law into account. . . . The Convention should so far as possible be interpreted in harmony with other rules of international law of which it forms part, including those relating to the grant of immunity to a State (the Court would add: or to an international organisation). . . .

(f) Measures taken by a High Contracting Party which reflect generally recognised rules of public international law on State immunity (the Court would add: or the immunity of international organisations) cannot in principle be regarded as imposing a disproportionate restriction on the right of access to a court as embodied in Article

> 6 § 1. Just as the right of access to a court is an inherent part of the fair trial guaranteed in that Article, so some restrictions on access must likewise be regarded as inherent. Examples are those limitations generally accepted by the community of nations as part of the doctrine of immunity from domestic jurisdiction, whether it concerns the immunity of a foreign sovereign State or that of an international organisation. . . .
>
> When creating new international obligations, States are assumed not to derogate from their previous obligations. Where a number of apparently contradictory instruments are simultaneously applicable, international case-law and academic opinion endeavour to construe them in such a way as to coordinate their effects and avoid any opposition between them. Two diverging commitments must therefore be harmonised as far as possible so that they produce effects that are fully in accordance with existing law.[164]

Before the ECtHR applied the principles from its case law to the nature of the immunity enjoyed by the United Nations, it noted that previous cases before it concerned the jurisdictional immunity of international organizations in disputes between the organization and members of its staff,[165] or the request to impute the acts of international organizations to State Parties to the ECHR who are members of those international organizations.[166] It differentiated this case from those cases because the dispute in this one involved a dispute between the applicants and the United Nations arising out of the action of the United Nations Security Council under Chapter VII of the United Nations Charter. As a result, the Court held that because of the fundamental mission of the United Nations to secure international peace and security, Article 6 of the Convention cannot be interpreted to deny the United Nations jurisdictional immunity for the acts and omissions of the Security Council: "To bring such operations within the scope of domestic jurisdiction would be to allow individual States, through their courts, to interfere with the fulfillment of the key mission of the United Nations in this field, including with effective conduct of its operations."[167]

164. *Id.*, para. 139 [citations omitted].

165. See *Waite and Kennedy, and Beer and Regan.*

166. See *Behrami v. France, and Saramati v. France,* Application Nos. 71412/01, 78166/01.

167. *Stichting Mothers of Srebrenica,* para. 154 [citations omitted].

Regarding the applicant's contention that the cloak of immunity protecting the United Nations should be removed for claims based on genocide, as the prohibition of genocide was a rule of jus cogens, the Court stated:

> International law does not support the position that a civil claim should override immunity from suit for the sole reason that it is based on an allegation of a particularly grave violation of a norm of international law, even a norm of *ius cogens*. In respect of the sovereign immunity of foreign States this has been clearly stated by the ICJ in *Jurisdictional Immunities of the State (Germany v. Italy: Greece intervening)*, judgment of 3 February 2012, §§ 81–97. In the Court's opinion this also holds true as regards the immunity enjoyed by the United Nations.[168]

With respect to the applicant's contention about the absence of any alternative jurisdiction to entertain their claim against the United Nations, the Court recalled that in *Waite and Kennedy*, it had "considered it a 'material factor', in determining whether granting an international organisation immunity from domestic jurisdiction was permissible under the Convention, whether the applicants had available to them reasonable alternative means to protect their rights under the Convention."[169] But it ruled that its judgment in *Waite and Kennedy* cannot be interpreted in absolute terms as it does not follow that the absence of an alternative remedy automatically constitutes a violation of the right of access to a court, and that the ICJ has similarly ruled in respect of State immunity in *Jurisdictional Immunities of the State (Germany v. Italy: Greece Intervening)*.[170] In conclusion, the Court held that the grant of immunity to the United Nations in the case served a legitimate purpose and was not disproportionate.[171]

The Canadian Supreme Court has taken the following position on access to court: "The absence of a dispute resolution mechanism or of an internal review process is not, in and of itself, determinative of whether [an international organization] is entitled to immunity."[172] In a case implicating the immunity of an international organization, it ruled that the "fact that the appellant has no forum in which to air his grievances and seek remedy is unfortunate. However, it is the

168. *Id.*, para. 158.

169. *Id.*, para. 163.

170. *Id.*, at para. 164.

171. *Id.*, para. 169.

172. *Amaratunga v. Northwest Atlantic Fisheries Organization*, 2013 SCC 66, [2013] 3. S.C.R. 866 (Can.), para. 60.

nature of an immunity to shield certain matters from the jurisdiction of the host state's courts."[173] It noted that "it is an 'inevitable result' of a grant of immunity that certain parties will be left without legal recourse, and this is a 'policy choice implicit' in the legislation."[174]

To a submission that immunity "is unconstitutional to the extent that it prevents access to an effective remedy for gross human rights violations," and an argument that "it is a principle of fundamental justice that 'where there is a right, there must be a remedy for its violation,'" the Canadian Supreme Court responded:

> "While I agree that 'where there is a right, there must be a remedy for its violation' is a legal maxim, I cannot accept that it necessarily constitutes a principle of fundamental justice. While rights would be illusory if there was never a way to remedy their violation, the reality is that certain rights do exist even though remedies for their violation may be limited by procedural bars. Remedies are by no means automatic or unlimited; there is no societal consensus that an effective remedy is always guaranteed to compensate for every rights violation."[175]

173. See *id.*, para. 63.

174. *Id.*

175. *Kazemi Estate v. Islamic Republic of Iran*, [2014] 3 S.C.R. 176; 2014 SCC 62, para. 159. Justice LeBel delivered the opinion of the court which is joined by Chief Justice McLachlin and Justices Rothstein, Cromwell, Moldaver and Karakatsanis, with Justice Abella dissenting.

PART THREE

Cross-Cutting and Confused Concepts

9

Similarities and Differences among Immunities

ORIGIN AND NATURE OF DIPLOMATIC IMMUNITY

For a better understanding of State immunity and immunity of international organizations, it is important to equally understand diplomatic immunity because of the relationship among the three related but different immunities.

Diplomatic immunity had developed as an aspect of sovereign immunity when the diplomatic envoy or agent was considered as the personal representative of the sovereign, but diplomatic immunity is now a distinct and well-developed rule of international law. Over the years, diplomatic immunity, which covers both diplomatic missions and agents, has been founded on the following three principles: extraterritoriality, personal representation, and functional necessity.

The theory of extraterritoriality was the first and oldest legal basis for diplomatic immunity.[1] Ancient writers, such as Hugo Grotius,[2] have based diplomatic immunity on the fiction of extraterritoriality, which considers the diplomatic mission to be outside of the territory of the receiving State. The idea of extraterritoriality

1. See B. Sen, A Diplomat's Handbook of International Law and Practice 80 (Martinus Nijhoff 1965).

2. *De Jure Belli et Pacis.*

Jurisdictional Immunities of States and International Organizations. Edward Chukwuemeke Okeke.

also meant that a diplomat accredited to a receiving States was actually situated within the territory of the sending State. Extraterritoriality as the basis for diplomatic immunity has been discredited and has fallen into desuetude.

The diplomatic agent is the representative of the sovereign or the State. On the basis of personal representation, the immunity of the diplomat was equated with that of the sending State. As a result, a diplomatic agent as the representative of a sovereign State is entitled to the same privileges and immunities as the sovereign. The major shortcoming of this rationale for diplomatic immunity is that it does not consider the difference in the nature and scope of the respective immunities of the State and the diplomat. Also, the personal representation basis for diplomatic immunity does not account for the immunity enjoyed by the diplomat in his or her personal capacity as opposed to official acts.

The most reasonable and defensible of the three bases for diplomatic immunity is functional necessity. Under this rationale, diplomatic immunity is necessary for a diplomatic agent to perform his or her functions. The immunity allows the diplomatic agent to perform functions efficiently, freely, and independently in the receiving State. To this effect, the Preamble of the Vienna Convention on Diplomatic Relations ("Vienna Convention or VCDR") states "that the purpose of such privileges and immunities is not to benefit individuals but to ensure the efficient performance of the functions of diplomatic missions as representing States."

> The rules of diplomatic law, in short, constitute a self-contained regime which, on the one hand, lays down the receiving State's obligations regarding the facilities, privileges and immunities to be accorded to diplomatic missions and, on the other hand, foresees their possible abuse by members of the mission and specifies the means at the disposal of the receiving State to counter any such abuse. These means are, by their nature, entirely efficacious, for unless the sending State recalls the member of the mission objected to forthwith, the prospect of the almost immediate loss of his privileges and immunities, because of the withdrawal by the receiving State of his recognition as a member of the mission, will in practice compel that person, in his own interest, to depart at once. But the principle of the person of the diplomatic agents and the premises of diplomatic missions is one of the very foundations of this long-established regime. . . .[3]

The customary international law of diplomatic immunity, which is long-standing, is now codified in the Vienna Convention with almost universal participation

3. *United States Diplomatic and Consular Staff in Tehran ("United States v. Iran")*, Judgment, I. C. J. Reports 1980, p. 3, 40, para. 86.

by States.[4] The Preamble of the Convention "recall[s] that people of all nations from ancient times have recognized the status of diplomatic agents." It also states that the purpose of the Convention is "the development of friendly relations among nations, irrespective of their differing constitutional and social systems" and "that the rules of customary international law should continue to govern questions not expressly regulated by the provisions of the . . . Convention." The Convention provides the rules for the establishment, maintenance, and termination of diplomatic relations. It is in the mutual interest of State parties as they are both sending and receiving States in their diplomatic relations, which are based on mutual consent and reciprocity. As noted by the International Court of Justice (ICJ), it is an "edifice of law carefully constructed by mankind over a period of centuries, the maintenance of which is vital for the security and well-being of the complex international community of the present day, to which it is more essential than ever that the rules developed to ensure the ordered progress of relations between its members should be constantly and scrupulously respected."[5]

The Convention contains 53 articles that govern the behavior of diplomatic agents, 13 of which address the issue of immunity. With respect to diplomatic missions, the key provisions for purposes of jurisdictional immunity are Articles 22 and 24, which provide respectively for the inviolability of the premises of the diplomatic mission, and of its archives and documents.[6] Inviolability protects the premises of the diplomatic mission from unauthorized entry by authorities of the receiving State. It also imposes an obligation of protection by the receiving State against any intrusion or external interference even from third parties. "The inviolability of diplomatic archives followed as a logical consequence of the inviolability of mission premises."[7] It protects the archives and documents of a

4. Vienna Convention on Diplomatic Relations (VCDR), Apr. 18, 1961, 500 U.N.T.S. 95; 23 U.S.T. 3227. The treaty entered into force on April 24, 1964, and has 189 State parties.

5. *United States v. Iran*, p. 43, para. 92.

6. Article 22 of VCDR provides: "1. The premises of the mission shall be inviolable. The agents of the receiving State may not enter them, except with the consent of the head of the mission.

2. The receiving State is under a special duty to take all appropriate steps to protect the premises of the mission against any intrusion or damage and to prevent any disturbance of the peace of the mission or impairment of its dignity. 3. The premises of the mission, their furnishings and other property thereon and the means of transport of the mission shall be immune from search, requisition, attachment or execution."

Article 24 of VCDR provides: "The archives and documents of the mission shall be inviolable at any time and wherever they may be."

7. Eileen Denza, Diplomatic Law: A Commentary on the Vienna Convention on Diplomatic Relations 108 (Oceana 1976).

diplomatic mission from any coercion, such as search and seizure, or infringement on their confidentiality and privacy, which means that their production and use cannot be compelled in any legal proceedings. The inviolability of archives covers information and documents that are neither on the diplomatic premises nor in diplomatic pouches.

In the case of diplomatic agents, Article 29 provides for the inviolability of the person of the diplomat, which means that he or she is not liable to any form of arrest or detention in the receiving State.[8] As part of the inviolability of the person of the diplomat is the duty of protection owed by the receiving State to the diplomat. The principle of inviolability is so fundamental that it must be respected by the receiving State even in the case of armed conflict or break in diplomatic relations.[9] "The inviolability of the diplomatic agent is certainly the oldest established and most fundamental rule of diplomatic law."[10] "Personal inviolability is, of all the privileges and immunities of missions and diplomats, the oldest established and the most universally recognized."[11] The age-old principle of inviolability was at the center of the Iran Hostage Crisis when the United States embassy in Tehran was occupied by Iranian militants who also held embassy staff hostage, where the ICJ reiterated:

> Whereas there is no more fundamental prerequisite for the conduct of relations between States than the inviolability of diplomatic envoys and embassies, so that throughout history nations of all creeds and cultures have observed reciprocal obligations for that purpose; and whereas the obligations thus assumed, notably those for assuring the personal safety of diplomats and their freedom from prosecution, are essential, unqualified, and inherent in their representative character and their diplomatic function;
>
> Whereas the institution of diplomacy, with its concomitant privileges and immunities, has withstood the test of centuries and proved to be an instrument essential for effective co-operation in the international community, and for enabling States, irrespective of their differing constitutional and social systems, to achieve mutual understanding and to resolve their differences by peaceful means.[12]

8. Article 29 of VCDR provides: "The person of a diplomatic agent shall be inviolable. He shall not be liable to any form of arrest or detention. The receiving State shall treat him with due respect and shall take all appropriate steps to prevent any attack on his person, freedom or dignity."

9. See *United States of America v. Iran*, para. 86; Articles 44 and 45 of the VCDR.

10. DENZA, at 135.

11. SATOW'S DIPLOMATIC PRACTICE 122 (Ivor Roberts ed., 6th ed. Oxford University Press 2009).

12. *United States v. Tehran*, Order of 15 December 1979, 1979 I.C.J. Rep. 19, paras. 38–39.

Article 31 grants a diplomatic agent immunity from criminal jurisdiction without any exceptions, and from civil and administrative jurisdictions with three enumerated exceptions.[13] The exceptions are: (1) with respect to immovable property in the receiving State; (2) if the diplomat is acting as an administrator, executor, heir, or legatee in his personal capacity; or (3) if the diplomat undertakes a commercial or professional activity that is not part of his official functions. The immunity from civil and administrative jurisdictions covers family law issues such as divorce or custody. "The immunity of an ambassador from criminal jurisdiction and later from the civil jurisdiction of the receiving State was, after inviolability, the earliest to be established of the basic rules of diplomatic law. Immunity from criminal jurisdiction was originally regarded as an aspect of inviolability."[14]

Article 32 sets out the rules for waiver of immunity.[15] As the immunity of a diplomatic agent belongs to the sending State, it is for that State to waive the immunity. A sending State cannot revoke a waiver made by an official with actual or apparent authority.[16] As a general rule, the head of a diplomatic mission is deemed to have the authority to waive immunity. A waiver of immunity must be express. However, where a diplomatic agent institutes proceedings in a national court, the immunity is deemed waived in regard to any set-off or counterclaim

13. Article 31 of VCDR provides: "1. A diplomatic agent shall enjoy immunity from the criminal jurisdiction of the receiving State. He shall also enjoy immunity from its civil and administrative jurisdiction, except in the case of: (*a*) A real action relating to private immovable property situated in the territory of the receiving State, unless he holds it on behalf of the sending State for the purposes of the mission; (*b*) An action relating to succession in which the diplomatic agent is involved as executor, administrator, heir or legatee as a private person and not on behalf of the sending State; (*c*) An action relating to any professional or commercial activity exercised by the diplomatic agent in the receiving State outside his official functions. 2. A diplomatic agent is not obliged to give evidence as a witness. 3. No measures of execution may be taken in respect of a diplomatic agent except in the cases coming under subparagraphs (*a*), (*b*) and (*c*) of paragraph 1 of this article, and provided that the measures concerned can be taken without infringing the inviolability of his person or of his residence. 4. The immunity of a diplomatic agent from the jurisdiction of the receiving State does not exempt him from the jurisdiction of the sending State."

14. Denza, at 149.

15. Article 32 of VCDR provides: "1. The immunity from jurisdiction of diplomatic agents and of persons enjoying immunity under article 37 may be waived by the sending State. 2. Waiver must always be express. 3. The initiation of proceedings by a diplomatic agent or by a person enjoying immunity from jurisdiction under article 37 shall preclude him from invoking immunity from jurisdiction in respect of any counterclaim directly connected with the principal claim. 4. Waiver of immunity from jurisdiction in respect of civil or administrative proceedings shall not be held to imply waiver of immunity in respect of the execution of the judgement, for which a separate waiver shall be necessary."

16. See Denza, at 184.

that is directly connected with the principal claim, and any appeal by the defendant. Execution of judgment requires a separate waiver.

A diplomat may be declared persona non grata by the receiving State under Article 9 of the Convention.[17] The declaration is an expression by the receiving State that a diplomat is personally unacceptable to it, but it does not necessarily signal displeasure with the sending State. The receiving State has no obligation to give reasons for the declaration, and the sending State must grant the request for recall.[18] A sending State is therefore required to recall the diplomat or terminate his functions in the receiving State. If the functions of the diplomat are terminated, then the diplomat is no longer shielded by immunity *ratione personae*.

Diplomatic immunity is both status-based (*rationae personae*) and conduct-based (*rationae materiae*). Status-based immunity depends on the person's present status as a diplomat and ends when the individual's status as a diplomat ceases.[19] Conduct-based immunity, on the other hand, attaches only to the conduct performed in an official capacity and continues after the diplomat has left the office in which the act was done. It must be pointed out that the jurisdictional immunity of a diplomat does not exempt the holder from legal liability, but only from judicial process in the receiving State. This exemption extends only to official acts for which she cannot incur legal liability under the law of the receiving State during and after her diplomatic service. However, the diplomat may be sued, when her diplomatic status ends, for any civil or criminal liability that she has incurred. Of course, the diplomat has no immunity in the sending State.

Although the abuse of diplomatic immunity invites opprobrium, it should not detract from its purpose and proper use. The immunity is to protect the diplomatic function, not to place the diplomat above the law. "More recently attacks have come from scholars concerned at the conflict between immunity and human rights access to justice, or at immunity for violators of international criminal law and in particular torturers."[20]

17. Article 9 of VCDR provides: "1. The receiving State may at any time and without having to explain its decision, notify the sending State that the head of the mission or any member of the diplomatic staff of the mission is *persona non grata* or that any other member of the staff of the mission is not acceptable. In any such case, the sending State shall, as appropriate, either recall the person concerned or terminate his functions with the mission. A person may be declared *non grata* or not acceptable before arriving in the territory of the receiving State. 2. If the sending State refuses or fails within a reasonable period to carry out its obligations under paragraph 1 of this article, the receiving State may refuse to recognize the person concerned as a member of the mission."

18. See DENZA, at 40.

19. *Id.*, Art. 39 (2).

20. EILEEN DENZA, VIENNA CONVENTION ON DIPLOMATIC RELATIONS, UNITED NATIONS AUDIOVISUAL LIBRARY OF INTERNATIONAL LAW 4 (2009).

DIPLOMATIC IMMUNITY AND STATE IMMUNITY

> If ambassadors and diplomatic agents are accorded immunities under international law in their capacity as representatives of States or foreign sovereigns, *a fortiori* the States or the sovereigns they represent should be entitled to no lesser a degree of favored treatment. Immunities belong to a category of favorable treatment. Diplomatic immunities may be said to have given an added reason for State immunities. It is true that in the practice of States the immunities of ambassadors had been well-established before those of States, and that diplomatic immunities are functional in foundation; yet the two concepts are not totally unrelated. Diplomatic immunity is accorded not for the benefit of the individual, but for the benefit of the State in whose service he is. There is no immunity if the diplomat ceases to represent a sovereign State.[21]

Diplomatic immunity and State immunity are not analogous even though the immunity of the diplomat derives from the immunity of the State whom the diplomat represents. Diplomatic immunity cannot be waived except by the sovereign, but a sovereign can waive its own immunity.[22] Although diplomatic immunity is a distinct and separate rule of international law, the immunity ultimately appertains to the sending State. State immunity is multilateral and applies erga omnes in relation to all States. Diplomatic immunity, on the other hand, is bilateral and applies in relation to sending and receiving States, subject to mutual consent and accreditation. Reciprocity is at the core of diplomatic immunity.

Diplomatic immunity is based on functional necessity but State immunity is based on the independence and equality of States. Diplomatic immunity and (restrictive) State immunity both have exceptions. Article 31(1)(a) and (c) of VCDR provides exceptions for immovable property, and commercial activity (outside of official function) respectively. Article 32(2) provides for waiver, which must be express, and Article 32(2) provides that there is no immunity for a counterclaim. The exceptions to State immunity are much more extensive. The restrictive State immunity recognizes an exception for employment contracts, but that exception is circumscribed with respect to employment at diplomatic missions.[23]

21. Second Report on the Jurisdictional Immunities of States and Their Property, U.N. Document A/CN.4/331 and Add.1, p. 229, para. 122 [citation omitted] (11 April 11 and 30 June 1980).

22. See *The Charkieh (6200)* [1873] [L.R.] 4 A & E. 59, p. 70.

23. See *Fogarty v. United Kingdom.*

DIPLOMATIC IMMUNITY AND IMMUNITY OF INTERNATIONAL ORGANIZATIONS

Historically, the privileges and immunities of international organizations originated by analogy to diplomatic privileges and immunities.[24] For example, Article 7(4) of the Covenant of the League of Nations conferred diplomatic privileges and immunities on the agents of the League and representatives of the member States of the League. In the same vein, Article 3 of the Headquarters Agreement of the International Labour Organization (ILO) provides that the organization "enjoys the immunities known in international law as diplomatic immunities." Although Articles 104 and 105 of the Charter of the United Nations were a departure from the precedents of the League of Nations and ILO, diplomatic privileges and immunities remained a point of reference for the scope of immunity accorded their premises, communication, archives, and senior officials of the United Nations and its specialized agencies. The General Convention and the Specialized Agencies Convention refer variously to diplomatic envoys, missions, and couriers.[25] In a departure from the concept of diplomatic immunity, Section 18 of the General Convention and Section 19 of the Specialized Agencies Convention provide immunity only for official acts. However, Section 19 of the General Convention entitles certain senior officials of the United Nations to the same privileges and immunities as diplomatic envoys.[26] Similarly, Section 21 of the Specialized Agencies Convention provides that the executive heads of the specialized agencies shall be accorded the same privileges and immunities as diplomatic envoys. This means that these senior officials also benefit from the provisions of the Vienna Convention, and those of the General Convention and the Special Agencies Convention, as applicable.[27]

24. See Josef L. Kunz, *Privileges and Immunities of International Organizations*, 41 Am. J. Int'l L. 842 (1947); Linda S. Frey & Marsha L. Frey, The History of Diplomatic Immunity 539 (1999).

25. See Articles III, IV, V, VI, and VII of the General Convention, and Articles IV, V, VI, VII, and VIII of the Specialized Agencies Convention. Most headquarters agreements of international organizations refer to diplomatic privileges, immunities, and facilities, for example, Agreement between France and UNESCO (Paris 2 July 1954).

26. High-level officials, such as the Secretary-General, Under-Secretaries-General, and the Assistant Secretaries-General, as well as representatives of member States receive diplomatic immunity, whereas the rest of the officials, as well as experts on mission, have only functional immunity, that is, immunity for acts undertaken in an official capacity.

27. Section 18(a) of the General Convention provides: "Officials of the United Nations shall be immune from legal process in respect of words spoken or written and all acts performed by them in their official capacity." Section 19 provides: "In addition to the immunities and privileges specified in Section 18, the Secretary-General and all Assistant Secretaries-General shall be accorded in

The resort to analogy of the privileges and immunities of international organizations and their officials to those of diplomatic missions and agents was a matter of convenience during the nascence of international organizations. Although both diplomatic immunity and the immunity of international organizations share the rationale of functional necessity, the analogy failed to account for their conceptual difference. Foremost in the difference is that the immunity of international organizations and their officials was intended to ensure their independence from all States and to enable them to perform their functions. The immunity of officials of international organizations derives from that of the organizations, and not the home States of the officials of the international organization, and extends to the jurisdiction of their home States. The purpose of the immunity of international organizations is to protect the officials from all States in the performance of their official functions. Diplomatic agents, on the other hand, are not immune from the jurisdiction of their home State, that is, the sending State. Also, if the sending State waives the immunity of the diplomatic agent, then the diplomat would be subject to the jurisdiction of the receiving State.

Reciprocity, which is permissible under Article 47 of VCDR,[28] is a golden rule where a State treats the diplomats of another State in the same way that its diplomats are treated by that other State. Under the practice, both sending and receiving States can disallow certain privileges to each other. Reciprocity is usually applied with respect to privileges as a matter of comity, and those privileges are not considered essential to the fulfillment of the diplomatic function. Unlike States who can resort to reciprocity as a "substantial measure of protection against partial treatment, denial of justice or unreasonable interference by each other or each other's courts," international organizations are "completely at the mercy of their member States, both collectively and individually" absent

respect of themselves, their spouses and minor children, the privileges and immunities, exemptions and facilities accorded to diplomatic envoys, in accordance with international law."

Sections 19(a) of the Specialized Agencies Convention provides: "Officials of the specialized agencies shall be immune from legal process in respect of words spoken or written and all acts performed by them in their official capacity." Section 21 provides: "In addition to the immunities and privileges specified in Sections 19 and 20, the executive head of each specialized agency, including any official acting on his behalf during his absence from duty, shall be accorded in respect of himself, his spouse and minor children, the privileges and immunities, exemptions and facilities accorded to diplomatic envoys, in accordance with international law."

28. Article 47 of VCDR provides: "1. In the application of the provisions of the present Convention, the receiving State shall not discriminate as between States. 2. However, discrimination shall not be regarded as taking place: (*a*) Where the receiving State applies any of the provisions of the present Convention restrictively because of a restrictive application of that provision to its mission in the sending State; (*b*) Where by custom or agreement States extend to each other more favourable treatment than is required by the provisions of the present Convention."

jurisdictional immunity.[29] Reciprocity does not and should not apply in the relationship between an international organization and a State because international organizations do not have receiving and sending States even though they have host States. International organizations have only member States and host States. Since diplomatic privileges are based on the mutual consent of both the receiving and sending States, reciprocity and retaliation are, therefore, unavailing to international organizations with respect to their privileges and immunities.

Declaration of persona non grata is the process of removing a "diplomatic agent" who is personally unacceptable to the receiving State. A person may be *declared persona non grata* even before arrival at the receiving State. The concept of persona non grata has a permissible purpose, in cases of abuse of privilege, but it is not unheard of that States use it also for impermissible purposes. The concept, which is an acceptable feature of diplomatic immunity, would be inimical to the independence of international organizations if applied to their officials. A State may use it to address its difference or displeasure with an official of the international organization or the organization itself, thereby undermining their independence. Persona non grata has no place in the immunity of officials of international organizations because the functions of diplomats and officials are very different. Diplomats represent national interest, whereas officials of international organizations represent international interest, so to say.

Related to principle of persona non grata is that of prior notification, which imposes a duty of notification of appointment and movement of diplomatic staff.[30] In the case of international organizations, for purposes of immigration and alien registration host States are notified of appointment of officials. Prior notification is also related to the diplomatic principle of *Agrément*, where although the sending State appoints its diplomats, it has to seek the agreement of the receiving State for the person it proposes for accreditation as head of the diplomatic mission.[31] The practice has been imported from diplomatic immunity with respect to resident representatives or heads of office of international organizations in host States because those officials are accorded diplomatic status in those States. Since a State can refuse any particular official, that is, deny its *agrément*, the practice may bring a national influence over the appointment of officials of an international organization. To ensure their independence, all officials of international organizations

29. C.W. Jenks, International Immunities 40–41 (Oceana 1961).

30. See Article 10 of VCDR.

31. Article 4 of VCDR provides: "1. The sending State must make certain that the *agrément* of the receiving State has been given for the person it proposes to accredit as head of the mission to that State. 2. The receiving State is not obliged to give reasons to the sending State for a refusal of *agrément*."

should be appointed by the organizations themselves with no requirement for agreement by a State. *Agrément* seems to be a trade-off for conferring diplomatic status on certain officials of international organizations.

Under the principle of national discrimination, nationals and permanent residents of the receiving State do not enjoy certain privileges and immunities in their home State.[32] National discrimination is a limitation on diplomatic immunity in the sense that members of the diplomatic staff of a mission may be appointed from among the nationals of the receiving State only with the express consent of their home State. Such nationals, with the exception of the inviolability and immunity from jurisdiction in respect of official acts performed in the exercise of their functions, enjoy only such privileges and immunities as may be granted by the receiving State. The rationale is that diplomatic agents do not require immunity from the jurisdiction of their sending State in the performance of their diplomatic functions for their home State. This is not the case with officials of international organizations who perform functions for the organization and, as such, require privileges and immunities from all member States, including their home State.

To sum up, immunity of diplomatic agents is well founded on customary international law, whereas the immunity of officials of international organizations is largely based on treaty law. The application of diplomatic immunity to officials of international organizations is inapt because the bases of the immunities of diplomats and officials of international organizations are different. Of particular importance is that the immunity of officials of international organizations is intended to ensure their independence and to protect them from interference by all member States, including that of the host States and their States of nationality. In carrying out their duties, officials of international organizations owe their duty and loyalty to no one but the organization that employs them. Articles 4 and 9 of the Vienna Convention should have no place in the immunity of officials of international organizations. Also, the nationality criterion of the Vienna Convention is inconsistent with Article V, Section 18, of the General Convention, and Article VI, Section 19, of the Specialized Agencies Convention. The logic of sending and receiving States is inapplicable with respect to the

32. Article 38 of VCDR provides: "1. Except insofar as additional privileges and immunities may be granted by the receiving State, a diplomatic agent who is a national of or permanently resident in that State shall enjoy only immunity from jurisdiction, and inviolability, in respect of official acts performed in the exercise of his functions. 2. Other members of the staff of the mission and private servants who are nationals of or permanently resident in the receiving State shall enjoy privileges and immunities only to the extent admitted by the receiving State. However, the receiving State must exercise its jurisdiction over those persons in such a manner as not to interfere unduly with the performance of the functions of the mission."

immunities of officials of international organizations. The relationship between officials of international organizations and the States where they perform their functions is different from the relationship between a diplomat and the receiving State of accreditation. The analogy of the immunity of international organizations to diplomatic immunity and the application of diplomatic immunities and privileges to international organizations and their officials is surely problematic.

STATE IMMUNITY AND IMMUNITY OF INTERNATIONAL ORGANIZATIONS

The jurisdictional immunities of States and international organizations have different rationales. In this regard, the Legal Counsel of the United Nations, in a Note to the Minister of Foreign Affairs of a member State concerning certain labor claims filed against the United Nations by former individual contractors, stated:

> The Legal Counsel wishes to point out that the concepts of jurisdictional immunities of states and the privileges and immunities of international organizations have a different nature and origin. The jurisdictional immunities of states are a part of customary international law that has evolved through the years and recently was codified in the United Nations Convention on Jurisdictional Immunities of States and their Property, 2004. Under customary international law, when a state acts as a private person in a commercial context (*jure gestionis*), it is not immune from the jurisdiction of the state in which it is acting in that capacity. In such a case, since the state is acting outside of its role as a sovereign power, the immunity does not apply.
>
> Unlike the case with sovereign states, the privileges and immunities of the United Nations are of a treaty law nature and, as explained above, originated in the United Nations Charter and the General Convention. The exception to state immunity in situations where the state is undertaking commercial activities is not provided for under the United Nations Charter or the General Convention with respect to the United Nations. Instead, pursuant to article VIII, section 29 of the General Convention, the Organization shall make provisions for appropriate modes of settlement of, *inter alia*, "disputes arising out of contracts or other disputes of a private law nature to which the United Nations is a party." Accordingly, there is no "commercial activity" exception under the General Convention that would be applicable with respect to the United Nations.[33]

33. United Nations Juridical Yearbook 2012, Chapter VI, p. 461 (November 20, 2012) [citation omitted].

Although immunity of international organizations had been conceived in terms of State immunity, States and international organizations are different, and their immunities cannot be equated. The difference between States and international organizations was articulated in the *Amicus Curiae* brief of the United Nations in *Broadbent v. Organization of American States*:

> (a) States have sovereignty, but international organizations do not; (b) States have territory, international organizations do not, but function within the territory of States; (c) States have citizens, but international organizations merely have officials who are generally citizens of their member States, though freed of certain responsibilities toward such States; (d) States are considerably protected from undue intrusion of other States by their ability to invoke the principle of reciprocity, or can protect themselves by their ability to retaliate; international organizations, not standing on a parity with States, cannot depend on reciprocity, nor are they in a position to retaliate against any violation of their integrity; (e) More particularly, States can grant to or withhold immunity from each other, and generally do so on the basis of agreements or principles of comity embodied in international law; international organizations normally do not exercise jurisdiction over anyone except, and only to a limited extent, their own officials, and thus are not in a position to grant to or withhold immunity from States; (f) States are protected from interference by international organizations in their affairs by provisions in the constitutions of these organizations (for example, United Nations Charter, Article 2(7)) and by the fact that representatives of States constitute the political organs and control the administrative organs of these organizations; international organizations are protected from interference by States principally by the immunities provided for by international law; (g) Consequently, the immunities of States are those attributable to sovereigns and those reflect those that States reserve to themselves, whether absolute or relative; those of international organizations are functional and thus reflect their needs, which require complete protection from national jurisdiction.[34]

In short, a major distinction between States and international organizations is that States possess all the rights and responsibilities under international law, whereas international organizations possess only those that are granted them by their constituent treaty. Unlike States, which are political entities pursuing their own self-interest, international organizations exist and operate for the benefit of all their member States.

34. 1980 United Nations Juridical Yearbook 224, 229–30, UN Doc. ST/LEG/SER.C/18 (1983).

State immunity is based primarily on the principle of sovereign equality, whereas the immunity of international organizations is based on functional necessity. The immunity of international organization is informed by a different consideration from that of States. To this effect, in its determination of the immunity of an international organization, the Canadian Supreme Court saw fit to "highlight certain differences between state immunities on the one hand and immunities granted to international organizations on the other."[35] It noted that States enjoy immunity from the jurisdiction of other States as a matter of customary international law, whereas with respect to international organizations, "the prevailing view at present is that no rule [customary] of international law confers immunity on them. International organizations derive their existence from treaties and the same holds true for their rights to immunities."[36] Thus, the dissimilarities between States and international organizations, as well as the conceptual bases of their respective immunities, should militate against the assimilation of the scope of immunity of States to international organizations.

PITFALLS OF ANALOGIES BETWEEN IMMUNITIES

The immunity of international organizations is a composite, with some elements of diplomatic and State immunities. There are parallels among diplomatic immunity, State immunity, and immunity of international organizations. These parallels might have proved promising at the nascence of international organizations but is now fraught with pitfalls. At the time both diplomatic immunity and State immunity were extended to international organizations, the classical theory of absolute State immunity held sway. With the development of the doctrine of restrictive State immunity, which distinguished between *acta jure imperii* and *acta jure gestionis,* the pitfall of the analogy has been laid bare.

Two legislative acts in the United States provide an object lesson on the pitfall. The International Organizations Immunity Act (IOIA) was enacted in 1945, when absolute State immunity reigned supreme; it provides that international organizations shall enjoy the same immunities from suit as foreign States. The Foreign Sovereign Immunities Act (FSIA) was enacted in 1976 to codify restrictive State immunity. The latter legislation has led, or more aptly misled, some to argue that the doctrine of restrictive State immunity should be applied to international organizations.

35. *Amaratunga v. Northwest Atlantic Fisheries Organization,* 2013 SCC 66, [2013] 3 S.C.R. 866 (Can.), para. 27.

36. *Id.,* paras. 28 and 29 [citations omitted].

The pitfall of analogizing the immunity of international organization to State immunity was apparent in the case of *OSS Nokalva* (OSSN) *v. European Space Agency* (ESA), where the United States Court of Appeals for the Third Circuit ruled that the doctrine of restrictive State immunity, as codified in the FSIA, applied as well as to international organizations in the United States.[37] In this breach of contract action brought by OSSN, ESA moved for dismissal for lack of subject-matter jurisdiction based on its assertion of immunity under the IOIA. The District Court denied ESA's motion to dismiss based on the court's determination that although ESA was immune under the IOIA, it had waived that immunity in this case. On appeal, the Court of Appeals agreed with the District Court that ESA was not entitled to immunity in this case, but based its conclusion on different reasons. It construed the IOIA to incorporate the exceptions to State immunity under the FSIA and found the commercial agreements at issue in the dispute between the parties to constitute "commercial activity" within the intendment of the FSIA.

The opinion of the Court of Appeals betrays a misunderstanding of the nature and source of the immunity of international organizations. The court asserts: "In light of the 'same immunity' language in the IOIA, it is unreasonable to assume that those international organizations that were established under the IOIA after foreign sovereign immunity had been altered by the FSIA would still be subject to that level of immunity enjoyed by foreign governments and international organizations in 1945."[38] The Court must be mistaken about its statement that international organizations are "established under the IOIA" because that is not the case. IOIA does not establish international organizations, but confers immunity on them under the national law of the United States. IOIA does not abrogate or derogate the immunity already conferred on an international organization under international law by its constituent instrument—where the United States is a member of that particular international organization.

To support its conclusion that ESA was not entitled to immunity as it stood for States in 1945, the Third Circuit Court of Appeals states: "We find no compelling reason why a group of states acting through an international organization is entitled to broader immunity than its member states enjoy when acting alone. Indeed, such a policy may create an incentive for foreign governments to evade legal obligation by acting through international organizations."[39] Contrary to the Court's statement, the compelling reason is that the immunity of international organizations has a different justification or purpose than that of States.

37. *OSS Nokalva v. European Space Agency*, 617 F.3d 756 (3d Cir. 2010),

38. *Id.* at 764.

39. 617 F. 3d at 764.

An international organization is not the sum of its constituent member States; it has a separate legal existence under both international and national laws. The immunity of international organization should not be equated with State immunity, as the different rules of immunity have different origins and serve different purposes. The purpose of the immunity of international organizations is not for its constituent member States to evade their own obligations.

If the Court's statement about immunity and obligation is credited, then there is no justification for the creation and existence of corporations under national laws. "A body which, as distinct from the natural persons composing it, can have rights and be subject to duties and can own property must be regarded as having personality, whether it is or is not called a corporation."[40] International organizations have distinct and separate international and legal personality from their member States and consequently, their obligation belongs to them: "it is elemental that the only persons liable and entitled under a contract, in the absence of trust or agency, are the parties to the contract."[41]

To justify its holding that FSIA's exception to immunity for commercial transactions "is equally applicable to international organizations and is incorporated into the IOIA," the Court argues:

> If Congress wanted to tether international organization immunity to the law of foreign sovereign immunity as it existed at the time IOIA was passed, it could have used language to expressly convey this intent. For example, Congress could have simply stated that international organizations would be entitled to the "same immunity as of the date of this Act." Or, it could have just specified the substantive scope of the immunity it was conferring. Because it did neither, we interpret the IOIA in light of the Reference Canon to mean that Congress intended that the immunity conferred by the IOIA would adapt with the law of foreign sovereign immunity.[42]

The flaw in the Court's argument is that a similar counterargument is equally, if not more, plausible. To be sure, the IOIA is a reference statute, and the product of lazy and harried legislation. The reference of the immunity of international organizations to that of States was a legislative convenience, as the IOIA was hurriedly

40. *Rayner (J.H.) (Mincing Lane) Ltd v. United Kingdom (Department of Trade and Industry)*, House of Lords, [1990] 2 AC 418, [1989] 3 WLR 969, [1989] Ch 72, [1989] 3 All ER 523, para. 69, citing *Chaff and Hay Acquisition Committee v. J.A. Hemphill & Sons Proprietary Ltd.* (1947), 74 C.L.R. 375, 385, per Latham, C.J.

41. *Id.*, para. 72.

42. *Nokalva*, 617 F.3d at 764.

enacted for the imminent seating of the United Nations headquarters in the United States.[43] However, lazy legislation should not lead to lazy judicial interpretation of a statute.[44] The Court of Appeals' argument is too simplistic and fails to take account of the circumstances surrounding the enactment of the IOIA. Most important, it is not enough for the Court to state that the IOIA now incorporates the FSIA without also examining whether Congress intended the FSIA to also apply to international organizations. Following the Court of Appeals' syllogism, if Congress wanted to apply the doctrine of restrictive State immunity, as codified in FSIA, to international organizations, it would have used language to expressly convey that intent. Instead, the only mention of international organization in FSIA is in respect of the protection from attachment of the property of an international organization that is immune under IOIA in an action against a foreign State under the FSIA.[45]

If the interpretation of the FSIA by the Supreme Court in *Samantar*[46] is any guidance, then the FSIA and the restrictive State immunity that it codified does not apply to international organizations by altering their immunity under the IOIA. In *Samantar*, the Supreme Court considered the text, history, and purpose of the FSIA, and decided that the Act did not cover the immunity of foreign officials. It held that the term "foreign state" in the Act does not encompass officials because Congress did not expressly mention officials where their acts would have counted as equivalent to those of the foreign State. "There is therefore little reason to presume that when Congress set out to codify state immunity, it must also have, *sub silento*, intended to codify official immunity."[47] Considering *Samantar*, a foreign official is not a foreign State under the FSIA. Similarly, an international organization and its officials are not a foreign State under the FSIA and, as such, the FSIA is not applicable to them. In sum, according to the Supreme Court, the FSIA only says what it says: nothing more, nothing less.

In fact, the primary purposes of the FSIA are to codify the customary international law doctrine of restrictive State immunity and to shift the decision or determination of immunity of foreign States from the State Department to the

43. See 91 Cong. Rec. 12,530-31 (daily ed. Dec. 21, 1945).

44. See *Atkinson v. Inter-American Development Bank*, 156 F 3d 1335, 1342 (D.C. Cir. 1998) ("Obviously, the 1945 Congress was legislating in shorthand, referring to another body of law—the law governing the immunity of foreign governments—to define the scope of immunity of the new immunity for international organizations.")

45. See 28 U.S.C. § 1611(a) (2006).

46. *Samantar v. Yousuf*, 560 U.S. 305 (2010).

47. *Id.* at 322.

courts.[48] The FSIA, where it applies, also provides the "sole basis for obtaining jurisdiction over a foreign state in federal court."[49] Considering the purpose of the FSIA, it would be anomalous to apply it to international organizations. Thus, the FSIA neither enacted a rule of restrictive immunity for international organization nor amended the IOIA.

If the FSIA were applied to international organizations, for example, with respect to employment disputes, it would be discordant: under contemporary international law, immunity of international organizations in employment matters is the rule, whereas an employment contract is an exception to the rule of State immunity. In *Broadbent v. Organization of American States*,[50] former staff members of the Organization of American States (OAS) sought damages for wrongful termination, arguing essentially that the FSIA should be applied to international organizations because the IOIA granted them the "same immunity" as foreign governments. Without necessarily deciding whether the restrictive State immunity is applicable to OAS, the District of Columbia Court of Appeals held that employment relations of international organizations was not the kind of commercial activity exempted from immunity by FSIA.[51]

The opinion by the Third Circuit Court of Appeals might be an invitation for the Supreme Court to resolve the split that the opinion has created with the jurisprudence of the District of Columbia Court of Appeals. In *Nyambal v. International Monetary Fund*,[52] the plaintiff invited the District of Columbia Circuit to revisit its interpretation of the IOIA in *Atkinson v. Inter-American Development Bank* in light of the Third Circuit's decision, but the District of Columbia Court of Appeals declined to do so and declared that "*Atkinson* remains vigorous as Circuit law."[53] Nyambal petitioned for a writ of certiorari and presented the following question: "Whether the present-day scope of immunity enjoyed by international organizations is absolute and unrestricted, as it was for foreign states prior to the enactment of FSIA; or whether it is now limited by the commercial

48. See *id.* at 313.

49. *Id.* at 314, citing *Argentine Republic v. Amerada Hess Shipping Corp.*, 488 U.S. 428, 439 (1989).

50. 628 F.2d 27 (D.C. Cir. 1980).

51. *Id.* at 34.

52. *Nyambal v. Int'l Monetary Fund*, 772 F.3d 277, 281 (D.C. Cir. 2014).

53. *Id.* In *Atkinson v. Inter-American Development Bank*, 156 F.3d 1335 (D.C. Cir. 1998), the plaintiff brought an action to garnish the salary of her ex-husband, after he had defaulted on a judgment for alimony and child support. The Court interpreted IOIA, and concluded that Congress intended to incorporate the regime of foreign sovereign immunity as it had existed when IOIA was enacted.

activities exception to sovereign immunity contained in FSIA."[54] He argued that the opinion of the District of Columbia Circuit and the Third Circuit regarding the scope of immunity of international organizations cannot be reconciled, but the United States Supreme Court denied certiorari.[55]

A dissension has, however, appeared within the ranks of the District of Columbia Court of Appeals, where a concurring opinion in *Jam v. International Finance Corp.*[56] was of the view that *Atkinson* and *Mendaro* were wrongly decided, and invited the Circuit to revisit them. The dissent stated:

> Reading the *IOIA* to dynamically link organizations' immunity to that of their member states makes sense. The contrary view we adopted in *Atkinson* appears to allow states, subject to suit under the commercial activity exception of the *FSIA*, to carry on commercial activities with immunity through international organizations. Thus, the Canadian government is subject to suit in United States courts for disputes arising from its commercial activities here, but the Great Lakes Fishery Commission—of which the United States and Canada are the sole members—is immune from suit under *Atkinson*. Neither the *IOIA* nor our cases interpreting it explain why nations that collectively breach contracts or otherwise act unlawfully through organizations should enjoy immunity in our courts when the same conduct would not be immunized if directly committed by a nation acting on its own.
>
> Were I not bound by *Atkinson*, I would hold that international organizations' immunity under IOIA is the same as the immunity enjoyed by foreign states. *Accord OSS Nokalva, Inc. v. European Space Agency*, 617 F.3d 756, 762–64 (3d Cir. 2010) (declining to follow Atkinson and holding that restricted immunity as codified in the FSIA, including its commercial activity exception, applies to international organizations under the IOIA).[57]

The argument by the dissent betrays a misunderstanding of the nature of the international organizations and the purpose of their immunity. An international organization is not the sum of its member States. An international organization possesses its own international personality, separate and apart from that of its member States. The immunity of an international organization is not coterminous with that of its member States. The dissent's argument about a State acting

54. *Nyambal v. International Monetary Fund*, 2014 U.S. Briefs 1037 (2015).

55. *Nyambal v. International Monetary Fund*, 135 S. Ct. 2857 (2015).

56. *Jam v. Int'l Fin. Corp.*, 860 F.3d 703 (D.C. 2017).

57. *Id.* at 710 (Pillard J. concurring) [citation omitted].

alone versus States acting collectively is akin to asking why the immunity of State officials or entities of the State is different from that of the State itself. Although the immunity of a State official derives from that of the State, it is not dependent on whether the State itself is immune for the underlying act. Under the doctrine of restrictive State immunity, a State is immune for its *acta jure imperii*, and its officials have immunity *ratione materiae* for official acts on behalf of the State. At any rate, an international organization is not a mere collection of States and, as such, the scope of its immunity is different than that of its member States because both immunities have different rationales

The relation between national laws, for example, IOIA, and international law, that is, treaties and conventions, on the immunity of international organizations bears examination. In a suit against the United Nations, the plaintiffs had argued that the Convention on the Privileges and Immunities of the United Nations ("General Convention") that entered into force with respect to the United States on April 29, 1970, should not be enforced by the American courts because it is not self-executing.[58] The Second Circuit Court of Appeals disagreed and held that the General Convention "is self-executing and applies in American courts without implementing legislation."[59] The plaintiffs had invoked national legislation of the United States, arguing that international organizations "no longer have absolute immunity in all cases" with the enactment of FSIA, "which strips foreign sovereigns of their immunity in certain circumstances."[60] The court noted that the plaintiffs' argument had been rejected by the District of Columbia Circuit Court of Appeals and decided that it need not resolve whether plaintiffs' argument was correct. It, however, decided that "whatever immunities are possessed by other international organizations, [the General Convention] unequivocally grants the United Nations absolute immunity without exceptions."[61]

Assuming that there is a conflict between the IOIA, or FSIA for that matter, and any treaty on the immunity of international organizations to which the United States is a member, the United States Supreme Court has held that "a treaty will not be deemed to have been abrogated or modified by a later statute unless such purpose on the part of Congress has been clearly expressed."[62]

58. See *Brzak v. United Nations*, 597 F. 3d 107, 111 (2d Cir. 2010).

59. *Id.* at 112.

60. *Id.*

61. *Id.*

62. See *Sadikoglu v. United Nations Development Programme*, 2011 U.S. Dist. LEXIS 120205, citing *Weinstein v. Islamic Republic of Iran*, 609 F 3d 43, 53 (2d Cir. 2010) quoting *Trans World Airlines Inc. v. Franklin Mint Corp.*, 466 U.S. 243, 251–52 (1984).

According to the *Charming Betsy* canon of statutory construction, an ambiguous statute should be construed to be consistent with international law.[63] The effect of the FSIA is not to continue tethering the immunity of international organizations to State immunity. Nothing in either the language or legislative history of the FSIA gives any indication that the United States Congress intended the FSIA to modify the IOIA.

If an analogy is permitted, States now have restrictive immunity, whereas international organizations still have absolute immunity. It is a different issue whether international organizations should continue to have absolute immunity when States no longer have it. When the IOIA was enacted, the immunity of international organizations was coextensive with that of State, but as the customary international law of restrictive State immunity evolved or developed, there is no such evolution or development with respect to immunity of international organizations, which is primarily based on treaty law. Thus, under contemporary international law, the immunity of international organizations is no longer coterminous with State immunity.

It is still debatable whether a customary international law on the immunity of international organizations has developed. As stated in *The Paquete Habana*:

> International law is part of our law, and must be ascertained and administered by the courts of justice of appropriate jurisdiction, as often as questions of right depending upon it are duly presented for their determination. For this purpose, where there is no treaty, and no controlling executive or legislative act or judicial decision, resort must be had to the customs and usages of civilized nations; and, as evidence of these, to the works of jurists and commentators, who by years of labor, research and experience, have made themselves peculiarly well acquainted with the subjects of which they treat. Such works are resorted to by judicial tribunals, not for the speculations of their authors concerning what the law ought to be, but for trustworthy evidence of what the law really is.[64]

Where the United States is a member of an international organization and party to any convention or treaty on the immunity of that organization, the IOIA must be construed to be in harmony with the international legal instrument. The District of Columbia Court of Appeals has taken this correct approach.

63. See *Murray v. Schooner Charming Betsy*, 6 U.S. (2 Cranch) 64, 118 (1804), Chief Justice Marshall ("an act of Congress ought never to be construed to violate the law of nations if any other possible construction remains.")

64. *The Paquete Habana*, 175 U.S. 677, 700 (1900) [emphasis added].

Unfortunately, the debate about the precise scope of the jurisdictional immunity of international organizations has often been couched in the parlance of State immunity: absolute versus restrictive. This characterization is nothing but a vestige of the relationship between both immunities. Considering that the immunity of international organizations, including the prototypical United Nations, is founded on functional necessity, courts and commentators should eschew employing in their description of it "absolute versus restrictive" terminology of State immunity.

In the determination of the immunity of international organizations and their officials, the paramount consideration should be the functional necessity test, rather than an analogy to sovereign immunity. Actually, the jurisdictional immunity of international organization is both "absolute" and "functional," except where specific exceptions are made in the constituent text of the organization as is the case with multilateral development banks (MDBs) such as the World Bank. Although absolute is not the opposite of functional, critics of the immunity of international organization have questioned the functional necessity doctrine, claiming that "it might result in immunity being granted to international organisations in all circumstances, given that international organisations will always be deemed to act within the scope of their duties."[65] They also argue that the doctrine "is only an empty shell; it hardly plays a role in circumscribing the immunity of international organizations."[66]

At any rate, the immunity of the United Nations and of its specialized agencies is based on the doctrine of functional necessity. Even the exception to the immunity of MDBs under their charter cannot be equated with the commercial activities exception to the restrictive State immunity because the distinction between *acta jure imperii* and *acta jure gestionis*, which is the fulcrum of the doctrine, cannot be properly applied to the activities of these international organizations. If the distinction were applicable, then such activities where the MDBs are amenable to suit would surely be characterized as *acta jure imperii* because they are "sovereign" or charter-based functions of the organization. Thus, it is absurd to apply the doctrine of restrictive State immunity to international organizations. The rationale for restrictive State immunity is that fairness demands that if States decide to enter the market arena, they should do so under the same conditions as other participants in the market. Thus, private parties engaging in commercial activities will not be frustrated by the immunity of States and denied judicial

65. E. Gaillard & I. Pingel-Lenuzza, *International Organizations and Immunity from Jurisdiction: To Restrict or Bypass*, 51 International and Comparative Law Quarterly 1, 10 (2002).

66. Cedric Ryngaert, The Immunity of International Organizations Before Domestic Courts: Recent Trends, Working Paper No. 143—December 2009, Institute for International law, K.U. Leuven.

remedy. To be sure, this may be all good and well in the case of States because they exist for their sovereign acts, and not their commercial acts. However, because an international organization carries out activities that if engaged in by States would be considered commercial should not detract from the principle of functional necessity that underpins the immunity of international organizations.

In sum, there is no rational basis for the application of the doctrine of restrictive State immunity to international organizations because any distinction between *acta jure imperii* and *acta jure gestionis* regarding the immunity of international organizations is not workable.

10

Conclusion

If all you read were the polemics on jurisdictional immunity of States and international organizations, you would be forgiven if you were left with the impression that impunity is running rampant in the world and denial of justice is the order of the day. However, the state of affairs is not as gloomy as painted by the polemics. There is no gainsaying that immunity may lead to inequity. The world is imperfect. In a perfect world, there would be international courts and tribunals with jurisdiction to adjudicate claims against or involving States and international organizations, which will obviate the adjudication of such claims in national courts. If the experience with the International Criminal Court (ICC) is any guidance, it shows that existence of an international court with compulsory or universal jurisdiction is a pious hope or pipe dream.[1] The jurisdictional immunities of States and international organizations as rules of international law reflect the preference of

1. The ICC was established by the Rome Statute and has jurisdiction over genocide, crimes against humanity, war crimes, and crimes of aggression. The United States government actively participated in the creation of the ICC but has so far refused to join the court because it would like the Security Council of the United Nations to screen cases to be prosecuted by the court where it could exercise veto over possible charges against its nationals. The ICC has also been reproached for targeting mostly Africans and some African States have threatened withdrawal from the court. (International) justice does not have double standards and should apply equally to all nations and their nationals.

Jurisdictional Immunities of States and International Organizations. Edward Chukwuemeke Okeke.

internationalism over nationalism. States conceded an aspect of their sovereignty, that is, jurisdiction, for the overall good of international relations. A disdain for jurisdictional immunity represents a threat to, if relapse or retreat from, internationalism and a resurgence of perilous nationalism. It is ironic that some of the States that championed the internationalism that gave birth to the United Nations system, for instance, are the same ones that are taking actions that may undermine the internationalist and multilateral systems that they had a hand in building.

States and international organizations are the most important actors on the world stage. The world order is built and sustained on international law. "One of the challenges of present-day international law is to provide for stability of international relations and effective international intercourse while at the same time guaranteeing respect for human rights."[2] States and international organizations are subjects of international law, and are neither lawless entities nor above the law. "International law then cannot itself prevent conflict or injustice, and cannot create order, but it can help to organize, rationalize and extend that order."[3] The international community, represented by States themselves, have made the policy choice of conferring jurisdictional immunities on States and international organizations.

The law of immunities precedes the existence of the modern State and international organizations. International law recognizes diplomatic immunity, consular immunity, head of State immunity, State immunity, and international organizations immunity. Diplomatic immunity, which is the granddaddy of all immunities in international law, has influenced the development of both State immunity and the immunity of international organizations, for better or for worse. It is also the immunity most susceptible to abuse and invites the most opprobrium. "The immunities and privileges of the diplomat often come in for envy and disapproval, and legislatures are jealous of their extension; but, while their abuse is to be condemned, it is only fair to judge them by the purpose and extent of their proper use."[4] Most of the criticism of the immunity tend to lose sight of why there exists the immunity in the first place.

> It is worth remembering that there is a point and purpose to immunity. The foundations of diplomatic and consular immunity, in both law and practice, are functionality and reciprocity. A host state accords immunities to accredited diplomats and other representatives of foreign governments so that—and frequently to the extent—its own diplomats and representatives are treated similarly by the foreign government within its territory. It does so because recognizing these immunities facilitates the conduct of vital government

2. Arrest Warrant of 11 April 2000 (Democratic Republic of the Congo v. Belgium), Judgment, I.C.J. Rep. 2002, p.3, Joint Separate Opinion of Judges Higgins, Kooijmans, and Buergenthal, para.5.

3. J.E.S. Fawcett, The Law of Nations 17 (Penguin 1971).

4. *Id.* at 72–73.

> business. Immunity from legal process, civil suit, and criminal prosecution is a time-honored protection granted to foreign governmental representatives to shield them from harassment, punishment, or other actions that would interfere with their representational functions. It is this mutuality of interest that makes the system of diplomatic and consular immunity work.[5]

Debates about State immunity underscore its complexity. For example, the Canadian Supreme Court noted: "State immunity is a complex doctrine that is shaped by constantly evolving international relations. Determining the exceptions to immunity requires a thorough knowledge of diplomacy and international politics and a careful weighing of national interests."[6] Similarly, the International Court of Justice (ICJ) has noted: "State immunity occupies an important place in international law and international relations."[7] Conversely, jurisdictional immunity has been assailed as anachronistic and anathematic:

> In present democratic society an absolute immunity from judicial proceedings appears to be an anachronistic doctrine incompatible with the demands of justice and the rule of law. The international law immunities originated at a time when individual rights were practically non-existent and when States needed greater protection from possible harassment through abusive judicial proceedings. The doctrine of State immunity has in modern times been subjected to an increasing number of restrictions, the trend being to reduce its application in view of developments in the field of human rights which strengthen the position of the individual.[8]

The ICJ recognizes the need to strike the proper balance between two very important norms of international law:

> These trends reflect a balancing of interests. On the one scale, we find the interest of the community of mankind to prevent and stop impunity for perpetrators of grave crimes against its members; on the other, there is the interest of the community of States to allow them to act freely on the inter-State level without unwarranted interference. A balance therefore must be struck between two sets of functions which are both valued by the international community. Reflecting these concerns, what is regarded as a permissible

5. David P. Stewart, Immunity and Accountability: More Continuity than Change?, 99 Am. Soc'y Int'l L. Proc. 228–29 (2005).

6. Kazemi Estate v. Islamic Republic of Iran, 2014 SCC 62 ¶ 169, [2014] 3 S.C.R. 176 (Can.).

7. Jurisdictional Immunities of the State (*Germany v. Italy: Greece Intervening*), Judgment I.C.J. Rep. 2012, p. 99, para. 57.

8. *McElhinney v. Ireland* [GC], no. 31253/96, ECHR 2001-XI (Dissenting Opinion of Judge Loucaides).

> jurisdiction and what is regarded as the law on immunity are in constant evolution. The weights on the two scales are not set for all perpetuity. Moreover, a trend is discernible that in a world which increasingly rejects impunity for the most repugnant offences, the attribution of responsibility and accountability is becoming firmer, the possibility for the assertion of jurisdiction wider and the availability of immunity as a shield more limited. The law of privileges and immunities, however, retains its importance since immunities are granted to high State officials to guarantee the proper functioning of the network of mutual inter-State relations, which is of paramount importance for a well-ordered and harmonious international system.[9]
>
> We wish to point out, however, that the frequently expressed conviction of the international community that perpetrators of grave and inhuman international crimes should not go unpunished does not *ipso facto* mean that immunities are unavailable whenever impunity would be the outcome.... But immunities serve other purposes which have their own intrinsic value.... International law seeks the accommodation of this value with the fight against impunity, and not the triumph of one norm over the other.[10]

The United Nations Convention on Jurisdictional Immunities of States and Their Property seeks to harmonize the international law of State immunity. Even though it has not gone into effect as a treaty, some courts do have recourse to some of its provisions as codification or evidence of customary international law. Ratification of the Convention by States has stalled, and it appears there is no momentum for its entry into force. Absent a treaty of universal application, national legislation and judicial decisions have become the most important source of the law of State immunity, with the augury that the international law of State immunity will degenerate into the comparative law of State immunity. The future is more fragmentation through national legislation than harmonization through the entry into force of the Convention. Such a development may undermine the international law of State immunity, unless there's judicial dialogue in the interpretation of these national legislation for the twin purpose of developing and applying customary international law. Judicial dialogue takes place when courts refer to and analyze decisions of other national and international courts and tribunals. This will lead to a coalescence of interpretation and application of international law principles, especially considering Lord Denning's observation regarding international law: "International law knows no rule of *stare decisis*."[11] The law and practice

9. Arrest Warrant of 11 April 2000 (Democratic Republic of the Congo v. Belgium), Judgment, I.C.J. Rep. 2002, p. 3, Joint Separate Opinion of Judges Higgins, Kooijmans, and Buergenthal, paras. 74–75.

10. *Id.*, para. 79.

11. *Trendtex Trading Corporation v. Central Bank of Nigeria* [1977] 2 WLR 356, 554.

of one State alone do not international law make: Treaty law requires the consent of more than one State and customary international law requires the practice of States with the requisite *opinio juris*.

The prevalence of the restrictive doctrine has diminished the disaffection with State immunity, and the focus of the discontent toward immunities has shifted to international organizations. There is no gainsaying that jurisdictional immunity, without access to court, may operate to deny justice in some situations. However, there is equally no denying that it is a necessary evil for the benefit of international relations and cooperation. Immunity ensures the unimpeded and independent performance of functions—global public goods—by the international organizations. It is inaccurate to assert that international organizations lack accountability, considering that they could be called to answer for their actions, without being subjected to suits in national courts, in international tribunals, through alternative modes of dispute settlement. In addition, international organizations have established international administrative tribunals for the adjudication of employment disputes with their staff. With respect to other private law disputes with third parties, international organizations normally provide arbitration clauses in commercial contracts. The problem remains with disputes concerning tort, or where human rights are implicated, and the international organizations do not waive their immunity. Because international organizations have immunity does not mean that they are not held accountable for their actions and decisions. There are various accountability mechanisms to which an international organization may be subjected, but the elimination of immunity is not the right remedy to achieve accountability.

An international law luminary had observed in 1961, the same year that the United Nations General Assembly adopted the Vienna Convention on Diplomatic Relations:

> [I]mmunities are apt to be regarded either as one of the housekeeping problem [*sic*] of international organizations or as insidious encroachment on the rule of law, the liberty of the subject, and the equality of man. They are neither. In the present stage of development of world organisation they are an essential device for the purpose of bridling unilateral and sometimes irresponsible control by particular governments of the activities of international organisations. These organisations have been created by agreement among governments to discharge important and in some cases vital responsibilities on behalf of the world community as a whole with freedom, with independence, and with impartiality.[12]

12. C. Wilfred Jenks, International Immunities, Preface, at xiii. (1961). Jenks, a British international lawyer, was the legal adviser of the International Labour Organization and its sixth Director-General.

Even the European Court of Human Rights, which has been in the vanguard of the proposition that a corollary of jurisdictional immunity is the availability of alternative means of dispute resolution, has also held that the jurisdictional immunity of international organizations is "an essential means of ensuring the proper functioning of such organizations free from unilateral interference by individual governments."[13]

Although the law of the immunity of international organizations is virtually treaty law, judicial dialogue by national courts is also called for in the interpretation of the legal instruments regarding their jurisdictional immunity. "The general rule is that international treaties should, so far as possible, be construed uniformly by the national courts of all states."[14]

The European Court for Human Rights has noted: "While the Court is not formally bound to follow its previous judgments, it is in the interests of legal certainty, foreseeability and equality before the law that it should not depart, without good reason, from precedents laid down in previous cases."[15] International law is dynamic; it develops and evolves. Its dynamism might appear glacial sometimes but the law can and does change. The development of customary international law develops "at first a trickle, then a stream, last a flood."[16] What was once acceptable yesterday might not be tomorrow. An example is the development of the doctrine of restrictive State immunity out of the quest for justice and fairness occasioned by the involvement of States in commercial activities. "Most of the time, when a law is found to be 'inadequate' the reason is that its goal is valued less than some other goal. The remedy then is not to manipulate laws but to change the evaluation of goals."[17] Thus, if the international community finds the international law of jurisdictional immunities of States and international organizations to be illegitimate or inadequate, then the proper course of action is to re-evaluate the goals served by the law, not manipulate or misapply the law as is.

13. *Case of Waite and Kennedy v. Germany* (Application no. 26083/94), ECtHR Judgment of 18 February 1999, para. 63.

14. See *R v. Bow Street Metropolitan Stipendiary Magistrate and others, ex parte Pinochet Ugarte (Amnesty International and others intervening) (No 3)*, ("*Ex Parte Pinochet 3*"), [2000] 1 AC 147, [1999] 2 ALL ER 97, [1999] 2 WLR 827 (Judgement of Lord Hope of Craighead).

15. *Jones v. United Kingdom*, [2014] ECHR 34356/06, para. 194.

16. See *Trendtex Trading v. Central Bank of Nigeria*, [1977] QB 529, 556.

17. Werner Levi, Contemporary International Law: A Concise Introduction 1 (Westview Press 1979).

Bibliography

Andrew Dickinson, Rae Lindsay & James P. Loonam, State Immunity: Selected Materials and Commentary (Oxford University Press, 2004).

Anne Peters, Evelyne Lagrange, Stefan Oeter & Christian Tomuschat, Immunities in the Age of Global Constitutionalism (Brill Nijhoff, 2015).

Anthony Aust, Handbook of International Law, 2nd Edition (Cambridge University Press, 2008).

Anthony Miller, The Privileges and Immunities of the United Nations, 6 International Organizations Law Review 7 (2009).

Arthur Watts, The Legal Position in International Law of Heads of States, Heads of Government and Foreign Ministers, 247 Recueil des cours de l'Académie de droit international de La Haye, 9 (Martinus Nijhoff 1995).

A.S. Muller, International Organizations and Their Host States: Aspects of Their Legal Relationships (Martinus Nijhoff, 1995).

August Reinisch, International Organizations before National Courts (Cambridge University Press, 2000).

August Reinisch & Ulf Andreas Weber, In the Shadow of Waite and Kennedy, 1 International Organizations Law Review 59–110 (2004).

Barry E. Carter & Phillip R. Trimble, International Law, 2nd Edition (Little, Brown and Company, 1995).

Biswanath Sen, A Diplomat's Handbook of International Law and Practice (Martinus Nijhoff, 1965).

Blaise Knapp, Les Privièges et Immunités des organisations internationales et leurs agents devant les tribunaux internationaux, 69 Revue Générale de Droit International Public 651–681 (1965).

C. F. Amerasinghe, Principles of the Institutional Law of International Organizations (Cambridge University Press, 2005).

Cedric Ryngaert, Ige F Dekker, Ramses A Wessel & Jan Wouters, Judicial Decisions on the Law of International Organizations (Oxford University Press, 2016).

Charles Brower II, International Immunities: Some Dissident Views on the Role of Municipal Courts, 41 Virginia Journal of International Law 1 (2000).

Jurisdictional Immunities of States and International Organizations. Edward Chukwuemeke Okeke.

Christian Dominicé, L'immunité de juridiction et d'exécution des organisations internationales, 187 Recuiel des cours de l' Académie de Droit International 149–238 (1984).

Christoff Schreuer, State Immunity: Some Recent Developments (Cambridge University Press, 1988).

Daniel Bradlow & David Hunter, International Financial Institutions and International Law (Kluwer, 2010).

David J. Bederman, Christopher J. Borgen & David A. Martine, International Law: A Handbook for Judges (American Society of International Law, 2013).

Eileen Denza, Diplomatic Law: Commentary on the Vienna Convention on Diplomatic Relations (Oxford University Press, 2016).

Emmanuel Gaillard & I. Pingel-Lenuzza, International Organisations and Immunity from Jurisdiction: To Restrict or to Bypass, 15 International and Comparative Law Quarterly 1 (2002).

Ernest K. Bankas, The State Immunity Controversy in International Law: Private Suits against Sovereign States in Domestic Courts (Springer, 2005).

Ernesto J. Sanchez, The Foreign Sovereign Immunity Act Deskbook (American Bar Association, 2013).

Finn Seyersted, Common Law of International Organizations (Martinus Nijhoff, 2008).

Finn Seyersted, Objective International Personality of Intergovernmental Organizations: Do Their Capacity Really Depend Upon Their Constitutions? (Krohns Bogtrykkeri, 1963).

Geoffrey Marston, The Personality of International Organisations in English Law, 2 Hofstra Law & Policy Symposium 75 (1997).

Hazel Fox & Philippa Webb, The Law of State Immunity, 3rd Edition (Oxford University Press, 2013).

Henry G. Schermers & Niels M. Blokker, International Institutional Law: Unity within Diversity (Martinus Nijhoff, 2004).

Hersch Lauterpacht, The Problem of Jurisdictional Immunities of Foreign States, 28 British Yearbook of International Law 220 (1951).

Ignaz Seidl-Hohenveldern, L'Immunite de juridiction et d'execution des etats et des organisations internationales (Pedone, Paris, 1981).

Ivor Roberts, Satow's Diplomatic Practice (Oxford University Press, 2017).

Jan Klabbers, An Introduction to International Organizations Law, 3rd Edition (Cambridge University Press, 2015).

Jean Cambacau & Serge Sur, Droit international public (Montchrestien, Paris, 2001).

Jean Duffar, Contribution à l'Etude des Privilèges et Immunités des Organisations Internationales (Librairie Generale de Droit et de Jursiprudence, 1982).

Jean-Flavien Lalive, L'Immunité de juridiction des états et des organisations internationales, 84 Recueil des cours de l'Académie de Droit International, 205–396 (1953).

Jean-Luc Fagnart, L'immunité de juridiction des organisations internationales, Mélanges Jacques van Compernolle. 181–200 (Bruylant, 2004).

Josef Kunz, Privileges and Immunities of International Organizations, 41 American Journal of International law 828–862 (1947).

Kathleen Cully, Jurisdictional Immunities of International Organizations, 91 Yale Law Journal, 1167–1195 (1982).
Kuljit Ahluwalia, The Legal Status, Privileges and Immunities of the Specialized Agencies of the United Nations and Certain Other International Organizations (Martinus Nijhoff, 1964).
Lee M. Caplan, State Immunity, Human Rights, and Jus Cogens: A Critique of the Normative Hierarchy Theory, 97 American Journal of International Law 741 (2003).
Linda S. Frey & Marsha L. Frey, The History of Diplomatic Immunity (Ohio State University Press 1999).
Mark E. Villiger, Customary International Law and Treaties (Springer Netherlands, 1985).
Mark E. Villiger, Customary International Law and Treaties: A Manual on the Theory and Practice of the Interrelation of Sources (Martinus Nijhoff, 1997).
Michael Singer, Jurisdictional Immunity of International Organizations: Human Rights and Functional Necessity Concerns, 36 Virginia Journal of International Law 53 (1995).
N.C.H. Dunbar, "Controversial aspects of sovereign immunity in the case law of some states," 132 Collected Courses of the Hague Academy of International Law 197, The Hague Academy of International Law (Martinus Nijhoff, 1971).
P.H.F. Bekker, The Legal Position of Intergovernmental Organizations: A Functional Necessity Analysis of Their Legal Status and Immunities (Martinus Nijhoff, 1994).
Philippe Sands & Pierre Klein, Bowett's Law of International Institutions, 6th Edition (Sweet & Maxwell, 2009).
Richard Garnett, State Immunity in Employment Matters, 46 International and Comparative Law Quarterly 81 (1997).
Richard Oparil, Immunity of International Organizations in United States Courts: Absolute or Restrictive?, 24 Vanderbilt Journal of Transnational Law 689–710 (1991).
Roberto Virzo & Ivan Ingravallo, Evolutions in the Law of International Organizations (Brill Nijhoff, 2015).
Steven Herz, International Organizations in U.S. Courts: Reconsidering the Anachronism of Absolute Immunity, 31 Suffolk Transnational Law Review 471 (2008).
Sucharitkul, Sompong, Immunities of foreign states before national authorities, 149 Recueil des cours/*Collected Courses of the Hague Academy of International Law* 87 (The Hague Academy of International Law, 1976).
W.C. Jenks, International Immunities (Stevens & Sons Ltd., 1961).
Werner Levi, Contemporary International Law: A Concise Introduction (Westview Press, 1979).
Xiaodong Yang, State Immunity in International Law (Cambridge University Press, 2012).

Index

www.ingramcontent.com/pod-product-compliance
Lightning Source LLC
LaVergne TN
LVHW091534200926
848483LV00002B/393

* 9 7 8 0 1 9 0 6 1 1 2 3 1 *